Contents

8   IBM Direct File Organization   183

9   COBOL Indexed I–O Files   199

10   Physical Organization of Indexed Sequential Files   230

11   VSAM Concepts   244

Preface
to the
Second Edition

We are more than pleased with the wide acceptance that the First Edition of this book has received. From comments by instructors, we have discovered that users fall into three main groups. There are those who like the first half and wish it were expanded. There are those who would like us to drop the first half and expand the second half, which contains the really important part of their course. Finally, there are the middle-of-the-roaders who would like both ends dropped and the center expanded! This leads us to believe that if we delete as advised there would be no book, whereas if we add as advised we would be following in the footsteps of the venerable Knuth, and the book would never be finished. Neither alternative is acceptable so we have redesigned the book on the basis of its known and projected use as a text. Fortunately, this follows our original philosophy, and we believe that the result is a much improved treatment of file processing, which retains the qualities of the original edition.

Essentially there are four uses of the book as a text:

- First half: Introduction to files
- Middle: File and data structures
- Second half: Design and implementation of file systems
- All of book: Two-semester file processing course for undergraduates, or one-semester course for graduate students.

The detailed requirements of different instructors varied somewhat from our own use of the text. Several chapters were originally written mainly as reference material for readers who may not have had certain background material which our own students had. We now know that this material represents parts of courses offered by others, so we have revised these chapters to increase content and have added several new chapters to give instructors more choice in selecting course material from the book.

File processing is a significant practical problem that is becoming increasingly more complex. Nevertheless, it is a neglected part of many computing programs. There appear to be two main reasons. It has generally been considered part of another course because historically it was neither as important nor as complex as it is today. Sequential files were a natural part of any COBOL course, and techniques of direct files were dealt with in a data structures course.

Since it was not treated as a subject in itself, no books were written with file processing as the central theme. Thus, no courses were developed from a dominant file aspect; rather, the topic of files was appended to existing courses. We wrote the First Edition of this book to address file processing as a central theme with COBOL and data structures as valuable and essential topics but subordinate to the central problem of how to organize computer files.

There have been two main approaches to teaching file material. Theoretical departments have treated file structures as a minor topic in data structures, neglecting necessary practical aspects of file processing. Practical departments have treated file processing as part of an advanced programming course (usually COBOL), neglecting the theoretical aspects of file structures.

We believe that file processing should be a core subject for all computing students: Students of applied computing must be able to efficiently process data stored in files; students of theoretical computing must realize that theory and analysis that do not model the constraints of the real word are ultimately of questionable value and that files are very real data structures.

A file designer needs a judicious mix of practice and theory in order to obtain a good understanding of how to expand knowledge in each area as required by the problem at hand. We believe that file processing techniques are the central problem and that COBOL and data structures provide useful but supporting tools for the major objective: the design of efficient files in the context of the resident computer system. This is the theme of the Second Edition. We have chosen COBOL and VSAM as our computer interface because of their widespread use in the computing industry.

For practically oriented programs, we suggest that the book be used following an introductory programming course. A file course based on the book can follow or be done in parallel with an advanced COBOL and program design course. We have included sufficient data structure material so that a data structure course can be postponed until the completion of file processing. Practically oriented students will then have a good motivational foundation for a theoretically oriented course in data structures, which can then be followed by a data base course.

For theoretically oriented programs, we suggest that the book be used following a data structures course and that file processing be used to illustrate the application and ultimate use of the theory provided in the data structures course. The practical problems of file design then give an appropriate background for advanced theoretical courses in data structures, data base, and algorithm analysis.

The book has been carefully partitioned into theoretical and practical chapters to allow the instructor the flexibility to select course topics suitable to the context of a department's program. In so far as possible, chapters are independent of each other, and this edition should suit a wide variety of needs but of course cannot be optimal in all cases.

We have attempted where possible to keep terminology close to its normal English meaning. We have also tried to avoid jargon and to restrict the use of special terms that do not significantly contribute to ease of exposition. In general we follow the terminology of Martin with due consideration to Knuth unless we have good reasons to do otherwise. Now that computing has developed structured programming, perhaps the time has come to invent structured terminology and control the unrestrained tendency to GO TO new meanings of old words, when our grasp of English fails our reach.

REVISIONS

While we have fiddled here and there with minor improvements to the text, there are a number of significant revisions and additions.

Chapter 2, "Data Management": Completely rewritten to provide the basic hardware-related concepts required by the file designer. More detail than is provided here should be obtained from manufacturer's literature in a specific design situation.

Chapter 5, "Practical Considerations": This new chapter provides detail on how to deal with device characteristics at the programming level. Since many students will already have studied sequential files and sorting, this is a good point at which to begin a file processing course.

Chapter 7, "Record Addressing Techniques": Modified to include more technical detail.

Chapter 9, "COBOL Indexed I–O Files": Substantially revised to add alternate keys and a new case study. The full use of the COBOL Indexed I–O module is now discussed for VSAM-based files.

Chapter 10, "Physical Organization of Indexed Sequential Files": VSAM has been removed from this chapter. The coverage of ISAM is not integral to the text and can be skipped.

Chapter 11, "VSAM Concepts": This new chapter replaces the former brief coverage in Chapter 10. It can be omitted, and practical courses can move directly to Chapter 12. Theoretical courses can examine VSAM as an example of B-trees, ignoring the actual use of VSAM in Chapter 12.

Chapter 12, "VSAM Applied": This new chapter allows students to use VSAM without reading Chapter 10 or 11.

Chapter 13, "Data Structures": Revised to add more detail; however, we have omitted detailed analytical analysis because this should be done in advanced data structures or algorithm analysis. There is, nonetheless, sufficient detail so that students need not have taken a data structures course before studying file processing.

Chapter 14, "Index Organization": This new chapter deals with applied data structures.

Chapter 17, "File Design": Some detail has been added to give a more analytical basis for file design calculations.

Chapter 18, "File Implementation": Substantially revised to provide a more realistic case study that brings together various topics of the book.

ACKNOWLEDGMENTS TO THE SECOND EDITION

Professors A. M. Stevens and W. R. Knight provided insight and incisive comments for which we are grateful. Graduate student Bill Hyslop helped with the new programs. Ray Strong gave, albeit from a distance, his usual strong comments. Nevertheless, all errors and omissions that remain are entirely the fault of the other author!

Preface
to the
First Edition

The material in this book was developed mainly because our experience with students and professionals indicated a real need for such an approach. As teachers, we found that students, as prospective programmers, had trouble relating the general theory of data structures to the effective implementation of files. In our consulting, we found to our surprise that professional programmers and analysts often had a faulty understanding of the various file systems and were not fully aware of their design parameters. The result was often a specialization in the use of one system to the exclusion of all other solutions. This is understandable, for many professionals cut their teeth on sequential tape systems, so the change to direct access methods can be traumatic when done on the job, with the pressures caused by pressing deadlines and the elusive "one remaining bug."

Accordingly, the book is aimed at these two groups, and the efforts made to satisfy their differing demands have provided interesting constraints, which have greatly improved our original class notes.

This text is intended to be used for a second course in COBOL programming and file processing at the university level and for independent study by professionals. It is intended to provide an introduction to advanced COBOL language features for file handling and data base management. The discussion of COBOL is based on the ANSI standard manual and relevant CODASYL documents.

The basic material has been class tested at the University of New Brunswick in various courses taken by upperclass students and by graduate students, many of whom enter the professional areas of computing. Their input has strongly influenced the book's scope and intent.

This book is directed to the student of computing who works, or will work, with files in some capacity. We consider ourselves students of computing also, and as such, identifying with our audience, we have tried to write a book we would have liked to read when we began to learn about files. By no means have we exhaustively covered file techniques, but we have included what we feel is basic and should prove useful in the future.

At times we will refer to various functions performed by people involved with files, using the following terminology. A *user* is a consumer of a system product. A *programmer* is a language specialist. An *analyst* is a system specialist. *Designer* is a general term for a person making intelligent decisions that affect the design of the system at any level.

We regret that with the exception of words such as "one" there are no pronouns that address both men and women. We adopt the convention of using "he" and "his" and do so sparingly as the demands of the language require.

Although we have tried to deal with the subject in a broad and acceptable manner, we would be naive to expect complete accord with our selection and presentation of material. We believe that instructors who have alternate views of the subject will only enhance the learning experience of their students. Our views are contained herein; instructors have the classroom in which to present theirs. We hope the debate will be lively and rewarding.

ACKNOWLEDGMENTS

It is a pleasure to acknowledge the help we have received in preparing this book. First, we would each like to thank the other author.

In addition we had help from Pat Emin, Rufus McKillop, Professors Albert M. Stevens and Fred Cogswell, and a host of students, in particular Ron Ho, Joe Marriot, Jim Carmont, Luc Frenette, Jamie Campbell, Mike Good and Ronnie Loiser.

The book was carefully reviewed by Ray Strong and by Prentice-Hall's reviewers. Thank you for being cruel. Karl Karlstrom of Prentice-Hall deserves a round of applause, because he made the book possible and was great to work with.

A warm thanks to Dr. William Knight, our resident statistician, for his oblique and random encouragements at all hours of the day and night. Our sincere thanks to Mrs. Anna Anderson, who typed endless versions and who now knows that a final draft is final in name only.

All of these people contributed to improving the book you are reading, and we are most grateful to them.

This product neither states the opinion of, nor implies concurrence of, the sponsoring institutions.

The authors and copyright holders of the copyrighted material used herein

FLOW-MATIC (trademark of Sperry Rand Corporation), Programming for the UNIVAC I and II, Data Automation Systems copyrighted 1958, 1959, by Sperry Rand Corporation; IBM Commercial Translator Form No. F 28-8013, copyrighted 1959 by IBM; FACT, DSI 27 A5260-2760, copyrighted 1960 by Minneapolis-Honeywell

have specifically authorized the use of this material in whole or in part in the COBOL specifications. Such authorization extends to the reproduction and use of COBOL specifications in programming manuals or similar publications.

Introduction

As the computing field has matured, those in the field have changed their attitude to data, realizing that data exists independently of the programs that access it and that files can be more valuable than the individual programs that access them. The development of data management techniques has tended to isolate applications programmers from the physical storage structures of the data their programs access and even from the programs' logical structure in a data base. Nevertheless, in his own programs the applications programmer must deal with files that are ultimately mapped to a physical storage structure resident on some physical storage medium. Thus the logical and physical limitations of the data base are ultimately present in every program, and their effects may seriously degrade it.

Although a data base may alleviate the programmer's need to construct physical files, he must still construct logical files. Since data bases cannot at present manipulate data in a completely arbitrary way, a knowledge of physical file structure will be to the programmer's advantage. Similarly, a deep understanding of file techniques will always be important because applications are neither completely general nor physically independent. On the other hand, someone must ultimately construct the physical files that store the data base. Therefore, the current trend toward large data base systems only accentuates the need for file techniques, for it is upon techniques discussed in this book that data base systems ultimately depend for implementation.

Although the vast data base argument is persuasive, considerable argument exists for distributed data bases and some enterprises are returning to distributed computing. Basic file techniques will remain fundamentally important, since the data base management system philosophy is, in general, of large scale. No matter what the future brings, there will be large systems with data base management and small systems without.

It is not possible to do language-independent computing; at best, in the search for generality, a deep understanding of the particular is required. One approach is to use a pseudocode. We do not believe, however, that a pseudocode that cannot be run on a computer and is used by few people is superior, for teaching of file techniques, to a commonly used programming language—both can be improved upon. The techniques of this book are illustrated using COBOL, for while we do not always love COBOL, the fact that it is *the* business language makes all counterargument spurious. Since design is really just the search for optimal choice subject to the constraints of the real world, we trust that the reader will accept COBOL as one example of a real system of constraints that he is likely to encounter frequently in the business world. Practical file techniques have been difficult to acquire not because of any intrinsic difficulty but because the requisite information is scattered among many sources. The purpose of this book is to gather in one source a description of basic methods for the logical and physical description of files along with the appropriate COBOL statements for definition and access. We discuss the effective use of file techniques while relating our discussion to data base organization.

We stress the how and why of good design and demonstrate style by example rather than precepts. Our approach is to provide a good background in the fundamentals along with sufficient detail to allow immediate use in a COBOL work environment. By no means will the reader become an instant expert, but he should acquire the ability to approach and solve file problems in a reasonable time. On the one hand, the book can be considered as an intermediate COBOL text; on the other hand, the book is basically about file techniques and uses COBOL simply as an extended example of how one language handles fundamental file techniques.

We would be remiss if we did not apply our principles of design and style to the organization of the book. The essence of the approach is to move from a specific example to a generalization of the concept suggested by the example, then to a COBOL instance of their use. We move from a creation and discussion of logical structure to the realization and storage of the logical structure as a physical structure. This mapping is the fundamental problem of file design. Only after we have provided a firm grasp of the various major techniques do we attempt to discuss their interrelationship and their role in the file design process.

In our view, it can be quite traumatic for a student to move from a general concept to his first realization of that concept in a programming language. However, once this first dichotomy has been bridged, the student rapidly gains facility with the concept. In substance, we move from the particular to the general and back to the particular because this is how one creates.

Some authors believe in the multiple-language approach. We do not. In our experience, given a thorough understanding of a single language, language skills are transferable. We believe in a thorough and workable conceptual structure for files expressed in one language which may be worked with directly and which may be used indirectly as a stable frame of reference for future needs.

COBOL

This book uses COBOL as defined in ANSI X3.23-1974. Other books which refer to ANSI COBOL may refer to earlier versions of the standard. In additon, manufacturers' compilers that claim to be ANSI COBOL may in fact differ by including features not in the standard. Where possible, programs should conform to the standard; although the standard is not an instructional text, the programmer is advised to refer to it.

It must also be noted that various levels of implementation exist. Thus a compiler may not have all the features necessary to implement a given subset of COBOL. To this purpose COBOL refers to eleven processing modules. Those of main concern for this book are Sequential I–O, Relative I–O, Indexed I–O, and Sort–Merge. Each module has two or three levels of implementation. Lower levels are subsets of higher levels in that module. The null level has *no* features.

The COBOL standard not only gives the language description but also provides information to the implementer and leaves certain decisions to him. In actual use the implementer provides a translator that transforms the COBOL program to a language or to another translator (usually a compiler) that the machine understands. Since programming in COBOL cannot be divorced from the computer, we will refer to the IBM OS/VS COBOL compiler (operating in a VSAM environment) and JCL for the IBM 370 system control language in our examples. There are two reasons for this choice: first, this is the COBOL implementation at our installation; and second, it is in wide use. We will differentiate between the standard and the IBM implementation where necessary. Those readers who use other implementations should experience no difficulties; rather they should find this approach a useful exercise in the variations in interpretation of the standard.

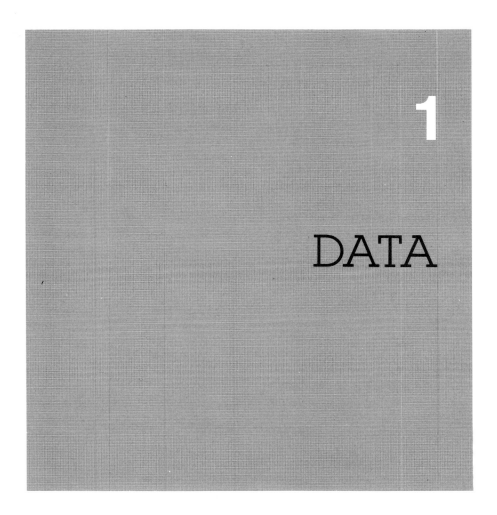

DATA

What is data? How is it related to computing? Why are we concerned with it? Although these are elementary questions, the answers are neither simple nor static. For our purposes, *data* is that information manipulated by programs and stored external to those programs. Because of the high cost of main memory compared to secondary or external memory, data resides in main memory only temporarily. It is most often stored on external, secondary memory such as disks or magnetic tapes.

The view that stored data belongs to a particular program has gradually shifted to the view that stored data exists independently of the programs that manipulate it. This shift has occurred as a result of the change in several factors. As programming systems became more complex, it was realized that the same data was present in various files of different programs (or even the same program) and that the cost of collecting, storing, and accessing data was becoming an increasingly major component of the overall system cost. In addition, the inevitability of organizational change leads to the need to lessen its impact on programming systems. The separation of data from the programs that manipulate it is intended to reduce the impact of change by reducing the software maintenance effort required to accommodate such change. Thus a new importance was placed on the relation of data to the algorithms that manipulate it.

The shift in the ways we view data has been made possible by advances in computer technology and this shift in turn has influenced the development of stored data technology. Increases in the cost of data in relation to the total computing cost combined with the need to protect data from future organizational changes require a more general view of stored data; however, only recent significant advances in computer technology have made a more general view possible.

A growing realization of the true cost of data has forced a reconsideration of its role in effective, cost-conscious computing. The rapid increase in demand for data and the consequent growth in storage is well known. The result of this growth is a serious compounding of the problems of efficient data management. Although the data problem is intrinsic to information processing, solutions have been technological in nature.

Because of the constant change in technology, solutions to problems once considered effective are now obsolete. In effect, computer programs, like automobiles, deteriorate with time and use, and just as it may ultimately cost less to buy a new car than to keep an old car running, some computer solutions are best improved by throwing the old programs away. Unfortunately, as for certain automobiles, the effective life of software and hardware can be very short indeed. The cost of data can leave us with, in effect, an automobile we cannot afford to keep and yet cannot afford to throw away. The data base concept, which considers data independently of the programs that use it, is an attempt to solve such a dilemma by keeping the data while changing its apparent structure so that it can be used by a new set of programs. Informally, a *data base* is a collection of data files that are in some way related and serve many application programs. A *data base management system* (DBMS) consists of a data base and the necessary software to manipulate and relate the data files. This description is an oversimplification, but it is sufficient for now.

A rapidly decreasing cost per bit has led to increased on-line and interactive use of data. Because of this the cost of acquiring, changing, and providing rapid access to vast amounts of data has a tremendous impact on the total cost of computing. That is, managing data for such systems is a significant part of the total cost. It is the major costs of a system that determine our degree of concern, and so today data has a high profile as a problem area. Since file handling is fundamental to data, the more design alternatives the systems analyst and programmer have, the better will be the cost-effective use of data. *Data base organization* refers to the formal interactions and relationships of the data files that constitute the data base. The field of data base organization is vast, growing, and the technology rapidly evolving; however, we believe that a firm grasp of basic file techniques and principles will be of continuing use and value.

Accordingly, the thrust of this book is on the techniques and the principles of files: their use in COBOL and their relationship to data bases.

In designing files a question must be continually asked. How should data be related to programs? Three basic answers are: it should be possible to use data easily for a variety of programs; data should be independent of programs; and it should be easy to examine the data as required. Not all the techniques we examine will satisfy these requirements, but they will ultimately lead to methods that can do so.

1.1 INFORMATION

The advent of the computer with its ability to provide easy access to large quantities of data has made the use and storage of vast amounts of data not only practical but a common occurrence. However, it is one thing to collect volumes of data but quite another matter to be able to access and interpret this data in a meaningful manner. The many recorded bankruptcies of businesses as a direct consequence of implementing a data processing system is stark evidence of the difficulties that can be encountered. Of course, many data processing failures have not been as severe, but they have been costly nevertheless. As a result, the collecting of large amounts of data must be approached with a considerable degree of respect and attention to the needs of the organization as well as its ability to support the costs that will arise.

The purpose of computing is *not* to collect data but to enable the making of decisions. A *decision* is the choice of a particular course of action among alternatives. If a decision is not to be haphazard or illogical, then it must be based on information that indicates one alternative as preferable. In some instances decisions can be made by the computer with the provision of a suitable algorithm. For example, if an account is outstanding 60 days, the computer can automatically send a form letter requesting payment or threatening legal action. More complex decisions may require human interaction. The importance of information determines the effort we are willing to expend to obtain it. Various file techniques have been developed in an attempt to match the cost of this to the ultimate importance of the information.

The Cost/Benefit Tradeoff

What then is the value of information? Why is it important? Certainly, the costs of obtaining information can be extremely high. Consider a data form that requires 15 minutes to fill out under ideal conditions. Suppose that the 10 supervisors of a company complete the form once a month. Since they are not readily familiar with the form, they take 30 minutes, and because they dislike filling out the form, another 30 minutes is required for them to cool off and return to normal. If each supervisor earns $40,000 a year, a rough cost to the company of filling out the form each month is twice his hourly rate or approximately $40. The costs have hardly begun. Imagine an error that requires return of the form once, twice, ...

In the decision to acquire a data processing system, the possible benefits to be derived must be weighed against the cost of obtaining these benefits. This is called a *cost/benefit tradeoff.* In order to determine this, the system is broken into its component parts. The more a component contributes to total cost, the more important are the benefits obtained from that component. Simply stated, do the benefits derived justify the cost? Insofar as the cost/benefit tradeoffs are largely determined by the computing system, this relationship is a fundamental question in the design of files and data bases. In the subsequent study of file techniques, the cost/benefit tradeoffs will be of particular concern.

Although this discussion of cost may appear to digress from the technical aspects of file design and data bases, we cannot overstress its important influence in the ultimate choice of technical alternatives for an implementation. Cost is an important constraint of any system implementation, and it is not always apparent in dollars. Hidden costs not directly assigned to a project may not be discovered until too late. Every data manager knows that customers will suggest changes and additions to their original request that were unthought of in the absence of working output. The cost of these unplanned changes will be very real when they occur, for rarely do the original constraints of time and money allow the initial design to accomodate these changes easily. The determination of cost is complex and uncertain; the cost of what is not done must be considered in addition to the cost of what is done.

1.1.1 The Information Asset

In examining the assets of a company, accountants consider only those things to which a meaningful dollar value can be assigned, while managers are just as likely to consider their staff as a critical asset. Of course, a good stock market analyst will consider both in his evaluation of the assets of a company. But the most important asset that many companies have does not appear on the balance sheet nor on the organizational chart; it is the knowledge of its business that resides in the organization independently of the individuals that constitute that organization.

Operating a business requires capital, people, and information. The fundamental importance of each is illustrated by the fact that any single element can generate the other two. For example, capital or information can be used to attract good people because people want to be well paid and wish to acquire knowledge. Indeed, good technical people will often accept a lower salary in order to be able to work with the latest concepts in an area.

For the knowledge within an organization to be effective, it must be possible to put this knowledge to use as information readily available to the individuals of the organization. How to accomplish this is a difficult problem, and although file techniques have contributed immensely to solutions, the problem is far from solved. The all-knowing computer that responds to and anticipates verbal requests exists as yet only in science fiction.

In the past, information was regarded primarily as a byproduct. Financial information resided in the accounting department, marketing information in the sales department, engineering information in the design and production departments, and so on. The technology of manual filing systems effectively limited other choices. Since, from the management view, money is the essential raw material, early computing functions began in the accounting departments, which provided the basic information for management decisions, and data processing reported through that function. This ignored the essential importance of the common requirements for information. Recognizing this as a deficiency, many companies have revised the reporting structure of computing to make it independent of any particular departmental bias. Although the user must influence the design of files and, ultimately, the system should be biased in the direction of profits, the undue pressures of more powerful users may warp the system to such an extent that this degrades the overall return to the organization.

That the critical information inherent in an organization be independent of individuals is extremely important to the ongoing success of the organization. Compare an organization to biological organisms consisting of cells; they live, are made up of individuals, yet they are independent of individual cells that die and are replaced or change function. This illustrates one of the reasons for the survival of large organizations and the high fatality rate of small organizations. The larger the organization the less significant any one person is to the whole. For this reason, the threat of resignation based on indispensability is a dangerous tactic. The organization hires a replacement and, thus repaired, lives on.

Such repairs nevertheless are not without cost. People leaving the organization constitute an information leakage and the loss of organizational energy. Such leakage along with the inability to access and apply information effectively can be the prime causes of the decline of a once successful organization. Data must be stored in files to prevent this, but what data?

1.1.2 Information Systems

The determination of the value of information is a major difficulty in deciding what data to collect and how to store it. The failure to determine the proper value of information has been the basis of many programming system failures. It is impossible to collect all available data and, indeed, unnecessary. Our concern with data, then, arises from the use we can make of it, or the information we can derive from the raw data so to speak.

As facts increase in volume, they soon become incomprehensible and are thus of little use by themselves. It is the meaningful interpretation of facts that give rise to their utility. *Information* can be thought of as an interpretation or use of data that is meaningful to a person. Thus in the broad or generic sense, an *information system* is one that provides for the collection and storage of suitable raw facts or data and provides for the means to manipulate this data to produce output suitable for direct human use.

Figure 1.1 shows the outline of several possible features of an information system. Four main divisions of any information system are: input, system processors, external data storage, and output.

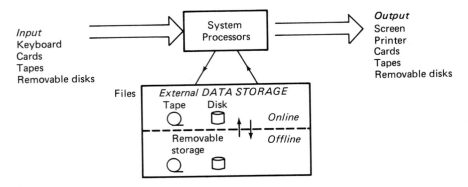

Figure 1.1   Information systems.

The following list gives an idea of some of the diverse applications of information systems:

- accounting
- airline reservations
- charge cards
- customer records
- income tax records
- insurance records
- inventory control
- land registration records
- patient's medical records
- production control

It is not difficult to imagine the diversity of such applications and that the performance requirements may themselves be just as diverse. For instance, Table 1.1 indicates three broad levels of the requirements for information: operational, managerial, and executive. Of course, all three levels may be present in a single system.

System Performance

For any job, certain performance criteria or measurements must be defined in order to determine the best system design. For instance, an airline reservation system has a critical response time for booking and checking reservations. Essentially, information is required in a demand time measured in seconds. Solutions that are inexpensive but slow are unacceptable. Updating of the data must also be essentially instantaneous since several seat requests on a particular flight may arrive simultane-

Table 1.1 Activity Levels in Information Systems

Level	Activity
Executive decision	Intellectual Unpredictable Browsing
Management control	Interpretation Summary Statistical
Operational control	Automatic Factual Predictable

ously. The cost to obtain a reservation system that meets the performance require-ments is tremendous but so too are the cost of a plane and the cost of moving empty seats through the air. Of course, once an airline upgrades service with an efficient reservation system, others are forced to follow to remain competitive.

Performance criteria must be determined before a system is defined and will form part of the system definition. For instance, that the data should be error free, timely, and current and that the system should satisfy the user and meet cost objectives are obvious criteria, which, however, are seldom met.

When the criteria can be quantified, then we have a performance measure. If we specify that the data error rate is to be less than one per thousand requests, we have a measure. Similarly, the criterion of timeliness could be stated as: 80% of requests will be answered in 30 sec and 95% in 60 sec with no request exceeding 2 minutes.

Ultimately, performance of a system is measured in terms of user satisfaction with the quality of the service provided by the system. Of course user satisfaction is achieved by more specific systems performance such as mean search time of a file, mean response time for random access to a record, and minimum throughput of transactions per day.

The *purpose* of data processing is twofold:

1. to organize vast amounts of data for efficient machine consumption
2. to organize interpretations of the data for efficient human consumption

With earlier information systems, or classical data processing, these two purposes were intertwined. It is now generally realized that to a large degree they can be separated and that in fact it is advantageous to do so.

In response to the first purpose, machine-stored data is now usually referred to informally as a data base. In response to the second purpose, programs that provide the algorithms to obtain information are called applications programs. The efficiency referred to can only acquire meaning within the criteria set for the system, not as a result of criticism from those ignorant of the basis for design. A study of the first purpose is in large part the subject of the rest of this book.

1.2 FILES

The need to organize the storage of data for efficient access was recognized long before computers arrived. The scroll, devised by the ancients, is an example of a sequential file. Unfortunately, a scroll has severe disadvantages. One must carefully unroll it to access information. If it is very long, the part unrolled gets rolled into a second roll, making it inconvenient to glance back at what was read. Changes can only be accomplished by recopying to a new scroll. Its advantage, however, is simplicity: all that is needed is a continuous sheet of paper. The disadvantages outweighed the advantages, and the scroll gave rise to the bound book, allowing random access to chapters and pages. The innovations of the bound book required not only a change in the physical organization of the recording media but also in the technology to provide for printing and binding of the pages. On a more modern note, we have filing cabinets, card index systems, and other mechanical aids to storage retrieval.

There are a number of reasons for using a computer file system as a source of information:

- expected reduced costs of operation
- faster access
- increased demand for data
- increased flexibility over manual systems
- government reporting requirements

Depending on the user, the source and importance of the reasons used to justify a file system will vary. However, we can express the basic reason and measure of value as that of profit to the organization, although the profit expected may be impossible to measure in dollars. The reasons put forward may be technically sound, result from the pressures of hardware and software salesmen, or simply be based on prestige requirements. Basically our concern is with technical reasons, but one must be aware of the political reasons that usually come disguised in pseudotechnical terms.

1.2.1 Data Subgroups

Data is a collection of facts. These facts are obtained though observation or measurement. For purposes of storage and processing, well-defined subgroupings of data are necessary. In computing, a number of subgroupings have acquired common usage and a relatively common terminology. They are summarized in Table 1.2.

Table 1.2 File Terminology

Term	Definition
Data	Collection of facts in an accessible form
Data base	Organized collection of related files
File	Organized collection of related data grouped in individual elements called records
Record	Collection of related data identified as the element of a file
Item	Smallest accessible unit of named data in a file
Aggregate	Named set of items in a record referred to as a whole
Group	Named set of *contiguous* items in a record referred to as a whole
Bit	Smallest unit of information storage (binary digit)
Byte	Smallest addressable group of bits (usually a unit consisting of eight bits)

A precise and common computing terminology has not yet been developed, particularly in the data processing area where a proliferation of manufacturer-spawned names has added to the usual confusion of conflicting terms in a new and developing academic area. In Table 1.2 and throughout the book, we give only a single name for a concept because we believe that once understood it will be recognized by other names. In the beginning, a profusion of alternate names can be confusing.

The subgroupings of data in Table 1.2 that is of prime concern and used as the unit for processing reference is the *record*. A collection of similar records, that is, records having a similar structure, is called a computer *file*. A collection of related files is now usually referred to as a *data base,* but more about that later. The smallest accessible unit of data that we refer to by a name is an *item*. We may now redefine a record as a collection of data items that is identified as a file element. It is possible for the computer to refine the data in an item. For instance, a byte can be extracted from an item, but this goes beyond a discussion of files.

It is often useful or necessary to have subgroupings of the items of a record. *Aggregate* refers to such a subgrouping. If, in addition, we require the items to be contiguous, then we call such an aggregate a *group*. The distinction between a record and a group is that a record is an element of a file while a group is an element of a record. This hierarchy of the definitions is usually quite clear in actual application.

As an illustration, suppose that an enterprise requires *data* on the people employed. For each person a *record* is kept in a personnel *file*. *Items* of a record would be name, personnel number, salary, and so on. An *aggregate* could be all data items of a personal nature. A *group* could be all positions held in the company by one employee. There could be many other files such as one for job description records. The collection of all files in the personnel office form a *data base*.

A more important distinction is in the number of occurrences of each subgrouping. The size of a record is fixed, or if it is variable, then it has an upper limit. Thus the number of groups in a record is limited. The number of records, however, is unbounded; that is, given more hardware, more records can be added to the file. It is characteristic of files that the number of records increases, and provision for this should always be incorporated in the design.

Within a record certain items called *keys* are used to identify the record or some property of the record. In some cases the key is unique to a record, in which case it is then called a *primary key*. For example, in a personnel file the social security number provides a primary key for the individual record. The item "sex," on the other hand, can be used as a key to identify all the records of male employees. Obviously, this would not be a primary key.

Basically it is the size of files that warrants the techniques discussed in this book. Presently, large files require secondary storage. The cost per bit of secondary storage is much less than that of main memory, and it would appear that this differential will be maintained since the speed of main memory must match or approach that of the central processor unit (CPU) in order to make effective use of the CPU's processing capability. Attaining such speed is expensive, thus limiting the size of main memory used in a computer system. Of course, another reason for using secondary storage is the need to remove the storage media from the system for back-up, security, transportation, and so on.

1.2.2 File Organization

Files can be characterized by the methods used to organize their records. Well-known file organization methods are sequential, indexed sequential, direct, and indexed. Each of these has different system performance characteristics when used for storage and processing. Associated with these organizations are access methods for adding, updating, and deleting records. The decisions as to which organization and access methods to use are based on the two fundamental measures of computing: *space* and *time*. Space refers to the amount and cost of hardware; in the case of files, this means the amount of storage media which is related to the size of the file and the method of organization used. Time is the processing speed; in the case of files, this refers to the time required to fetch an arbitrary record, add a record, update a record, or delete a record. The file design problem arises from the time/space tradeoff, which says, essentially, that you can have more of one at the expense of the other but not both for the same cost. The basic constraint on a file system is the cost limit. As the cost of hardware decreases, the main source of cost is time, and this is increasingly a function of people costs.

There are other performance measures as observed by the user; the data should be error free, timely, current, and the system should provide satisfaction in its use. The system performance measures we have indicated provide for the attainment of these more general performance characteristics but do not guarantee them. The user ultimately does not really care about the wonderful technical performance; he wants the data when he wants it and he wants it to be usable. However, such performance can only be attained if particular care is taken to see that the subsystems have the appropriate performance characteristics. Perhaps most crucial are the file subsystems because the performance of secondary devices is the weakest link in the computing chain.

1.2.3 Integrity and Security

To obtain satisfactory performance from the system files, there are a number of considerations beyond the organization of data and access to it that must be considered. The *integrity* of a file concerns the extent that the data is accurate at all times. This is a complex question for there are limits to maintaining integrity. For instance, it is not always possible to verify the correctness of an individual entry, but bound checks may be employed such as numeric type, upper bound on a number, sign, and so on. When the same item appears in various files, its value may differ among files because of difficulties in updating all occurrences. One hopes that this is only temporary, but it can still have serious consequences. Thus integrity, like freedom from errors, is not an absolute but a performance objective at which to aim.

The loss of integrity arises from three main areas: hardware failure, human error, and programming errors that allow invalid modification of data. By data *security* we mean the protection of data against unauthorized access. Such access may involve disclosure, alteration, or even destruction of data. No system is totally secure; all that can be hoped for is that the cost of penetration exceeds the value of penetration. Since this is expensive to achieve, the cost of security is related to the value of the data files to be protected. Unfortunately, the best technical security will not protect against careless human procedures that allow security mechanisms to be opened or whole files to be copied.

Integrity and security can be treated together in many aspects. It is important to be able to detect and recover from alterations and destruction of data by whatever cause. Procedures to do so must be designed into a file system and may well be its most important feature.

1.3 LOGICAL ORGANIZATION

Given a set of named objects, we may wish to consider how the names are organized and recorded. In lieu of any information concerning the objects, it is highly likely that the names would be ordered alphabetically. This recognizes that, if nothing else, at least the symbols that represent the objects (i.e., alphabetic names) have a logical relationship of alphabetic order.

Another possibility could be the order derived from listing the names sequentially. For example, we might ask for the sixth name and, because of the integer ordering conventions we all learn from an early age, chances are we would know where to find that name. The relationship in this case is one of physical position.

Although the names are physically organized, by the act of constructing the written list, they may have no logical organization. However, names may appear to be disorganized merely because the ordering function is not recognized. For instance, the names of acquaintances may be arranged in the order they were first met.

Thus there are two major ways to organize data: *logically,* whereby the data items are arranged according to some abstract relationship; and *physically,* whereby the data items are arranged by the physical adjacencies.

The purpose of files is to provide a representation of data and the relationships among the data items. The organization or structure of data that we store in files is logical, but because the structure of the file in storage is physical, the file ultimately has a physical organization. It is advantageous to preserve the logical nature of the ways in which the organizing of future data can be perceived as distinct from its present physical organization. The pure logical view is as a *data structure* which is a model for data, and we will briefly consider some examples that provide a constrast to the file structures of COBOL.

1.3.1 Linear Ordering Structures

When we speak of structure, we mean that some relationship of order is present. The alphabetic and integer orders are linear orders. They have the form of a straight line: every element is related by the order to every other element. The importance of these two orders is signified by the fact that they are the first two formal orders taught to children. There are many linear orders, and we spend a great deal of time learning them and being asked to recognize them.

Linear orders all have the important property of sequentiality. That is, an element in the order is located by position with respect to its logically adjacent elements: each element is in forward order from the preceding element and in reverse order from the following element. Thus, although the linear orders may differ, they can all be recognized as having a serial structure, and any linear order can be stored quite naturally in a sequential file.

Data can, however, often have more than one linear relationship present, and it is unlikely that they can all be simultaneously expressed in one serial list. Sorting is one answer to this problem. The purpose of linear sorting is to rearrange a sequential list of objects so as to obtain in explicit form a linear order we know to be implicitly present among the list elements. This is the basis of sequential file processing.

This multiple ordering of data allows us to view different relationships of the data. For instance, while a personnel file may be ordered on a personnel number, it makes more sense for it to be ordered on names. If we wish to examine the effect of age on salary, we may wish to order the file on age and on salary for a given age. Reports are always more useful when appropriately ordered.

To express order, a model or representation of the order is required. Data structures are representations and thus *models* of the structure of data. Many representations have been discerned and formally defined. A brief overview will indicate the pattern and a more detailed consideration is given in Chapter 13. Common representations for linear orders are the stack, queue, and the linear linked list. The distinctions among these representations are in the access methods: how we locate, add, and delete elements, as illustrated in Fig. 1.2.

Stack

A *stack* is a serial list of records where access is restricted to one end of the list. This end is usually called the *top*. Thus we may think of a stack conceptually as having a variable upper boundary and a fixed lower boundary.

Queue

A *queue* is a serial list of records with restricted access where deletions occur at one end called the *front* and additions at the other end called the *back*. Theoretically the lineup for a movie is a queue. Line crashers illustrate that the real world does not always obey the nice distinctions of theory. In computer storage, unlike a movie lineup, the records do not move each time there is a record deleted, rather the front of the queue recedes.

Linear Linked List

A linear linked list is a general form of a list with unrestricted access. Additions, deletions, and record access can occur anywhere in the list. For instance, in the line of people in Fig. 1.2(c), access can occur at any point where hands are joined. The physical order does not have to bear any relation to the logical order of the list. This is achieved by pointer variables in each record that point to the next record in the list, as shown in Fig. 1.3. Nonlinear lists have multiple pointers and

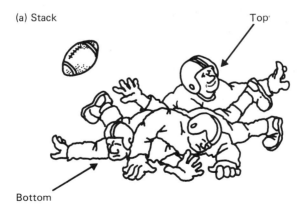

(a) Stack Top

Bottom

Football pile-up

Figure 1.2 Access to data structures: (a) stack; (b) queue; (c) linear linked list.

(b) Queue

Front   Movie line-up   Back

(c) Linear linked list

(Person enters or
leaves where hands
are joined.)

Group of people joining hands

Figure 1.2 (cont.)

shall be discussed later. The linear linked list can be used as a stack or a queue if desired, and thus the latter are special cases of the general linked list. Linked lists are very important in file organization both logically and physically.

1.3.2 Nonlinear Ordering Structures

Some orderings cannot be simply expressed as a linear sequence. A number of nonlinear relational structures have been devised to describe such orderings. Perhaps the simplest and best known is the tree.

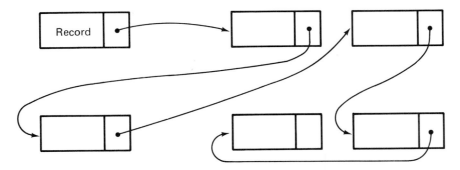

Figure 1.3 Linked list.

Tree Structure

Consider the set of male descendants of Adam to the third generation. If we wish to illustrate the descendants of Adam and at the same time show both the ancestors and descendants of each of Adam's male descendants, we require a structure more complex than a linear list. The structure of Fig. 1.4 gives the required ordering and this structure is called a *tree*. Any descendant is reached in a downward direction. Given a descendant only his ancestors can be reached in an upward direction.

The point or *vertex* labeled "Adam" is a distinguished vertex called the *root* of the tree. The lines or *edges* joining the names have an implied downward direction. Such a tree is called a *rooted tree,* and it is a very common relationship in computing. An important property of a tree is that there are no circular relationships. A rooted tree is a hierarchical structure.

Trees are a special class of a more general structure called a *graph*. Although the tree structure may appear to be very simple, its properties are mathematically complex, and its use in computing fundamental. Many files are naturally structured as trees.

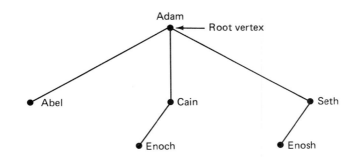

Figure 1.4 Tree structure of some male descendants of Adam.

Plex Structure

Many structures contain circular relationships. Because these are nonhierarchical, they cannot be expressed as trees. For example, in a retail store the owner may find that rather complex relationships exist among inventory items, their classification, and the suppliers. In Fig. 1.5, items are classified by supplier and by type, such as glassware. The complex structure obtained is called a *plex*. A plex is a labeled graph or network and is the most general type of data structure. The term ''plex'' is reserved for those structures that cannot be represented by trees or other simple data structures. Few computer languages have storage structures for defining plexes, and so the programmer must resort to their definition within the program.

Partial Orderings

What kind of order is represented by trees and plexes? *Partial ordering* is a concept that is applicable. In a partial ordering some elements may not be ordered with respect to one another; they are in effect incomparable. Some subsets of the set of elements are linearly ordered. However, if X is ordered with respect to Z and Y is also ordered with respect to Z, then X and Y may be incomparable. The subset relation on a set is a partial ordering. In effect a partial ordering may be thought of as a collection of linear orderings that are in some sense connected. A tree is a partial order on the vertices where every element is ordered with respect to at least one element, namely, the root.

The nature of data structures is far more complex than the file structures that have so far been provided in computer languages.

The intent of these comments is merely to indicate the place of data structures

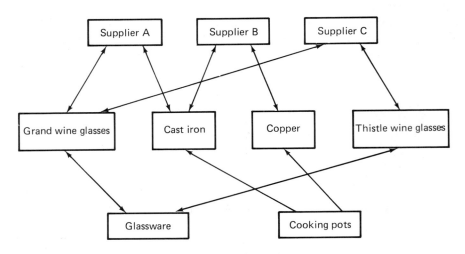

Figure 1.5 Plex structure of inventory records.

in the organization of data and their relation to files. A more detailed consideration is provided in Chapter 13. The reader should realize that the best organization of the data may not be directly expressible in a file organization.

1.3.3 Data Structure Synopsis

In summary, a *data structure* is an organized representation of data that is explicitly intended to display certain interrelationships among the data items. The central problem of the theory of data structures is how to provide representations that express most simply those interrelationships of the data, or structures, that we perceive as important and to analyze the consequences of such structures. Thus data structures provide models for data bases.

Unfortunately, the logical organizations a programmer devises cannot always be directly defined in the programing language we may wish to use. Nor do the physical organizations possible on a computer system's available external storage devices always correspond to the data structure we choose. The basic problem of file design is to determine how *best* to move from the perceived logical organization of the data to its ultimate physical organization on a storage device, where "best" is determined by some performance measure chosen for the design. We shall examine this problem and performance measures in some detail within a COBOL context in subsequent chapters.

1.3.4 Language Data Structures

The purpose of data structures, as we have discussed, is to provide as simply as possible a suitable representation of the logical relationships of the data that concern us. In other words, data structures provide abstract models of the structure of the data. The various data structures are devised without any great concern for how or where individual records and items are to be physically inserted or deleted, for how the computer system works, and for how these structures might be created within a programming language context. Indeed, this lack of concern is necessary for the theory of data structures to develop, since it is not at all clear what kind of computing systems will be available in future. In fact, the theory of data structures will strongly influence the development of future systems. Because a language may only have certain data structures incorporated, we will refer to such data structures as *language data structures*.

Since the computer system cannot be ignored in the representation of data, certain mechanisms for storing data on external storage have been devised for most programming languages. These mechanisms, taking into account the physical properties of external storage, provide means of access, insertion, deletion, and modification of records. In addition, they determine the physical organization of the data on the external storage media. Thus these mechanisms determine the physical representation of a data structure and provide for the creation and manipulation of the resulting physical storage organization. Such a mechanism is termed a *storage structure* to differentiate it from a data structure; in the case of external devices it is usually referred to as a *file structure*.

How the logical relations of a language data structure correspond to the actual physical storage is determined by the software. It is quite possible for a language data structure to have a different physical organization in different systems. In a given system, the language data structures may be considered synonymous with the physical structure or organization; this assumption is a convenience that can be misleading.

In the early days of computing, a language data structure corresponded to the physical organization of the data in a very direct way. Sequential files on magnetic tape are a good example. The program considers records as being sequentially ordered, and they are physically placed on the tape in that order. A language data structure is simply the implementation of a data structure within the context of a programming language and the realities imposed by the need for efficient use of physical storage devices. Insofar as it is consistent in this context, a good language data structure attempts to provide a simple conceptual mechanism and it may, as in COBOL Indexed I–O files, hide a great deal of the actual physical organization from the programmer.

1.4 PHYSICAL ORGANIZATION

The actual way data is stored on a physical device may bear little resemblance to how the programmer has organized it or how the language data structure appears to organize it. This is primarily because the two objectives of physical organization are to conserve space and to optimize the speed at which storage locations can be accessed. In general, these requirements conflict and the difficulty of the design problem is to determine an acceptable trade off. In other words, you can have more of one only at the expense of the other.

A good file structure does not require that the programmer know how the data is physically organized nor even on what kind of device it may reside. However, more efficient use of a file structure can usually be made if the programmer is aware of the physical organization, the reasons for it, and the device to be used. As the amount of storage used increases, this knowledge assumes increasing importance because any attempt to conserve space degrades the access time, which is generally more important.

Let us consider how the physical characteristics of a device may affect the access time of records and a simple solution called *blocking*. A tape drive has a time delay before it reaches full speed. To examine this, play a tape recorder for a few minutes. Since reading or writing is done at full speed, the portion of the tape that moves past the read/write heads during the delay period is *unusable*, and it is called the *interblock gap*. To reduce the amount of unused tape, several records are written at one time. This group of records is called a *block* or physical record. The programmer must have knowledge of the storage device in order to determine the optimal block size. It is possible for the storage structure to determine the block size, however, this may not be ideal for the particular application. Figure 1.6 illustrates the physical organization of a sequential file on a tape with unblocked (a) and blocked (b) records.

A disk permits direct access to a record; therefore, a file need not be sequential. Nevertheless, the time required to physically locate a record may exceed the read or write time of the record and blocking may be advantageous. Figure 1.7

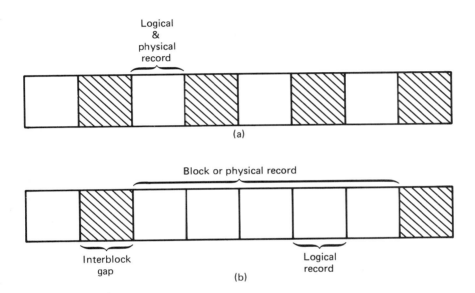

Figure 1.6 Physical organization of fixed-length logical records on a magnetic tape: (a) unblocked; (b) blocked.

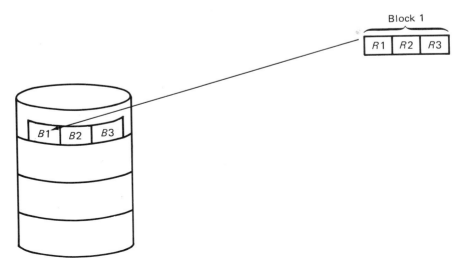

Figure 1.7 Consecutive blocks on a disk.

illustrates consecutive blocks on a disk. The unused portions of a disk may not be contiguous and, in order to use several such portions, a linked pointer system may be used. Figure 1.8 illustrates this concept. There are other reasons for the linked technique which shall be examined later.

1.5 WORKING WITH DATA

As we have seen, there are essentially two kinds of perceived relationships among data items. These are the logical relationships, or how the programmer wishes to view the structure of the data, and the physical adjacencies, or how the data items are physically stored with respect to each other.

Logical organization can be further subclassified into data structures and language data structures. The concept of a data base, as we shall see, suggests further subdivisions.

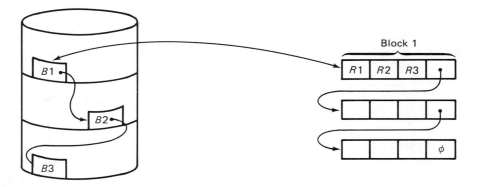

Figure 1.8   Linked blocks on a disk.

What is the correspondence among these various ways of viewing data? For simplicity, let us assume that the data structure and the language structure coincide. We consider then the relation between logical organization and physical organization. Ideally these two types of relationships should also coincide. This can occur in, for instance, sequential files. However, the fact that this is not always possible nor desirable poses a major difficulty in file design.

There exists then the set of physical organizations that are available in a computing system and the set of logical relationships that we can conceive. The object of data structures, as we have mentioned, is to provide explicit expression of the logical relationships we consider important; however, they are far more varied and extensive than the physical relationships presently available on storage devices.

Thus it is a major problem to derive a correspondence between how we wish to perceive the data and how we are forced to store it.

1.5.1 Mapping

To consider the way one view is transformed into another, we require a concept called a *mapping*. As an illustration let us consider the representation of a matrix in the main memory. Computer memory is generally a linear store, that is, it has the characteristics of a vector where the memory locations are where the data items are stored and the addresses of the location act as the index into the data. Storage of a matrix is achieved by mapping it into a vector.

In FORTRAN, for instance, a matrix is stored column by column, as illustrated by Fig. 1.9. The mapping of Matrix M to memory is defined by the following function f which, for simplicity, maps each matrix element to the locations 1 to 6 in memory:

$$f(i, j) = i + [m \cdot (j - 1)]$$

For practice with mapping, try Problem 11 at the end of the chapter. Conceptually a mapping is a correspondence of the elements of a set X to the elements of a set Y. There are several kinds of mappings according to the properties of the correspondence. Functions are mappings, and when the function has a unique inverse it is called a one-to-one function. In computing, mappings are always into *finite* sets. The reader can refer to a text on discrete structures for a more formal discussion of mappings.

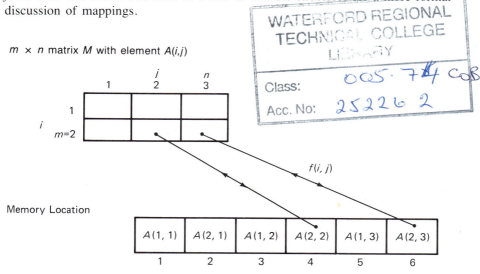

Figure 1.9 Matrix storage in FORTRAN.

The mapping of a language data structure to a physical storage organization is provided by the program language software. It may be possible for the programmer to influence the form of the mapping, for example, by specifying the blocking factor. In later chapters we examine how the mapping is done because the selection of a particular language data structure is determined to some extent by the physical organizations that result.

When the logical structure chosen by the programmer is not available as a language data structure provided by COBOL, the programmer must determine an appropriate mapping from the data structure to an available storage structure. This is done by controlling the program access to the language data structure records using suitable algorithms to perform the required mappings. Not all COBOL structures are available in all COBOL compilers.

Interestingly, all data structures can be mapped into a sequential file; it may not be very efficient, but it can be done.

1.5.2 Processing

How the data is to be processed influences how it should be organized. Basically there are two types of processes used to apply transactions to files.

Batch Processing

Batch processing applies to a set of transactions against a master file that they affect. Each transaction concerns a record of the master file and the transactions are first sorted in the order of the master records so sequential processing of the transaction file against the master file is possible. The major disadvantage of batch processing is the need to sort files before processing. When more than one master file is affected by the transactions, resorting of the transaction file may be required. In batch processing, a considerable amount of the total processing time is usually consumed by sorting. Knuth (1973) states that computer manufacturers claim over 25% of computer time is used for sorting. Since many programs do no sorting, some must do a great deal.

Another disadvantage of batch processing is that the processing is scheduled so that the transaction file is sufficiently large to make a run worthwhile. This is because the complete master file must be examined in sequential processing. If magnetic tape is the only external storage available, batch processing is necessary.

Transaction Processing

Transaction processing, sometimes called *inline* processing, applies a transaction against all master files before dealing with the next transaction. When no sorting of the transactions is involved, direct access is required, so files cannot be on tape while being processed. The major advantage then is that a transaction can be processed immediately online as received. However, transaction processing may be used in a batch system.

Computer processing has a jargon with which you should become familiar. *On demand* means the request for processing need not await a scheduled operation which could be as infrequent as monthly. Processing is then single transaction oriented. *Real time* means that the response is linked to a physical process as it occurs. *Interactive* processing means that the user can modify the processing in some manner in real time.

The file designer must know the type of processing to be used and anticipate future processing requirements.

1.6 DATA BASE

1.6.1 Overview

The concept of data as external to the program gives rise to the idea of a data base. There is some confusion about the meaning of the term "data base" because the scope of the idea is large and allows many specific instances. In brief, a *data base* is a collection of data consisting of multiple files arranged so that it may be readily accessed by different programs usually devised by different programmers.

In actual use this definition can and must be expanded. Other considerations are the level of redundancy allowed in the data, the degree of independence from application programs, the control of access to data, and the provision for optimal use of a set of application programs with conflicting requirements.

Martin (1976), among others, states that a data base must include the considerations mentioned to differentiate it from a collection of files. Because the boundary between a data base and a collection of files is vague, we relax this definition somewhat and use *data base management system* (DBMS) to refer to a data base with the software required to implement to a significant degree the considerations previously mentioned.

Primarily, the data base system concept is a result of the realization that, ideally, data and the files that contain data items exist independently of the program that accesses the data and should be treated accordingly. However, the complexity that arises from this view is immense and poses limits to a complete realization of the view, for carried to its ultimate the result would be one world data base. Thus the idea must be tempered by reality. Nevertheless, the limits of such a view are still to be explored. It should also be realized that the requirements of the large organization and the small organization do not necessarily coincide. We note that some corporations have compounded their data problems by premature implementations of data base systems.

The concept of a data base system does not lessen the need to consider physical files; rather, it says that the definition of physical files should not be located in the application program but in the data base system. The purpose of this transfer of location, as shown in Fig. 1.10, is to move from a static storage defined by the application program mapping to a dynamic storage mapping independent of the ap-

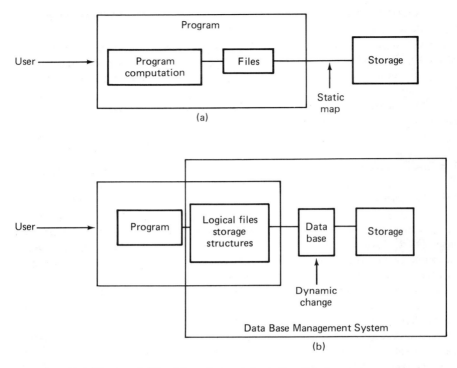

Figure 1.10   Mappings: (a) static; (b) dynamic.

plication program. This dynamic mapping is to be controlled by the data base software. Unfortunately in practice, such an idea has not been fully recognized.

In a data base system the data item is the main element of data rather than the file, and it is in the various ways that the data base system can organize the relational structure of these elementary elements of information that differentiate it from a simple collection of files. Of course, in the data base, as seen by the application program, it is the record structure that is of primary interest. Flexibility of organization and use is the key concept of data base systems, and data base management is the means by which it occurs. However, before such flexibility can be examined, it is necessary to understand static structures both logically and physically. We shall do this in subsequent chapters before returning to a consideration of the data base philosophy.

Virtual files and transparent files are two concepts toward which computing has been moving. A virtual file is one that appears to exist to the programmer but that is not normally present in the computer system. A simple instance is the logical file defined within a program that has a physical storage structure other than the one of which we are aware. A transparent file does not appear to the programmer to exist, but it does. The actual physical file in the above example is, ideally, transparent.

Because a data base system is simply a high-level file management technique, the development of data base systems has a good analogy in the development of high-level languages. The same pros and cons will be advanced and the same emotional debates will ensue. Of course, you still need an assembler language, but no one uses it unless it is absolutely necessary. Using file techniques, we can design file systems, in so far as it is possible, exactly the way we want them. Use of a given DBMS removes the flexibility to tailor the physical and logical properties of our files. The advantages of DBMS and their performance will increase with time, and it can be expected that a data base system will be in general the most cost-effective way to store data, just as high-level languages eventually became more cost effective than assembler languages. Nevertheless, it can happen that the use of the generality provided by a DBMS cannot be justified, or no system is satisfactory to the purpose; then it may be better to resort to file techniques to build your own data base. The point being that the simplest and most direct solutions are chosen unless *good* reasons are given to the contrary. Complex detail and so-called clever solutions should never be tolerated for their own sake.

1.6.2 History of Data Files

Basically, the history of data files can be viewed in three main stages of progression. These stages illustrate the move to isolate the physical storage of data from the applications program. This has been achieved by delaying the point at which the logical record is tied or bound to a physical address. This is called the *binding time*.

Stage 1: *Static physical organization*
The physical storage of data is performed by the applications programmer. Example: sequential files. Physical address used by programmer for direct access. Device sensitive.

Stage 2: *Dynamic physical organization and static storage structures*
The physical storage of data is performed by a software processor and data accessed indirectly by the applications program. Physical data restructured independently of the application program. Examples: relative files, indexed files. Device independent but a fixed logical view.

Stage 3: *Dynamic logical organization*
The logical structure of program files may change while the physical organization remains fixed. The logical files of the data base may change without affecting the application program's logical files. In other words, multiple logical files can be obtained from the same physical data. This is achieved by the data base system software.

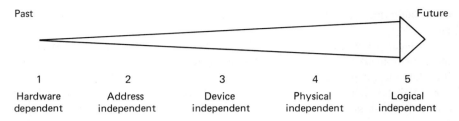

Figure 1.11   Trends in applications programming.

1.7 THE FUTURE

From the discussion so far, it is not difficult to see the future trend in storage techniques. The cost of acquiring and maintaining data will increase with respect to the costs of processing it. Thus greater and greater effort will be made to isolate the applications programmer from the impact of change in physical storage. At the same time the problem of storage utilization, time utilization, response time, complexity, and provision for anticipating use will be of major concern, continually requiring the need for complex tradeoffs that will be dynamic because of improvement in storage technology and the dynamic nature of the data base. To quote James Martin (1976):

> One of the most difficult tricks that we have to learn is how to introduce automation without introducing rigidity. The computer industry is only now beginning to glimpse how that can be done. Data base techniques are an important part of the answer.[1]

We might add that the telephone industry has dealt with this problem for many years. Its immense plant investment has forced new solutions to integrate with old solutions. The trend shown in Fig. 1.11 is developing rapidly.

The question remains. What will the applications programmer see in a file in the future? We believe that it will be the same file he now sees in his COBOL program but it may only be a logical figment of this program's imagination. Since the application programmer is usually concerned with records rather than with the individual data items manipulated by a data base management system, a thorough knowledge of a record-oriented application language such as COBOL should continue to be of value in approaching the new data technologies. Thus the file structures of COBOL will live on as long as COBOL does. Love it or hate it; COBOL may be aging, but it does not appear about to die.

---

[1]James Martin, *Principles of Data-Base Management* (Englewood Cliffs, N.J.: Prentice-Hall, Inc.,

REFERENCES FOR FURTHER READING

Mealy, A. H. "Another Look at Data." In *Proceedings of the AFIPS 1967 Fall Joint Computer Conference*. vol. 31. Montvale, N.J.: AFIPS Press, 1968.

Special Issue on Database. *ACM Computing Surveys* 8 (March 1976).

PROBLEMS

1. Explain the difference between data and information.

2. Determine measures of the value of information.

3. Determine ten functions that could be performed by an information system.

4. Discuss the information requirements of a small retail store.

5. Discuss the information requirements of a retail chain with central buyers and management.

6. Discuss the information requirements of a university. Is a single data base suitable? Is it necessary?

7. Suppose each home could afford a data terminal that could request computing service in the same way we now have telephone services.

(a) As the computer company, how would you charge for services?

(b) As the subscriber, how would you make use of this service?

8. Suppose you are engaged as a consultant to a small company that wishes to computerize their operations. What general advice would you give? Devise a feasibility study. Remember you do not know their business, but they do.

9. Comment on the human aspects of introducing a data processing system to an organization.

10. Does your installation have a data base? Write a brief report on its success.

11. (a) Change the function in Fig. 1.9 to begin at location k of memory.

(b) Map a three-dimensional array to memory and determine a function to describe your map.

2

Data
Management

The main purpose of this chapter is to provide essential device and system background for understanding file structures in general, COBOL file types in particular, and the relation of program files to hardware requirements. To do this, a knowledge of how and why data is managed in a computer system is necessary so that we may appreciate the form storage structures take and the reasons why files are processed in certain ways.

There are many forms of computer memory derived from the many technologies that have been developed to store data. Not all memory technologies have stood the test of time and many once important devices are no longer used, such as magnetic cores, or are declining in use, such as punched cards and paper tape. No one type of memory has yet to encompass all the diverse requirements of storage; therefore, computers tend to use several forms of memory to provide their storage requirements.

Computer memory is broadly classified into primary memory and secondary memory; each class may, and usually does, have several different types of memory devices. The distinguishing feature is that *primary memory* is directly accessible by the central processor (CPU) whereas *secondary memory* is only indirectly accessible by means of specific I/O data access instructions such as READ, WRITE, GET, and PUT.

We can add a third class called ternary memory; this is usually lumped with secondary memory. *Ternary memory* is only accessible through human intervention to initiate I/O access physically; in other words, it is normally off line. Main memory should not be confused with primary memory, as it may be only one of several primary memories. Of course, in computers with a single primary memory, the terms are interchangeable. Secondary memory is also called auxiliary memory or storage. Although these distinctions are not always made, when we use the term *memory,* we mean primary memory and usually main memory; and when we use the term *storage,* we mean secondary memory. We will always refer to secondary memory devices as *storage devices.* (See Fig. 2.1)

The two most important characteristics of memory devices are speed of access to storage and storage capacity. In general, the faster memory access is, the more that memory costs per byte and consequently the less we can afford to have of it. For a given amount of money, the basic tradeoff is between speed and storage capacity. Although the size and speed of main memory has rapidly increased year by year in hand with decreasing cost per byte, total storage requirements have always greatly exceeded available system capacity. Because we cannot afford to have a single memory type of uniform speed, we must interconnect several kinds of memory devices to supply the total storage requirements. In order to balance the conflicting requirements of cost, capacity, ease of use, and access speed, computer memory is organized as a hierarchy of devices, which ultimately communicate with each other via the main memory. The memory most directly accessible to the program is at the top of the hierarchy, and that least accessible to the program is at the bottom.

Files and data bases are stored on large-capacity storage devices. File data is moved as required through the memory hierarchy. This is the file processing problem: moving data about in secondary memory, and moving file data between main memory and its resident storage device. The movement of blocks of data in the hierarchy is quite complex, and the detailed physical movement is controlled by the operating system, even though it is initiated and terminated by the programmer via a file application program. The physical storage of data is a complex problem primarily because of the presence of the storage hierarchy, the need to move data between different levels of the storage hierarchy, and the desirability of making the different devices of the storage hierarchy and their interfaces as transparent to the user as possible in the process of data migration through the hierarchy.

Data management refers to the methods used to store and retrieve data, including input/output as well as external storage devices. It is data management software (as a part of the operating system) that conceals as much as possible the actual detail required to manage the storage hierarchy. Our concern with data man-

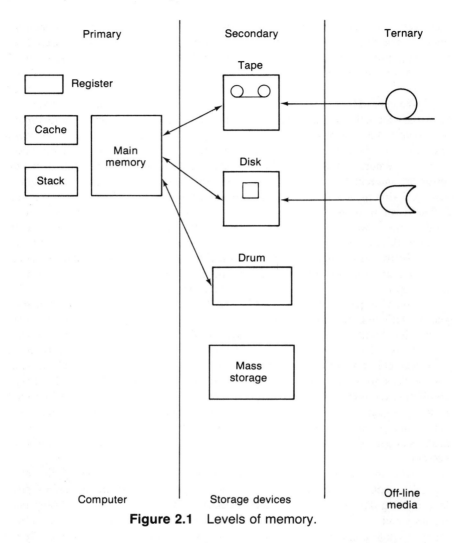

Figure 2.1   Levels of memory.

agement is limited mainly to the use of external storage for files; however, because data must be stored on a physical medium, data management necessarily also involves consideration of hardware. We restrict our discussion of hardware to the essential details of tape and disk drives that influence how and why data is managed on these devices.

2.1 STORAGE DEVICES

Intense competition by hardware technology manufacturers has provided a large variety of storage devices. For us, the important aspects of storage devices are cost per byte, storage capacity, and access speed. Indeed, the increasing use of data base technology is largely due to the availability of larger and larger storage capacity at a decreasing cost per byte. In addition, an ever-increasing reduction in access time has made many on-line systems possible.

Storage devices consist of a storage medium that physically holds the data and an access mechanism that does the reading and writing of data on the storage medium. Two storage media were already in use before 1900: the Hollerith card and paper tape. Since these media are permanently altered when data is stored, they can only be recorded on once. For both of these media, it is possible to read faster than it is to record. The use of magnetic media, on the other hand, allows rewriting. Furthermore, reading and writing are equally fast. Tape, disk, and drum are common examples of magnetic media. An important characteristic of a storage medium is whether or not it is volatile. A *nonvolatile* storage medium retains data until rewritten. A *volatile* storage medium requires a means of continually renewing the data stored. In other words, turn the power off and poof! Your data is gone. Primary memory today is usually volatile because of existing technology, while secondary memory is nonvolatile, a necessary condition for data protection in long term storage.

Use of a storage medium requires an access mechanism that locates the beginning of a physical record on the medium and provides the flow of data through either a READ, which is a copy of the existing record, or a WRITE, which is a replacement of the existing record by a new record. In primary memory, data access is direct and essentially independent of location. Access times on secondary memory vary depending on the physical location of the target record in relation to the present position of the access mechanism, which must be moved to the target record location. There are two kinds of access mechanism movement: serial access and direct access.

A sequential access storage device can only locate a record by moving from the location of a physically adjacent record. That is, the time to move from record X to record Y is a function of the number of records that sequentially lie between them on the medium. Examples of sequential devices are card readers and tape drives. Though tape drives normally move forward, some have a backspace capability.

Ideally, a direct-access storage device locates a record independently of the position of other records. The time to move from record X to record Y is related to their physical distance as measured by the motion of the access mechanism, which need not be related to the number of records that sequentially lie between X and Y. While access time varies, an average value, which gives a good approximation for random record retrieval, can be calculated for a direct-access device. Examples of direct-access devices are disks and drums. In practice, record access is not usually completely random as in memory. Disks locate the basic storage area, called the track, directly but sequentially scan the track for a record.

Magnetic media are relatively cheap and have large capacity. The access mechanisms are generally mechanical, which is much slower than electronic access but less expensive. Storage devices that use a magnetic medium have provided the best price performance and have dominated the secondary storage market.

Emerging optical technologies are expected to change these price and performance relationships.

2.1.1 Tape Devices

The first major large-capacity, external storage device was the magnetic tape drive, and today magnetic tape is still the primary off-line storage medium. The traditional data processing operation has been predominantly tape oriented, and the limitations of tape have resulted in processing procedures that are less than ideal on some other storage devices. From the mid-1960s there has been a general move away from tape-oriented processing. The weight or inertia of tradition has often caused programmers to apply tape processing procedures unnecessarily to more general devices when more efficient processes exist for these devices. Of course, the cost of conversion may also prevent existing processing procedures from being upgraded to new device capabilities.

Computer tape usually consists of a Mylar plastic base that is coated with a thin ferric oxide film, which is easy to magnetize. Tape comes on reels of different lengths in a range of 600 feet to 3600 feet; ½-inch, 2400-foot tapes have become standard for most use. Tapes are now often contained in self-loading cartridges, which are much faster to mount than reels because the operator need not manually feed the tape to the take-up reel. As the labor costs of tape mounts continue to grow, cartridges have become more popular, although they cost more initially than reel-to-reel tapes.

A tape drive has a tape reel mount and a take-up reel. As the tape is fed between reels, it moves past electromagnetic head sensors that can read or write characters (represented as binary bits) on the tape by means of the magnetic properties of tape. Fig. 2.2 illustrates the basic tape transport. A tape drive and its associated magnetic tape are similar in essence to an audio tape recorder. A drive can start, write (record), stop, rewind, start, read (play back), and stop. The tape only moves

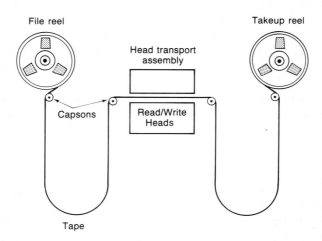

Figure 2.2   Tape transport mechanism.

while reading or writing a record, and this must be done at a fixed speed.

Like the audio recorder, a tape drive can work at different speeds. At present a typical tape speed is 125 in./sec, and 200 in./sec is now quite common. There are actually two speeds involved: the speed of the tape transport (or the rate at which the tape moves) and the speed of writing to the tape (or the rate at which characters are sent to the write head). These both determine the density of information on the tape, measured in bytes per inch (bpi). By standardizing the density of tape, it can be transferred to another drive with a different tape speed as long as the drive has the same recording density.

A density of 800 bpi was standard for many years, but it has been replaced by 1600 bpi. Improved drive technology has now placed 6250-bpi drives in wide use. To facilitate interchange of tapes, some drives have more than one recording density.

The speed of a tape and its density give the *data transfer rate*. For instance, a speed of 100 in./sec at a density of 1600 bpi gives a transfer rate of 160,000 bytes/sec. Choosing the highest recording density for a fixed drive speed maximizes the transfer rate but increases the cost of the drive as does increasing drive speed.

Recording density determines the amount of data a tape can store. Tapes store an immense amount of data. A standard 2400-foot tape at 1600 bpi potentially stores $1600 \times 12 \times 2400 = 46,080,000$ bytes. However, as we shall explain in more detail, the effect of interblock gaps (IBG; refer to Fig. 1.6) can significantly decrease the actual amount of data stored.

Table 2.1

Tape Drives	IBM 3420-8	IBM 3480 (1984)
Speeds		
Tape speed	200 in./sec	79 in./sec
Rewind time	40 sec for 2400-ft tape	48 sec
Start time	1.1 msec	
IBG time	3.0 msec at 1600 bpi 1.5 msec at 6250 bpi	
Data transfer	320 KB/sec at 1600 bpi 1.250 MB/sec at 6250 bpi	3 MB/sec at 38,000 bpi
IBG	0.6 in. at 1600 bpi 0.3 in. at 6250 bpi	0.08 at 38,000 bpi
Tracks	9	18
Capacity	165 MB/10.5-in. reel	200 MB/cartridge

Tape Data Organization

The standard nine-track tape contains nine parallel tracks running the length of the tape, with any character on a track recording a binary zero or one in each track. Looking at right angles to the tracks, we have nine binary bits, the eight-bit byte used to record a character and the ninth, called a *parity bit,* used to detect errors in the recorded character. Different codes are used for character representation; ASCII is an american standard accepted internationally, but IBM generally uses EBCDIC.

The basic data unit of a tape is the physical record or block. This is that portion of the tape on which data is recorded between a start and the following stop. Since a tape must move at full speed while writing or reading, not all of the tape contains data. It takes time for a drive to reach full speed, and this consumes space on the tape as does the time required to stop the tape when the data transfer is complete. This wasted space is known as the interblock gap, IBG, and is typically about ¾ in. An IBG of ½ in. at 1600 bpi would delete 800 bytes of storage. Thus, if recording blocks are 800 bytes long, the tape would use only 50% of its capacity for data. The design of the block size for a tape is an important efficiency parameter; we will consider this in detail in Chapter 5.

In addition to data, tape control information must also be present on a tape. The logical beginning of a tape is marked by a reflective strip of aluminum attached to the tape several feet from its physical beginning.

The first block of a tape is often a label used to describe the tape. It should contain such information as file identification, creation date, security date, retention date, and reel number if the file requires more than one tape. To indicate that there are no more file records, an *end-of-file* marker is written on a tape after the last file record is written. In the event that we try to write or read beyond the end of a tape, there must be an indicator to prevent the tape from running off the reel. A reflective strip of aluminum is used to indicate the logical end of the tape.

IBM 3480 Tape Drive

With the IBM 3480 tape drive, IBM has moved to a new generation of tape drives that use cartridges to replace reels. Tape is contained in a 4-in. by 5-in. easily handled cartridge, which is about ¼ the size of the standard 10 ½-in. reel it replaces, yet the cartridge stores up to 20% more data or about 200 MB. The new drives provide major reductions in space and power of about 60%.

The data transfer rate of 3 MB/sec is more than twice the rate of an IBM 3420. This is primarily achieved by using 18 recording tracks at a density of about 38,000 bpi. The error rate, determined by laboratory tests, is less than one permanent error for every trillion characters read. Maintenance costs are expected to be significantly less than that of an IBM 3420.

Tape Operational Considerations

Tapes are surprisingly durable and can be used thousands of times; however, their ability to function degrades with time and hostile environments. Some tapes of insufficient quality may degrade the tape drive on which they are used or degrade other tapes that are used afterwards on that drive. The manufacturer of a drive will usually provide specifications and tests for appropriate tapes (7). To reduce errors and the operating costs of tape, it is important to use high-quality tapes. Unless your organization is large enough to evaluate tapes, rely on published studies. The U.S. government maintains a list of tapes that meet their standards for data processing; that is a good place to start in selecting tapes.

Before use, tapes should be conditioned to the environment for 24 hours. High temperature or high humidity of tape may lead to degraded performance. Magnetic fields from electrical equipment can cause errors on tapes and must be avoided. Tape libraries should have controlled environments, and the environmental conditions of off-site storage should also be controlled. It is a good idea to rewrite long-term storage tapes once a year and to use archival quality tapes.

Tape errors are primarily caused by foreign deposits on the tape surface, by excessive tape wear, or by misadjusted drives. Drives should be cleaned regularly to avoid the dirt problem and the environment kept as dust free as possible. Drives are usually cleaned on a fixed cycle such as one per shift. A drive should always be cleaned after detection of a permanent error, and it is a good idea to clean a drive before mounting exceptionally important tapes. Cleaning an IBM 3480 is done by inserting a cleaning cartridge. This can take less than one minute per week as opposed to cleaning an IBM 3420, which takes two to five minutes and may be performed several times per day.

Tapes should not be cleaned unless they are dirty as the act of cleaning can degrade the medium. Tape performance statistics should be used to indicate the need for cleaning. Unfortunately, the ultimate solution to tape wear is to replace the tape. Drive adjustment is a maintenance problem; the fact that the drive appears to work does not mean it is within its adjustment standards.

Each tape should have an external label attached to the reel containing identification and important characteristics. Tapes have a write protection ring which when removed prevents writing on the tape, and they are stored without this ring. Normally, the operator should be given the instruction "ring in" when requesting a tape mount only if writing is intended.

The value of a tape is not its initial cost but the cost of the data stored on it and the cost of a run. The cost of reruns of a tape because of error can exceed 100 times the value of the tape.

Tape Usage

Because of the imprecise mechanical positioning of a tape, it is not possible to rewrite a block safely without overwriting the following block. Changes to a tape *must* be made by copying all records to another tape, modifying selected records in the transfer. However, it is possible to add records to the end of the tape data, but it is safer practice to copy to another tape and then add the new records.

Tapes were once the main source of secondary storage, and data processing techniques (discussed in Chapter 3) were designed to cope with the limitations imposed by the sequential nature of tape storage. Disk devices have since become cost competitive for high-use applications, and tape drives are used less and less during processing. Normally, sequential files are now stored on magnetic tape because of the relatively low cost of the medium, its compactness, and ease of removal from a drive. Tapes are mainly used today for off-line, backup, and archive storage. Tapes can be sent through the mail or delivered by courier because of their compact size and durability when stored on a reel. Although nonsequential files cannot be used on tapes, they can always be stored in sequential form as sequential files. Tapes can thus be used as a cheap, portable storage medium for all file structures, and, for this reason alone, tape will continue to be used.

It should be pointed out that insufficient knowledge of how to use tapes generally leads to the storage of infrequently used files on the more expensive mass-storage devices. This lazy approach often leads to the needless expense of purchasing more mass storage than is really necessary.

2.1.2 Disk Devices

The one-dimensional and mechanical nature of a tape drive limits it to sequential access. To obtain direct access memory, early computers used magnetic drum devices, which allowed two-dimensional access to the rounded surface of their drum cylinder, as in Fig. 2.3. While this permitted direct high-speed access (as well as sequential access), drums were of limited capacity, very expensive, and consumed a relatively large amount of physical space. Disk devices of greater capacity developed from the early drum technology, much as the phonograph record of today developed from the early cylinder phonograph of Edison. The basic principle of a disk is the same as that of a drum, and we can think of a disk as a rearrangement of the drum surface to use the flat ends of the cylinder, compressing the space between the ends. The use of drums has declined as disk technology has improved and the cost of disk storage decreased.

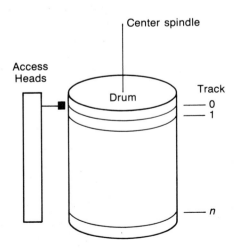

Figure 2.3 Drum with n tracks. The head access may have a movable head or a fixed head for each track.

The physical form of a disk recording medium is more complex than that of tape or drum; the basic physical unit is a platter, which resembles a phonograph record. A platter is a thin, rigid aluminum disk coated with a layer of magnetic oxide to retain data in magnetic form. Most IBM disks are 14 inches in diameter, although the IBM 3310 has 8-inch disks. In use, a platter rotates about its center passing under a read/write head that senses a narrow band of magnetic surface material. When the head is held fixed, it scans a circular band of the disk called a *track*. Since the head can only be located at fixed discrete points along the radius of a platter, these tracks form a fixed number of concentric circles, unlike the spiral tracks of a phonograph record, which result from the continuous motion of the record arm as it moves toward the center and end of the record.

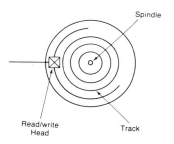

Spindle

Read/write
Head

Track

Figure 2.4   Platter.

The complete disk storage module consists of a stack of these platters mounted on a fixed spindle much like the stack of records on an automatic record player, except that there is sufficient space between the platters for the insertion of read/write heads. A typical storage module with 11 platters would have 22 surfaces. When a read/write head is inserted in the gap between platters, it can scan all tracks as it is moved towards the center; thus all surfaces can be accessed and platters recorded on both sides. This arrangement gives a large surface area in a small volume, so that a disk unit of equivalent physical volume has a much greater capacity than a drum.

The disk device sketched in Fig. 2.5 has a movable access arm resembling a

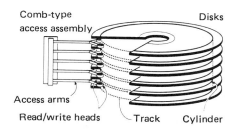

Comb-type
access assembly

Disks

Access arms

Read/write heads   Track   Cylinder

Figure 2.5   Disk device.

comb. The teeth of the comb can pass between the stacked platters, moving in and out along the diameter of the disks to seek any recording track desired. Each tooth contains two read/write heads: one for the platter above, and one for the platter below. Often the very top and bottom surfaces of the disk storage module are not used, because they are more subject to surface damage that can cause errors or head damage.

To read any point on the surface of any platter, the following three steps take place. First, the access arm moves toward the center spindle (or away from it, depending on its position relative to the track sought). Then the read head for the desired surface is activated. Finally, a waiting period takes place until the rotation of the platters brings the desired track location on the track under the head, at which time the data is read. Thus the clever rearrangement of the drum surface into a stacked set of platters leads to three-dimensional access. This discussion has neglected considerable device detail which need not concern us here. The intent is merely to understand how the capacity and speed characteristics arise from the physical construction.

Disk Characteristics

The advantage a direct access device has over a sequential device is speed of access. For a movable arm, disk drive access time has two components: the time required to move the head to the proper track, called the *seek time,* and the rotational delay time required to locate the beginning of the record on the track, called the *latency time*. We can ignore head selection time, as it is relatively insignificant. Seek time varies nonlinearly according to the initial position of the recording head. The manufacturer usually only provides an average seek value. Seek time can be reduced by clever programming, but multiple users of the disk in a multiprogramming environment will usually destroy the assumptions used to reduce seek time.

The only possible reduction of latency time is to speed up the rotation of the disk, a problem in the physics of dynamics and materials, but *seek time can be eliminated* by providing a separate head for each track. A fixed-head disk is simpler in that the access comb need not move, but more expensive because of the increased number of heads required. In addition, reduced capacity will result if we cannot pack the heads as closely as we can the tracks for a movable arm. Modern disks sometimes now mix these two types, placing fixed heads on a few tracks, typically for fast system access, while the remainder are accessed by a movable arm. A note of caution: sometimes fixed head disks are loosely referred to as drums; this is confusing terminology, avoid it.

The speed with which data can be read or written is known as the *transfer rate* and is usually measured in bytes per second. On disks the read and write rates are identical. The effective rate of data transfer is less than the transfer rate, since the track contains control information in addition to data and this control information is not useful to the program. The recording density of disks is very high. One might expect the inner tracks to store less information, since they have a smaller radius but all tracks can have the same capacity. This is achieved by increasing the recording density of the inner tracks. Track capacity is specified directly in bytes; thus density does not have the same importance to programmers as it does for tapes. The track capacity available to a user of an IBM 3380 is 47,476 bytes. The actual capacity depends on the type of recording block and the size of a block. The device manufacturer's specifications and the recording mode must be examined in order to determine the actual data capacity of a track, and this can be rather complicated.

The disk medium may be removable and is then called a *disk pack*. This not only allows off-line storage but effectively increases the capacity of the disk device. Unfortunately this is at the expense of drastically increased access time, which is not acceptable for an on-line system. Nevertheless, because the disk medium costs far less than the access mechanism, this is the cheapest way to expand system direct access capacity.

Table 2.2 Nominal Disk Characteristics

	IBM 3350	*IBM 3380*
Access speed		
Seek average (msec)	25	16
Rotation average (msec)	8.4	8.3
Disk speed (rpm)	3600	3600
Data transfer (Kbytes/sec)	1198	3000
Capacity (gigabytes)	0.635	2.52
Drives	2	2
Track capacity (user)(bytes)	19,069	47,476
Cylinder capacity (bytes)	572,070	712,140

Disk Data Organization

The basic physical storage unit of a disk is the track. The total physical storage unit is the set of all tracks. There are two natural subgroupings: all the tracks of a surface, and a cylinder. A *cylinder* is the set of tracks that can be accessed from a fixed position of the access arm. It is faster to process data by cylinder than by surface for a movable access arm, because the head need not move until every surface has been read and no rotational delay is required in passing from surface to surface. The cylinder has consequently become the most important conceptual organization of data on a disk.

A track is organized into a beginning, designated by an *index point* (this also serves as the end of the track), and one or more data blocks separated by physical gaps. It is the blocks of data which are the addressable storage units of the disk. A block address is obtained from the cylinder number, the head number, and the block number. In the simplest case, a block is a complete track, and we only need the track index point for control. Usually the track capacity is much larger than a desirable block size and some means of dividing the track into addressable storage units is required. Blocking a disk is more complex than blocking a tape because the block must contain control information for direct access. In order to identify blocks and determine their size, track data is organized in a pattern called a format. For illustration, we discuss three format patterns used by IBM: count-data format, count-key-data format, and fixed-block architecture (FBA).

Count-data format (Fig. 2.6) *does not* contain a record key. It begins with an *address marker* (2 bytes) written by the control unit to mark the beginning of a physical record. After a gap comes the *count area* (typically 13 bytes) used to identify the record location and type as well as provide required control information. A gap precedes the actual data that then follows.

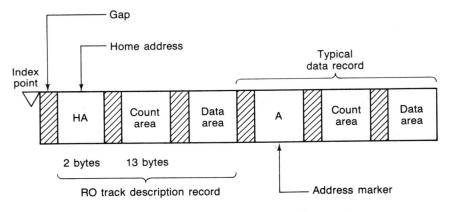

Figure 2.6   Count-data format.

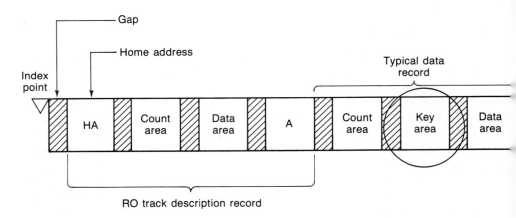

Figure 2.7   Count-key-data format.

In addition to an address marker and a count area, the *count-key-data* format (Fig. 2.7) contains a key area (from 1 to 255 bytes) for the key of the *logical record*. The key precedes the record data and contains a copy of the highest logical record key in the block.

An alternative to the variable-block format is to divide a track into a fixed number of addressable sectors (Fig. 2.8). Each sector is divided into an identification field followed by a data field both of fixed length. The identification field contains the sector address and control information. A typical data field is 512 bytes.

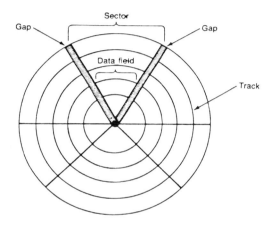

Figure 2.8   Sector format.

The selection of block size for a disk is rather complex compared to tape. This is because block size must also take into account the control information and gap sizes. Manufacturer's disk manuals provide detailed blocking information, which must be consulted for block calculations. Because direct access is logical record oriented, large block sizes may actually be more inefficient when the adjacent records are not required. When records are to be processed both sequentially and randomly, a compromise must be made in the choice of an efficient block size for both cases.

Disk Operational Considerations

Disk packs should avoid magnetic fields and be kept dust free (they are normally sealed in a container). The Winchester disk design, with its sealed construction, reduces exposure to environmental contamination and elminates preventive maintenance of heads and disks. Nonetheless, all disk packs should be treated carefully. Information on disks can be nonrecoverable because of errors or damage to the medium; thus back-up copies are required. Tape is most often used to back up disks, but demountable disk packs can also be used if the extra cost of the medium is acceptable.

Disk Usage

Disks have become the main source of large-capacity direct storage, and many installations now use disks solely as the processing external memory, limiting tapes to I/O, portable transfer of data, and off-line library storage. This has occurred because disks not only have relatively fast access times (on the order of milliseconds) and fast data transfer (on the order of megabytes per second) but also, and most important, provide storage at acceptable costs.

An operating system requires considerable storage, and some of the disks are reserved solely for its use, such as system catalogs and spooling.

Sequential file processing is usually done on disk, if disk space is available. On-line systems are based on direct access processing techniques and require disks if the system is too large to reside in main memory.

Disks differ with respect to mechanical construction, the number of recording surfaces, the number of cylinders, and the track data capacity. In short, there are wide variations in speed, capacity, and, as a consequence, cost. Any variation in characteristics can make it difficult to do a comparative analysis of disk drives. The costs of on-line and off-line storage can be difficult to determine, but estimates provide a useful relative comparison for making decisions.

2.1.3 Floppy Disk

In the search for cheap, mass, direct access storage, IBM developed, in the early 1970s, a flexible storage medium resembling a phonograph record. This has since developed into the now familiar floppy disk and drive unit.

A *floppy disk* is a flexible disk of mylar plastic coated with a magnetic oxide film enclosed within a permanent protective jacket. The diameters are 8, 5¼, and 3¼ in. Access to the medium is through a slit in the jacket for a read/write head to sense track data.

The disk in its envelope is inserted into a slot in the drive and the center of the disk is clamped to a rotating spindle that rotates the disk within its protective jacket passing by the read/write head, which can move in and out to seek a recording track. Rotation, in the order of 300 rpm, is slow compared to disks and there is continual wear on the surface because the read/write head is held in physical contact with the medium surface.

Some of the disadvantages of floppy disks have been overcome by a 3½-disk cartridge developed by Sony and adapted by Hewlett-Packard. In 1983, ANSI X3B8 began developing a 3½ standard based on use by Hewlett-Packard. These cartridges provide improved reliability, since the hard polymer case with an automatic metal shutter greatly decreases contamination of the disk surface. Writing on the label cannot damage the medium.

After the first year of testing, Hewlett-Packard found the 3½ cartridge to be four times more reliable than their preceeding 5¼ disk. Future improvements are expected to increase capacity to several megabytes, and every indication points to the 3½ cartridge as the emerging storage standard for personal computers.

Diskette Data Organization

The organization of data can be preformatted, called hard-sectored, or formatted by the user's operating system, called soft-sectored. A soft-sectored disk must be preformatted before use by the system on which it is to be used. We will describe here the format of the IBM PC DOS 2.0.

There are 40 tracks numbered from outer track 0 to inner track 39. Each track is divided in 512 byte sectors, and the sector is the minimum block size. An integer number of sectors compose a block.

There are a maximum of 9 sectors a track for 4608 bytes per track. Not all track capacity is available, as DOS reserves a portion of track 0 for system use.

Data is addressed by side (0 or 1), by track (0–39), and by sector (0–8). However, the DOS operating system provides symbolic addressing, so that this direct numeric addressing need never be used by an applications programmer.

Diskette Operational Considerations

Diskettes are fragile and can be easily damaged. The surface must be kept protected from dust, fingers, and pressure. They should be stored in envelopes and storage boxes away from heat and magnetic fields. Do not write on them except lightly with a felt pen.

Do not use master copies of software disks; run them only to make working copies. Because diskettes wear out from head-to-surface contact, at some point they can no longer be used.

Diskette Use

Because of their low cost, floppy disk drives are the main source of secondary storage for personal computers, word processors, and minicomputer applications where cost prohibits a hard disk.

Table 2.3 Diskette Drives

	IBM PC (1983)	Typical (1984)	Typical (1984)
	5¼	5¼	5¼
Access speed			
Average access time		415	187
Seek average, t_s			
Rotation average, t_r	100 msec		
Disk speed (rpm)	300	300	600
Data transfer, D_r	30 KB/sec	250 KB/sec	500 KB/sec
Capacity (dual sided)	368,640 bytes	540 K	540 K
Sector	512 bytes	256 bytes	256 bytes
Track	4608 bytes		

They can be expected to have wider use with main frames to replace the traditional card and tape files of user. They will increasingly replace magnetic tape as a portable off-line storage medium for those applications that do not require the bulk capacity of tape.

2.2. I/O CONCEPTS

Computers have become so complex that they manage themselves through a software program called an operating system. An *operating system* is the primary software program that supervises and manages all the resources available to a computer and provides user interfaces to these resources. Memory in all its forms is the most significant of a computer's resources. Therefore, all access to data is via the operating system; thus, an understanding of its I/O facilities is necessary for the proper design and evaluation of file and data base systems. The performance of such systems depends not only on the underlying hardware but also on the underlying software, that is, the operating system and all its data management facilities.

Computers are attached to terminals, printers, card readers, tape drives, disks, drums, and so on. How can the CPU communicate with all these peripheral devices whose characteristics and operating parameters vary drastically? In essence they all speak different languages. The solution is a translation unit, called an interface unit, placed between the CPU and the peripheral device.

There are many solutions to this interface problem. Personal computers usually provide one interface unit for each peripheral device. On large systems, such as the IBM 370 architecture, the interface problem is divided up into device-independent and device-dependent considerations. To relieve the CPU from detail control of I/O, a unit called a *channel* is used to handle device-independent functions of I/O control and data flow. To handle the different physical and design characteristics of peripheral devices, a unit called a *device controller* is used to manage device-dependent functions of I/O control and data flow. Thus a channel interfaces between the CPU via main memory and device controllers. A device controller provides the interface betweeen a device and a channel to the CPU.

Channels

A *channel* is a device that controls the flow of data between main memory and auxiliary data devices. A channel has direct access to main memory and operates independently of the CPU, except that they cannot both access the same memory at the same time. A channel is connected to a storage device through a device controller that directly controls one or more devices. Though a channel may be able to access more than one controller, it can only service one storage device at a time.

A channel is in essence a special-purpose computer that can execute programs within its special instruction set. Channel programs are stored in main memory, and channels have direct access to main memory. Channels communicate to the CPU via interrupt signals that initiate the appropriate action to be taken. The main function of channels is the routing of data between main memory and a device controller; this consists of establishing the data flow paths followed by the assembly and disassembly of data to travel the path. Data flows through the channel in user-specified amounts of data called data blocks, under the control of channel programs provided by the operating system. Channels control this flow by

1. fetching channel program commands from main memory
2. testing for availability of the selected storage device
3. starting and stopping data flow

It is the READ and WRITE instructions of a COBOL or other file application program that initiate these complex channel responses, which are transparent to the application program.

There are two main classes of channels, dedicated and time-sharing. A *selector* channel can only service a single device at a time; selector channels are usually reserved for fast devices in order to keep the channel busy. A *multiplexer* channel can service two or more devices by giving them turns to transmit units of data, which could be bytes or blocks depending on the type of channel.

Device Controllers

A device controller interprets the channel commands and translates them into operational commands of the controlled device and returns control information to the channel. It does validity checks on data to detect errors. It assembles data for the channel and disassembles it for the device, when data widths differ.

There are four types of controller commands: locate, search, read, and write. Locate commands position a device read/write mechanism to a physical address. For instance, a disk seek would be positioned by a locate command. Search commands compare a data search key against physical data to locate an address. Write commands cause data to be transferred onto the storage medium, and read commands cause data to be copied from the storage medium and transferred to the channel.

Buffers

We have noted that records are written and read from physical files in groups called blocks, but application programs deal in single records. How is a logical record accessed by the application program when device access is by physical record, which is a block of logical records? The difference in the program record access and the device access is resolved by a concept called a *buffer,* which is an area of main memory that is equal in size to the maximum block size and used to store blocks for program reference. The buffer problem arises because usually the program record size is much smaller than an economical block size for the storage device in use. Data management software provides and uses buffers for the blocking and deblocking of records. Good management of the buffers maximizes the use of both memory and the storage device.

If a READ statement that is used to obtain a record from a buffer is executed when the file buffer is empty, then a block of records is moved from external storage to the file buffer. However, if the buffer contains the required record, then the execution of a READ statement causes the next record to be moved from the buffer to the data area.

Similarly, the execution of a WRITE statement moves program data to the buffer when space is available. As soon as the buffer contains a complete block, it is immediately written to the file storage device.

The foregoing procedure is called single buffering, and it has major limitations. When a buffer is full, it is not available to a WRITE; and when it is empty, it is not available to a READ. To empty or fill a buffer, access to the device controller via a channel is required. Until a path is established and the movement of a data block is completed, the application program is *locked out*. If we increase the size of the buffers, then this lockout will occur less often, but buffers are reserved areas of main memory; thus, this solution consumes memory, the very problem we are trying to avoid by placing files on external storage devices.

A common solution to the problem of buffer lockout is to provide two buffers, one used by the application program and the other used by the storage device, where the buffers alternate between uses as required. Suppose we are writing to buffer A; when A becomes full, we simply switch the program to buffer B (assuming it is empty) and request a block transfer to empty buffer A. If we are lucky, buffer A will be empty and available by the time we fill buffer B; this switching process can then continue uninterrupted.

Suppose we have full buffers A and B. We read from A until it is empty and then switch to buffer B and request a block transfer to fill buffer A. Now if all goes well, A will be again full when we find B empty and we can then switch back to buffer A; this switching process can then continue uninterrupted.

The use of a single buffer means that the application program must wait whenever fully processed buffers require a block transfer to be completed. Double buffering allows overlap of logical record access and physical record access, thus speeding up the access of logical records. In practice a program may have to wait because it has processed a buffer faster than a data block transfer can be completed. More complicated buffer strategies are available, but they do not concern us here.

Optimal block size, which determines the buffer size, is determined by the size of logical records, the memory available for buffers, and the storage device in use. Some devices limit blocking choices. We shall examine blocking calculations in more detail in Chapter 5. Choice of block size is complicated by the fact that in modern systems one may not necessarily determine the device to be used nor even be able to. Nevertheless, because blocking is such an important component of program efficiency, it cannot be ignored. Perhaps more ideally the data management software should determine the blocking factor.

2.3 FILE MANAGEMENT

Since files usually reside externally to main memory, file access necessarily involves the physical location of that file on an external device followed by the establishment of data flow between main memory and the selected external device. Communication with a file requires that the file exist, be identifiable, be accessible through a data path, and that system resources be available to establish the required data path. A file is created by having the operating system allocate secondary storage for the number of records expected and by reserving this file space only for as long as the file exists. How the operating system does this is not our concern, whereas how the creation or existence of a file is defined for the operating system is an important concern of the file user. File content detail is defined in a COBOL program within an FD description. The system file description is only concerned with the physical storage parameters and location, not the logical records, and these physical parameters are conveyed by means of an operating system language, which in the IBM system 370 is called JCL (for Job Control Language). Files must be defined to exist within the operating system before COBOL can access them. The system manages the files known to it through a directory.

In System 370 a tape reel or a disk pack is referred to as a volume. A *volume* is a single complete physical unit of storage medium. For instance, neither a platter nor a cylinder is a volume, but all the platters on a spindle constitute a volume. Volumes usually have labels, and each file stored on a volume should have a file label. Normally on a disk volume, the labels of all the files stored on that volume are grouped together as a volume directory stored on the first cylinder. This directory, usually called the volume table of contents (VTOC), is used to find the physical location of a file on the volume. Multiple files on disk are the norm, whereas they are the exception on tape; you may need to give some thought to a tape directory when using multiple files on tape.

Communication between a program and a file involves two kinds of information: file control parameters and actual file data. Our concern in this section is with file control; the handling of file data is the subject of the rest of the book. First of all, files are identified by file names that must be known to the operating system. COBOL programs use two file names: the program, or COBOL file name, and the operating system file name. A COBOL file name is determined in its file definition by an FD declaration. The system file name is defined by the operating system language, which IBM JCL does in a DD (data definition) statement. The correspondence between the two names for the same file is established through the COBOL ENVIRONMENT DIVISION using an ASSIGN clause. COBOL files are explicitly connected to and disconnected from programs through OPEN and CLOSE statements.

Before a file can be accessed by a program, a number of events must take place in order to establish a data path between the program and the file. This is known as *opening* a file, and in COBOL the OPEN verb is used to initiate a file for program use. The file is first located in the system directory, or, if necessary, a message is sent to the operator to mount the required file volume. A sequential file is positioned to the first record and labels checked or created. The operating system creates the necessary access method control programs, assigns an area of main memory to the file buffers, and performs any other preconditions for processing that file.

In order to release the system resources assigned to a program by opening a file, the data path between the file and the program must be disconnected; this is known as *closing* a file. In COBOL the CLOSE verb is used to initiate file closing. For an output file, the last block is written to the file; for sequential output files an end-of-file label is written. The file buffer and any associated control areas are released. Tape drives are rewound, and the file storage device released to the system.

It should be obvious by now that connecting files to programs consumes system resources and that a charging algorithm may be assigning system overhead costs to your program. Files should only be opened before intended use; however, remember that it takes time and costs overhead just to open a file. Files should be closed as soon as they are no longer expected to be active or when sufficient time will elapse between use; this is a design decision and the answer may not be obvious.

2.4 CONCLUSIONS

Our discussion of devices has been brief because it is necessarily of a general nature. Our main point is that the physical characteristics of storage devices can determine the kind of logical or abstract file characteristics of the solutions we choose. Since storage devices are continually being improved, we should be careful to avoid ignoring the fundamental reasons for past solutions when those reasons no longer exist.

The reader should note that manufacturers generally reserve the right to change specifications at any time. Therefore, parameter values used for design calculations should be obtained from the most recent manufacturer's manuals. Since many units have several models with corresponding variations in operational parameters, some care is required in obtaining correct values.

Devices come and go, but concepts of access speed, capacity, transfer rates, and physical organization of data will continue to apply. It may well be that the reader will gain a deeper appreciation by a more detailed study of a particular device. Unfortunately, no device that we choose to examine here can satisfy the detailed requirements of all our readers. In our view such detailed study should only be on need-to-know and when-required basis. Life is too unpredictable and short for any other approach.

Device access involves the operating system, which provides access method support programs. File access requires not only device management support but also file management support that deals with all files, not just those of a single user. In order to evaluate the costs of file access in real time and in execution time, an understanding of the involved sequence of events that lead to actual device read and write operations is necessary. The actual sequence of events and their cost depend upon the operating system in use and the access utilities provided. These are subject to change and can affect a file system's operation, sometimes drastically. Logical files that are independent of the physical details of their resident computer system can only be obtained at the cost of software overhead to manage the detail transparent to the application programmer.

REFERENCES FOR FURTHER READING

ANSI X3.27-1977, Magnetic Tape Labels and File Structures for Information Interchange. New York: American National Standard Institute, Inc., 1977.

ANSI X3.39-1973, Recorded Magnetic Tape for Information Interchange. New York: American National Standards Institute, Inc., 1973.

Bohl, M. *Introduction to IBM Direct Access Storage Devices.* Chicago: SRA, 1981.

Davis, W. S. *Operating Systems: A Systematic View.* 2nd ed. Reading, Mass.: Addison-Wesley, 1983.

IBM. *Channel Characteristics and Configuration Guide.* Order Form GA22-7077.

IBM. *Input/Output Device Summary.* Order Form GA32-0039.

IBM. *Magnetic Tape Subsystems.* Order Form GA32-0021.

IBM. *Magnetic Tape Subsystems, IBM 3480.* Order Form GA32-0041.

IBM. *Tape Requirements for IBM One-Half Inch Tape Units.* Order Form GA32-0006.

PROBLEMS

1. Select the five most important characteristics of storage devices and explain your choices.

2. List the storage devices used at your computer center. Discuss why there should only be one type.

3. Obtain the characteristics of the most common tape drive in your computer center. List in decreasing order of importance any characteristics important to programmers. If there is more than one tape drive in the center, determine the best one to use.

4. Determine the essential programming characteristics of the disk drives in your computer center. Which drive is best? Comment on this question.

5. Suppose physical records 800 bytes in length are written on a tape of density 800 bytes/in. If the interblock gap is ½ in., how much of the tape available is used for physical records?

6. Suppose records 50 bytes in length are blocked in groups of 100 and written on a tape of density 1600 bytes/in. If the interblock gap is ¾ in., how much of the tape is consumed by interblock gaps?

7. How long would it take to read a 3600-foot, 1600-bpi tape at 125 in./sec, assuming one block on the tape?

8. How long would it take to read a 2400-foot tape (with 11-inch blocks) at 200 in./sec if an IBG is 1 in. and consumes 1 sec?

9. How many punched card records can be stored on an 800-bpi, 2400-foot tape blocked at 240 characters? Assume IBG of ½ in.

10. How many punched card records can be stored on a 1600-bpi 2400-foot tape blocked at 480 characters? Assume IBG of ½ in.

11. If a disk has 10 platters with 20 tracks and the very top and bottom platter surfaces are not used, what is the cylinder size (in tracks)? If a track stores 4000 bytes, what is the disk capacity?

12. A disk unit using the sector method with 12 sectors of 512 bytes per track has 11 platters. If each platter has 100 tracks, how many cylinders are there and what is the capacity of a cylinder in bytes?

13. Suppose records are 92 bytes long and an I/O buffer is available with 1000 bytes. You have a choice of tape recording densities of 800 and 1600 bpi. What blocking factor and density would you use to get the highest recording density of records on the tape? To get the lowest recording density of records on the tape?

14. (a) What is the importance of the surface area of the recording medium?

(b) What is the importance of the transfer rate?

(c) For which kind of access is the seek time important?

(d) How can seek time be eliminated?

15. Investigate two storage devices that we have not considered; discuss their operation and list the advantages and disadvantages of these devices.

16. Invent a mass storage device of very large capacity. List the advantages and disadvantages of your device.

COBOL Sequential Files

3.1 INTRODUCTION

A *sequential file* is a serial list of records where, except for the first and last records, each record has a unique predecessor and a unique successor record. This serial order is established when the file is created, by physically storing the records one following the other in the order of writing. The records are physically stored in their logical sequential order. Essentially, a sequential file has a static linear physical order, records are accessed in the order that they were originally written.

A file is *sequentially organized* when its records are sequenced and are stored and accessed in consecutive order according to this sequence. A set of COBOL statements with sequence numbers from 1 to 100 stored in this sequence is an example of a sequentially organized file. The file would still be sequentially organized if the statements were numbered 10, 20, 30, to 1000 or even if stored in the same order without the sequence numbers being present. On the other hand, a file is said to be *sequentially accessed* when the records are processed in the consecutive order in which they are physically located on a storage device. A sequentially organized file *must*, by definition, be sequentially accessed, but as we shall see, it is possible to sequentially access files that are not sequentially organized.

The set of statements mentioned above is sequentially accessed by the COBOL compiler during compilation. If the program statements are shuffled, destroying their sequence, the program will not execute properly. Note that a deck of playing cards is usually shuffled before being used. This is done in order to achieve a random distribution but playing cards are dealt sequentially, one card at a time (one would hope, off the top of the deck). Thus a deck of playing cards is randomly organized but sequentially accessed.

There are many examples of *sequentially organized* files, such as

1. a list of all employees of a company in ascending order by social security number
2. a list of all students in a high school in decreasing order by student ID number
3. a list of the hit parade songs played by a radio station during one hour, arranged in the order in which they were played.

With regard to data base organization, there are two major reasons for using sequential access to records. First, the occurrence of records is sequentially organized for purposes of the application; hence, sequential access to the records is a necessary requirement. Second, the cost or availability of equipment requires the use of magnetic tape drives or other devices that permit only sequential access to the records.

Sequentially organized files are found most often in batch-oriented data processing. Transactions relevant to some application are collected into a batch and kept until enough have accumulated to warrant their processing as a group. An example of this is the recording of purchases made with credit cards. Each purchase is not immediately debited to a credit card account by a clerk. Rather, it is forwarded by mail to a central clearing house where it is batched together with many other credit slips before being processed. These transactions are arranged in some sequence (usually in increasing order by corresponding credit card number) and then processed by a program to each individual account where the accounts are stored in the same sequence.

Batch-oriented data processing is also performed when data is to be processed for monthly billings, semiannual inventories, quarterly tax reports, and other applications. A major factor is that processing is scheduled by the cyclic nature of the application. Thus the need for data is not a sudden demand; rather it is known in advance and can be planned for. Batch can be very efficient in such cases. Sudden demand reports tend to require organization of the data base in a manner other than sequential.

Reading a sequential file normally begins with the first record. However, some systems allow an offset, and reading may begin with the *n*th record. In

COBOL a START instruction is used to obtain the offset. Records can be added to the end of the file, but some installations forbid such operations, requiring a new file copy to be made. This is really a matter of the file back-up procedures in use, since an error in the program could inadvertently wipe out a portion of the file. A sequential file record can be rewritten on a direct access device. Records *cannot* usually be rewritten in place on *magnetic* tape as there is *no* guarantee that they can be returned to the same physical location and, consequently, adjacent records may be overwritten, destroying them.

Whether sequential access to the records is required because the data is sequentially organized or whether the storage devices permit only sequential access, most operating systems provide routines that store and retrieve records from storage devices sequentially. Such routines, called *access methods* are responsible for transferring data between primary memory of the machine and a storage device. These routines are usually complicated, machine dependent, and very sophisticated. Normally, the details required to use them need not be known directly by the programmer as most of the higher-level languages and in particular, COBOL contain language statements that invoke their execution. When the programmer is unaware of the access method, we say it is *transparent*.

> In COBOL, the language elements necessary for handling sequential files are termed the *Sequential I–O module*. This is the ANSI term; it may or may not be used by a particular manufacturer's implementation. The Sequential I–O module has two levels of implementation called *Level 1* and *Level 2*. Level 1 contains the basic facilities for the definition and access of sequential files as well as specification of check points. Level 2 provides full facilities. Although we cannot examine every feature, we have not restricted our discussion to Level 1. Since Level 1 does not provide for the full capabilities of COBOL sequential files, the programmer must determine the level of the compiler he is to use.

In summary, *sequential organization* means that the file records are stored consecutively on the file media and can only be retrieved serially in the order that they are stored. Records are thus addressed implicitly. Sequential access moves records between the program and the file media in the physical order of storage. *Sequential processing* refers to the use of sequentially accessed files.

3.2 CASE STUDY: MUSIC LOG

The disc jockeys of radio station XJBC maintain a written report that lists the music selections they play during their radio programs. This report is known as the *music log* and is very useful to management for determining advertising costs and daily programming content. This log is also studied to advise the government's radio and television authority of the amount of air time allocated to music of national and international origin and to help the station's listeners obtain the names of selections and performers of music they have enjoyed.

The increased use of the log, particularly the statistics required by government, has excessively increased administrative costs. Protests to the government officials concerned have been to no avail. And in view of last year's submissions being lost in the mail, management has decided that it is essential to improve present procedures by placing the music log on a computer.

3.2.1 Logical Analysis: Music Log

Each entry of the manual music log contains the name of the music selection, the name of the performer, the time the music was played, the name of the recording label, and the duration of the selection. To satisfy new government regulations, country of origin of both the record and the artist need to be added. The music log grows with the passing of time, but since each record of the log records a historical event, it is never changed unless an error was made.

The musical selections are naturally ordered by the playing sequence, and random retrieval is not required; therefore, a sequential file is a natural choice of file organization. This file can be stored on tape or disk. To provide statistics on the type and mix of music, management has decided to classify the music into country, classical, popular, jazz, teenage, and folk. This is encoded into a single field of the record.

Program 3.1 Narrative.   Program 3.1 enters records into the sequential music log file. The COBOL procedure contains four paragraphs whose order of execution is determined by the first paragraph in a top down structured manner. The reader should examine this program skimming over points he does not understand, as the next section introduces the Sequential I–O module of COBOL and will clarify this program.

Exercise (Program 3.1)

There is a problem with Program 3.1. Suppose a record is entered incorrectly. How do we correct it? First, we must find it. To do this, the record must be uniquely identified. Determine what changes should be made to the music log record definition in order to solve the problem.

When discussing COBOL programs we shall not be unduly concerned with those segments of the programs not pertinent to the discussion at hand. No attempt will be made to use files as detailed as those encountered in the real world, but the reader should constantly realize that he may well need to operate with records containing many more fields and files containing many more records.

Program 3.1

```
00001          IDENTIFICATION DIVISION.
00002          PROGRAM-ID. PROG3PT1.
00003      *    ** CREATES THE MUSIC LOG **
00004          DATE-WRITTEN. 85/05/31.
00005          AUTHOR. R H COOPER.
00006          ENVIRONMENT DIVISION.
00007          CONFIGURATION SECTION.
00008          SOURCE-COMPUTER. IBM-370.
00009          OBJECT-COMPUTER. IBM-370.
00010
00011          INPUT-OUTPUT SECTION.
00012          FILE-CONTROL.
00013              SELECT INPUT-FILE
00014                      ASSIGN TO UT-CARD-S-SYSIN
00015                      ORGANIZATION IS SEQUENTIAL
00016                      ACCESS MODE IS SEQUENTIAL.
00017              SELECT MUSIC-LOG
00018                      ASSIGN TO UT-DISK-S-MUSIC
00019                      ORGANIZATION IS SEQUENTIAL
00020                      ACCESS MODE IS SEQUENTIAL.
00021              SELECT PRINTER
00022                      ASSIGN TO UT-PRNT-S-SYSOUT
00023                      ORGANIZATION IS SEQUENTIAL
00024                      ACCESS MODE IS SEQUENTIAL.
00025
00026
00027          DATA DIVISION.
00028          FILE SECTION.
00029
00030          FD  INPUT-FILE
00031              BLOCK CONTAINS 1 RECORDS
00032              RECORD CONTAINS 80 CHARACTERS
00033              LABEL RECORDS ARE OMITTED
00034              DATA RECORD IS CARD-IMAGE.
00035          01  CARD-IMAGE.
00036              02  FILLER                PIC X(80).
00037
00038          FD  MUSIC-LOG
00039              BLOCK CONTAINS 100 RECORDS
00040              RECORD CONTAINS 149 CHARACTERS
00041              LABEL RECORDS ARE STANDARD
00042              DATA RECORD IS MUSIC-LOG-RECORD.
00043          01  MUSIC-LOG-RECORD.
00044              02  FILLER                PIC X(149).
00045
00046          FD  PRINTER
00047              BLOCK CONTAINS 1 RECORDS
00048              RECORD CONTAINS 133 CHARACTERS
00049              LABEL RECORDS ARE OMITTED
00050              DATA RECORD IS PRINT-LINE.
00051          01  PRINT-LINE.
00052              02  FILLER                PIC X(133).
00053
00054
00055          WORKING-STORAGE SECTION.
00056          77  EOF-CARD-FLAG             PIC X(3).
00057              88  EOF-CARD VALUE IS 'ON'.
00058
00059          01  WS-MUSIC-LOG-RECORD.
00060              02  FIRST-CARD.
00061                  03  NAME-OF-SELECTION  PIC X(30).
```

Program 3.1   (cont.)

```
00062                          03  NAME-OF-ARTIST      PIC X(30).
00063                          03  NAME-OF-RECORDING-LABEL
00064                                                  PIC X(20).
00065                      02  SECOND-CARD.
00066                          03  TIME-PLAYED         PIC 9(4).
00067                          03  DURATION            PIC 9(4).
00068                          03  ORIGIN-OF-RECORD    PIC X(30).
00069                          03  ORIGIN-OF-ARTIST    PIC X(30).
00070                          03  MUSIC-CLASSIFICATION
00071                                                  PIC X.
00072
00073
00074             PROCEDURE DIVISION.
00075
00076                 PERFORM INITIALIZATION.
00077                 PERFORM PROCESS-CARDS UNTIL EOF-CARD.
00078                 PERFORM TERMINATION.
00079                 STOP RUN.
00080
00081             INITIALIZATION.
00082                 OPEN INPUT INPUT-FILE
00083                      OUTPUT PRINTER
00084                             MUSIC-LOG.
00085                 MOVE 'OFF' TO EOF-CARD-FLAG.
00086                 READ INPUT-FILE RECORD INTO FIRST-CARD
00087                      OF WS-MUSIC-LOG-RECORD
00088                      AT END MOVE 'ON' TO EOF-CARD-FLAG.
00089                 IF NOT EOF-CARD THEN
00090                     READ INPUT-FILE RECORD INTO SECOND-CARD
00091                          OF WS-MUSIC-LOG-RECORD.
00092
00093             PROCESS-CARDS.
00094                 WRITE MUSIC-LOG-RECORD FROM WS-MUSIC-LOG-RECORD.
00095                 WRITE PRINT-LINE FROM FIRST-CARD OF
00096                       WS-MUSIC-LOG-RECORD.
00097                 WRITE PRINT-LINE FROM SECOND-CARD OF
00098                       WS-MUSIC-LOG-RECORD.
00099                 READ INPUT-FILE RECORD INTO FIRST-CARD
00100                      OF WS-MUSIC-LOG-RECORD
00101                      AT END MOVE 'ON' TO EOF-CARD-FLAG.
00102                 IF NOT EOF-CARD THEN
00103                     READ INPUT-FILE RECORD INTO SECOND-CARD
00104                          OF WS-MUSIC-LOG-RECORD.
00105
00106             TERMINATION.
00107                 CLOSE INPUT-FILE
00108                       PRINTER
00109                       MUSIC-LOG.
```

3.3 SEQUENTIAL I–O MODULE OF COBOL

The statements of the sequential I–O module of COBOL can be divided into three classes:

1. those that describe the file
2. those that describe the records of the file

3. those that access the file

In the first class are statements that *name* the file, *define* its mode of organization and access, and that *link* the file to a physical storage device.

In the second class are statements that *describe* the data layout of the records comprising the file.

In the third class are statements that *prepare* the file for use, *write* records to the file, *read* records from it once created, and, lastly, *disconnect* the file from the program once work with it is completed.

The allocation of physical storage—that is, the labeling and selection of a magnetic tape, the reservation of space on a disk. or the setting aside of some of the capacity of any storage device—is not a function that can be done within the COBOL language. This is a function of the operating system. For help in this matter consult a systems analyst at your installation. (See Chapter 12 for more details.)

Today many installations forbid users reserving physical storage space and police its availability. This is done in an effort to provide increased reliability, integrity, and security for all the users of data at an installation.

The COBOL program to create the music log (Program 3.1) is unexpectedly complex, but this is typical of COBOL. Unfortunately, the flexibility allowed by COBOL in defining files and the desire for system independence makes COBOL a wordy language. Though this makes COBOL programs long, it also makes them self-documenting. A carefully written COBOL program using appropriately chosen variable names can quickly be mastered by another programmer. This feature has done much to make COBOL an industry standard. The following description of COBOL corresponds to the order in which a program is written and concentrates on the statements concerned with the definition and processing of a sequential file. The reader should refer to Program 3.1 for examples in the following discussion.

The program must communicate to the operating system the necessary information for it to handle the input output operations required. COBOL statements are provided to describe the file name, record size, block size, record format, and type of file organization. The INPUT-OUTPUT section describes the file environment; this may only be the system file name or it may also specify the type of storage device. A file on external storage must also include control information for system use; IBM refers to a file and its control information as a *data set*. The program file description is provided in a COBOL FD entry.

3.3.1 INPUT-OUTPUT SECTION: Defining the File

The FILE-CONTROL paragraph of the INPUT-OUTPUT SECTION defines the name of a file, its organizational type, and the type of access permitted. In addition, it provides a link between the internal COBOL name of a file and the physical storage address of the file itself. A standard ANSI COBOL entry form is[1]

```
FILE-CONTROL.
    SELECT file-name
        ASSIGN TO implementor-name
        ORGANIZATION IS SEQUENTIAL
        ACCESS MODE IS SEQUENTIAL.
    SELECT . . .
```

File-name is the name by which the file will be known within the COBOL program and is a user-defined word. Such words are at most 30 characters in length. *Implementor-name* is a system-name COBOL word that is used to communicate with the operating system environment and whose definition may differ among installations.

As an example, a typical IBM COBOL entry for the INPUT-OUTPUT SECTION defines the MUSIC-LOG file of Program 3.1. The ASSIGN clause entry UT-DISK-S-MUSIC specifies that this file is to be stored on a disk device, that it is a sequential file ('S'), and that the *ddname* on the job control language card associated with this file is MUSIC.

Finally, in the preceding COBOL entry form, ORGANIZATION IS SEQUENTIAL specifies that the file is sequentially organized, and ACCESS MODE IS SEQUENTIAL specifies that the file is to be sequentially accessed.

3.3.2 FD Entry: Describing the Records

The FD entry furnishes information concerning the identification, record names, and physical structure of a file. A standard ANSI COBOL entry is

```
FD file-name
    BLOCK CONTAINS integer RECORDS
    RECORD CONTAINS integer CHARACTERS
    LABEL RECORDS ARE STANDARD
    DATA RECORD IS data-name.
```

These clauses may appear in any order but, for consistency, it is advisable to follow the order used in the standard.

The BLOCK CONTAINS clause designates how many logical records constitute one physical record. This grouping is transparent to the user and is entirely handled by the compiler and the operating system.

---

[1]Since COBOL is very flexible and quite complex, the ANSI standard and manufacturers' manuals provide very general entry skeletons. To do so here would provide unwarranted detail. We give the basic structure that is normally used and refer the reader to the appropriate manuals for special options.

The BLOCK CONTAINS clause is used with the record size to determine the buffer size.

The BLOCK CONTAINS clause is not required in the event that a physical record and a logical record are of the same size or where the hardware device assigned to the file, such as a printer, has a fixed physical record size. If the block size is unknown, then code BLOCK CONTAINS 0 RECORDS.

The RECORD CONTAINS clause specifies the number of characters in a data record. This clause is optional as the size of each data record can be obtained by an examination of the PICTURE clauses of the level 01 entry that follow its FD entry. However, most COBOL implementations compare the length of a record as stated with the sum of the record's elementary item PICTURE clauses and warn of a discrepancy.

The LABEL RECORDS clause indicates whether or not the physical file has a label. It is a *required* clause. STANDARD indicates that the file has a label and that it conforms to the specifications for labels at the installation. In the event that labels are not present, as, for example, card and print files,

LABEL RECORDS ARE OMITTED

must be coded. (See Program 3.1.)

The DATA RECORD clause is optional and serves only as documentation. It associates the level 01 entry record description whose record name is *data-name* with the file with which it is associated.

3.3.3 PROCEDURE DIVISION: Accessing the File

The OPEN Statement for a Sequential I-O File

The following form of the OPEN statement should be used when records are to be written to a sequential file.

OPEN OUTPUT *file-name*

If the records are to be read from a sequential file, the following form is used.

OPEN INPUT file-name

The OPEN statement indicates that the file is to be prepared for processing. No statements may be executed that reference a file until an OPEN has been performed on that file (except in the sort module). After an OPEN has been issued, the program is positioned at the beginning of the sequential file.[2]

[2]This is not the case if records are being appended to the end of an existing file where DISP=MOD is specified in the file DD card.

The WRITE Statement

The general form of the WRITE statement is

```
WRITE record-name  [FROM identifier]
```

The *record-name* is the name of a logical record in the FILE SECTION FD entry of the file in question and may be a qualified name. If the optional FROM is used, the record is first moved from the WORKING-STORAGE SECTION area, denoted *identifier,* to *record-name* before writing.

The READ Statement

The general format of the READ statement is

```
READ file-name  [INTO identifier]
AT END imperative statement
```

The execution of this statement causes one logical record to be made available to the program. In the event that the optional INTO clause is added, the record will be transferred from the buffer to the area in the WORKING-STORAGE SECTION named *identifier* by a group MOVE.

The *imperative statement* following the key words AT END is required and is executed in the event that an attempt is made to read beyond the end of the file. Once this imperative statement, indicating what action is to be taken, is executed, control is returned to the statement following the READ, and this READ statement should not be executed again.

The CLOSE Statement

A CLOSE statement should be issued whenever all WRITE statements to the file are completed or once end-of-file has been reached on reading. Once a file has been closed, it can be repositioned for more processing at the beginning by issuing another OPEN statement. The CLOSE statement disconnects the file from the program, thus making it available to other users. A CLOSE also ensures that any logical records left in a buffer for writing to the file (even if they do not exactly complete a physical record) are transferred to the file. In addition, an end-of-file marker is placed on the file if the file has been opened for OUTPUT. The general form of the CLOSE statement is

```
CLOSE file-name
```

If a file is opened for OUTPUT, the previous contents of the file are lost. A START statement (discussed in Chapter 6) can also be used to position a file prior to a READ.

3.4 SEQUENTIAL FILE PROCESSING

Sequential file processing can be classified into four basic functions: edit, sort, update, and report. *Edit* involves the creation of a valid set of transactions to be applied to update a file or files. *Sorting* is required to make the update process more efficient or to rearrange the order of a report. *Update* involves any change to a file. The *report* function is the ultimate purpose for which the files exist and for which the other functions are required.

How these functions are performed varies greatly; however, there are some fairly common types of procedures for sequential files known as *batch processing*. These procedures have been developed to deal efficiently with the limitations of sequential organization. Basically, processing is arranged to occur in large blocks of records. For instance, input transactions are collected into large batches before being entered into the computer. There are two kinds of files in a batch system: transaction and master.

A *transaction* is the recording of an enterprise event that produces data. Before transactions are applied to a master file to update it, they are collected in a transaction file. Such a file could well be simply a deck of cards. A transaction file is temporary, unless it must be saved for historical purposes. The stored data of an enterprise resides in *master* files; these files are permanent except as the records they contain are modified by transactions. A master file is sequenced on a primary key.

The classical method of applying transactions to a sequential master file is to order the transactions on the same key as the master and then to search the master file for the record that matches the transaction record. Since transactions can be insertions or deletions as well as changes, the master file is rewritten to a new master. Incidently, the old master in conjunction with this transition file automatically provides a backup for the new master. When a record update is made, the master record is changed and rewritten to the new master and the next transaction obtained before proceeding. Records are deleted by failing to rewrite them. Records are inserted by writing to the new master before the following record of the master is written. We formalize this procedure in the next section.

A general batch processing cycle on a single master file is indicated in Figs. 3.1–3.4. The first step of the cycle consists of creating a transaction file. Input transactions are examined by the edit program shown in Fig. 3.1. Valid transactions are written to the transaction file and invalid transactions are printed on an error file, with the errors indicated usually by flags. The errors are corrected by the user and these corrected transactions are resubmitted to the edit process.

When the transaction file is ready for processing, it is sorted to match the key sequence of the master to which it will be applied. This step is indicated by Fig. 3.2 (sorting is discussed in the next chapter). The update process of Fig. 3.3 merges the transaction file into the old master to create a new master. The error report is necessary to indicate invalid update attempts. For instance, we cannot correct a master record that does not exist. This could indicate loss of a master record or an invalid

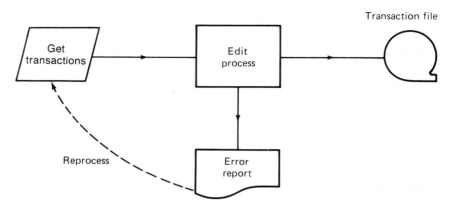

Figure 3.1   Creation of a transaction file.

key in a transaction record. The programmer must take care to allow for recovery from processing errors.

When the master file is updated, which may take more than one run because of errors, we are ready to produce a report. A simple report process is shown in Fig. 3.4. It is parameter driven by the type of report requested. Often the report phase also updates the master (father), producing, for instance, year to date totals, and then we have a new master (son). If the file is on disk and only existing record values need be changed, copying can be avoided and the changes written in place. This may not provide the saving it appears to, as the need for a copy of the old master may require a copy to be made at this time anyway. Of course, most systems

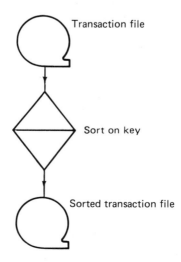

Figure 3.2   Sort process.

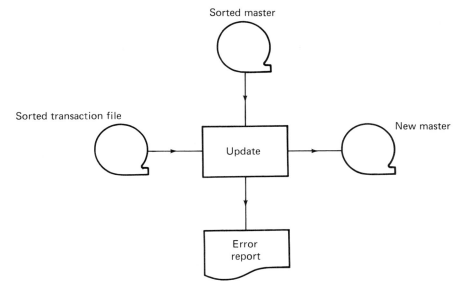

Figure 3.3   Update process.

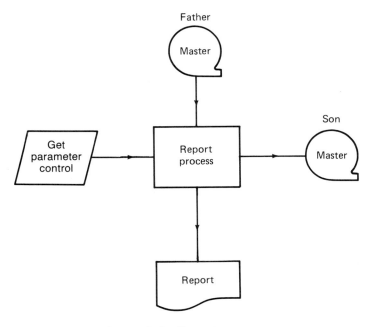

Figure 3.4   Report process.

will require more than one file and more than one report. Often the same report is sorted on different keys at various levels of detail.

While the data of an enterprise changes continuously, batch processing delays the effect of such change on master files into lengthy discrete steps. Change is recognized usually on a regular cycle or after some determined interval. The time chosen between processing transactions is important. The smaller the interval, the more costly the process of updating becomes because of the overhead associated with a run. Since all records of a sequential file must be examined, a small number of transactions will cause less efficient processing of the master file. On the other hand, a greater time between runs decreases the value of the information obtained by the enterprise. Second, because the volume of transactions is increased, the run will be more complex, which could also increase the cost of the run.

3.5 UPDATING A SEQUENTIAL FILE: THE BALANCE LINE ALGORITHM

In Program 3.1 we have seen the creation of a sequential file. This program is not too useful as a production program because it assumes that the records entered are correct. The correct assumption with files is to assume that, no matter what, bad records will occur.

The *balance line algorithm* is a standardized approach to updating a sequentially ordered master file by one or more transaction files. It should more properly be called a process as it gives rise to many specific algorithms. It is a structured generalization of the update process discussed in the previous section. Many examples are given in the work by Cooper *et al.* (1973).

The balance line algorithm requires at least three files: a transaction file, an original master, called the *father,* and a new master, called the *son.* Transaction files and the master *must* be sorted in ascending order on the same key, and this key is a primary key of the master file. There are four kinds of transactions: additions, changes, deletions, and verifications. Additions create and add a new master record. Changes modify specified fields of an existing master record. Deletions remove a master record from the file. Verifications request a copy of a master record for checking; this may only be a request to print a copy. A transaction can affect only one record of a master file, but several transactions may be applied to the same master record. The key of the transaction file is called the *transaction key* and that of the master file the *master key.* A transaction record may only update a master record if the current transaction key matches the current master key. Before proceeding to the algorithm proper it is useful to consider what can happen to both types of records.

A master record is read into the WORKING-STORAGE SECTION and it is either

(a) copied as is to the new master file or

(b) copied with changes to the new master file or

(c) not copied at all to the new master file.

Each master record is thus left alone, changed, or deleted.

A transaction record is read into the WORKING-STORAGE SECTION and it is either

(a) used to create a new master record or

(b) used to change the contents of a master record or

(c) used to delete a master record, by not transferring it to the new master file.

The fundamental idea of the balance line algorithm is to synchronize the interaction of master and transaction records in a standard manner so that the appropriate actions can be taken. The process is in two parts: an initialization phase and a process phase.

3.5.1 Initialization

The following steps are taken in the initialization phase:

1. Read a master file record. If end-of-file is reached, set the master key to HIGH-VALUES.

2. Read a transaction record from each transaction file and set the transaction key to HIGH-VALUES for each file that is positioned at end-of-file.

3. Extract the smallest key from among the master and transaction keys and place this value in a separate key called the *active key*.

3.5.2 Process Phase

In the process phase the following steps are repeated until the value of the active key is HIGH-VALUES.

4. If the master key matches the active key, move the master record to the output area and read another master record. Set the master key to HIGH-VALUES if end-of-file is reached.

5. For each separate transaction file whose current transaction record has a transaction key that matches the active key, process the transaction. By process is meant the following:

   (a) If the transaction is a change, modify the record in the output area.

   (b) If the transaction is an addition, create a new record in the output area.

   (c) If the transaction is a deletion, set a switch to indicate that the record in the output area must not be copied to the new master file.

(d) If the transaction is a verification, make a copy of the record in the output area and move the copy to a report file.

After processing read the transaction file. If end of file is reached, set the transaction key to HIGH-VALUES. If the new transaction key matches the active key, repeat the process.

6. Write the record in the output area if the WRITE is not inhibited.

7. Redetermine a new active key setting as in step 3.

The active key acts like a policeman directing traffic at a busy intersection. Only those records whose keys equal the active key are allowed to participate in the update process. Of course, eventually all the keys on all the files will equal HIGH-VALUES and the algorithm will terminate. Rush hour through the intersection is then over.

3.6 CASE STUDY: PROFIT INC.

O. R. Capital, the president of Profit, Inc., a small company, has realized continued growth of his company will soon be limited by lack of current detailed information on its operations. Realizing that computer systems will eventually be required, he wishes to move slowly in that direction before the need becomes pressing. He has contacted an old school friend, R. Matrix, who owns a small consulting company. Matrix also has a problem; she has specialized in scientific programming but wishes to move into the data processing area. They have met together to discuss their mutual problems. They have come to the conclusion that a process of incremental design, supported by manual assistance will give them both the required experience and ultimately develop the systems needed by Profit Inc. By building usable subsystems with close cost controls on development, there will not only be early results but also immediate payback on the company's investment. As a result of these meetings, the correspondence shown in Figs. 3.5-3.7 takes place.

3.6.1 Logical Analysis: Profit Inc.

We need only understand those aspects of Profit Inc.'s accounting process that will be manipulated by the computer. While the more the analyst understands about accounting the more she can contribute to the design of an effective accounting system, it must be realized that she will often be called upon to develop systems for areas in which she is *not* an expert. Thus she must work with the user or another professional expert in the area and use her skills to determine by careful questioning what is important to the computer solution.

Any accounting system must record the flow of money in an enterprise. For example, *expenses* are those goods and services consumed by Profit Inc., *cash* are those monies paid out or a debt incurred; *sales* result in income, which is cash received or money owed Profit Inc. These events result in accounting transactions that

Profit Incorporated

14 WEST OHIO STREET
NEW YORK, NY 10011

May 10, 1986

Ms. R. Matrix, President
Matrix & Associates
65001 Pennsylvania Ave.
Washington, DC 20028

Dear Ms. Matrix,

Further to our meeting on May 5 concerning computer
systems for my firm, please find attached a summary of my
thoughts on the matter.

My present concern is that while our revenue is currently too low to support extensive computer work, our
projected revenues should be sufficient to cover this investment. In order to achieve this projected revenue, very
close management control is needed to optimize our resources.
I am hopeful that your work will be directed to benefiting
us in this area.

In terms of project funds, I feel that 1% of revenue is
the most that we can spend outside the firm. However, I
can devote considerable time to this project provided that
it is productive.

Sincerely yours,

O.R. Capital
President

ORC:aa
Attachment

Figure 3.5

must be recorded as they happen. Then they are classified by accountants to provide meaningful information and summarized in reports to control cash flow and determine profits. Debts are *liabilities*. The resources owned by the enterprise are *assets*. The money invested in the enterprise is its *capital*. The fundamental accounting equation relating these terms is

$$\text{Assets} = \text{Liabilities} + \text{Capital}$$

Every accounting transaction in a double entry bookkeeping transaction is expressed in terms of how it effects this accounting equation. Obviously, if we add to assets, we must have an identical increase in either liabilities or capital. Thus we talk of *balance*. Assets and liabilities are grouped into accounts of like transactions. Each account has two entries for increase and decrease. The first entry is called a *debit entry* and the second a *credit entry*. It is important to realize that debit does not necessarily decrease an account; in fact if it is an asset account, a debit increases it. Simply think of a debit as the left entry and credit as the right entry of an account.

MEMO TO: Ms. R. Matrix, President
             Matrix & Associates

FROM: O.R. Capital, President, Profit Inc.

DATE: May 10, 1986

SUBJECT: Problem Area Definition for Computer Systems

     Profit Incorporated is a small retail firm which is growing
past the current limitations imposed by its manual bookkeeping
and accounting system. I have decided that further growth cannot be maintained unless accounting, inventory, and personnel
computer systems are introduced. Because our firm must currently
be viewed, however, as a relatively small enterprise, the basic
restriction to this advanced strategy must be considerations of
capital outlay. It should be specifically understood at the
outset that I am not prepared to hire additional staff with a
computer science background. Any systems designed must keep
this fact in mind. Profit has grown in large measure because of
the dedication of a very few hardworking and loyal individuals,
and I am not prepared to consider their replacement to support
the introduction of computer systems. I am vitally concerned
at this time with growth maximization, tight monetary control
and increased profits.

     The objective of the systems you are to design is to provide
support for ensuring tight monetary control through the monitoring
of cash flow. Information output by these systems will be used
to gauge the firm's performance. At the outset I would envisage
the following limited systems being converted to computer:

     (a)   general journal

     (b)   income statement

     (c)   balance sheet

     (d)   company accounts.

     The idea behind putting these items on computer is to make it
possible to calculate trial balances quickly. Further modifications
can be considered as our relationship matures.

Figure 3.6

Any accounting transaction affects two accounts, one on each side of the accounting equation in order to keep the equation balanced. Thus an accounting transaction debits an account and credits a balancing account. We need not worry how
this is done; Profit Inc. will provide the proper accounting transactions. We need
only concern ourselves with their *form*. For instance, if the rent is paid, the amount
is debited to the account RENT and since the money came from somewhere, the
account CASH is credited if the rent is paid by check. Remember, for our purpose
we need not know how to create a proper accounting transaction but only how to
manipulate it in a computer system.

Profit Inc. records all transactions chronologically in a General Journal as
shown in Table 3.1. In order to better relate like entries, a separate ledger is kept for
each account and this contains the record of entries for that account obtained from
the General Journal. The transfer from journal to ledger account is called *posting*.
Accounts are posted once a month. Each account has the form shown in Table 3.2.

The first summary of accounting transactions is the trial balance; from this the
two most important summaries are made: the income statement that determines
profit or loss and the balance sheet that indicates the financial health of the enter-

MATRIX & ASSOCIATES
65001 PENNSYLVANIA AVENUE
WASHINGTON, DC 20028

May 15, 1986

Mr. O.R. Capital, President
Profit Incorporated
14 W. Ohio Street
New York, NY 10011

Dear Mr. Capital,

Initially, we propose to provide as main output a trial balance from which your accountant can then determine the adjusted trial balance and income statement. Hopefully you should be able to produce these reports monthly instead of semi-annually as is the case at present. When this is working well, we will discuss further improvements.

Changes will be as per our standard rates which I have enclosed.

Because of our lack of experience in this area I will not myself directly take charge of this phase.

I would appreciate a letter of intent to proceed before I send an analyst to your firm. Delivery of Phase One will be six months from your letter.

Sincerely,

R. Matrix
President

RM:lj
Enclosure

Figure 3.7

prise. The main problem that Profit Inc. has is in quickly determining the trial balance, as this is the most time-consuming part of determining the two latter summaries.

To this end a Phase One solution by Matrix & Associates is to create the General Journal as a sequential file, and from this file to find the total or balance of each account and provide a trial balance. The accounts are created as a sequential file and

Table 3.1 Sample of General Journal Entries

Date	*Comments*	*Check No.*	*Debit*	*Credit*
'date'	'debit account name'		'amount'	
	'credit account name'			'amount'
	Comments			
86/01/5	RENT		1000.00	
	CASH	2001		1000.00
	RENT FOR JAN 1980			
	Note 10% increase			

Table 3.2 Sample of Account Ledger Posting

RENT Account Ledger

Date	Comment	Debit	Credit	Code	Balance
86/01/5	Jan	1000		D	1000.00

they carry only the account total. This is not a satisfactory long-term solution (see the Problems at the end of this chapter) because account detail is not provided except as scattered in the General Journal: however, a trial balance is obtained in a simple manner with minimal programming and consequent cost. The system is to be expanded in Phase Two, where a sequential file of accounts with transaction detail will be maintained.

The trial balance of accounts, as shown in Table 3.3, consists of a list of all accounts, ordered according to accounting principles, along with their balances and an indication of whether these balances are debit or credit entries. The sum of the debits *must* equal the sum of credits of the accounts in the trial balance. This indicates that all entries have been properly made and that totals are correct. In effect, a double entry bookkeeping system is an *error*-detecting system.

3.6.2 Profit Inc.'s Accounting System

The system for Phase One consists of four programs as illustrated in Figs. 3.8–3.11, and the accounting cycle is on a monthly basis.

Accounting transactions are assigned a transaction number as a unique

Table 3.3 Trial Balance

		Debit	Credit
Assets			
	Cash	10,000	
	Equipment	5,000	
	Inventory	6,000	
Liabilities			
	Loans		3,000
	Capital		20,000
Income			8,000
Expenses			
	Rent	3,000	
	Supplies	1,000	
	Wages	6,000	
		31,000	31,000

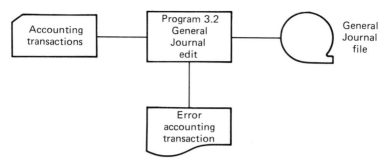

Figure 3.8 Creation of a General Journal transaction file for Profit, Inc.

identifier and are entered on the General Journal file as in Fig. 3.8 until transactions are complete for the period just ended. The General Journal file will be used to update a master file of account information. This account directory file is initialized in Fig. 3.9.

When the General Journal is complete for the period just ended, the accounts are totaled and entered in the master account directory file. This is indicated in Fig. 3.10. A trial balance report can be obtained as in Fig. 3.11. This trial balance covers the period or periods represented by the totals in the master account file.

Note

The following program examples use a simple-minded approach that works only for the very first accounting period. To run subsequent periods, Program 3.4 must make provision to carry through previous account balances. As well, new account transactions must be added onto the previous General Journal file. At this point it is convenient to generate an expense report for the expense account totals as they are found. The dashed lines in the figures indicate that this is not present in the program examples.

Program 3.2 Narrative.   The purpose of Program 3.2 is to read an input file containing accounting transactions to be entered in the General Journal of Profit Inc. Debit and credit entries are punched on separate cards, and each debit-credit pair is

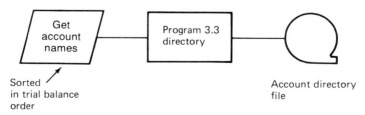

Figure 3.9   Creation of an account directory file.

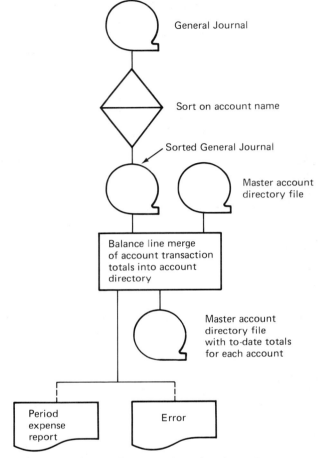

General Journal

Sort on account name

Sorted General Journal

Master account directory file

Balance line merge of account transaction totals into account directory

Master account directory file with to-date totals for each account

Period expense report

Error

Figure 3.10 Update of account totals of master account file.

followed by any number (including zero) of comments. The general format of a debit or credit entry data card is as follows:

1. an 8-digit transaction number
2. a 'D' or 'C' for debit or credit, respectively
3. the date of the entry in the form

    Month 3 alphabetic characters

    Day 2 digits from 01 to 31

    Year 2 digits from 00 to 99

4. the name of the account to which the entry is posted using at most 30 characters

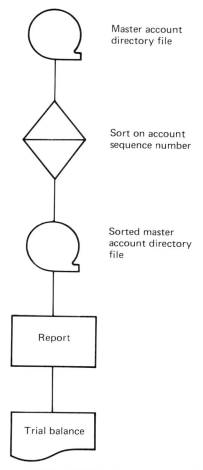

Master account
directory file

Sort on account
sequence number

Sorted master
account directory
file

Report

Trial balance

Figure 3.11   Trial balance generation.

5. the transaction amount
6. a 3-digit batch number

An input card will be posted to the General Journal provided that it is a valid
member of a debit-credit pair or a valid comment. A debit-credit pair is a set of two
data cards, the first of which is a debit entry and the second the corresponding credit
entry. A credit entry corresponds to a debit entry if it has the same transaction number and the same amount field as the debit. No posting of a debit entry is made
unless a corresponding credit directly follows it in the data. A debit entry is saved in
WS-DEBIT-ENTRY before the corresponding credit is processed. In the event that
a corresponding credit entry cannot be found, an error condition is raised and an
error handling routine (not actually coded) is entered. This error routine should void

Program 3.2

```
00001          IDENTIFICATION DIVISION.
00002          PROGRAM-ID. PROG3PT2.
00003          *  ** POSTS TRANSACTIONS TO GENERAL JOURNAL **
00004          DATE-WRITTEN. 85/05/31.
00005          ENVIRONMENT DIVISION.
00006          CONFIGURATION SECTION.
00007          SOURCE-COMPUTER.  IBM-3081.
00008          OBJECT-COMPUTER.  IBM-3081.
00009
00010          INPUT-OUTPUT SECTION.
00011          FILE-CONTROL.
00012
00013              SELECT CARD-READER
00014                 ASSIGN TO CARD-S-SYSIN
00015                 ORGANIZATION IS SEQUENTIAL
00016                 ACCESS MODE IS SEQUENTIAL.
00017              SELECT GENERAL-JOURNAL-FILE
00018                 ASSIGN TO DISK-S-DD1
00019                 ORGANIZATION IS SEQUENTIAL
00020                 ACCESS MODE IS SEQUENTIAL.
00021
00022
00023          DATA DIVISION.
00024          FILE SECTION.
00025
00026          FD  CARD-READER
00027                 BLOCK CONTAINS 1 RECORDS
00028                 LABEL RECORDS ARE OMITTED
00029                 RECORD CONTAINS 80 CHARACTERS
00030                 DATA RECORDS IS CARD-READER-RECORD.
00031          01  CARD-READER-RECORD.
00032              02 FILLER                       PIC X(80).
00033
00034          FD  GENERAL-JOURNAL-FILE
00035                 BLOCK CONTAINS 1 RECORDS
00036                 LABEL RECORDS ARE STANDARD
00037                 RECORD CONTAINS 80 CHARACTERS
00038                 DATA RECORD IS GENERAL-JOURNAL-FILE-RECORD.
00039          01  GENERAL-JOURNAL-FILE-RECORD.
00040              02 FILLER                       PIC X(80).
00041
00042
00043          WORKING-STORAGE SECTION.
00044
00045          77  ERROR-IN-INPUT-FLAG             PIC X(3).
00046              88 ERROR-IN-INPUT VALUE IS 'ON'.
00047          77  NO-MORE-COMMENTS-FLAG           PIC X(3).
00048              88 NO-MORE-COMMENTS        VALUE IS 'ON'.
00049          77  NO-MORE-ENTRIES-FLAG            PIC X(3).
00050              88  NO-MORE-ENTRIES        VALUE IS 'ON'.
00051              88  MORE-ENTRIES           VALUE IS 'OFF'.
00052          77  NUMBER-OF-ERROR-RECORDS         PIC 9(5)
00053                              USAGE IS    COMP SYNC.
00054          77  NUMBER-OF-RECORDS-TO-WRITE      PIC 9(5)
00055                              USAGE IS    COMP SYNC.
00056          77  PROCEED-FLAG                    PIC X(3).
00057          77  VALID-DEBIT-ENTRY-FLAG          PIC X(3).
00058              88  VALID-DEBIT-ENTRY      VALUE IS 'ON'.
00059              88  INVALID-DEBIT-ENTRY    VALUE IS 'OFF'.
00060          77  READ-BUFFER-EMPTY-FLAG          PIC X(3).
00061              88  READ-BUFFER-EMPTY      VALUE IS 'OFF'.
00062          77  VALID-CREDIT-ENTRY-FLAG         PIC X(3).
00063              88  VALID-CREDIT-ENTRY     VALUE IS 'ON'.
```

Program 3.2 (cont.)

```
00064               88  INVALID-CREDIT-ENTRY     VALUE IS 'OFF'.
00065
00066        01  WS-COMMENT-RECORD.
00067            02  TRANSACTION-NUMBER              PIC X(8).
00068            02  COMMENT-ASTERISK               PIC X.
00069                88  COMMENT                VALUE IS '*'.
00070            02  COMMENT-ENTRY                  PIC X(71).
00071
00072        01  WS-CREDIT-ENTRY.
00073            02  TRANSACTION-NUMBER             PIC X(8).
00074            02  DEBIT-OR-CREDIT                PIC X.
00075                88  CREDIT-RECORD          VALUE IS 'C'.
00076            02  ENTRY-DATE.
00077                03  MONTH                      PIC X(3).
00078                03  ENTRY-DAY                  PIC 9(2).
00079                03  YEAR                       PIC 9(2).
00080            02  NAME-OF-ACCOUNT                PIC X(30).
00081            02  CREDIT-AMOUNT                  PIC 9(5)V9(2).
00082            02  FILLER                         PIC X(24).
00083            02  BATCH-NO                       PIC 9(3).
00084
00085        01  WS-DEBIT-ENTRY.
00086            02  TRANSACTION-NUMBER             PIC X(8).
00087            02  DEBIT-OR-CREDIT                PIC X.
00088                88  DEBIT-RECORD           VALUE IS 'D'.
00089            02  ENTRY-DATE.
00090                03  MONTH                      PIC X(3).
00091                03  ENTRY-DAY                  PIC 9(2).
00092                03  YEAR                       PIC 9(2).
00093            02  NAME-OF-ACCOUNT                PIC X(30).
00094            02  DEBIT-AMOUNT                   PIC 9(5)V9(2).
00095            02  FILLER                         PIC X(24).
00096            02  BATCH-NO                       PIC 9(3).
00097
00098
00099        PROCEDURE DIVISION.
00100
00101            PERFORM INITIALIZATION.
00102            PERFORM ADD-ENTRIES-TO-GENERAL-JOURNAL
00103                    UNTIL NO-MORE-ENTRIES.
00104            PERFORM TERMINATION.
00105            STOP RUN.
00106
00107        INITIALIZATION.
00108            OPEN INPUT   CARD-READER
00109                 OUTPUT  GENERAL-JOURNAL-FILE.
00110            MOVE SPACES TO WS-DEBIT-ENTRY.
00111            MOVE SPACES TO WS-CREDIT-ENTRY.
00112            MOVE SPACES TO WS-COMMENT-RECORD.
00113            PERFORM ZERO-COUNTERS-SET-FLAGS.
00114            MOVE 'OFF' TO READ-BUFFER-EMPTY-FLAG.
00115            PERFORM OBTAIN-JOURNAL-ENTRIES.
00116
00117        ADD-ENTRIES-TO-GENERAL-JOURNAL.
00118            PERFORM ERROR-PRESENT-ROUTINE.
00119            IF NOT ERROR-IN-INPUT
00120                THEN PERFORM WRITE-GENERAL-JOURNAL-RECORD
00121                ELSE PERFORM ERROR-RTN.
00122            IF MORE-ENTRIES
00123                PERFORM ZERO-COUNTERS-SET-FLAGS
00124                PERFORM OBTAIN-JOURNAL-ENTRIES.
00125
00126        TERMINATION.
```

Program 3.2   (cont.)

```
00127                        IF NUMBER-OF-RECORDS-TO-WRITE
00128                            IS GREATER THAN ZERO THEN
00129                            PERFORM WRITE-GENERAL-JOURNAL-RECORD.
00130                        IF NUMBER-OF-ERROR-RECORDS
00131                            IS GREATER THAN ZERO THEN
00132                            PERFORM ERROR-RTN.
00133                        CLOSE CARD-READER
00134                            GENERAL-JOURNAL-FILE.
00135
00136                   ERROR-PRESENT-ROUTINE.
00137                        IF INVALID-DEBIT-ENTRY
00138                           OR INVALID-CREDIT-ENTRY
00139                           THEN
00140                                MOVE 'ON' TO ERROR-IN-INPUT-FLAG
00141                           ELSE
00142                                MOVE 'OFF' TO ERROR-IN-INPUT-FLAG.
00143
00144                   WRITE-GENERAL-JOURNAL-RECORD.
00145                        PERFORM WRITE-DEBIT-ENTRY.
00146                        PERFORM WRITE-CREDIT-ENTRY.
00147                        PERFORM WRITE-COMMENT-RTN
00148                            UNTIL NO-MORE-COMMENTS OR NO-MORE-ENTRIES.
00149                        MOVE SPACES TO WS-CREDIT-ENTRY.
00150
00151                   ERROR-RTN.
00152                        EXIT.
00153
00154                   ZERO-COUNTERS-SET-FLAGS.
00155                        MOVE ZERO TO NUMBER-OF-RECORDS-TO-WRITE.
00156                        MOVE ZERO TO NUMBER-OF-ERROR-RECORDS.
00157                        MOVE 'OFF' TO ERROR-IN-INPUT-FLAG.
00158                        MOVE 'ON' TO PROCEED-FLAG.
00159                        MOVE 'OFF' TO VALID-DEBIT-ENTRY-FLAG.
00160                        MOVE 'OFF' TO VALID-CREDIT-ENTRY-FLAG.
00161                        MOVE 'OFF' TO NO-MORE-ENTRIES-FLAG.
00162                        MOVE 'OFF' TO NO-MORE-COMMENTS-FLAG.
00163
00164                   OBTAIN-JOURNAL-ENTRIES.
00165                        PERFORM GET-DEBIT-ENTRY.
00166                        PERFORM VERIFICATION-OF-DEBIT-ENTRY.
00167                        IF VALID-DEBIT-ENTRY
00168                           PERFORM PREPARE-DEBIT-RECORD
00169                           ELSE
00170                                PERFORM INVALID-DEBIT-ENTRY-ROUTINE.
00171                        IF PROCEED-FLAG EQUAL 'ON'
00172                           THEN
00173                                PERFORM GET-CREDIT-ENTRY
00174                                IF MORE-ENTRIES THEN
00175                                PERFORM VERIFICATION-OF-CREDIT-ENTRY
00176                                IF VALID-CREDIT-ENTRY
00177                                    PERFORM PREPARE-CREDIT-RECORD.
00178
00179
00180                   GET-DEBIT-ENTRY.
00181                        IF READ-BUFFER-EMPTY
00182                           THEN
00183                                PERFORM READ-DEBIT-ROUTINE
00184                           ELSE
00185                                PERFORM COPY-DEBIT-ROUTINE.
00186
00187                   VERIFICATION-OF-DEBIT-ENTRY.
00188                        IF DEBIT-RECORD
00189                           MOVE 'ON' TO VALID-DEBIT-ENTRY-FLAG.
```

Program 3.2   (cont.)

```
00190
00191          PREPARE-DEBIT-RECORD.
00192              ADD 1 TO NUMBER-OF-RECORDS-TO-WRITE.
00193              MOVE 'OFF' TO READ-BUFFER-EMPTY-FLAG.
00194
00195          INVALID-DEBIT-ENTRY-ROUTINE.
00196              MOVE 'OFF' TO READ-BUFFER-EMPTY-FLAG.
00197              MOVE 'OFF' TO PROCEED-FLAG.
00198
00199          GET-CREDIT-ENTRY.
00200              IF READ-BUFFER-EMPTY
00201                 THEN
00202                       PERFORM READ-CREDIT-ROUTINE
00203                 ELSE
00204                       PERFORM ERROR-RTN.
00205
00206          VERIFICATION-OF-CREDIT-ENTRY.
00207              IF CREDIT-RECORD AND CREDIT-AMOUNT
00208                 IS EQUAL TO DEBIT-AMOUNT
00209                 AND TRANSACTION-NUMBER OF WS-DEBIT-ENTRY
00210                 IS EQUAL TO TRANSACTION-NUMBER
00211                 OF WS-CREDIT-ENTRY
00212                 THEN
00213                       MOVE 'ON' TO VALID-CREDIT-ENTRY-FLAG.
00214
00215          PREPARE-CREDIT-RECORD.
00216              ADD 1 TO NUMBER-OF-RECORDS-TO-WRITE.
00217              MOVE 'OFF' TO READ-BUFFER-EMPTY-FLAG.
00218
00219          READ-DEBIT-ROUTINE.
00220              READ CARD-READER RECORD
00221                   AT END MOVE 'ON' TO NO-MORE-ENTRIES-FLAG.
00222              MOVE 'ON' TO READ-BUFFER-EMPTY-FLAG.
00223              IF MORE-ENTRIES
00224                 MOVE CARD-READER-RECORD
00225                      TO WS-DEBIT-ENTRY.
00226
00227          COPY-DEBIT-ROUTINE.
00228              MOVE CARD-READER-RECORD
00229                   TO WS-DEBIT-ENTRY.
00230
00231          READ-CREDIT-ROUTINE.
00232              READ CARD-READER RECORD
00233                   AT END MOVE 'ON' TO NO-MORE-ENTRIES-FLAG.
00234              MOVE 'ON' TO READ-BUFFER-EMPTY-FLAG.
00235              IF MORE-ENTRIES
00236                 MOVE CARD-READER-RECORD
00237                      TO WS-CREDIT-ENTRY
00238              ELSE
00239                 SUBTRACT 1 FROM NUMBER-OF-RECORDS-TO-WRITE
00240                 MOVE 'OFF' TO VALID-DEBIT-ENTRY-FLAG.
00241
00242          WRITE-DEBIT-ENTRY.
00243              MOVE WS-DEBIT-ENTRY
00244                   TO GENERAL-JOURNAL-FILE-RECORD.
00245              WRITE GENERAL-JOURNAL-FILE-RECORD.
00246              MOVE SPACES TO WS-DEBIT-ENTRY.
00247              MOVE SPACES TO WS-COMMENT-RECORD.
00248
00249          WRITE-CREDIT-ENTRY.
00250              MOVE WS-CREDIT-ENTRY
00251                   TO GENERAL-JOURNAL-FILE-RECORD.
00252              WRITE GENERAL-JOURNAL-FILE-RECORD.
```

Program 3.2 (cont.)

```
00253
00254          WRITE-COMMENT-RTN.
00255              READ CARD-READER RECORD INTO WS-COMMENT-RECORD
00256                  AT END MOVE 'ON' TO NO-MORE-ENTRIES-FLAG.
00257          IF COMMENT AND TRANSACTION-NUMBER
00258              OF WS-COMMENT-RECORD
00259              EQUAL TRANSACTION-NUMBER OF WS-CREDIT-ENTRY
00260              THEN
00261                      WRITE GENERAL-JOURNAL-FILE-RECORD
00262                          FROM WS-COMMENT-RECORD
00263                      MOVE SPACES TO WS-COMMENT-RECORD
00264              ELSE
00265                      MOVE 'ON' TO NO-MORE-COMMENTS-FLAG
00266                      MOVE 'ON' TO READ-BUFFER-EMPTY-FLAG.
```

all data with the current transaction number. Processing will resume on the first new transaction number that is found on a debit entry. Following the posting of a debit-credit pair, any number of comments are posted to the journal provided they are valid. A comment is valid if it directly follows a debit-credit pair and has the same transaction number as the pair or if it directly follows a valid comment with the same transaction number. Processing is continued until the data is exhausted.

Since a debit-credit pair can be followed by any number of comments, the number of logical records used to record a single business transaction can vary. There is thus a variable amount of space used on the storage device to store the results of a single business transaction. The actual size of the logical records, however, remains fixed at 80 characters. Later we shall study a method whereby even the logical records of the file themselves may vary in length.

Before entering a transaction, it must be tested for correctness; if an error is found, the transaction is rejected. An error report will list such transactions, and they must be found, corrected, and reentered. The most obvious test is that the debit amount equal the credit amount. Data verification is treated in Chapter 16.

Program 3.3 Narrative. The purpose of 3.3 is to create the account directory file, a listing of all the accounts named in the General Journal with added fields for debit and credit totals for the trial balance and the adjusted trial balance. A sequence number is carried with each account to specify the order of printing of accounts in the Trial Balance Report (to be written later). The sequence number is taken to be the order in which the account names are read from the input data. This input must be in the order that accounts appear in the trial balance.

Program 3.3 has three phases: initialization, building the directory, and sorting it.

During initialization the ACCOUNT-DIRECTORY and CARD-READER files are opened for OUTPUT and INPUT, respectively.

The BUILD-DIRECTORY paragraph initializes totals to zero, assigns the sequence number to each card read, writes the ACCOUNT-DIRECTORY-RECORD, and reads another card. Processing of this paragraph halts when end-of-file is encountered on the CARD-READER.

Program 3.3

```
00001              IDENTIFICATION DIVISION.
00002              PROGRAM-ID. PROG3PT3.
00003          *    ** CREATE ACCOUNT DIRECTORY FILE **
00004              DATE-WRITTEN. 85/05/31.
00005              ENVIRONMENT DIVISION.
00006              CONFIGURATION SECTION.
00007              SOURCE-COMPUTER. IBM-3081.
00008              OBJECT-COMPUTER. IBM-3081.
00009
00010              INPUT-OUTPUT SECTION.
00011              FILE-CONTROL.
00012
00013                  SELECT ACCOUNT-DIRECTORY
00014                      ASSIGN TO DISK-S-DD1
00015                      ORGANIZATION IS SEQUENTIAL
00016                      ACCESS MODE IS SEQUENTIAL.
00017                  SELECT ACCOUNT-DIRECTORY-SORT-FILE
00018                      ASSIGN TO DISK-S-SORTWK01
00019                      ORGANIZATION IS SEQUENTIAL
00020                      ACCESS MODE IS SEQUENTIAL.
00021                  SELECT CARD-READER
00022                      ASSIGN TO CARD-S-SYSIN
00023                      ORGANIZATION IS SEQUENTIAL
00024                      ACCESS MODE IS SEQUENTIAL.
00025
00026
00027              DATA DIVISION.
00028              FILE SECTION.
00029
00030              FD  ACCOUNT-DIRECTORY
00031                  LABEL RECORDS ARE STANDARD
00032                  RECORD CONTAINS 63 CHARACTERS
00033                  DATA RECORD IS ACCOUNT-DIRECTORY-RECORD.
00034              01  ACCOUNT-DIRECTORY-RECORD.
00035                  02  FILLER                   PIC X(63).
00036
00037              SD  ACCOUNT-DIRECTORY-SORT-FILE
00038                  RECORD CONTAINS 63 CHARACTERS
00039                  DATA RECORD IS ACCOUNT-DIRECTORY-SORT-RECORD.
00040              01  ACCOUNT-DIRECTORY-SORT-RECORD.
00041
00042                  02 SEQUENCE-NUMBER           PIC X(3).
00043                  02 NAME-OF-ACCOUNT           PIC X(30).
00044                  02 FILLER                    PIC X(30).
00045
00046              FD  CARD-READER
00047                  LABEL RECORDS ARE OMITTED
00048                  RECORD CONTAINS 80 CHARACTERS
00049                  DATA RECORD IS CARD-IMAGE.
00050              01  CARD-IMAGE.
00051                  02 NAME-OF-ACCOUNT           PIC X(30).
00052                  02 TYPE-OF-ACCOUNT           PIC X.
00053                  02 EXPENSE-ACCOUNT-FIELD     PIC X.
00054                  02 FILLER                    PIC X(48).
00055
00056
00057              WORKING-STORAGE SECTION.
00058
00059              77  COUNTER                      PIC S9(8)
00060                                               COMPUTATIONAL
00061                                               SYNCHRONIZED.
00062              77  EOF-CARD-FLAG                PIC X(3).
```

Program 3.3   (cont.)

```
00063                        88  EOF-CARD VALUE IS 'ON'.
00064
00065                    01  WS-ACCOUNT-DIRECTORY.
00066                        02 SEQUENCE-NUMBER            PIC S9(3).
00067                        02 NAME-OF-ACCOUNT            PIC X(30).
00068                        02 TYPE-OF-ACCOUNT            PIC X.
00069                        02 EXPENSE-ACCOUNT-FIELD      PIC X.
00070                        02 TRIAL-DEBIT-TOTAL          PIC 9(5)V9(2).
00071                        02 TRIAL-CREDIT-TOTAL         PIC 9(5)V9(2).
00072                        02 ADJUSTED-DEBIT-TOTAL       PIC 9(5)V9(2).
00073                        02 ADJUSTED-CREDIT-TOTAL      PIC 9(5)V9(2).
00074
00075
00076                    PROCEDURE DIVISION.
00077
00078                        PERFORM INITIALIZATION.
00079                        PERFORM BUILD-DIRECTORY UNTIL EOF-CARD.
00080                        CLOSE CARD-READER
00081                              ACCOUNT-DIRECTORY.
00082                        PERFORM SORT-DIRECTORY.
00083                        STOP RUN.
00084
00085                    INITIALIZATION.
00086                        OPEN INPUT CARD-READER
00087                             OUTPUT ACCOUNT-DIRECTORY.
00088                        MOVE 'OFF' TO EOF-CARD-FLAG.
00089                        MOVE 0 TO COUNTER.
00090                        READ CARD-READER RECORD
00091                             AT END MOVE 'ON' TO EOF-CARD-FLAG.
00092
00093                    BUILD-DIRECTORY.
00094                        ADD 1 TO COUNTER.
00095                        MOVE CORRESPONDING CARD-IMAGE
00096                             TO WS-ACCOUNT-DIRECTORY.
00097                        MOVE ZERO TO TRIAL-DEBIT-TOTAL.
00098                        MOVE ZERO TO TRIAL-CREDIT-TOTAL.
00099                        MOVE ZERO TO ADJUSTED-DEBIT-TOTAL.
00100                        MOVE ZERO TO ADJUSTED-CREDIT-TOTAL.
00101                        MOVE COUNTER TO SEQUENCE-NUMBER
00102                             OF WS-ACCOUNT-DIRECTORY.
00103                        WRITE ACCOUNT-DIRECTORY-RECORD
00104                            FROM WS-ACCOUNT-DIRECTORY.
00105                        READ CARD-READER RECORD
00106                             AT END MOVE 'ON' TO EOF-CARD-FLAG.
00107
00108                    SORT-DIRECTORY.
00109                        SORT ACCOUNT-DIRECTORY-SORT-FILE
00110                             ASCENDING KEY
00111                             NAME-OF-ACCOUNT
00112                             OF ACCOUNT-DIRECTORY-SORT-FILE
00113                             USING ACCOUNT-DIRECTORY
00114                             GIVING ACCOUNT-DIRECTORY.
```

The SORT-DIRECTORY paragraph sorts the records of ACCOUNT-DIRECTORY in NAME-OF-ACCOUNT order. Note that the input and output files to the sort routine are identical. (See Chapter 4 for sorting.)

Program 3.4 Narrative. The first step in Program 3.4 is to sort the GENERAL-JOURNAL file on NAME-OF-ACCOUNT. Recall that the ACCOUNT-DIRECTORY is already sorted in this order by Program 3.3

Program 3.4

```
00001           IDENTIFICATION DIVISION.
00002           PROGRAM-ID.  PROG3PT4.
00003           *    ** CREATE TRIAL BALANCE **
00004           DATE-WRITTEN. 85/05/31.
00005           ENVIRONMENT DIVISION.
00006           CONFIGURATION SECTION.
00007             SOURCE-COMPUTER.  IBM-3081.
00008             OBJECT-COMPUTER.  IBM-3081.
00009
00010           INPUT-OUTPUT SECTION.
00011           FILE-CONTROL.
00012
00013               SELECT ACCOUNT-DIRECTORY
00014                 ASSIGN TO DISK-S-DD1
00015                 ORGANIZATION IS SEQUENTIAL
00016                 ACCESS MODE IS SEQUENTIAL.
00017               SELECT ACCOUNT-DIRECTORY-SORT-FILE
00018                 ASSIGN TO DISK-S-SORTWK01
00019                 ORGANIZATION IS SEQUENTIAL
00020                 ACCESS MODE IS SEQUENTIAL.
00021               SELECT GENERAL-JOURNAL
00022                 ASSIGN TO DISK-S-DD2
00023                 ORGANIZATION IS SEQUENTIAL
00024                 ACCESS MODE IS SEQUENTIAL.
00025               SELECT GENERAL-JOURNAL-SORT-FILE
00026                 ASSIGN TO DISK-S-SORTWK01
00027                 ORGANIZATION IS SEQUENTIAL
00028                 ACCESS MODE IS SEQUENTIAL.
00029               SELECT PRINTER
00030                 ASSIGN TO DISK-S-DD3
00031                 ORGANIZATION IS SEQUENTIAL
00032                 ACCESS MODE IS SEQUENTIAL.
00033               SELECT SORTED-GENERAL-JOURNAL-FILE
00034                 ASSIGN TO DISK-S-DD4
00035                 ORGANIZATION IS SEQUENTIAL
00036                 ACCESS MODE IS SEQUENTIAL.
00037               SELECT TRIAL-BALANCE
00038                 ASSIGN TO DISK-S-DD5
00039                 ORGANIZATION IS SEQUENTIAL
00040                 ACCESS MODE IS SEQUENTIAL.
00041
00042
00043           DATA DIVISION.
00044           FILE SECTION.
00045
00046           FD  ACCOUNT-DIRECTORY
00047               BLOCK CONTAINS 1 RECORDS
00048               LABEL RECORDS ARE STANDARD
00049               RECORD CONTAINS 63 CHARACTERS
00050               DATA RECORD IS ACCOUNT-DIRECTORY-RECORD.
00051           01  ACCOUNT-DIRECTORY-RECORD.
00052               02 SEQUENCE-NUMBER          PIC X(3).
00053               02 NAME-OF-ACCOUNT          PIC X(30).
00054               02 TYPE-OF-ACCOUNT          PIC X.
00055               02 EXPENSE-FIELD            PIC X.
00056               02 TRIAL-DEBIT-TOTAL        PIC 9(5)V9(2).
00057               02 TRIAL-CREDIT-TOTAL       PIC 9(5)V9(2).
00058               02 ADJUSTED-DEBIT-TOTAL     PIC 9(5)V9(2).
00059               02 ADJUSTED-CREDIT-TOTAL    PIC 9(5)V9(2).
00060
00061           FD  GENERAL-JOURNAL
00062               LABEL RECORDS ARE STANDARD
00063               BLOCK CONTAINS 1 RECORDS
00064               RECORD CONTAINS 80 CHARACTERS
```

Program 3.4 (cont.)

```
00065                    DATA RECORD IS GENERAL-JOURNAL-RECORD.
00066           01  GENERAL-JOURNAL-RECORD.
00067               02  TRANSACTION-NUMBER        PIC X(8).
00068               02  DEBIT-OR-CREDIT-FLAG      PIC X.
00069               02  ENTRY-DATE.
00070                   03  MONTH                 PIC X(3).
00071                   03  ENTRY-DAY             PIC 9(2).
00072                   03  YEAR                  PIC 9(2).
00073               02  NAME-OF-ACCOUNT           PIC X(30).
00074               02  AMOUNT                    PIC 9(5)V9(2).
00075               02  CARD-NO                   PIC 9(3).
00076               02  FILLER                    PIC X(24).
00077
00078           SD  GENERAL-JOURNAL-SORT-FILE
00079                   RECORD CONTAINS 80 CHARACTERS
00080                   DATA RECORD IS GENERAL-JOURNAL-SORT-RECORD.
00081           01  GENERAL-JOURNAL-SORT-RECORD.
00082               02  FILLER                    PIC X(16).
00083               02  NAME-OF-ACCOUNT           PIC X(30).
00084               02  FILLER                    PIC X(34).
00085
00086           SD  ACCOUNT-DIRECTORY-SORT-FILE
00087                   RECORD CONTAINS 63 CHARACTERS
00088                   DATA RECORD IS ACCOUNT-DIRECTORY-SORT-RECORD.
00089           01  ACCOUNT-DIRECTORY-SORT-RECORD.
00090               02  SEQUENCE-NUMBER           PIC X(3).
00091               02  FILLER                    PIC X(60).
00092
00093           FD  PRINTER
00094                   BLOCK CONTAINS 1 RECORDS
00095                   LABEL RECORDS ARE OMITTED
00096                   RECORD CONTAINS 133 CHARACTERS
00097                   DATA RECORD IS PRINTER-RECORD.
00098           01  PRINTER-RECORD.
00099               02  FILLER                    PIC X.
00100               02  DATA-AREA                 PIC X(132).
00101
00102           FD  SORTED-GENERAL-JOURNAL-FILE
00103                   BLOCK CONTAINS 1 RECORDS
00104                   LABEL RECORDS ARE STANDARD
00105                   RECORD CONTAINS 80 CHARACTERS
00106                   DATA RECORD IS SORTED-GENERAL-JOURNAL-RECORD.
00107           01  SORTED-GENERAL-JOURNAL-RECORD.
00108               02  TRANSACTION-NUMBER        PIC X(8).
00109               02  DEBIT-OR-CREDIT           PIC X.
00110               02  ENTRY-DATE.
00111                   03  MONTH                 PIC X(3).
00112                   03  ENTRY-DAY             PIC 9(2).
00113                   03  YEAR                  PIC 9(2).
00114               02  NAME-OF-ACCOUNT           PIC X(30).
00115               02  AMOUNT                    PIC 9(5)V9(2).
00116               02  CARD-NO                   PIC 9(3).
00117               02  FILLER                    PIC X(23).
00118               02  COMMENT-ENTRY             PIC X.
00119                   88  COMMENT          VALUE IS '*'.
00120
00121           FD  TRIAL-BALANCE
00122                   BLOCK CONTAINS 1 RECORDS
00123                   LABEL RECORDS ARE STANDARD
00124                   RECORD CONTAINS 63 CHARACTERS
00125                   DATA RECORD IS TRIAL-BALANCE-RECORD.
00126           01  TRIAL-BALANCE-RECORD.
```

Program 3.4   (cont.)

```
00127                02 SEQUENCE-NUMBER            PIC X(3).
00128                02 NAME-OF-ACCOUNT            PIC X(30).
00129                02 TYPE-OF-ACCOUNT            PIC X.
00130                02 EXPENSE-ACCOUNT-FIELD      PIC X.
00131                02 TRIAL-DEBIT-TOTAL          PIC 9(5)V9(2).
00132                02 TRIAL-CREDIT-TOTAL         PIC 9(5)V9(2).
00133                02 ADJUSTED-DEBIT-TOTAL       PIC 9(5)V9(2).
00134                02 ADJUSTED-CREDIT-TOTAL      PIC 9(5)V9(2).
00135
00136
00137        WORKING-STORAGE SECTION.
00138
00139            77  ACCOUNT-DIRECTORY-EOF-FLAG PIC X(3).
00140                88 END-OF-FILE-AD       VALUE IS 'ON'.
00141            77  ACTIVE-KEY                 PIC X(30).
00142                88 FINISHED             VALUE IS HIGH-VALUES.
00143            77  SORTED-JOURNAL-EOF-FLAG    PIC X(3).
00144                88 END-OF-FILE-SGJ      VALUE IS 'ON'.
00145            77  WRITE-SWITCH               PIC X(3).
00146
00147            01  WS-TRIAL-BALANCE-RECORD.
00148                02 SEQUENCE-NUMBER            PIC X(3).
00149                02 NAME-OF-ACCOUNT            PIC X(30).
00150                02 TYPE-OF-ACCOUNT            PIC X.
00151                02 EXPENSE-ACCOUNT-FIELD      PIC X.
00152                02 TRIAL-DEBIT-TOTAL          PIC 9(5)V9(2).
00153                02 TRIAL-CREDIT-TOTAL         PIC 9(5)V9(2).
00154                02 ADJUSTED-DEBIT-TOTAL       PIC 9(5)V9(2).
00155                02 ADJUSTED-CREDIT-TOTAL      PIC 9(5)V9(2).
00156
00157
00158        PROCEDURE DIVISION.
00159
00160                PERFORM SORT-JOURNAL-ACCOUNT-NAME.
00161                PERFORM INITIALIZE-BALANCE-LINE.
00162                PERFORM BALANCE-LINE UNTIL FINISHED.
00163                PERFORM TERMINATION.
00164                STOP RUN.
00165
00166        SORT-JOURNAL-ACCOUNT-NAME.
00167                SORT GENERAL-JOURNAL-SORT-FILE
00168                    ASCENDING KEY
00169                        NAME-OF-ACCOUNT OF GENERAL-JOURNAL-SORT-FILE
00170                    USING GENERAL-JOURNAL
00171                    GIVING SORTED-GENERAL-JOURNAL-FILE.
00172
00173        INITIALIZE-BALANCE-LINE.
00174                OPEN INPUT SORTED-GENERAL-JOURNAL-FILE
00175                           ACCOUNT-DIRECTORY
00176                     OUTPUT TRIAL-BALANCE.
00177                MOVE 'OFF' TO SORTED-JOURNAL-EOF-FLAG
00178                             ACCOUNT-DIRECTORY-EOF-FLAG.
00179                MOVE 'OFF' TO WRITE-SWITCH.
00180                PERFORM READ-SORTED-JOURNAL-RECORD.
00181                PERFORM READ-ACCOUNT-DIRECTORY-RECORD.
00182                PERFORM DETERMINE-ACTIVE-KEY.
00183
00184        BALANCE-LINE.
00185                IF NAME-OF-ACCOUNT OF ACCOUNT-DIRECTORY-RECORD
00186                   EQUAL ACTIVE-KEY
00187                  THEN
00188                     PERFORM PROCESS-MASTER-RECORD.
```

Program 3.4   (cont.)

```
00189                         PERFORM PROCESS-TRANSACTION-RECORD
00190                             UNTIL NAME-OF-ACCOUNT
00191                                 OF SORTED-GENERAL-JOURNAL-RECORD
00192                                 NOT EQUAL ACTIVE-KEY.
00193                         PERFORM WRITE-TRIAL-BALANCE-RECORD.
00194                         PERFORM DETERMINE-ACTIVE-KEY.
00195
00196                     TERMINATION.
00197                         CLOSE ACCOUNT-DIRECTORY
00198                                 SORTED-GENERAL-JOURNAL-FILE
00199                                 TRIAL-BALANCE.
00200
00201                     READ-SORTED-JOURNAL-RECORD.
00202                         READ SORTED-GENERAL-JOURNAL-FILE RECORD
00203                             AT END MOVE 'ON' TO
00204                                 SORTED-JOURNAL-EOF-FLAG.
00205                         IF END-OF-FILE-SGJ
00206                             MOVE HIGH-VALUES TO NAME-OF-ACCOUNT OF
00207                                 SORTED-GENERAL-JOURNAL-RECORD.
00208
00209                     READ-ACCOUNT-DIRECTORY-RECORD.
00210                         READ ACCOUNT-DIRECTORY RECORD
00211                             AT END MOVE 'ON' TO
00212                                 ACCOUNT-DIRECTORY-EOF-FLAG.
00213                         IF END-OF-FILE-AD
00214                             MOVE HIGH-VALUES TO NAME-OF-ACCOUNT OF
00215                                 ACCOUNT-DIRECTORY-RECORD.
00216
00217                     DETERMINE-ACTIVE-KEY.
00218                         IF NAME-OF-ACCOUNT OF
00219                                 SORTED-GENERAL-JOURNAL-RECORD
00220                                 IS LESS THAN
00221                                 NAME-OF-ACCOUNT OF ACCOUNT-DIRECTORY
00222                                 THEN
00223                             MOVE NAME-OF-ACCOUNT OF
00224                                     SORTED-GENERAL-JOURNAL-RECORD
00225                                     TO ACTIVE-KEY
00226                                 ELSE
00227                             MOVE NAME-OF-ACCOUNT OF ACCOUNT-DIRECTORY
00228                                     TO ACTIVE-KEY.
00229
00230                     PROCESS-MASTER-RECORD.
00231                         MOVE CORRESPONDING ACCOUNT-DIRECTORY-RECORD
00232                                 TO WS-TRIAL-BALANCE-RECORD.
00233                         MOVE 'ON' TO WRITE-SWITCH.
00234                         PERFORM READ-ACCOUNT-DIRECTORY-RECORD.
00235
00236                     PROCESS-TRANSACTION-RECORD.
00237                         IF DEBIT-OR-CREDIT OF
00238                                 SORTED-GENERAL-JOURNAL-RECORD
00239                                 EQUAL 'D' AND NOT COMMENT
00240                                 THEN
00241                             ADD AMOUNT OF SORTED-GENERAL-JOURNAL-RECORD
00242                                 TO TRIAL-DEBIT-TOTAL OF
00243                                 WS-TRIAL-BALANCE-RECORD
00244                                 ELSE
00245                             IF DEBIT-OR-CREDIT OF
00246                                     SORTED-GENERAL-JOURNAL-FILE
00247                                     EQUAL 'C' AND NOT COMMENT THEN
00248                                 ADD AMOUNT OF SORTED-GENERAL-JOURNAL-RECORD
00249                                     TO TRIAL-CREDIT-TOTAL OF
00250                                     WS-TRIAL-BALANCE-RECORD.
```

Program 3.4 (cont.)

```
00251                    PERFORM READ-SORTED-JOURNAL-RECORD.
00252                    PERFORM READ-SORTED-JOURNAL-RECORD
00253                        UNTIL NOT COMMENT OR END-OF-FILE-SGJ.
00254
00255          WRITE-TRIAL-BALANCE-RECORD.
00256             IF WRITE-SWITCH EQUAL 'ON' THEN
00257                WRITE TRIAL-BALANCE-RECORD
00258                    FROM WS-TRIAL-BALANCE-RECORD
00259             MOVE 'OFF' TO WRITE-SWITCH.
```

Next the SORTED-GENERAL-JOURNAL and ACCOUNT-DIRECTORY files are opened for INPUT and the TRIAL-BALANCE file is opened as an output file. An initial record is read from each of the input files and the lowest key of these records determined and placed in ACTIVE-KEY.

The balance line routine is now entered. Records on the ACCOUNT-DIRECTORY are treated as master records. They are copied into WS-TRIAL-BALANCE-RECORD. Records from the GENERAL-JOURNAL are treated as transaction records. When a transaction record is read, a debit entry is added to the TRIAL-DEBIT-TOTAL of WS-TRIAL-BALANCE-RECORD; a credit entry is added to the TRIAL-CREDIT-TOTAL of WS-TRIAL-BALANCE-RECORD. Comment records on the GENERAL-JOURNAL file are ignored. When all transaction records whose NAME-OF-ACCOUNT match the ACTIVE-KEY are processed, the WS-TRIAL-BALANCE-RECORD, which now contains the debit and credit totals for that account, is written to the TRIAL-BALANCE file. Processing is continued until the records of both files are exhausted. The ACTIVE-KEY will be set to HIGH-VALUES at this time. Files are then closed, and the program terminates.

3.7 CASE STUDY: MISSILE TARGET SYSTEM

A Titan missile can be armed with a MIRV (a multiple independently targeted reentry vehicle) for a retaliatory nuclear strike against a possible enemy. Basically this means that the rocket contains a package of several atomic weapons, each of which has a different selected target and all of which are released when she reaches a certain distance from the target area. A computer program is to be written to keep track of the targets assigned to each missile at a missile launch center.

3.7.1 Logical Analysis: Missile Target System

The number of warheads assigned to each individual Titan is variable and depends on the general area targeted. For example, a missile launched against a hydroelectric plant in the Ukraine may have no other targets in the general area whereas another launched against an industrial complex near Moscow may have several nearby vital targets. If each Titan Complex is capable of launching 25 such missiles and each missile carries a maximum of 5 warheads, there exists a potential of 25 to 125 possible first targets.

The nature of the defense against an incoming missile strike is not entirely known beforehand. Tactical counterdefense planning allows for each Titan to have a series of one or more secondary strike centers. This requires each of the individual MIRV warheads to carry various secondary targets.

The logical record in this case is the record associated with each individual missile at the launch site. The launch complex at Norman Falls, South Dakota, which we shall use for this study, has 25 missiles, each in its own silo. The missiles are labeled USAFN1, USAFN2, USAFN3, . . . , USAFN25. Each missile contains a MIRV with from 1 to 5 different warheads. The following information is kept for each warhead:

1. name of target
2. class of target
   (a) primary
   (b) secondary
3. expected time to target
4. warhead payload in megatonnage
5. expected nature of defense
   (a) ground-to-air missiles
   (b) air-to-air missiles
   (c) both of the above
   (d) none of the above
6. time required to launch
7. warhead number (a label from 1 to 5)
8. abort mission code (a secret number which, if telegraphed to the missile in flight, causes self destruct)

While each of the fields mentioned above, "name of target," "class of target," etc., is fixed in length, the number of targets associated with each Titan rocket is not. One rocket may carry a MIRV with three warheads, each with a secondary target, whereas another missile may have only two warheads, neither of which has a secondary target. The first rocket will thus have six targets (three warheads, two targets each) and the second rocket will have only two targets (two warheads, one target each). Thus the length of each record will not be fixed in length for each individual rocket but will vary with the number of targets.

One solution to this problem is to arrange for each record associated with an individual rocket to contain space for the maximum possible number of targets whether assigned or not. As this wastes a great deal of space and is not very imaginative, we term this a *bureaucratic solution.*

An alternate solution is to make use of variable-length records. This is more space efficient; and considering the large number of missiles and targets, we as taxpayers have implemented the second approach. The fact that such saving is insignificant in comparison to the cost of the missiles does not concern us here (after all they are not constructed according to ANSI standards).

3.8 VARIABLE-LENGTH RECORDS

Variable-length records permit a varying number of character positions. When the records in a file have fixed length, they are called *fixed-length records.*

3.8.1 Processing Variable-Length Records in COBOL

If a COBOL file contains variable-length records, the level 01 description of the records in the file FD or in the WORKING-STORAGE SECTION must reflect this variance in size. This can be accomplished in one of two ways. Either a different level 01 record description can be coded for each separate record size in the file FD or the format of the OCCURS clause containing the DEPENDING ON option can be used.

The former method is generally used when a file contains few different record sizes or when the records of differing size vary considerably in format. The following ANSI COBOL statements describe a file that contains 12 records of different length and a level 01 entry is included for each:

```
FD File-name
   LABEL RECORDS ARE STANDARD
   BLOCK CONTAINS integer RECORDS
   RECORD CONTAINS integer-1 TO integer-2 CHARACTERS
   DATA RECORDS ARE record-name-1
                    record-name-2
                    record-name-3
                       .
                       .
                       .
                    record-name-12.
01 record-name-1
   02 FILLER PIC X(n1).
01 record-name-2.
   02 FILLER PIC X(n2).
01 record-name-3.
```

```
02 FILLER PIC X(n3).
                    .

                    .

                    .
01 record-name-12.
   02 FILLER PIC X(n12).
```

As with all FD file descriptions the LABEL RECORDS clause is required.

The BLOCK CONTAINS clause specifies the length of each physical record. It will be assumed that the size of each block is *integer* times the size of the largest of the various individual record sizes.

The RECORD CONTAINS clause indicates the size of the smallest of various variable record sizes in characters (*integer-1*) and the size of the largest (*integer-2*) of the record sizes in characters. In the above, then,

$$integer\text{-}1 = min\ \{n1, n2, n3, \ldots, n12\}$$
$$and\ integer\text{-}2 = max\ \{n1, n2, n3, \ldots, n12\}$$

The DATA RECORDS clause specifies the record names of each of the individual record descriptions. It is assumed that at least two of the integers, *n1*, *n2*, *n3* . . . , *n12* are different; otherwise, each will be considered an automatic redefinition of *record-name-1* and strictly speaking we would not then be dealing with variable-length records.

The following IBM COBOL statements describe a variable length record file containing records of three different types:

```
FD AIRPLANE-FILE
   LABEL RECORDS ARE STANDARD
   BLOCK CONTAINS 5 RECORDS
   RECORD CONTAINS 30 TO 50 CHARACTERS
   DATA RECORDS ARE CARGO-PLANE
                    PASSENGER-PLANE
                    MILITARY PLANE.
01 CARGO-PLANE.
   02 FILLER PIC X(40).

01 MILITARY-PLANE.
   02 FILLER PIC X(30).

01 PASSENGER-PLANE.
   02 FILLER PIC X(50).
```

This FD describes a variable-length record file called AIR-PLANE. There are three different record descriptions for records of 30, 40, and 50 characters. Actual elementary field descriptions have not been included.

In order to understand the action initiated by the BLOCK CONTAINS *integer*

RECORDS clause in IBM OS/VS COBOL, it is important to realize that it does not specify what its meaning in English would imply. BLOCK CONTAINS 5 RE-CORDS does not mean that each physical record actually contains five logical records (as it does with fixed-length records) but rather that the physical record shall take up no more space on the storage device than would be occupied by five records of the largest possible size. Several bytes are added to the physical record size in order to maintain internal bookkeeping. This extra storage space amounts to

1. four bytes for each logical record in the block *plus*
2. four additional bytes

Thus the statement BLOCK CONTAINS 5 RECORDS actually allows a maximum physical record size of 274 bytes in the above example. This is calculated from the fact that the largest variable-length record permitted is 50 bytes long; there are 5 of these for a total of $5 \times 50 = 250$ bytes; for each of these 5 records there are 4 additional bytes, $5 \times 4 = 20$ making a total of $250 + 20 = 270$ bytes; and, lastly, an additional 4 bytes is added for a grand total of 274 bytes. The maximum physical record that could be stored is thus 274 bytes.

A physical record may not actually contain this number of bytes as the logical records are not all of the same length. A physical record is completed and written to the storage device whenever the sum of the number of bytes in each logical record in the block, plus 4 bytes for each of these records, plus 4 additional bytes is subtracted from the maximum physical record size and the difference does not leave enough space for a variable-length record of the maximum size. An example will make this clear.

The BLOCK CONTAINS clause permitted a maximum physical record size of 274 bytes. Suppose the user wishes to write one 30-byte record followed by five 40-byte records. The sum of space occupied by these logical records is

$$
\begin{array}{rcl}
1 \times 30 & = & 30 \\
5 \times 40 & = & 200 \\
6 \times 4 & = & 24 \\
1 \times 4 & = & 4 \\
\hline
\text{Total} & & 258
\end{array}
$$

The amount of space remaining is $274 - 258 = 16$, which is not enough for a record of 50 bytes, the maximum variable-record length. As a result, a 258-byte physical record is written.

It should be noted that BLOCK CONTAINS 5 RECORDS was chosen for illustrative purposes and that the number 5 may be a very poor choice depending on the storage device used and the amount of space available for storing logical records prior to their being written on a storage device. The correct choice of this number is discussed in Chapter 5.

3.8.2 Variable-Length Records in the Missile Target System

In the missile target system each record contains information about one or more targets associated with a Titan rocket. Thus the length of each varies with the number of targets. The fields associated with each target are identical and what actually varies is the group item of targeting information. For each rocket, this group item will occur as many times as there are targets and what is needed is a variable form of the OCCURS clause which permits the length of the group item to vary from record to record.

OCCURS DEPENDING ON

The following code, valid for IBM COBOL, describes the record associated with each missile:

```
01 TITAN-MISSILE.
02 NUMBER-OF-TARGETS PICTURE 99.
02 TARGET OCCURS 0 TO 5 TIMES
      DEPENDING ON NUMBER-OF-TARGETS.
   03 NAME-OF-TARGET PIC X(20).
   03 CLASS-OF-TARGET PIC X(9).
   03 EXPECTED-FLIGHT-TIME PIC 9(4).
   03 WARHEAD-PAYLOAD PIC 9(3).
   03 EXPECTED-DEFENSE PIC 9.
   03 LAUNCH-TIME PIC 9(3).
   03 WARHEAD-NUMBER PIC 9.
   03 ABORT-CODE PIC 9(5).
```

Each of the level 03 elementary items describes one unit of information concerning the target. The level 02 group item thus contains all the information concerning each target and it is itself a table. For any record this table may have from 0 to 5 entries. The number of entries varies from record to record but is given in the elementary data item named NUMBER-OF-TARGETS. If this data item contains 5, then the group item TARGET is a table of 5 entries. If NUMBER-OF-TARGETS is 3, the group item TARGET is a table of 3 entries. In the example given, the entry TARGET for any record cannot have more than 5 entries.

Program 3.5 Narrative: Missile Target. The input to Program 3.5 consists of keypunched data cards because of budget cuts. Each card contains a 7-character missile identification code called MISSILE-IDENTIFICATION and carries the information about one particular target. As any missile can have up to five first strike targets, there are a maximum of five data cards having the same missile identification code. We shall refer to a group of five or less such data cards as the "target group" of one missile. To aid in processing, the data cards are sorted by hand into target groups.

Program 3.5

```
00009          /  ** MISSILE TARGET PROGRAM **
00010
00011          INPUT-OUTPUT SECTION.
00012          FILE-CONTROL.
00013
00014              SELECT CARD-READER
00015                  ASSIGN TO CARD-S-SYSIN
00016                  ORGANIZATION IS SEQUENTIAL
00017                  ACCESS MODE IS SEQUENTIAL.
00018              SELECT PRINTER
00019                  ASSIGN TO PRNT-S-SYSOUT
00020                  ORGANIZATION IS SEQUENTIAL
00021                  ACCESS MODE IS SEQUENTIAL.
00022              SELECT  MISSILE-FILE
00023                  ASSIGN TO DISK-S-MISSILE
00024                  ORGANIZATION IS SEQUENTIAL
00025                  ACCESS MODE IS SEQUENTIAL.
00026
00027
00028          DATA DIVISION.
00029          FILE SECTION.
00030
00031          FD  CARD-READER
00032              BLOCK CONTAINS 1 RECORDS
00033              LABEL RECORDS ARE OMITTED
00034              RECORD CONTAINS 80 CHARACTERS
00035              DATA RECORD IS CARD-READER-RECORD.
00036          01  CARD-READER-RECORD.
00037              02 MISSILE-IDENTIFICATION   PIC X(7).
00038              02 NAME-OF-TARGET           PIC X(20).
00039              02 CLASS-OF-TARGET          PIC X(9).
00040              02 EXPECTED-FLIGHT-TIME     PIC 9(4).
00041              02 WARHEAD-PAYLOAD          PIC 9(3).
00042              02 EXPECTED-DEFENCE         PIC 9.
00043              02 LAUNCH-TIME             PIC 9(3).
00044              02 WARHEAD-NUMBER           PIC 9.
00045              02 ABORT-CODE               PIC 9(5).
00046              02 FILLER                   PIC X(27).
00047
00048          FD  MISSILE-FILE
00049              BLOCK CONTAINS 5 RECORDS
00050              LABEL RECORDS ARE STANDARD
00051              RECORD CONTAINS 55 TO 239 CHARACTERS
00052              DATA RECORD IS MISSILE-FILE-RECORD.
00053          01  MISSILE-FILE-RECORD.
00054              02 MISSILE-IDENTIFICATION  PIC X(7).
00055              02 NUMBER-OF-TARGETS       PIC 99.
00056              02  TARGET OCCURS 0 TO 5 TIMES
00057                  DEPENDING ON NUMBER-OF-TARGETS
00058                          OF WS-MISSILE-FILE-RECORD.
00059                  03 NAME-OF-TARGET       PIC X(20).
00060                  03 CLASS-OF-TARGET      PIC X(9).
00061                  03 EXPECTED-FLIGHT-TIME PIC 9(4).
00062                  03 WARHEAD-PAYLOAD      PIC 9(3).
00063                  03 EXPECTED-DEFENCE     PIC 9.
00064                  03 LAUNCH-TIME          PIC 9(3).
00065                  03 WARHEAD-NUMBER       PIC 9.
00066                  03 ABORT-CODE           PIC 9(5).
00067
00068          FD  PRINTER
00069              BLOCK CONTAINS 1 RECORDS
00070              LABEL RECORDS ARE OMITTED
```

Program 3.5 (cont.)

```
00071                    RECORD CONTAINS 132 CHARACTERS
00072                    DATA RECORD IS PRINTER-RECORD.
00073            01  PRINTER-RECORD.
00074                02 FILLER                    PIC X(5).
00075                02 NAME-OF-TARGET            PIC X(20).
00076                02 FILLER                    PIC X(5).
00077                02 MISSILE-IDENTIFICATION    PIC X(7).
00078                02 FILLER                    PIC X(95).
00079
00080
00081            WORKING-STORAGE SECTION.
00082
00083            77  ACTIVE-KEY                   PIC X(7).
00084            77  COUNTER                      PIC S9(8).
00085            77  EOF-CARD-FLAG                PIC X(3).
00086                88 EOF-CARD VALUE IS 'ON'.
00087
00088            01  WS-MISSILE-FILE-RECORD.
00089                02 MISSILE-IDENTIFICATION    PIC X(7).
00090                02 NUMBER-OF-TARGETS         PIC 99.
00091                02  TARGET OCCURS 0 TO 5 TIMES
00092                    DEPENDING ON NUMBER-OF-TARGETS
00093                                OF WS-MISSILE-FILE-RECORD.
00094                    03 NAME-OF-TARGET        PIC X(20).
00095                    03 CLASS-OF-TARGET       PIC X(9).
00096                    03 EXPECTED-FLIGHT-TIME PIC 99.
00097                    03 WARHEAD-PAYLOAD       PIC 9(3).
00098                    03 EXPECTED-DEFENCE      PIC 9.
00099                    03 LAUNCH-TIME           PIC 9(3).
00100                    03 WARHEAD-NUMBER        PIC 9.
00101                    03 ABORT-CODE            PIC 9(5).
00102
00103
00104            PROCEDURE DIVISION.
00105
00106                PERFORM INITIALIZATION.
00107                PERFORM READ-AND-COPY-TO-FILE-ROUTINE
00108                        UNTIL EOF-CARD.
00109                PERFORM TERMINATION.
00110                STOP RUN.
00111
00112            INITIALIZATION.
00113                OPEN INPUT   CARD-READER
00114                     OUTPUT PRINTER
00115                            MISSILE-FILE.
00116                MOVE 'OFF' TO EOF-CARD-FLAG.
00117                MOVE ZERO TO NUMBER-OF-TARGETS
00118                        OF WS-MISSILE-FILE-RECORD.
00119                READ CARD-READER RECORD
00120                    AT END MOVE 'ON' TO EOF-CARD-FLAG.
00121                IF NOT EOF-CARD THEN
00122                    MOVE MISSILE-IDENTIFICATION
00123                        OF CARD-READER TO ACTIVE-KEY
00124                    MOVE MISSILE-IDENTIFICATION
00125                        OF CARD-READER TO
00126                        MISSILE-IDENTIFICATION
00127                        OF WS-MISSILE-FILE-RECORD.
00128
00129            READ-AND-COPY-TO-FILE-ROUTINE.
00130                PERFORM COPY-CARD-TO-WORKING-STORAGE
00131                        UNTIL MISSILE-IDENTIFICATION
00132                            OF CARD-READER
```

Program 3.5 (cont.)

```
00133                        NOT EQUAL ACTIVE-KEY
00134                        OR EOF-CARD.
00135         MOVE NUMBER-OF-TARGETS
00136              OF WS-MISSILE-FILE-RECORD
00137              TO NUMBER-OF-TARGETS
00138              OF MISSILE-FILE-RECORD.
00139         DISPLAY NUMBER-OF-TARGETS
00140                 OF WS-MISSILE-FILE-RECORD.
00141         WRITE MISSILE-FILE-RECORD
00142              FROM WS-MISSILE-FILE-RECORD.
00143         IF NOT EOF-CARD  THEN
00144            MOVE MISSILE-IDENTIFICATION
00145                 OF CARD-READER TO ACTIVE-KEY
00146            MOVE ZERO TO NUMBER-OF-TARGETS
00147                          OF WS-MISSILE-FILE-RECORD
00148            MOVE MISSILE-IDENTIFICATION
00149                 OF CARD-READER
00150                 TO MISSILE-IDENTIFICATION
00151                 OF WS-MISSILE-FILE-RECORD.
00152
00153      COPY-CARD-TO-WORKING-STORAGE.
00154         ADD 1 TO NUMBER-OF-TARGETS
00155                 OF WS-MISSILE-FILE-RECORD.
00156         MOVE NUMBER-OF-TARGETS OF WS-MISSILE-FILE-RECORD
00157                 TO COUNTER.
00158         MOVE NAME-OF-TARGET OF CARD-READER-RECORD
00159                 TO NAME-OF-TARGET
00160                 OF TARGET
00161                 OF WS-MISSILE-FILE-RECORD (COUNTER).
00162         MOVE CLASS-OF-TARGET OF CARD-READER-RECORD
00163                 TO CLASS-OF-TARGET
00164                 OF TARGET
00165                 OF WS-MISSILE-FILE-RECORD (COUNTER).
00166         MOVE EXPECTED-FLIGHT-TIME
00167                 OF CARD-READER-RECORD
00168                 TO EXPECTED-FLIGHT-TIME
00169                 OF TARGET
00170                 OF WS-MISSILE-FILE-RECORD (COUNTER).
00171         MOVE WARHEAD-PAYLOAD OF CARD-READER-RECORD
00172                 TO WARHEAD-PAYLOAD
00173                 OF TARGET
00174                 OF WS-MISSILE-FILE-RECORD (COUNTER).
00175         MOVE EXPECTED-DEFENCE OF CARD-READER-RECORD
00176                 TO EXPECTED-DEFENCE
00177                 OF TARGET
00178                 OF WS-MISSILE-FILE-RECORD (COUNTER).
00179         MOVE LAUNCH-TIME OF CARD-READER-RECORD
00180                 TO LAUNCH-TIME
00181                 OF TARGET
00182                 OF WS-MISSILE-FILE-RECORD (COUNTER).
00183         MOVE WARHEAD-NUMBER
00184                 OF CARD-READER-RECORD
00185                 TO WARHEAD-NUMBER
00186                 OF TARGET
00187                 OF WS-MISSILE-FILE-RECORD (COUNTER).
00188         MOVE ABORT-CODE OF CARD-READER
00189                 TO ABORT-CODE
00190                 OF TARGET
00191                 OF WS-MISSILE-FILE-RECORD (COUNTER).
00192         PERFORM PRINT-VERIFY-ROUTINE.
00193         READ CARD-READER RECORD
00194              AT END MOVE 'ON' TO EOF-CARD-FLAG.
```

Program 3.5   (cont.)

```
00195
00196              PRINT-VERIFY-ROUTINE.
00197                  MOVE SPACES TO PRINTER-RECORD.
00198                  MOVE MISSILE-IDENTIFICATION OF CARD-READER
00199                      TO MISSILE-IDENTIFICATION OF PRINTER.
00200                  MOVE NAME-OF-TARGET OF CARD-READER
00201                      TO NAME-OF-TARGET OF PRINTER.
00202                  WRITE PRINTER-RECORD
00203                      AFTER ADVANCING 2 LINES.
00204
00205              TERMINATION.
00206                  CLOSE CARD-READER
00207                        MISSILE-FILE
00208                        PRINTER.
```

As each card of the target group is read, its targeting information is moved to the array TARGET in MISSILE-FILE- RECORD. The array TARGET is defined with an OCCURS DEPENDING ON clause which has as its object a variable called NUMBER-OF-TARGETS. As the variable controls the size of the array TARGET, it is stored in the fixed part of the record. Before any information from a data card is moved to the array, the variable NUMBER-OF-TARGETS is incremented by 1 to allow the array to expand by one or more entries to hold the additional information.

The missile identification code of the first data card within a target group is stored in a variable called ACTIVE-KEY and only cards whose codes match the ACTIVE-KEY are processed to the same MISSILE-FILE-RECORD. The ACTIVE-KEY is updated to another code when the target group is written.

Processing is terminated when end-of-file is encountered on the card reader.

It should be noted that the elementary item NUMBER-OF-TARGETS which expresses the size of the corresponding OCCURS clause is found in that part of the record that does not itself vary in size, this is usually referred to as the *fixed part of the record*. The data item referred to by the DEPENDING ON option of the OCCURS clause should always occur within the fixed part of the record. In addition, it should be described as a positive unsigned integer item that is defined with either USAGE IS DISPLAY (the default option) or as a COMPUTATIONAL or COMPUTATIONAL-3 item. It must never be a table entry or exceed in value the maximum size specified in the TIMES portion of the OCCURS clause. Note that the former of these restrictions prohibits the DEPENDING ON option of an OCCURS clause from naming a data item within another OCCURS DEPENDING ON clause.

ANSI COBOL does not permit an OCCURS clause of any format to describe an item whose size is variable, that is, an item containing an OCCURS DE-PENDING ON clause or having subordinate to it an item containing an OCCURS DEPENDING ON clause. IBM COBOL has relaxed this restriction. Check your manual for details.

The OCCURS DEPENDING ON option can be used either in the WORKING-STORAGE SECTION or in the FD entry for a given file. For either case, the object of the DEPENDING ON option, that is, the number that specifies how large the variable table is in size, should be updated to the correct value in order to reflect this size before any data is moved into the variable table. The table length is changed to reflect the updated value whenever the value of the data item that specifies this size is changed. This is done automatically when data is read into a buffer by a READ statement.

It is particularly important to note that if there is any data item that follows a portion of a group description containing an OCCURS DEPENDING ON option, because the contents of this subsequent item will be destroyed as the variable table grows and overwrites it. For example, in the following code the value of data item C will be lost if a new value is moved to A as this will change the size of variable table B.

```
01 RECORD-DESCRIPTION.
   02 A PIC 99.
   02 B OCCURS 0 TO 10
      TIMES DEPENDING ON A
      PIC X(4).
   02 C PIC X(2).
```

The contents of C can be saved in a temporary location and returned once A has been updated. The size of B changes as soon as the value of A is modified.

The user must employ caution when executing group moves to storage areas containing subordinate items described with the OCCURS DEPENDING ON option. This is best explained by describing the result of a MOVE operation to the following group item A:

```
01   A.
   02 B PIC 9(2).
   02 C OCCURS 5 TO 10
      TIMES DEPENDING ON
      B PIC X(5).
01   W.
   02 FILLER PIC X(50).
```

If the statement

```
                    MOVE W TO A
```

is executed, the size of variable table C is determined by the previous contents of B. After the MOVE is executed, if the data moved to the area defined by B within A is of the correct format (i.e., it can legally be defined as PIC 99) then the length of table C will be updated. In the event that the data transferred to B is not of the correct format, the value within B will be ignored and the length of table C will not change.

As a WRITE statement with the FROM option and a READ with the INTO options involve group moves, the user is cautioned that care must be taken to ensure that any variable-length tables within the receiving field are of the correct size. It may be advisable to avoid using these two options if confusion arises and move data to and from the buffer areas with individual MOVE statements after correctly updating the object data items of any DEPENDING ON options involved.

3.8.3 A Final Note

Variable-length records are not fully defined in the 1974 ANSI COBOL standard, and in the standard neither an OCCURS DEPENDING ON clause nor multiple FD level 01 entries of differing sizes really allow for logical records of variable length to be stored. Recent work of the COBOL CODASYL Committee would seem to indicate that future revisions of the standard will permit an approach very similar to that employed in IBM OS/VS COBOL. If you are using another COBOL compiler, careful reading of the manuals supplied is highly advisable.

3.9 POSTSCRIPT: A WORD ON PROGRAM STYLE

We would like to draw attention to the fact that none of the programs in this chapter contain a GO TO statement. Although we do not insist that GO TO's be forbidden, we adhere to the belief that GO TO's should only be used with care, as in most programs an overabundance of GO TO's can and does lead to unnecessary program complexity. Satisfying as it may be to a programmer's ego, program complexity is not a desirable attribute of *good* programming style. Our experience has shown that the decision to avoid GO TO's does not magically transform a bad program into a good program, but such a decision does bring discipline to the programming process. Certainly, there are many techniques that lead to good programming. If having a coffee, sharpening a pencil, or avoiding nested IF's (a good idea) do the same for our reader, so be it. Style arises from good and consistent habits. Choose a method and stick to it. Although good style requires hard work, the benefits that result are so profitable you cannot afford to neglect it. Programming takes effort, brains, and time; sloppy work leads to more effort and time than expected. The history of missed deadlines in the manufacture of software speaks for itself.

REFERENCES FOR FURTHER READING

Grauer, R. T. *Structured Methods through COBOL.* Englewood Cliffs, N.J.:Prentice-Hall, 1983.

Weinberg, G. M. et al. *High Level COBOL Programming.* Cambridge, Mass.: Winthrop Publishers, 1977.

PROBLEMS

1. Discuss the limitations of sequential files as you see them.

2. What is the major disadvantage of batch processing?

3. Write a COBOL program to access the MUSIC LOG file and determine the amount of time records have been played, the number of records, and the average duration of a record.

4. The purpose of this exercise is to master the concepts of a case study by doing.

Case Study: Fire Statistics

The city council of Johnsonburg has delegated the responsibility of drafting a new budget for the city's fire department to a small subcommittee. This decision was taken as a result of complaints brought forward by the Ratepayers' Association concerned with the alarming increase in fire losses suffered by the city. The Association has charged that the recent introduction of a large cereal factory and an addition to the pulp and paper mill necessitate appropriate expansion of the city's firefighting equipment. A recent newspaper report has further agitated the situation by suggesting that arson is increasing with the current growth in population. As a first step, the subcommittee has requested that the fire chief keep statistics on the nature and extent of all new fires. He is to provide a quarterly report to the committee.

Logical Analysis: Fire Statistics

The prime directive is to collect data on city fires. To this end a report form is prepared to collect details on the various areas of concern. A completed sample of this report, shown in Fig. 3.12, is based on the data items of Table 3.4, and is to be filled out as soon after a fire as possible. Manpower does not permit a more detailed report at this time.

Since these forms will be used to prepare quarterly reports, it is decided to store them on a magnetic tape file once a week. No one has requested instant access to any of these reports, therefore, storage on direct access devices is not required. Magnetic tape storage is expected to be less expensive for this application.

Several decisions are required concerning what information is to be written to the sequential tape file. The fires are first classified as to cause. Each fire cause is assigned a code, and it is decided that for purposes of reporting neither the type of injury nor the names of the injured need be recorded. The latter decision protects the privacy of the individuals from the city council subcommittee, and the exact extent of injuries can only be determined by a competent examining physician.

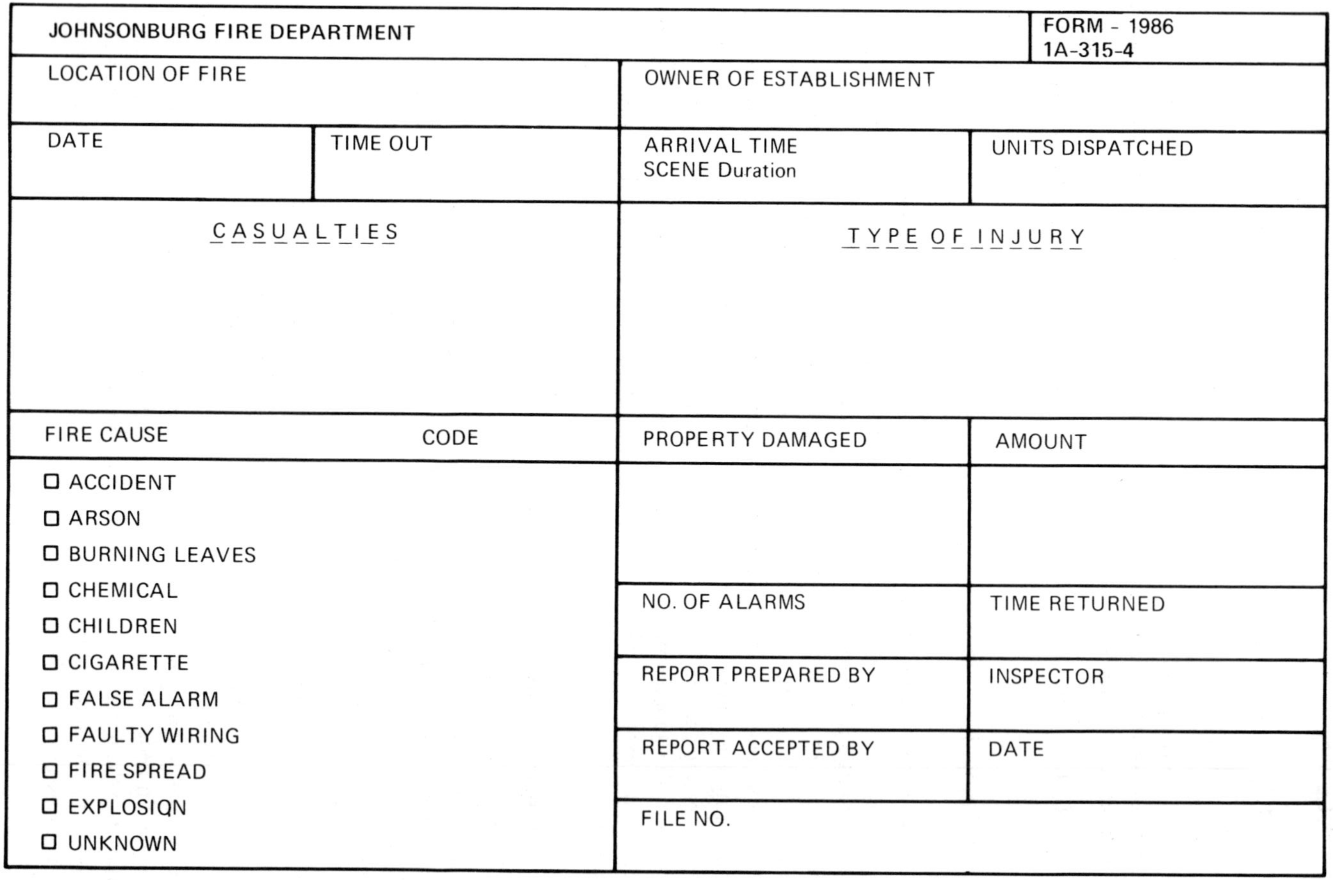

JOHNSONBURG FIRE DEPARTMENT FORM - 1986 1A-315-4

LOCATION OF FIRE | OWNER OF ESTABLISHMENT

DATE | TIME OUT | ARRIVAL TIME SCENE Duration | UNITS DISPATCHED

C A S U A L T I E S | T Y P E O F I N J U R Y

FIRE CAUSE | CODE | PROPERTY DAMAGED | AMOUNT

☐ ACCIDENT
☐ ARSON
☐ BURNING LEAVES
☐ CHEMICAL
☐ CHILDREN
☐ CIGARETTE
☐ FALSE ALARM
☐ FAULTY WIRING
☐ FIRE SPREAD
☐ EXPLOSION
☐ UNKNOWN

NO. OF ALARMS | TIME RETURNED

REPORT PREPARED BY | INSPECTOR

REPORT ACCEPTED BY | DATE

FILE NO.

Figure 3.12 Sample form for Fire Statistics Case Study.

Table 3.4   Data to be Stored in Fire-Statistics File

Entry	Number of Characters
Fire location	30—alphabetic
Owner of building	20—alphabetic
Date of fire	6—digits
Time of alarm	4—military (24-hour) time
Time at scene	4—military time
Duration of fire	4—digits
Number of trucks dispatched	2—digits
Dollar damage estimate	7—digits
Number of casualties	3—digits
Cause of fire	2—digit code
Number of fire alarms	1—digit
Time returned from fire	4—military time
File number	6—digits
	93—total

(a) Write a program to create a sequential FIRE-STATISTICS file on disk.

(b) Write an update program that rewrites in place. Are there any back-up problems? How would you solve them?

5. Whenever cash is paid out, it should be done by check. To control checks, they are assigned consecutive check numbers. Missing check numbers must be explained—perhaps they have been stolen. Show how to add check numbers to the transaction records of the GENERAL JOURNAL file. How could you detect missing check numbers?

6. Program 3.2 assumes that entries reaching the file are correct. This is not a valid assumption. Accounting errors are corrected by entering a *correcting entry*.

(a) Revise Program 3.2 so that transactions on the General Journal can be corrected.

(b) If the amount of a transaction was found a month later, how could you correct it?

7. Write a program to print out the GENERAL JOURNAL file.

8. At the end of the fiscal year, Profit Inc.'s expense accounts are zeroed. Explain how you might do this. Is a knowledge of accounting required or can the programmer just see that zeros get entered?

9. Profit Inc.'s accountant, John Figures, is pleased with the speed at which he gets his trial balance and with the fact that he no longer has to do posting and total accounts. However, last month there was an error in the supplies account, and it took him quite a while to find it in the General Journal. He wonders if it would be possible to print out the Account entries as well as the totals. He also feels it will be easier for him to audit entries in Accounts rather than the General Journal.

    (a) Advise him of solution, cost, and delivery.

    (b) Implement solution.

    (c) Propose a test of the solution.

    10. Investigate which files in your computer installation make use of variable-length records. Why are they used in these cases? What part of the records in these files vary in size?

    11. Make a list of your favorite baseball, hockey, or football players and indicate which teams they have played for. Write a program that reads in this data and prints it out. Make use of variable-length records to record the teams. If you dislike sports, try to design a file that would require variable-length records.

    12. Describe the contents of the record you think the income tax department keeps concerning you. Draw a diagram of the record indicating the various fields and the lengths that would be needed in characters for the information in each field. This is called making a *record layout*. Can you think of any part of this file that would require variable-length records? Is it likely or even reasonable that every field you fill out on your income tax form is included? Often individuals write letters to the tax department trying to clarify what level of tax to pay on certain incomes or questioning a decision of the government that affects the amount they are assessed. How would you keep track of this form of data? Remember you are not the only taxpayer and no two letters are the same.

    13. One thing many students often fail to get is enough experience presenting their material in public. Imagine that you are a member of the tax department and are asked to explain and justify the record layout in Problem 12 to management. Ask your fellow students or your teacher to arrange for a small public talk. If you cannot do this, try to lecture to yourself in a mirror or even to an empty classroom. Your future employers will often ask you to explain to them or another group what you are planning to do in your programming, and valuable experience can be had now without penalty.

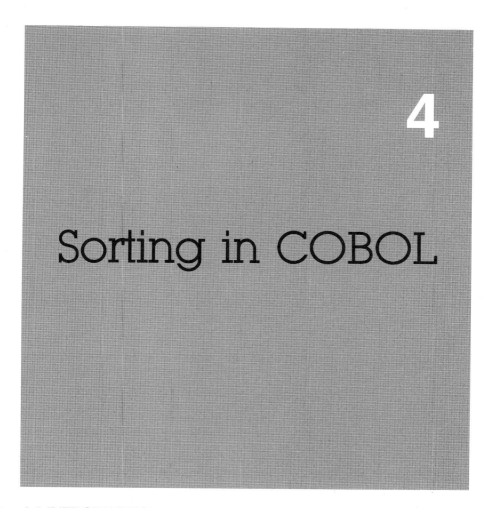

Sorting in COBOL

4.1 INTRODUCTION

Sorting a file consists of arranging the file records in the sequence of a key contained in the records. This key is referred to as a *sort key*. For instance, if the sort key is numeric, then the records can be placed in numeric order, either ascending or descending. Since the sort key need not be unique, it may be necessary to sort those records with the same value of the sort key on yet another sort key field.

The fact that a file to be sorted may not fit into memory poses an additional problem of considerable magnitude. Sorting methods that assume that all records to be sorted are stored in memory are called *internal sorts*. A method that need not have all records in memory at the same time is called an *external sort*.

Most data processing files cannot be placed in the available memory, and thus external sort methods are required. This is a serious restriction and affects the efficiency of the methods used for sorting. Efficiency of sorting is a function of the structure of the unsorted records, and no best method is known.

Some systems, particularly batch systems, often spend most of their processing time sorting. Thus sorting, while not a major topic of this book, is a very important technique for file processing. Our purpose here is to develop the essential background for the use of sorting in this book. The reader who wishes to may skip this chapter.

When two or more files are already sorted, combining them to form a single sorted file can be done by a process called a *merge*. Merging is more efficient because it assumes that the files to be combined are already in order. Most computer installations have a software system for sorting, called a Sort–Merge package, which provides a wide range of sorting techniques. Each Sort–Merge package has its own command statements or language, and a program can be written in this language to solve a particular sorting problem. The user must designate which file is to be sorted, on which keys the records are to be sorted, and where the file, once sorted, is to be stored.

The COBOL language has constructs for describing the necessary sorting information within a program. The COBOL compiler will provide a call to the Sort–Merge package and translate COBOL sort instructions into the command language of the Sort–Merge package. When the sort is described in COBOL, there are several immediate advantages realized. First, the user need only know COBOL; he need not learn the language of the Sort–Merge package. Second, the sort statements within COBOL are standardized by the ANSI Language Committee, whereas the command language often differs from one Sort–Merge package to another. This makes the program written in COBOL portable; that is, it can be run on different machines to attain the same result, and it also isolates the program from system changes. Third, the sorting statements can be embedded in a COBOL program. This enables a programmer to write COBOL statements that will govern when the sorting routines are to be called and which records in the file are to be sorted. It is also possible to write one's own sort in a COBOL program. This is not likely to be necessary, but a situation could occur, such as a limit on memory, in which it would be advantageous to do so. However, chances are that someone will have a COBOL sort, which he or she will be pleased to give you.

> The SORT–MERGE module of COBOL provides the capability to sort the records of a file according to the sort keys of the records specified by the user. Special procedures provide the flexibility to edit the files and to increase the efficiency of the sort phase. COBOL Level 1 limits the sorting of a file to once per program execution; COBOL Level 2 allows multiple sorting of files.

4.2 SORTING

In order to understand the process of sorting, we examine a simple yet reasonable sort algorithm which we refer to as the *simple selection sort*. Assuming that the records before the current record position are in order, select from the remaining records the one that belongs in the current position. Record selection from the yet unsorted records consists of simply selecting the maximum or minimum key of these records. The process is illustrated in Figure 4.1. Here the pointer *top* indicates the first of the as yet unsorted records. Initially no records are sorted, but when top points to the last record, the set of records must be sorted in ascending order from the first record.

The number of operations used by this algorithm is proportional to n^2, where n is the number of records. More efficient algorithms provide far better bounds for the size of the number of operations; Heapsort, discovered by J. W. J. Williams

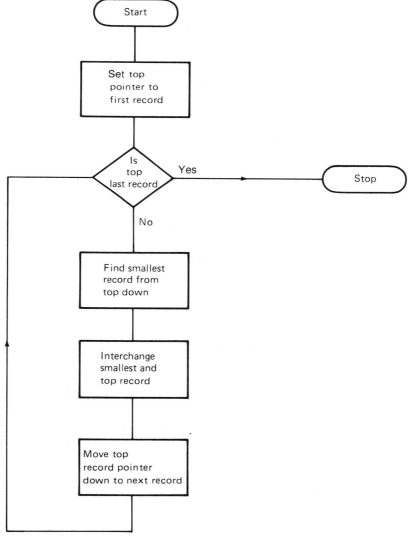

Figure 4.1 Simple selection sort.

(1964), is one such sort. One of the best all-around internal sorts is that proposed by Hoare (1962), called Quicksort. Its average processing time is very good; unfortunately, it can run poorly in the worst case.

When all the records do not fit into available memory, we can only sort subsets.We then require a method of combining two sorted subsets, while maintaining their sorted nature. This process is called *merging*. In Figure 4.2 we give the basic logic flow to merge two sorted tapes into a single sorted tape. It is easily done by keeping a pointer to each file that indicates the next record to be removed from that file. Simply determine which of these records pointed to is next, move it to the sorted file, and update that record pointer; then repeat the selection. Merging as part of a single sort is more complicated, as two output tapes may be required to contain the data on the two input tapes.

When using an external sort, the largest blocking factor possible should be used to reduce the number of I/O operations. Increasing the number of tapes being merged can be advantageous. However, there is usually a limit to the number of files that can be opened, and the results are system dependent, especially in a multiuser environment.

4.3 EXTERNAL SORTING IN COBOL

Sorting in COBOL requires that certain statements be added to each of the three main divisions of a COBOL program, namely, the ENVIRONMENT, DATA, and PROCEDURE DIVISIONs. These statements indicate which file is to be sorted, what fields within the records of this file are the sort keys, and where the sorted file is to be stored.

The program requirements for sorting can be more easily understood when it is realized that COBOL asks the Sort–Merge package to sort a special file known in COBOL as a sort file. This sort file is not the file you wish to have sorted. It is a special internal file *that the program may not open or close* but into which the records to be sorted are placed for actual sorting. This internal sort file, once it contains the records that are to be sorted, is turned over to the Sort–Merge package. Upon completion of sorting, the internal file is returned in sort order. Because this internal file is central to the whole idea of COBOL sorting, we shall begin with those COBOL statements used to describe it.

The file you wish to have sorted and the file in which you wish to store the sorted result are defined in the normal way except that in the FILE-CONTROL paragraph they must contain the clause ACCESS IS SEQUENTIAL. The internal sort file is described in the FILE-CONTROL paragraph as a sequential file. As an example, if the internal sort file is to be called INTERNAL-SORT-FILE, its SELECT clause might appear as

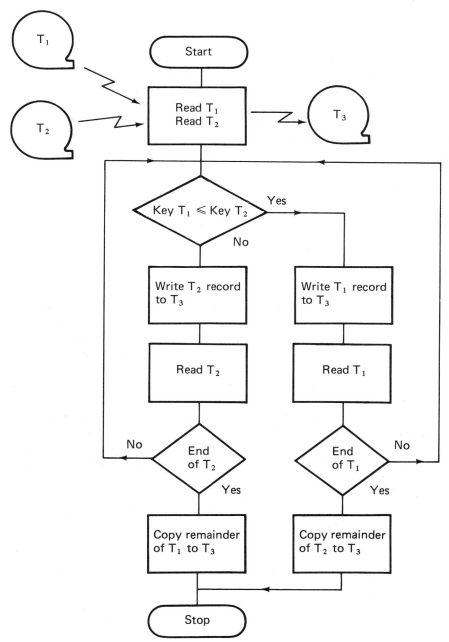

Figure 4.2   Merging sorted tapes into ascending order.

```
SELECT INTERNAL-SORT-FILEII
    ASSIGN TO UT-DISK-S-SORTWKII
```

The most important change in describing this internal sort file comes in the FILE SECTION of the DATA DIVISION, where *it receives the special designator SD instead of the normal FD*. This informs the COBOL compiler that this particular file is to be treated as a special internal sort file. The rest of the SD entry is, in other respects, the same as an ordinary FD entry except that *neither a* BLOCK CONTAINS *clause nor a* LABEL RECORDS *clause can appear*. For example, a typical SD entry might appear as follows:

```
SD  INTERNAL-SORT-FILE
    RECORD CONTAINS 100 CHARACTERS
    DATA RECORD IS INTERNAL-SORT-FILE-RECORD.
01  INTERNAL-SORT-FILE-RECORD
    02 LICENSE-NUMBER PIC X(6).
    02 FILLER         PIC X(17).
    02 COLOR          PIC X(9).
    02 FILLER         PIC X(68).
```

This entry acts in most respects just like a buffer for an ordinary file. Each record that is to be sorted will first be moved to INTERNAL-SORT-FILE-RECORD and then written to the INTERNAL-SORT-FILE. Later we shall see exactly how this writing (or releasing, as it is called) to an internal sort file is accomplished.

Each record is sorted on selected fields within the record. For example, we might wish to sort a vehicle file by license number or color of car or perhaps first by color of car and then within each color by license number. Since the Sort–Merge package must know exactly where in each record the sort keys are located, these fields must be described in the 01 entry of the SD. Other fields not used as sort keys may be described as FILLER items. In the SD example for INTERNAL-SORT-FILE, only the fields LICENSE-NUMBER and COLOR have been shown. Presumably one or both of these fields might be used as sort keys.

In the PROCEDURE DIVISION, sorting is initiated by the verb SORT, which must specify the following:

1. which field(s) within each record are to act as sort keys
2. which records of which file are to be moved to the internal sort file before sorting takes place
3. once sorting is completed, to which file the sorted records on the internal sort file are to be transferred for program access.

The SORT verb, which may be used anywhere within the PROCEDURE DIVISION, has several formats which can best be illustrated by example. The following illustrates the simplest form:

```
            SORT INTERNAL-SORT-FILE
            ON ASCENDING KEY LICENSE-NUMBER
            USING POLICE-FILE
            GIVING SORTED-POLICE FILE.
```

This instruction asks that all the records on POLICE-FILE be transferred to the INTERNAL-SORT-FILE, where they are to be sorted into ascending sequence by the field LICENSE-NUMBER. Upon completion, *all* the records are to be transferred to the file SORTED-POLICE-FILE (see Program 4.1).

Program 4.1

```
00014         /    ** THIS PROGRAM SORTS THE POLICE-FILE **
00015
00016         INPUT-OUTPUT SECTION.
00017         FILE-CONTROL.
00018
00019             SELECT INTERNAL-SORT-FILE
00020                 ASSIGN TO DISK-S-SORTWK01
00021                 ORGANIZATION IS SEQUENTIAL
00022                 ACCESS MODE IS SEQUENTIAL.
00023             SELECT OUTPUT-FILE
00024                 ASSIGN TO DISK-S-DD1
00025                 ORGANIZATION IS SEQUENTIAL
00026                 ACCESS MODE IS SEQUENTIAL.
00027             SELECT POLICE-FILE
00028                 ASSIGN TO DISK-S-POLICE
00029                 ORGANIZATION IS SEQUENTIAL
00030                 ACCESS MODE IS SEQUENTIAL.
00031
00032
00033         DATA DIVISION.
00034         FILE SECTION.
00035
00036         SD  INTERNAL-SORT-FILE
00037             RECORD CONTAINS 100 CHARACTERS
00038             DATA RECORD IS INTERNAL-SORT-FILE-RECORD.
00039         01  INTERNAL-SORT-FILE-RECORD.
00040             02  LICENSE-NUMBER          PIC X(6).
00041             02  FILLER                  PIC X(94).
00042
00043         FD  OUTPUT-FILE
00044             LABEL RECORDS ARE OMITTED
00045             BLOCK CONTAINS 0 RECORDS
00046             RECORD CONTAINS 100 CHARACTERS
00047             DATA RECORD IS OUTPUT-FILE-RECORD.
00048         01  OUTPUT-FILE-RECORD.
00049             02  FILLER                  PIC X(100).
00050
00051         FD  POLICE-FILE
00052             LABEL RECORDS ARE STANDARD
00053             BLOCK CONTAINS 100 RECORDS
00054             RECORD CONTAINS 100 CHARACTERS
00055             DATA RECORD IS POLICE-FILE-RECORD.
00056         01  POLICE-FILE-RECORD.
00057             02  FILLER                  PIC X(100).
00058
00059         WORKING-STORAGE SECTION.
```

Program 4.1 (cont.)

```
00060
00061
00062          PROCEDURE DIVISION.
00063
00064              SORT INTERNAL-SORT-FILE
00065                  ASCENDING KEY LICENSE-NUMBER
00066                      OF INTERNAL-SORT-FILE-RECORD
00067                  USING POLICE-FILE
00068                  GIVING OUTPUT-FILE.
00069              STOP RUN.
```

Sometimes we may wish to sort a file on more than one key. Suppose, for instance, that we have a directory of employees working in various departments of various factories. We might wish to sort all employees by factory, then within the factory by department, and within the department by name. A typical SORT statement to do this might be:

```
SORT INTERNAL-SORT-FILE
ON ASCENDING KEY
    FACTORY, DEPARTMENT, NAME
USING DIRECTORY-FILE
GIVING DIRECTORY-FILE-SORTED
```

This instruction asks that *all* the records on the file DIRECTORY-FILE be transferred to the INTERNAL-SORT-FILE, where they are to be sorted by factory, then within factory by department, and finally within department by name. On conclusion of sorting, all the records are to be placed in a file named DIRECTORY-FILE-SORTED.

Suppose we want to sort the directory of the preceding example, by factory, by department, and instead of sorting within department by name, by descending salary within department. The output might appear as in Figure 4.3. The SORT statement to do this is:

```
SORT INTERNAL-SORT-FILE
ON ASCENDING KEY
    FACTORY, DEPARTMENT
ON DESCENDING KEY.
```

We emphasize here the meaning of the words USING and GIVING. These two words indicate that *all* the records stored on DIRECTORY-FILE are to be transferred to the INTERNAL-SORT-FILE, and, once sorting is finished, *all* the records are to be transferred to the file DIRECTORY-FILE-SORTED. The word to note here is *all*. In the next section, we shall discuss a method that will allow us control over which records on the file are moved to the internal sort file and which records on completion of sorting are copied from the internal sort file.

Factory	Department	Name	Salary
.	.	.	.
.	.	.	.
.	.	.	.
1	2	Johnson	$250,000
1	2	Anderson	50,000
1	2	Penton	2,000
1	2	Hardy	1,000
1	2	Cooper	0
1	3	Emin	90,000
1	3	Jones	17,000
.	.	.	.
.	.	.	.
.	.	.	.
2	1	Carmen	25,000
2	1	Frenette	40,000
2	1	Smith	10,000
2	2	White	16,000
2	2	Lee	15,999
.	.	.	.
.	.	.	.
.	.	.	.

Figure 4.3   Output for Directory-File-Sorted.

4.3.1 INPUT AND OUTPUT PROCEDURES

In the previous section, we discussed the simplest form of the SORT verb, which is the form containing USING and GIVING. The word USING caused *all* file records to be transferred to the internal sort file for processing. Similarly, the word GIVING caused *all* sorted records to be copied from the internal file. COBOL provides for more complex sort procedures, some of which we discuss next.

Selecting Sort Input

Sometimes it is desirable to exclude certain records from the sorting process. A detective might request a list of those automobiles stolen since the first of January; but the file of stolen vehicles may contain automobiles dating back several years. Computer time is wasted when these old records are sorted. If the word GIVING is used, all records will move to the internal sort file; a filter of some kind is needed to sift out the unwanted records.

Surprisingly enough, there may even be occasions when the file has been sorted but we do not want to have a copy of all of it. Suppose, as an example, that we wish to ensure that our file contains no duplicated license numbers. One simple way of locating duplicates is to sort the file by license number. Any two that are the same will occur together. The internal sort file can then be read record by record and each license number matched with the one preceding it. The duplicates, if they exist, can then be identified.

COBOL provides for these requirements by letting the user write the records to the internal sort file himself (before sorting commences) and by permitting him to copy selected records from the internal sort file once sorting has been completed. To do this, a new form of the SORT verb is required. We begin by illustrating a SORT verb with the additional features and illustrate what happens.

As an example, suppose we wish to sort the stolen vehicle file by color of vehicle, deleting red ones from the sorting phase. Then, once sorting is accomplished, we shall print out the entire internal sort file and exclude all yellow vehicles. As a result neither red nor yellow cars should appear. Reds are not sorted; yellows are not printed. The following SORT statement appears in Program 4.2:

```
SORT INTERNAL-SORT-FILE
ASCENDING KEY COLOR
INPUT PROCEDURE REMOVE-RED-RECORDS
OUTPUT PROCEDURE SELECT-NON-YELLOW-RECORDS.
```

The key words INPUT PROCEDURE name a group of one or more paragraphs headed by the words REMOVE-RED-RECORDS SECTION within the PROCEDURE DIVISION. (Recall that one or more paragraphs are made into a SECTION by giving them a name followed by the word SECTION.)

Within the REMOVE-RED-RECORDS SECTION the following actions take place:

1. The POLICE-FILE is OPENed for INPUT. (Remember that the internal sort file must never be OPENed by the programmer.)

2. Records are read from the POLICE-FILE, and, provided that the COLOR field does not indicate a RED vehicle, these records are MOVEd one by one to the SD area of the internal sort file.

3. After each record is moved to the SD area of the internal sort file, it is written to the internal sort file.

4. After all records have been written to the internal sort file, control is transferred to the last paragraph within the REMOVE-RED-RECORDS SECTION, thereby terminating the INPUT PROCEDURE. (Note that the programmer may not CLOSE the internal sort file.)

Two of these steps require further clarification.

Once a record has been MOVEd to the internal sort file, it must be written to the internal file with the word RELEASE. The key word RELEASE can be thought of as a command to give the record to the Sort-Merge package. We can also employ the word FROM and have the MOVE to the SD area done automatically. We might, for instance, write

```
            RELEASE INTERNAL-SORT-FILE-RECORD
               FROM POLICE-RECORD
```

As with WRITE statements, this will cause a group move of the record from the 01 entry POLICE-RECORD to the 01 entry INTERNAL-SORT-FILE-RECORD.

To terminate the INPUT-PROCEDURE, control must be transferred to the last paragraph in the SECTION. The reader should think of a SECTION as a "super-paragraph" that is being PERFORMED by the SORT verb. A PERFORM is not termi-nated until the last statement of a paragraph or SECTION is reached. It is often con-venient to have a paragraph labeled END-PARAGRAPH or some equivalent at the end of the SECTION. Once control is passed to this paragraph, the input procedure is ter-minated. This paragraph could contain a CLOSE of the POLICE-FILE or the single statement EXIT (which does nothing).

Program 4.2

```
00015          /   ** SORT POLICE-FILE USING AN INPUT PROCEDURE **
00016
00017          INPUT-OUTPUT SECTION.
00018          FILE-CONTROL.
00019
00020              SELECT POLICE-FILE
00021                  ASSIGN TO DISK-S-POLICE
00022                  ACCESS IS SEQUENTIAL.
00023              SELECT INTERNAL-SORT-FILE
00024                  ASSIGN TO DISK-S-SORTWK01.
00025              SELECT PRINTER
00026                  ASSIGN TO PRNT-S-SYSOUT.
00027
00028
00029          DATA DIVISION.
00030          FILE SECTION.
00031
00032      SD  INTERNAL-SORT-FILE
00033          RECORD CONTAINS 100 CHARACTERS
00034          DATA RECORD IS INTERNAL-SORT-FILE-RECORD.
00035      01  INTERNAL-SORT-FILE-RECORD.
00036          02  LICENSE-NUMBER           PIC X(6).
00037          02  MAKE-OF-VEHICLE          PIC X(15).
00038          02  FILLER                   PIC X(2).
00039          02  COLOUR                   PIC X(9).
00040          02  FILLER                   PIC X(68).
00041
00042      FD  POLICE-FILE
00043          LABEL RECORDS ARE STANDARD
00044          DATA RECORD IS POLICE-FILE-RECORD
00045          RECORD CONTAINS 100 CHARACTERS.
00046      01  POLICE-FILE-RECORD.
00047          02  LICENSE-NUMBER           PIC 9(6).
00048          02  MAKE-OF-VEHICLE          PIC X(15).
00049          02  YEAR-OF-MODEL            PIC 9(2).
00050          02  COLOUR                   PIC X(9).
00051          02  TYPE-OF-CAR              PIC X(6).
00052          02  DATE-REPORTED-STOLEN     PIC 9(6).
00053          02  OWNER-ADDRESS            PIC X(18).
00054          02  CITY                     PIC X(10).
00055          02  STATE-QR-PROVINCE        PIC X(7).
00056          02  OWNER                    PIC X(16).
00057          02  FILLER                   PIC X(5).
```

Program 4.2   (cont.)

```
00058
00059          FD  PRINTER
00060              LABEL RECORDS ARE OMITTED
00061              DATA RECORD IS PRINT-LINE
00062              RECORD CONTAINS 101 CHARACTERS.
00063          01  PRINT-LINE.
00064              02  CARRIAGE-CONTROL          PIC X.
00065              02  DATA-LINE                 PIC X(100).
00066
00067
00068          WORKING-STORAGE SECTION.
00069
00070          77  INTERNAL-SORT-FILE-EOF        PIC X(3).
00071              88  SORT-FILE-EMPTY VALUE IS 'ON'.
00072                88  SORT-FILE-NOT-EMPTY VALUE IS 'OFF'.
00073          77  POLICE-FILE-EOF               PIC X(3).
00074              88  POLICE-FILE-EMPTY VALUE IS 'ON'.
00075              88  POLICE-FILE-NOT-EMPTY VALUE IS 'OFF'.
00076
00077          01  WS-POLICE-FILE-RECORD.
00078              02  LICENSE-NUMBER            PIC 9(6).
00079                02  DUMMY-RECORD-FIELD REDEFINES LICENSE-NUMBER.
00080                    03  FIRST-CHARACTER PIC X.
00081                      88  DUMMY-RECORD VALUE IS HIGH-VALUES.
00082                    03  FILLER            PIC X(5).
00083              02  MAKE-OF-VEHICLE           PIC X(15).
00084              02  YEAR-OF-MODEL             PIC 9(2).
00085              02  COLOUR                    PIC X(9).
00086              02  TYPE-OF-CAR               PIC X(6).
00087              02  DATE-REPORTED-STOLEN      PIC 9(6).
00088              02  OWNER-ADDRESS             PIC X(18).
00089              02  CITY                      PIC X(10).
00090              02  STATE-OR-PROVINCE         PIC X(7).
00091              02  OWNER                     PIC X(16).
00092              02  FILLER                    PIC X(5).
00093
00094          01  WS-PRINT-LINE.
00095              02  FILLER                    PIC X.
00096              02  FILLER                    PIC X(5).
00097              02  LICENSE-NUMBER            PIC X(6).
00098              02  FILLER                    PIC X(5).
00099              02  MAKE-OF-VEHICLE           PIC X(15).
00100              02  FILLER                    PIC X(5).
00101              02  COLOUR                    PIC X(9).
00102              02  FILLER                    PIC X(34).
00103
00104
00105          PROCEDURE DIVISION.
00106
00107          MAIN-LINE SECTION.
00108              PERFORM INITIALIZATION.
00109              PERFORM SORT-THE-RECORDS.
00110              STOP RUN.
00111
00112          INITIALIZATION.
00113              MOVE 'OFF' TO INTERNAL-SORT-FILE-EOF.
00114              MOVE 'OFF' TO POLICE-FILE-EOF.
00115              OPEN INPUT POLICE-FILE.
00116              READ POLICE-FILE RECORD
00117                  INTO WS-POLICE-FILE-RECORD
```

Program 4.2   (cont.)

```
00118                            AT END MOVE 'ON' TO POLICE-FILE-EOF.
00119
00120              SORT-THE-RECORDS.
00121                 SORT INTERNAL-SORT-FILE
00122                    ASCENDING KEY COLOUR
00123                       OF INTERNAL-SORT-FILE-RECORD
00124                    DESCENDING KEY LICENSE-NUMBER
00125                       OF  INTERNAL-SORT-FILE-RECORD
00126                    INPUT PROCEDURE REMOVE-RED-RECORDS
00127                    OUTPUT PROCEDURE SELECT-NON-YELLOW-RECORDS.
00128
00129              REMOVE-RED-RECORDS SECTION.
00130                 PERFORM SELECT-RED-ONES
00131                    UNTIL POLICE-FILE-EMPTY.
00132                 GO TO END-PARAGRAPH.
00133
00134              SELECT-RED-ONES.
00135                 IF COLOUR OF WS-POLICE-FILE-RECORD EQUAL 'RED'
00136                    OR
00137                    DUMMY-RECORD
00138                    THEN
00139                    NEXT SENTENCE
00140                    ELSE
00141                    PERFORM GIVE-SORT-THE-RECORD.
00142                 READ POLICE-FILE RECORD
00143                    INTO WS-POLICE-FILE-RECORD
00144                    AT END MOVE 'ON' TO POLICE-FILE-EOF.
00145
00146              GIVE-SORT-THE-RECORD.
00147                 MOVE WS-POLICE-FILE-RECORD
00148                    TO INTERNAL-SORT-FILE-RECORD.
00149                 RELEASE INTERNAL-SORT-FILE-RECORD.
00150
00151              END-PARAGRAPH.
00152                 EXIT.
00153
00154              SELECT-NON-YELLOW-RECORDS SECTION.
00155                 PERFORM INITIALIZATION.
00156                 PERFORM READ-AND-PRINT-RECORDS
00157                    UNTIL SORT-FILE-EMPTY.
00158                 CLOSE PRINTER.
00159                 GO TO END-PARAGRAPH.
00160
00161              INITIALIZATION.
00162                 OPEN OUTPUT PRINTER.
00163                 RETURN INTERNAL-SORT-FILE
00164                    AT END MOVE 'ON' TO INTERNAL-SORT-FILE-EOF.
00165
00166              READ-AND-PRINT-RECORDS.
00167                 IF COLOUR OF INTERNAL-SORT-FILE-RECORD
00168                    NOT EQUAL 'YELLOW'
00169                 THEN
00170                    PERFORM PRINT-RECORD
00171                 ELSE
00172                    NEXT SENTENCE.
00173                 RETURN INTERNAL-SORT-FILE
00174                    AT END MOVE 'ON' TO INTERNAL-SORT-FILE-EOF.
00175
00176              PRINT-RECORD.
00177                 MOVE SPACES TO WS-PRINT-LINE.
```

Program 4.2   (cont.)

```
00178                    MOVE CORRESPONDING INTERNAL-SORT-FILE-RECORD
00179                        TO WS-PRINT-LINE.
00180                    WRITE PRINT-LINE FROM WS-PRINT-LINE
00181                        AFTER POSITIONING 2 LINES.
00182
00183            END-PARAGRAPH.
00184                EXIT.
```

Selecting Sort Output

As with the INPUT PROCEDURE the OUTPUT PROCEDURE is a SEC-TION within the COBOL program. In the SELECT-NON-YELLOW-RECORDS SECTION the following procedures are performed:

1. OPEN the PRINTER file for OUTPUT.
2. READ each record from the internal sort file.
3. Provided the COLOR field value is not YELLOW move the record to the FD for the PRINTER and write it.
4. CLOSE the printer after all records have been examined.
5. Terminate the OUTPUT PROCEDURE by transferring to the last paragraph within the SECTION containing the statement EXIT.

The reader should examine this SECTION within Program 4.2. The only new statement the reader will not have encountered before is the command RETURN. An internal sort file because of its special nature cannot be read. The verb RETURN is used to read records from the internal file. The programmer may, if desired, use the word INTO, which has the effect of transferring a record from the 01 record of the internal sort file to another level 01 item.

Previously we noted our inclination to avoid the GO TO instruction. The IN-PUT PROCEDURE and OUTPUT PROCEDURE have forced us to break this rule. Here, however, because we must get to the end of these sections before the SORT verb can complete its functions, we have no choice. This is perfectly fine with us; our rules do not say *never* use GO TO's; rather they say *avoid* GO TO's when possible. Here the GO TO is used as a forward jump and cannot cause any confusion.

4.4 MERGE

The verb MERGE can, in a similar manner, be used in place of the verb SORT to merge several sorted input files into a single output file having this order. The following example would be used when file 1 and file 2 are already sorted:

```
MERGE file 1
ON ASCENDING
KEY key 1
USING file 2
GIVING file 3
```

4.5 CONCLUSIONS

The COBOL SORT verb is to be preferred when following the rules of simplicity and portability. However, there can be advantages to a sort routine external to the COBOL program. Since the external sort is invoked as a separate job step, less memory may be required; also the COBOL program might not need to be recompiled when the sort is changed. In the event that the sort is a single module, use of an external sort saves writing a COBOL program.

The costs of sorting increase nonlinearly with the number of records sorted. When sorts account for a significant portion of the system run time (it is worthwhile to time sorts and provide a run time statistic), program efficiency may best be improved by a careful consideration of the sorts. Are they necessary? Are the records properly blocked? Are the proper sorting features implemented? When only a small portion of the file records are to be processed, it may be better to extract these records first and then sort the smaller file so obtained. The input-output procedures of COBOL do just this. It is also important to note that for the paying user, cost efficiency is usually determined by the charging algorithm of an installation and not by the run time. Again as a charging algorithm will be changed from time to time, it is worthwhile to have sort cost indicators built into the program run report. Because of the importance of timing sorts for efficient use of machine resources, we would suggest that in general sorting should be considered a separate job step. This will make it easier to make changes and to localize the source of the inevitable errors made in doing so.

REFERENCES FOR FURTHER READING

Hoare, C. A. R. "Quicksort" *Computer Journal* 5 (April 1962) :10–15.

Knuth, D. E. *The Art of Computer Programming Vol III: Sorting and Searching.* Reading, Mass.: Addison-Wesley, 1973.

Lorin, H. *Sorting and Sort Systems.* Reading, Mass.: Addison-Wesley, 1975.

Williams, J. W. J. "Algorithm 232 Heapsort" *Communications of the ACM* 7 (June 1964) :347–48.

PROBLEMS

1. (a) Investigate the Sort–Merge package provided at your installation.

(b) Use it to sort a file.

2. Sort the file in problem 1 using the COBOL verb. Which method do you prefer? What differences are there?

3. If you have never written a sort program, investigate Quicksort and write a COBOL program for it. For references see Hoare (1962) and Knuth, Vol. III (1973). How large a file can you sort?

4. Discuss the differences between internal and external sorting.

5. Devise a flowchart to merge three sorted tapes giving two sorted tapes as output.

5

Practical Considerations

Conceptually, files are not complex. The COBOL constructs for files are based on principles that are neither complicated nor difficult to learn. However, file design can be a nontrivial problem and intricate in detail. The file designer encounters difficulty in two main areas: the design of a file data structure that is efficient for the programs that use it, and the implementation of the resulting file as an efficient storage structure. In this chapter we consider some practical requirements that must be considered in the development and implementation of an efficient computer file structure. This chapter may be skipped or skimmed on a first reading.

5.1 SPACE

There are two fundamental questions concerning space on a medium: How much raw space is there? And how much of the medium can be used to store user data?

While it seems sensible to measure capacity directly in characters, the peculiarities of devices lead to other measures from which the character capacity must be calculated. For example, tapes are measured in feet, which is a constant for a reel; however, character capacity of tape varies with recording density and is, therefore, a function of the tape drive used. The capacity of a disk is based on track capacity in characters; and from this, cylinder and pack capacity can be derived. The standard unit of measure is *de facto* the byte (which is synonymous for character in most systems), and we will use byte because of established usage.

There are two practical questions concerning file space: Given a file of x characters, how much medium is required? And conversely, given the capacity of a medium, what is the number of file data characters that can be stored? These questions are complicated by the mechanisms chosen to block logical records into physical records, and by the fact that 100% utilization of a medium by data is not possible. The percent utilization of a medium for file data depends on many design choices at both application and system levels.

In addition to the IBG there may also be control blocks embedded in a file to provide "file control." A file plus its control data (the storage overhead) is called a data set. That is, we have the "logical" file of the user and the "physical" file in the system, which is the data set containing the user's file and the necessary control information.

$$\text{Data set} = \text{File control} + \text{File data}$$

Space is consumed by

1. the user
2. the file system
3. the storage device

To find how much space is used for a file, the overhead of the hardware and the system must be added to that required by the records. This can get quite complicated. Our purpose in this chapter is to develop a basic and consistent approach that should enable a file designer to do appropriate space calculations to predict file requirements. Our formulas are derived from the following basic relationship, which must be particularized in a given system.

$$\text{Total space} = \text{Device control} + \text{System control} + \text{User data} + \text{Unused space}$$

5.1.1 Blocking

Efficient use of storage usually requires that physical records have some minimum size in relation to their associated device overhead. Yet, a natural logical record size may be much smaller than the optimum physical record size. The correspondence (or mapping) between the logical records of a file and the physical records of that file on a storage medium is known as *blocking*. The number of re-cords in a block is the *blocking factor*, B_f.

There are many ways records can be mapped into physical records, but in practice only a few basic methods are used. In essence, there are three basic kinds of blocking: blocked records, $B_f > 1$; unblocked records, $B_f = 1$; and spanned records, $B_f < 1$.

When two or more records are placed in the physical record, it is said to be *blocked,* and the file is called a *blocked* file. The most common method, fixed blocking, is to use a fixed integer number of constant-size records to fill the data area of each physical record completely. Then B_f is an integer constant greater than 1 for a fixed-blocked file.

When the logical record corresponds to the physical record, it is an *unblocked* record, and the file is called an *unblocked file*. Some devices have a maximum-size physical record, and when a logical record exceeds this size, more than one physical record is required to store it. In this case, the record is said to span the blocks and is called a *spanned record*. Some systems do not support spanned records, but a pro-gram can create its own spanned records. In many disk systems the physical record is fixed as the track size, and the programmer must then accept a fixed block size.

5.1.2 Block and Capacity Calculations

Medium capacity is best measured in bytes for comparisons between devices. Byte capacity can be easily converted to other dimensions as required, such as card images, feet (for tape), tracks (for disks), and number of records for a file. The number of bytes in a record is determined by programming considerations, which are sometimes determined by device considerations. We assume that R, the number of bytes in a logical record, is constant.

A block must contain at least $B_f \times R$ bytes. We say "at least" because a physical record may contain nondata information to control processing of the block's records. The *nominal size, B,* of a block is the number of bytes in the phys-ical record. The *effective size, $\hat{B}$,* of a block is the byte area reserved for data. In some cases the data area may not be completely used (i.e., see variable-length re-cords) and $\hat{B} > B_f \times R$. Then we speak of the *actual size*, $B_f \times R$, which is the amount of data stored in a block.

These are related by

$$B \geq \hat{B} \geq B_f \times R$$

All blocks are separated by an interblock gap, g; thus each block requires $B + g$ bytes. The effective block size $\hat{B}$ is the most the programmer gets, and it is a func-tion of block overhead, b, resulting from the type of device and the physical record format, where $B = \hat{B} + b$.

The overhead associated with blocked records means that a file cannot use all of the nominal capacity, C_M, of a storage medium available to the user. The problem is, given R and N_r, what value of C_M is required to store the file and its block overhead on the system? There are different measures of utilization of a medium, but the following formula holds in general.

$$\text{Percentage of utilization} = \frac{\text{Size used}}{\text{Size used} + \text{Size of overhead}} \times 100$$

We need only determine the size used, a function of the blocking factor, and the size of the overhead for a given device (reference must be made to the manufacturer's specifications). Figure 5.1 shows the overhead relationships.

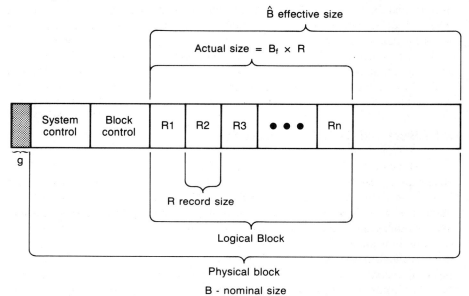

Figure 5.1   Block layout of a physical block $B_f = n$

The nominal utilization factor of a block is:

$$U = \frac{B}{B + g}$$

The nominal block capacity of a file is

$$C = U \times C_M = N_b \times B$$

The effective utilization factor of a block is

$$\hat{U} \geq \frac{B_f \times R}{B + g}$$

The effective file capacity of a file is

$$\hat{C} = \hat{U} \times C_M \geq N_r \times R$$

From these formulas we see that *U determines the utilization of the device and $\hat{U}$ determines the utilization of the file storage structure for data records.* In both cases utilization approaches 1 as $B_f \rightarrow \infty$, indicating that B_f should be made as large as possible. However, other factors limit the efficiency of increasing block size. A block cannot be larger than the maximum available buffer size and should equal the buffer size (usually a power of 2). Devices have maximum-size physical records, and any attempt to make a block larger than this increases device overhead. For instance, a track is usually the maximum-size physical record on a disk.

$$C_M = \frac{1}{U} \times N_b \times B$$

Utilization is a function of B_f, and we can extend the basic formula to a tape, several tapes, track, cylinders, and disks. *We restrict our calculations to blocks* because once the basic theory we develop is understood, it can be extended to any particular case. The following formula holds for devices in general.

$$U = \frac{g(B_f)}{f(B_f) + \text{Overhead}}$$

We can plot a relationship that holds for all devices. We now examine particular cases of this formula for tapes and disks.

5.1.3 Tape

There are two essential questions for tape: Given a tape of length L in feet, how many records of R bytes can be stored? And given N_r records of R bytes, how much tape is required? To answer these questions, we must know not only the density d but also the data utilization factor of the tape, which is a function of the blocking. If we assume that $B = B_f \times R$, then the calculations are simple because for tapes $b = g$.

$$g = \text{IBG} \times d \quad \text{bytes}$$

$$U = \frac{B}{B + g}$$

| Tape capacity | $C_M = 12 \times L \times d$ bytes |
| Tape data capacity | $C = U \times C_M$ bytes |

Number of blocks $\qquad N_b = \lfloor C_T/B$

Number of records $\qquad N_r = B_f \times N_b$

Required medium capacity $\qquad \boxed{C_M = \dfrac{1}{U} \times N_b \times B} = N_b \times (B + IBG \times d)$

If you do not have a specific device in mind, the parameters of Table 5.1 can be used for tape calculations.

Table 5.1 Tape Parameters

Symbol	Parameter	Typical	Dimension
s	speed	200	in./sec
t_{ss}	start/stop time	1	msec
IBG	interblock gap	0.75	in.
T_{RW}	rewind time	40	sec
L	length (capacity)	600–3600	ft
	Derived		
$g = IBG \times d$	interblock gap		bytes
$D_r = s \times d$	data transfer rate		bytes/sec

5.1.4 Disk

The recording capacity of a disk pack is developed from the capacity of a track, the number of disk surfaces, N_c (a cylinder), and the number of tracks, N_T. Track medium capacity, given in bytes, is fixed and identical for all tracks. The calculations of nominal and actual capacity is more involved for disks because the nondata portion of a track varies with format and device.

Each track may have an identical control area that reduces the track capacity available to the user; disk pack data capacity is invariably less than the advertised raw capacity. For file calculations it is necessary to determine the *track user capacity, C_K,* and we use this as the medium capacity for our calculations. In addition to the data block area, $\hat{B}$, each physical record may contain a control area, c, and a key area, k. Thus, in general, $B = \hat{B} + c + k$.

The following formulas specify track utilization and file data capacity. Some storage device manufacturers give their own specific formulas as well as providing tables to select appropriate blocking factors and determine block capacity. By extracting the corresponding values for the formulas given here, you should be able to use a unified and consistent approach to calculations for all devices. This is particularly useful when comparing devices.

Nominal utilization factor $\quad U = \dfrac{B}{B + g} \quad$ Data utilization factor $\quad \hat{U} = \dfrac{B_f \times R}{B + g}$

Nominal block size $B = \hat{B} + c + k$

Number of blocks $N_b = \dfrac{U_k C \times}{B}$

Number of records $N_r = B_f \times N_b$

Nominal track capacity $C_T = N_b \times B$ Track data capacity $\hat{C}_T = N_r \times R$

Nominal track utilization factor $U_T = \dfrac{C_T}{C_k}$ Data track utilization factor $\hat{U}_T = \dfrac{\hat{C}_T}{C_k}$

Table 5.2 lists typical disk parameters that are needed for disk calculations.

Table 5.2   Disk Parameters

Symbol	Parameter	Dimension
t_s	seek time	sec
t	rotation time	sec
t_ℓ	latency time	sec
D_r	data rate of transfer	bytes/sec
C_d	track capacity $(\ell_i \times d_i)$	bytes
C_k	track user capacity	bytes
N_c	tracks per cylinder	
N_T	cylinders per disk	
c	block control overhead	bytes
k	block key overhead	bytes
b	block total overhead	bytes

5.2 TIME

The factors that influence the time required to process file records are complex and often difficult to determine precisely. Fortunately, analysis can show that many factors are insignificant and can be safely ignored in calculating a good approximate answer. Since file timing is a consequence of block timing, we begin analysis with timing calculations for blocks. A more general consideration of file timing is left to Chapters 16 and 17.

The time needed to process a record arises from three general sources: the time required from record request to physical access of the beginning of the block containing the record, the time required to transmit the block to a file buffer, and the time required by the program to process the required record in the block. For device timing, we may neglect the third source.

Block Timing

The time required by a device to process a physical record is called the *block transfer time*, B_t; this consists of the time for a position mechanism to access the physical start of a block, plus the time for the device to transmit the data of the block.

Block transfer time = Time to access start of block on a device
+ Time to scan block medium and transmit block to memory

$$\boxed{B_t = T_A + T_T}$$

Block access time, T_A, depends upon the storage device. *Block transmit time*, T_T is mostly determined by the rate at which the medium can be scanned. (This is the usual limiting factor.) The data transfer rate, D_r, specifies the rate at which the medium is scanned in bytes per second. Since the time to transmit data between a storage device and memory is usually much faster than scanning a medium, we can approximate T_T by B/D_r.

$$B_t \doteq T_A + \frac{B}{D_r}$$

Given any device, we need only determine T_A and D_r for the device in order to calculate a good approximation for B_t.

Tape

The data rate of magnetic tape is a result of transport speed and recording density.

$$D_r = d \times s = \text{bytes/in.} \times \text{in./sec} = \text{bytes/sec}$$

Example

$$D_r = 1600 \text{ bpi} \times 200 \text{ in./sec} = 320{,}000 \text{ bytes/sec}$$

Tape block access time, T_A, has two values: one for continuous mode, the other for stop start mode. At full speed this is the time to traverse the IBG.

$$\text{Gap traverse time} = \frac{g}{D_r} = \frac{d \times \text{IBG}}{d \times s} = \frac{\text{IBG}}{s}$$

Example

IBM 3420 at 1600 bpi:

$$t_g = \frac{0.6 \text{ in.}}{200 \text{ in./sec}} = 0.003 = 3 \text{ msec}$$

The continuous gap traverse time and the start/stop gap traverse time usually differ but are identical for some tape transports. We will assume that the start/stop time, t_{ss}, is the additional time required to traverse an IBG in stop/start mode; then T_A for tape is t_{ss} + g/D_r. Note that we neglect time between block requests because this is not part of the device access time.

$$\text{Tape} \quad \boxed{B_t = t_{ss} + \frac{g}{D_r} + \frac{B}{D_r}}$$

(Note: $t_{ss} = 0$ in continuous mode.)

Disk

The access time, T_A, of a disk can have three components: time to seek the cylinder, time to select the track (head selection time), and time for the disk to rotate to the start of the block to begin reading by the read/write head. For movable access arms, seek time varies with the distance traveled to reach the cylinder. Device manufacturers usually provide an average expected seek time t_s. Head selection time is ignored as insignificant. The *latency time* t_l is assumed as an average time and for a single access arm disk is one half of the rotation time t_r.

$$\text{Disk} \quad \boxed{B_t = t_s + \frac{t_r}{2} + \frac{B}{D_r}}$$

(Note: g/D is present but neglected.)

The average seek time, t_s, may not be valid in a multiprogramming system because competing accesses may result in average seek times that are a function of the competing access points and a function of the distance between the competing files. Conversely, subsequent accesses may be very close, such as in a sequential file, and the seek time may be much less than t_s.

5.3 CHOOSING A BLOCKING FACTOR

There are two reasons for blocking:

1. Less external storage is consumed.
2. File I/O time is reduced.

The reason less external storage is used in blocking is that each interblock gap is quite large compared to a byte. Thus, the more bytes we write together, the larger the physical record compared to the interblock gap. A large blocking factor can significantly reduce the ratio of wasted space. Since access time is slow relative to data transmission, increasing the block size decreases the average time to transmit a byte when access time is included. Indeed, the blocking factor for sequential files is the most significant efficiency parameter that is easily controlled. When blocking a disk, the blocking factor should integer divide the track size. Typically two or three blocks per track are used. In some cases there is no choice, as only a track can be accessed and this determines a fixed block size.

Optimal block size is determined by the size of the logical records, the memory available for buffers, and the storage device in use. Choice of block size is complicated by the fact that in modern systems one may not necessarily determine the device to be used. Nevertheless, because blocking is such an important component of program efficiency, it cannot be ignored. Perhaps more ideally the software should determine the blocking factor.

In general, $B_f \leq B/R$ because there may be overhead within a block and the data area may not be fully used by records.

For tapes B_f should be as large as possible consistent with a suitable buffer size. For disks the block size should be an integral divisor of the user track size to avoid waste at the end of a track, and thus the largest available block size may not be efficient for disk storage.

Fundamental Formulas for Blocking

Nominal utilization factor $U = \dfrac{B}{B + g}$ Data utilization factor $\hat{U} = \dfrac{B_f \times R}{B + g}$

Nominal capacity $C = d \times L$ Data capacity $\hat{C} = U \times C$

Nominal data transfer rate $D_r = d \times s$ Data transfer rate $\hat{D}_r = \hat{U} \times D_r$

$$B_t = T_A + \frac{B}{D_r}$$

$$T_A = t_{seek} + t_{locate}$$

5.4 RECORD FORMAT

Files consist of a collection of related records. Our main concern is with relationships between records rather than record content. Nevertheless, interrecord relationships are to a large extent a function of record structure. The essential internal structure of a record in relation to other records is called *record format*. The file designer is largely concerned with the logical record format, but since this is contained within physical records, the file designer cannot ignore physical record format, which may influence the ultimate choice of logical record format. We treat physical record format first because any file design must accept, as initial design constraints, the available formats of the file system to be used. Logical record formats are difficult to treat briefly as ultimately they are determined by the design parameters of the required file. Fortunately, the objectives are the same: to reduce file processing time and minimize space. Unfortunately, these objectives are invariably in conflict.

5.4.1 S/370 Data Record Formats

The record formats of System 370 are classified into three types: fixed-length, variable-length, and undefined-length. These types apply to both logical records and physical records. Fixed-length records, as the name implies, all have the same length. For variable-length records, four bytes prefix the logical record to specify the record length. An additional four bytes are used to specify the block size. Undefined-length records differ from variable-length records in that the record length is not contained in the record; rather, the records are separated physically by an interblock gap. Undefined-length records cannot be blocked.

In some cases a record is very long and exceeds the block size, requiring the logical record to be contained in two or more blocks (a form of inverse blocking if you like). Spanned records (in System 370) are actually a special form of fixed- or variable-length records.

5.4.2 IBM Physical Record Formats

The characteristics of the three record types vary with the particular computer system; we restrict the discussion here to IBM System 370. In any event the designer must examine the format specifications of the computer system to be used by reference to the manufacturer's manuals.

Tape Format

There is only one format for magnetic tape. Blocks are delimited by IBGs; thus, in essence, they can be thought of as undefined. However, this single format can also be treated as fixed-length (the usual case), or variable-length. Of course, any format can be used within the block by the programmer but would not be used by the tape unit.

Disk Format

We have already encountered count-data and count-key-data record formats.

Fixed Unblocked.   Each data area contains one logical record. For count-key-data the key need not be repeated in the logical record unless desired for processing. Normally sequential files are formatted without keys to preserve space.

Fixed Blocked.   The data area is a block of records. The key area of count-key-data usually contains the maximum data key in the block, and each logical record contains its key for processing. When the block size is fixed, this is called fixed block standard.

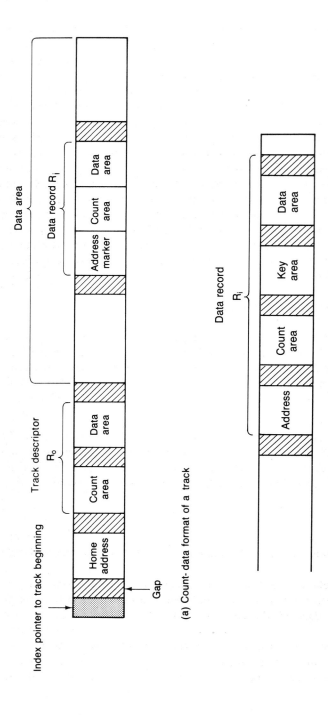

(a) Count- data format of a track

(b) Count-key-data format of a data record

Figure 5.2 Typical disk track format (IBM): (a) count-data format for a track; (b) count-key-data format of a data record.

Variable Unblocked. Each data area contains one logical record preceded by two fields to specify size. The block-length field, BL, specifies the number of bytes in the data area, including the block-length field; and the record-length field, RL, specifies the number of bytes in the record, including the record-length field. RL allows for spanned records and consistency with variable blocked.

Variable Blocked. The data area contains records of varying length each preceded by a record length field, RL. Essentially, variable fixed is a special case of variable blocked where there is only one record.

The disadvantages of variable-length records are increased processing overhead (because length is not a constant) and poor utilization of buffers (because the buffer size must be selected for the maximum length record). Blocking of variable-length records tends to average the block length and improve buffer utilization.

Undefined. Undefined-length records differ from variable-length records in that the record length is not contained in the record; rather, the records are separated physically by an interblock gap. Undefined-length records cannot be blocked.

5.5 TAPE LABELS

Tapes generally have special records, called labels, that are used to control the files stored on a tape. There are many possible formats for label records, and formats vary with the manufacturer. To facilitate the exchange of tapes between dissimilar computer systems, a national standard using ASCII characters (ANSI X3.27) is available. The IBM OS/VS system uses IBM standard labels as a default format but can specify ANSI standard, nonstandard (user defined), or no labels as required.

We restrict our discussion to IBM standard labels, which are similar in format to ANSI standard but, for 9 track tapes, use 80 character labels in EBCDIC with odd parity. The IBM volume label (VOL1) is always the first record on a tape; it identifies the volume and the owner. Although this information can be provided externally, a volume label enables the operating system to verify a requested tape mount internally.

IBM data set labels precede and follow each data set on a tape. These labels contain system information as well as identify and describe the associated data set, and thus they can be used to provide access security control.

The IBM header labels HDR1 and HDR2 can be followed by up to 8 user labels. The data set itself is preceded and followed by a *tape mark*, which is a special delimiter character used for control. After the data set tape mark, there occur trailer labels TDR1 and TDR2, which can then be followed by up to 8 user labels. Header and trailer labels are essentially the same; trailer labels permit a tape to be read backward.

The end of a single volume is signaled by two tape marks. If there is more than one volume, then the ends of intermediate volumes are signaled by substituting trailers EOV1 and EOV2 for the trailers EOF1 and EOF2 and using a single tape mark. The last volume in a multivolume set is the same as that of a single volume. IBM labels are created automatically by data management software. The reader who desires more information on labels should refer to the appropriate system manual.

REFERENCES FOR FURTHER READING

IBM. *Disk Storage Management Guide: Background Reference Information.* Order Form GA26-1675.

IBM. *Disk Storage Management Guide: Error Handling.* Order Form GA26-1672.

IBM. *Disk Storage Reference Summary.* Order Form GX20-1920.

IBM. *OS/VS Tape Labels.* Order Form GC26-3795.

ANSI X3.27-1977, Magnetic Tape Labels and File Structures for Information Interchange. New York: American National Standards Institute, Inc., 1977.

PROBLEMS

1. How many 80-byte records can a 2400-ft tape hold at 1600 bpi when $U = 0.8$?

2. What is the percentage of utilization of a tape that stores 80-byte records at 800 bpi?

3. What is N for a 1200-ft tape when $B_f = 5$, $B = 550$, and $d = 6250$ bpi?

4. If your file contains 100,000 records of 512 characters and $B_f = 10$, how many 600-ft tapes do you need to store the file?

5. How many 1-K blocks can a 3600-ft tape hold at 1600 bpi?

6. How many punched cards can be stored on a 3600-ft tape at 6250 bpi with $U = 0.98$? What would the blocking factor be? Is there a problem with your figures?

7. How long does it take to read a 600-ft tape at 125 in./sec?

8. How long does it take to read a 2400-ft tape at 800 bpi blocked at 2 KB on a 125 in./sec drive with a constant time of 100 msec for each IBG?

9. How long does it take to read a 100,000 record tape file? Assume that $B_f = 9$, $R = 128$ and $d = 1600$ bpi, $s = 200$ in./sec.

10. If t_{ss} = 1 sec, s = 150 in./sec, IBG = .75 in. and block size is 20 card images, what is the block transfer time for:

(a) an 800 bpi tape

(b) a 1600 bpi tape

(c) a 6250 bpi tape.

11. How many tracks are there in a cylinder of an IBM 3350? How many cylinders does a drive of an IBM 3380 have?

12. How long does it take to read a track of an IBM 3350? How long does it take to read 512K (contiguous) on an IBM 3380?

13. How long would it take to back up an IBM PC floppy (see Table 2.3)? Think about it and make assumptions, if necessary.

14. How long would it take to back up an IBM 3350 onto tape (see Table 2.2):

(a) using an IBM 3420-8?

(b) using an IBM 3480?

(Refer to Table 2.1.)

6

COBOL
Relative I-O
Files

6.1 INTRODUCTION

The need to access all the preceding records of a sequential file makes it not only complicated but slow to process a single record. The traditional batch processing methods, based on applying a transaction file against a master file, are an attempt to make the best of these disadvantages, and for many applications they provide a satisfactory solution. Although it is possible to design any on-line system to use sequential files, the result would generally be so slow as to disqualify it as on-line in most people's minds. Thus other solutions are necessary.

Direct access devices overcome the disadvantages of sequential access by permitting records to be stored and fetched independently of each other. Thus processing of records need not rely on any sequential ordering of the records; indeed, there may be no sequential ordering explicitly present. Direct access is often referred to as *random access,* although the retrieval of a record is not random. Direct access permits an increased flexibility in achieving system performance requirements.

The cost of direct access storage devices (DASD) has fallen dramatically since the first appearance of drums and disks. In fact, costs have fallen far enough that for many applications the increased performance provided now outweighs price as a design factor, and for many systems on-line is now chosen where once batch would most certainly have been the solution. There are, of course, other factors besides the cost of a DASD: one in particular is the availability of low-cost data entry terminals.

The increased flexibility of direct access, however, is obtained at the cost of explicit addressing of records as compared to the implicit addressing of sequential records. In a sequential file, one need only locate the address of the first record of the file, which is done implicitly by an OPEN statement. In a direct access file, the means to address each record must be present outside that record. Determining absolute physical addresses is complicated. Deciding how much information is needed and where extra information must be stored is a problem that can assume nightmare proportions.

With direct access, there are two generic address techniques: *explicit,* where the record is specified by address, and *implicit,* where the record is specified by the unique value of a key contained in the record. Of course, ultimately all records are located explicitly by physical address but here we are only concerned with the logical address as seen by a program.

In this book, three random access techniques are treated in COBOL: *direct, relative* and *indexed sequential.* We begin in this chapter with a discussion of the COBOL description of Relative I–O files.

Due to construction, the physical addressing of the storage locations of a device is complex and often the addresses may not be contiguous, which further confuses matters. Addressing within a device is tied to physical record locations, and it is quite complex to move physical records. Ideally, one would prefer to think of addresses as contiguous with simple names such as a set of integers. This is precisely the address scheme of a Relative I–O file. The initial record is assigned address 1, the next record is assigned address 2, and so on. Thus the address of a record is an integer value that reflects its position *relative* to the first record.

Historically, direct access (to be discussed in Chapter 8) came first. However, we choose to examine relative files first for two reasons: one, it is conceptually simpler to think of the addresses as integers (that is why it was devised); and two, direct access is not provided for in ANSI COBOL although it is available in some implementations.

Relative position is a logical concept and this position may not be preserved physically. By definition a *relative position* is a logical address or place name used by the system to locate the physical address. This is a problem of implementation. We should note, however, that because of the difficulties involved, Relative I–O incurs a software processing overhead cost.

The determination of the correspondence between the relative address integer and the physical address is provided by file access methods of the operating system, and the actual transferring of data to and from a storage device is handled entirely by them. Communication with these access methods is through the COBOL compiler. Thus the programmer is relieved of the need to know the intricate details of the access methods. Consequently, it is only necessary to describe the file and its storage structure to COBOL and to initiate access via the PROCEDURE DIVISION. The main disadvantage of Relative files is that the programmer must provide the relative address integer of a record for access but this integer is not always logically related to the content of the record.

Usually, each record must contain one or more keys that uniquely identify that record within the file, so we can associate the record with a unique relative address. Sometimes the record contains a key that can be used directly as the relative address. For instance, the records of a set of consecutive experiments numbered from 1 to n. In this chapter we assume that we are dealing with this simple case. In the more usual and difficult cases, the primary key must be mapped to its relative address. In some cases the record key we want to reference may not be unique, as, for example, an individual's name, and to guarantee uniqueness more qualifying information must be supplied.

In the next chapter we study techniques used to establish the mapping between the referenced record key and the relative address of that record. In Chapter 8 we examine the direct access method where we must provide the actual physical address rather than a relative key. In Chapters 9 and 10 we examine Indexed I–O files where this mapping is automatically provided. This last method is the simplest from the programmer's view; however, systems using it do not always give satisfactory performance characteristics and the other methods must be resorted to.

Relative addressing is a solution intermediate between direct physical addressing and primary key addressing. It has nearly the performance advantages of direct addressing with the advantage of simple integer addresses and independence of the need to know the physical addresses. For now, we assume simplistic relationships between the record key and the record address, ignoring efficient use of space. The main concern of this chapter is the definition and access of COBOL Relative I–O files rather than the use of Relative files in programming to construct more complex data files.

6.2 CASE STUDY: LICENSING OF VEHICLES

A state government wishes to maintain a computer record of every vehicle issued a state license plate. Each record will contain pertinent information about a licensed vehicle and will be updated whenever necessary. Updating is required whenever a vehicle is sold or scrapped, or whenever owner information is changed. The file of all these records is to be used to verify vehicle ownership, to provide statistics to government, to locate vehicle owners, and to aid police agencies.

6.2.1 Logical Analysis: Licensing of Vehicles

There are three questions that should be asked whenever a computer file is to be designed.

1. What are the various demands on the file that can be expected?
2. What file changes can be anticipated and how often are they likely to occur?
3. What constitutes a record and how can it be identified?

The first question (What are the various demands on the file?) helps determine whether to employ direct accessing procedures or sequential accessing procedures and ultimately forces the systems analyst to choose among possible storage devices. This question in itself does not provide the final answer, but it does provide an initial clue to the best form of solution.

In the case of licensing vehicles, we are told that the file is to be used to provide information on selected individuals and to provide vehicle statistics. These tasks can be accomplished using sequential access procedures, provided we are willing to search through large portions of the file to locate a single record. Two essential criteria determine the ultimate choice. How fast must the response be? How many records will the file eventually contain?

We assume the file is large (say, at least one million records) and the government desires speedy responses to its queries. Sequential procedures should only be used when queries can be batched together and applied to the file as a whole, preferably at a time convenient to the data processing department. There is a clearly defined requirement in this case: to select records quickly. This indicates that random accessing should be employed.

The second question (how is the file to be changed and how often?) provides information about the maintenance program that will have to be written to update the records and provides information for throughput analysis. In the present procedure, updating of records will be initiated when a vehicle owner fills out data request forms. A built-in delay is provided by issuing a temporary vehicle permit in the case of new ownership or whenever the information carried by a driver must be up to date as provided by law. Updating could thus be carried out using a procedure that batches changes and then applies them when convenient.

The third question (what constitutes a record and how is it identified?) is answered by deciding that each record on the file will contain the following fields:

1. make of vehicle
2. vehicle license number
3. color of vehicle
4. engine serial number
5. owner of vehicle
6. current address of owner
7. owner's driver license number
8. previous year's vehicle license number

Each record is identifed by assigning each vehicle a unique license number.

6.2.2 Relative File Processing: Vehicle File

An implementation of the vehicle file can be accomplished in COBOL using relative addressing. A file that can be relatively accessed is called in COBOL a *Relative I–O file*.

As with all direct access files (and a relative access file is only one type of direct access file), the operating system must be able to determine the physical address of any given record. With Relative I–O files this is done by assigning each record in the file a unique integer called a *relative record number* that designates the logical ordinal position of each record comprising the file relative to the first record of the file. Each record is thus ordered numerically within the file by its address. In order to store or retrieve any given record, COBOL passes its relative record number to an appropriate access method. A calculation involving this record number and the actual starting physical address of the file is performed by system software and is used to determine the physical address of the record.

6.2.3 The Relative I–O Module of COBOL

Program 6.1 creates a Relative I–O file called the VEHICLE-FILE. The reader should examine this program, skimming over those points not understood. The next section introduces the Relative I–O module and will clarify most points of COBOL usage.

Program 6.1

```
00008        /  ** CREATES THE VEHICLE FILE **
00009
00010           INPUT-OUTPUT SECTION.
00011           FILE-CONTROL.
00012
00013              SELECT CARD-READER
00014                  ASSIGN TO CARD-SYSIN
00015                  ORGANIZATION IS SEQUENTIAL
00016                  ACCESS MODE IS SEQUENTIAL.
00017              SELECT VEHICLE-FILE
00018                  ASSIGN TO DISK-LICENSE
00019                  ORGANIZATION IS RELATIVE
00020                  ACCESS MODE IS SEQUENTIAL
00021                  RELATIVE KEY IS VEHICLE-LICENSE-KEY.
00022
00023
00024           DATA DIVISION.
00025           FILE SECTION.
00026
00027        FD  CARD-READER
00028            BLOCK CONTAINS 1 RECORDS
00029            RECORD CONTAINS 80 CHARACTERS
00030            LABEL RECORDS ARE OMITTED
00031            DATA RECORD IS CARD-READER-RECORD.
00032        01  CARD-READER-RECORD.
00033            02  FILLER                  PIC X(80).
```

Program 6.1   (cont.)

```
00034
00035          FD  VEHICLE-FILE
00036              BLOCK CONTAINS 1 RECORDS
00037              RECORD CONTAINS 114 CHARACTERS
00038              LABEL RECORDS ARE STANDARD
00039              DATA RECORD IS VEHICLE-FILE-RECORD.
00040          01  VEHICLE-FILE-RECORD.
00041              02  OWNER-DATA.
00042                  03  NAME            PIC X(20).
00043                  03  PRESENT-ADDRESS.
00044                      04  STREET          PIC X(20).
00045                      04  CITY            PIC X(20).
00046                  03  DRIVER-LICENSE-NUMBER
00047                                          PIC X(8).
00048              02  VEHICLE-DATA.
00049                  03  MAKE-OF-VEHICLE     PIC X(20).
00050                  03  VEHICLE-LICENSE-NUMBER
00051                                          PIC X(6).
00052                  03  COLOUR-OF-VEHICLE  PIC X(6).
00053                  03  ENGINE-SERIAL-NUMBER
00054                                          PIC X(8).
00055                  03  LAST-YEAR-LICENSE-NUMBER
00056                                          PIC X(6).
00057
00058
00059          WORKING-STORAGE SECTION.
00060
00061          77  CARD-EOF-FLAG           PIC X(3).
00062              88  CARD-EOF            VALUE IS 'ON'.
00063          77  VEHICLE-LICENSE-KEY     PIC S9(8) COMP SYNC.
00064          77  WARNING-FLAG            PIC X(3).
00065
00066          01  WS-DATA-CARDS.
00067              02  CARD-1.
00068                  03  PART-1          PIC X(68).
00069                  03  FILLER          PIC X(12).
00070              02  CARD-2.
00071                  03  PART-2          PIC X(46).
00072                  03  FILLER          PIC X(34).
00073
00074
00075          PROCEDURE DIVISION.
00076
00077              PERFORM INITIALIZATION.
00078              PERFORM READ-AND-COPY-TO-FILE-ROUTINE
00079                  UNTIL CARD-EOF.
00080              PERFORM TERMINATION.
00081              STOP RUN.
00082
00083          INITIALIZATION.
00084              OPEN  INPUT  CARD-READER
00085                   OUTPUT VEHICLE-FILE.
00086              MOVE 'OFF' TO CARD-EOF-FLAG WARNING-FLAG.
00087              PERFORM READ-DATA-CARDS.
00088
00089          READ-DATA-CARDS.
00090              PERFORM READ-CARD-ONE.
00091              IF NOT CARD-EOF PERFORM READ-CARD-TWO.
00092
00093          READ-CARD-ONE.
00094              READ CARD-READER RECORD INTO CARD-1
00095                  AT END MOVE 'ON' TO CARD-EOF-FLAG.
00096          READ-CARD-TWO.
```

Program 6.1 (cont.)

```
00097                    READ CARD-READER RECORD INTO CARD-2
00098                       AT END MOVE 'ON' TO CARD-EOF-FLAG.
00099
00100          READ-AND-COPY-TO-FILE-ROUTINE.
00101               MOVE PART-1 TO OWNER-DATA.
00102               MOVE PART-2 TO VEHICLE-DATA.
00103               WRITE VEHICLE-FILE-RECORD
00104                    INVALID KEY MOVE 'ON' TO WARNING-FLAG.
00105               DISPLAY VEHICLE-LICENSE-KEY.
00106               PERFORM READ-DATA-CARDS.
00107
00108          TERMINATION.
00109               CLOSE CARD-READER VEHICLE-FILE.
```

Program 6.1 Narrative.   The purpose of Program 6.1 is to create a Relative I–O file called VEHICLE-FILE; see Fig. 6.1. The input to the program is a set of records containing the information to be stored in the file. Two data records are required to provide the information for one record of VEHICLE-FILE. The first record of a pair is read into CARD-1, the second into CARD 2. The first input record contains information about the owner of the vehicle and is moved from CARD-1 to OWNER-DATA of the VEHICLE-FILE-RECORD. The second card contains information about the vehicle itself and is moved from CARD-2 to VEHICLE-DATA of the VEHICLE-FILE-RECORD. Normally an edit check

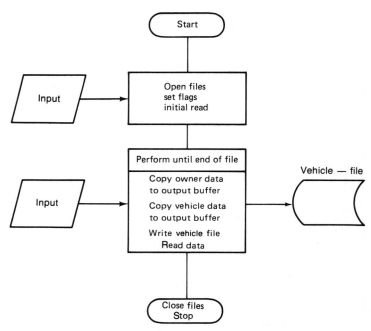

Figure 6.1   VEHICLE-LICENSE-FILE.

would be performed on CARD-1 and CARD-2 prior to these move operations to ensure that only correct data is transferred to the output buffer.

The output of the program is the VEHICLE-FILE. There is no printed output. A record is transferred to the VEHICLE-FILE by means of the following COBOL statement:

```
WRITE VEHICLE-FILE-RECORD
    INVALID KEY MOVE "ON"
    TO WARNING-FLAG.
```

This statement is found in the paragraph READ-AND-COPY-TO-FILE-ROUTINE.

The INVALID KEY clause will be invoked whenever an attempt is made to write a record beyond the physical boundary of the file. In the program 'ON' will be moved to WARNING-FLAG should this event occur. No check is made in the program to detect this occurence, but a program used for production purposes should contain an appropriate error routine.

Finally, it is important to note that the file is being created in SEQUENTIAL mode.

6.3 RELATIVE I–O MODULE OF COBOL: USED SEQUENTIALLY

6.3.1 Input–Output Section: Defining a Relative I–O File

A Relative I–O file is defined by a SELECT clause within the INPUT-OUTPUT SECTION of the ENVIRONMENT DIVISION. The following is a standard ANSI COBOL entry:

```
INPUT-OUTPUT SECTION.
FILE-CONTROL.
    SELECT file-name
    ASSIGN TO implementor-name
    ORGANIZATION IS RELATIVE
    ACCESS MODE IS SEQUENTIAL
    RELATIVE KEY IS data-name.
```

This SELECT clause indicates that the file named is a Relative I–O file that is to be accessed in a sequential mode and names the data item associated with the file that is to be considered as the relative key. If the ACCESS MODE clause is not specified, ACCESS MODE IS SEQUENTIAL is assumed. When the access mode is sequential, the records in the file are stored in the sequence dictated by the file organization. This sequence is the order of ascending relative record numbers.

Relative Key

In COBOL the relative record number variable is known as the RELATIVE KEY. This is an unsigned, positive, integer data item and is a primary key.

6.3.2 FD ENTRY: Describing the records of a Relative I–O File

A typical FD entry for a Relative I–O file would appear as follows in ANSI COBOL:

```
FD file name
      BLOCK CONTAINS integer RECORDS
      RECORD CONTAINS integer CHARACTERS
      LABEL RECORDS ARE STANDARD
      DATA RECORD IS record-name.
```

The clauses following the level indicator FD are optional and may appear in any order.

The BLOCK CONTAINS clause specifies the size of a physical record on the storage device. The physical records may be variable in size and the compiler manual should be consulted. The RECORD clause indicates the size of each record (this may also be variable and the compiler manual should be consulted). The LABEL RECORDS clause indicates in this example that the data set or file labels on the storage device have been created according to STANDARD conventions but ANSI COBOL also permits them to be OMITTED (not advised). The DATA RECORD clause names the level 01 record name(s) associated with this file.

6.3.3 PROCEDURE DIVISION: Accessing a Relative I–O File

The OPEN Statement

The following sequential form of the OPEN statement can be used to write records to an unloaded Relative I–O file in the sequential mode:

```
OPEN OUTPUT file-name
```

The WRITE Statement

The general form of the WRITE statement is:

```
WRITE record-name [FROM identifier]
      INVALID KEY imperative statement
```

The *record-name* is the name of the logical record in the FILE SECTION and may be qualified. If the optional FROM is used, the record is first moved from the WORKING-STORAGE SECTION before writing.

The INVALID KEY clause is invoked if an attempt is made to write a record beyond the physical boundary of the file on the storage device, and an *imperative statement* is used to define the action taken if this occurs.

After each WRITE statement, the relative record number of the record just written is placed in the data item named as the RELATIVE KEY.

Reading Records Sequentially

Two statements that are important to reading records sequentially are the START statement and the READ statement.

The START statement is used to provide a logical positioning in the file, or in other words it specifies where in the file sequential reading of the records is to commence. It has the general format:

```
START file-name KEY relation
      data-name INVALID KEY imperative statement
```

where *file-name* is the name of the file that is to be positioned and *relation* is one of the following:

```
IS EQUAL TO
IS =
IS GREATER THAN
IS >
IS NOT LESS THAN
IS NOT <
```

and *data-name* is the name of the data item specified in the RELATIVE KEY clause of the SELECT statement in the INPUT-OUTPUT SECTION.

An example will clarify the function of the START statement.

```
START VEHICLE-FILE
   KEY IS > VEHICLE-KEY
INVALID KEY MOVE "ON" TO
WARNING-FLAG
```

This statement asks that the file named VEHICLE-FILE be positioned at the first record whose relative record number is greater than the integer currently stored in the data item called VEHICLE-KEY which is, in fact, the RELATIVE KEY for this file. The INVALID KEY phrase is invoked when the comparison is not satisfied by any record in the file. Following execution of the INVALID KEY clause, execution returns to the statement following the START statement. If processing is to begin at the first record in the file, the START statement is not required.

Only one format of the READ statement is permitted with Relative I–O files when they are accessed sequentially, and this is

```
READ file-name RECORD [INTO identifier]
     AT END imperative statement
```

This is the same format of the READ statement used by the sequential I–O module. If the optional INTO clause is specified, the record once read into the buffer associated with the file is placed in the area of the WORKING-STORAGE SECTION specified as the *identifier*.

The *imperative statement* following the key words AT END is executed when there are no more logical records left to read in the file. Once this *imperative statement* has been executed, control is returned to the statement following the READ statement.

The CLOSE Statement

A CLOSE statement should only be issued for a file that is already in the OPEN state. It has the form:

```
CLOSE file-name
```

The CLOSE statement should always be issued when all records have been copied to the required file. Its execution assures that the file buffers are emptied, that all required label processing is completed, and an end-of-file marker is written on the file.

Creating a Relative I–O File

In IBM OS/VS COBOL, a file is referred to as an *unloaded* file if it has never at any time contained records. Once a record has been written (even if later it should be deleted), it becomes a *loaded* file. Normally a Relative file is created in the sequential access mode. In the sequential access mode, the file is opened for OUTPUT and new records written to the file for the first time. The records are automatically assigned relative key 1, 2, and so on. The file then becomes a loaded file. This file need not be filled, but any space left over cannot be accessed for reading purposes until records are placed there. A *file may only be opened once* in OUTPUT mode for the purpose of creation. Later, as we shall see, the file can be first opened in the I–O mode. A loaded file must never be opened for OUTPUT in the sequential access mode.

In ANSI COBOL, the records in a Relative I–O file can be of any length, and this length can vary from record to record. However, this may not always be true in the compiler being used. In IBM OS/VS COBOL, the space reserved for each record is the maximum record size specified.

It is important to stress that the relative record numbers constitute a sequential ordering of the records in the file. An individual record's relative record number is determined by the number of records preceding it in the file. In IBM OS/VS COBOL, the size of a file is determined by the amount of space made available. The number of logical records that can be stored is the amount of space available for records divided by the maximum record size.

Sometimes a programmer does not know in advance how large the file will eventually grow to be. In the event that the file becomes larger than the file space available, the file size must be redefined, and this is done by *recreating the file*. In order to overcome the difficulty inherent in recreating the file each time a new record is to be added, the programmer should make an estimate of how many records the file will have at some future time and create the file large enough to contain that many records. If, at a later date, it should become apparent that the number of records added at file creation was not sufficient, the programmer is forced to recreate the file to be of a more appropriate size. This is accomplished by creating a new Relative I–O file with records from the original.

6.4 PROCESSING A RELATIVE FILE SEQUENTIALLY

When the file space reserved is greater than that required by the file loaded, some compilers repeat the last record so that the file is larger than you thought and contains records you do not expect. One solution is to always create with "dummy" records so unexpected magical happenings do not occur in your programs.

If the updates to a file are collected together in a batch, then sequential processing can be efficient even for a direct access file. In this section we consider the sequential update of a Relative I–O file using the vehicle file as an example.

A transaction against a master file affects only one record although there may be more than one transaction for any given record. For example, a transaction file of a phone company may have three records affecting one telephone number. The first may advise that a customer has paid his account; the second that he is to be deleted from the file because he is moving; and the third that a new customer is to be added to the file with the same telephone number as the previous customer. It is a standard rule of thumb in sequential data processing, that no transaction should apply to more than one master record.

A transaction and a master file record are associated if they have the same primary key. In the case of the phone company, each customer is uniquely identified by phone number and each transaction contains the telephone number to which it applies. The primary key that labels each record on the master file is referred to as the *master key* and the primary key that identifies the master record to which a given transaction is to be applied is called a *transaction key*. As previously mentioned, the transaction file may contain many transactions with the same key; these are transactions that are to be applied to the matching record of the master file. The master file consists of only one record for each primary key. This is because a single customer is responsible for each telephone.

In order to carry out a sequential updating process, it is necessary that all files are sorted in the same order by primary key. The phone company would sort the master file and transaction file in ascending order by telephone number.

The update process uses the balance line algorithm introduced in Chapter 3. Updating involves the idea of balancing master and transaction records so that records are processed only if they have the same primary keys. Rather than comparing the key from a transaction file record against the key of a master record to determine whether or not updating should take place from one record to another, all keys are compared against an independent key, called, for want of a better name, the *active key*. The active key is the smallest record key of those pointed to by the current record pointer of each file. Each file is handled by a separate routine which is entered whenever a file's current record key matches the active key. If end-of-file is reached on any file, its record key is made equal to HIGH-VALUES.

Study the code shown in Fig. 6.2. Note that processing will halt when *both* files reach end-of-file, since ACTIVE-KEY will then become HIGH-VALUES in the DETERMINE-ACTIVE KEY routine. This coding for simplicity does not show initial reads for the two files. If more transaction files are desired, they can easily be added. Convince yourself of this before proceeding.

6.4.1 Sequential Processing of a Relative I–O File

Program 6.2 reads data containing additions and deletions to create an updated VEHICLE-FILE.

Program 6.2 Narrative.   The purpose of Program 6.2, as illustrated in Fig. 6.3, is to make additions and deletions to the VEHICLE-FILE created in Program 6.1. The balance line algorithm is used. VEHICLE-FILE is the master file; NEW-VEHICLE-FILE is the updated file. It is assumed that the VEHICLE-FILE is sorted by license number before Program 6.2 is executed.

The TRANSACTION-FILE contains records to be added and records to be deleted. Records to be added come in pairs as in Program 6.1 (two 80-byte records) and have the character string 'ADD' in column 7 of the first record of the pair. A DELETE record consists of only one record and contains the character string 'DE-LETE' in column 7. The delete transaction record contains a vehicle license number. Any record in the VEHICLE-FILE having this license number is to be deleted.

The balance line algorithm is initialized in the usual manner. First the master and transaction files are read. Then the lowest key (license number) becomes the ACTIVE-KEY.

The MASTER-ROUTINE is executed whenever the license number of the VEHICLE-FILE-RECORD matches the active key. The routine moves the VEHICLE-FILE-RECORD to a temporary area called WS-VEHICLE-FILE-RECORD in the WORKING-STORAGE SECTION. It then moves 'ON' to MASTER-SWITCH and reads another record.

.
.
.

```
PERFORM DETERMINE-ACTIVE-KEY.
    PERFORM BALANCE-LINE
        UNTIL ACTIVE-KEY EQUAL
            HIGH-VALUES.
```

.
.
.

```
BALANCE-LINE
    IF MASTER-KEY EQUAL
    ACTIVE-KEY PERFORM MASTER-RTN.
    IF TRANSACTION-KEY EQUAL
        ACTIVE-KEY
    PERFORM TRANSACTION-RTN
        UNTIL TRANSACTION-KEY
            NOT EQUAL ACTIVE-KEY.
    PERFORM DETERMINE-ACTIVE KEY.
```

.
.
.

```
DETERMINE-ACTIVE-KEY
    IF MASTER-KEY LESS THAN
    TRANSACTION-KEY
    MOVE MASTER-KEY TO ACTIVE-KEY
    ELSE
    MOVE TRANSACTION-KEY TO ACTIVE-KEY.
```

.
.
.

```
MASTER-RTN
```

.
.
.

```
    READ MASTER-FILE
        AT END
        MOVE HIGH-VALUES TO MASTER-KEY.
TRANSACTiON-RTN.
```

.
.
.

```
    READ TRANSACTION-FILE
        AT END
        MOVE HIGH-VALUES TO
        TRANSACTION-KEY.
```

Figure 6.2   Code for use of active key.

Program 6.2

```
00008          ** VEHICLE-FILE ADDITIONS AND DELETIONS **
00009
00010          INPUT-OUTPUT SECTION.
00011          FILE-CONTROL.
00012
00013              SELECT ERROR-FILE
00014                  ASSIGN TO DISK-ERROR
00015                  ORGANIZATION IS SEQUENTIAL
00016                  ACCESS MODE IS SEQUENTIAL.
00017              SELECT NEW-VEHICLE-FILE
00018                  ASSIGN TO DISK-NEW
00019                  ORGANIZATION IS RELATIVE
00020                  ACCESS MODE IS SEQUENTIAL.
00021              SELECT TRANSACTION-FILE
00022                  ASSIGN TO CARD-TRANS
00023                  ORGANIZATION IS SEQUENTIAL
00024                  ACCESS MODE IS SEQUENTIAL.
00025              SELECT VEHICLE-FILE
00026                  ASSIGN TO DISK-LICENSE
00027                  ORGANIZATION IS RELATIVE
00028                  ACCESS MODE IS SEQUENTIAL.
00029
00030
00031          DATA DIVISION.
00032          FILE SECTION.
00033
00034          FD  ERROR-FILE
00035              BLOCK CONTAINS 1 RECORDS
00036              RECORD CONTAINS 80 CHARACTERS
00037              LABEL RECORDS ARE STANDARD
00038              DATA RECORD IS ERROR-FILE-RECORD.
00039          01  ERROR-FILE-RECORD.
00040              02  FILLER                   PIC X(80).
00041
00042          FD  NEW-VEHICLE-FILE
00043              BLOCK CONTAINS 1 RECORDS
00044              RECORD CONTAINS 114 CHARACTERS
00045              LABEL RECORDS ARE STANDARD
00046              DATA RECORD IS NEW-VEHICLE-FILE-RECORD.
00047          01  NEW-VEHICLE-FILE-RECORD.
00048              02  FILLER                   PIC X(114).
00049
00050          FD  TRANSACTION-FILE
00051              BLOCK CONTAINS 1 RECORDS
00052              RECORD CONTAINS 80 CHARACTERS
00053              LABEL RECORDS ARE OMITTED
00054              DATA RECORDS ARE TRANSACTION-FILE-RECORD-1
00055                               TRANSACTION-FILE-RECORD-2.
00056          01  TRANSACTION-FILE-RECORD-1.
00057              02  TRANSACTION-KEY          PIC X(6).
00058              02  TRANSACTION-CODE         PIC X(6).
00059              02  TRANSACTION-DATA-1       PIC X(68).
00060          01  TRANSACTION-FILE-RECORD-2.
00061              02  FILLER                   PIC X(12).
00062              02  TRANSACTION-DATA-2       PIC X(46).
00063              02  FILLER                   PIC X(22).
00064
00065          FD  VEHICLE-FILE
00066              BLOCK CONTAINS 1 RECORDS
00067              RECORD CONTAINS 114 CHARACTERS
00068              LABEL RECORDS ARE STANDARD
00069              DATA RECORD IS VEHICLE-FILE-RECORD.
```

Program 6.2   (cont.)

```
00070          01  VEHICLE-FILE-RECORD.
00071              02  FILLER                  PIC X(88).
00072              02  MASTER-KEY              PIC X(6).
00073              02  FILLER                  PIC X(20).
00074
00075
00076          WORKING-STORAGE SECTION.
00077
00078          77  ACTIVE-KEY                  PIC X(6).
00079          77  MASTER-SWITCH               PIC X(3).
00080
00081          01  WS-VEHICLE-FILE-RECORD.
00082              02  DATA-1                  PIC X(68).
00083              02  DATA-2                  PIC X(46).
00084
00085
00086          PROCEDURE DIVISION.
00087
00088              PERFORM INITIALIZATION.
00089              PERFORM BALANCE-LINE-ROUTINE
00090                  UNTIL ACTIVE-KEY = HIGH-VALUES.
00091              PERFORM TERMINATION.
00092              STOP RUN.
00093
00094          INITIALIZATION.
00095              OPEN  INPUT  VEHICLE-FILE TRANSACTION-FILE
00096                    OUTPUT NEW-VEHICLE-FILE ERROR-FILE.
00097              MOVE 'OFF' TO MASTER-SWITCH.
00098              PERFORM READ-MASTER-FILE.
00099              PERFORM READ-TRANSACTION-FILE.
00100              PERFORM DETERMINE-ACTIVE-KEY.
00101
00102          READ-MASTER-FILE.
00103              READ VEHICLE-FILE RECORD
00104                  AT END MOVE HIGH-VALUES TO MASTER-KEY.
00105
00106          READ-TRANSACTION-FILE.
00107              READ TRANSACTION-FILE RECORD
00108                  AT END MOVE HIGH-VALUES TO TRANSACTION-KEY.
00109
00110          DETERMINE-ACTIVE-KEY.
00111              IF  MASTER-KEY < TRANSACTION-KEY
00112                  MOVE MASTER-KEY TO ACTIVE-KEY
00113                  ELSE MOVE TRANSACTION-KEY TO ACTIVE-KEY.
00114
00115          BALANCE-LINE-ROUTINE.
00116              PERFORM MASTER-ROUTINE.
00117              PERFORM TRANSACTION-ROUTINE
00118                  UNTIL TRANSACTION-KEY NOT = ACTIVE-KEY.
00119              PERFORM WRITE-RECORD-TO-NEW-FILE.
00120              PERFORM DETERMINE-ACTIVE-KEY.
00121
00122          MASTER-ROUTINE.
00123              IF  MASTER-KEY = ACTIVE-KEY
00124                  MOVE VEHICLE-FILE-RECORD
00125                      TO WS-VEHICLE-FILE-RECORD
00126                  MOVE 'ON' TO MASTER-SWITCH
00127                  PERFORM READ-MASTER-FILE.
00128
00129          TRANSACTION-ROUTINE.
00130              IF  TRANSACTION-CODE = 'ADD'
00131                  IF  MASTER-SWITCH = 'OFF'
```

Program 6.2   (cont.)

```
00132                        MOVE TRANSACTION-DATA-1 TO DATA-1
00133                        PERFORM READ-TRANSACTION-FILE
00134                        MOVE TRANSACTION-DATA-2 TO DATA-2
00135                        MOVE 'ON' TO MASTER-SWITCH
00136                     ELSE PERFORM ERROR-ROUTINE-1
00137               ELSE
00138               IF   TRANSACTION-CODE = 'DELETE'
00139                  IF   MASTER-SWITCH = 'ON'
00140                     MOVE 'OFF' TO MASTER-SWITCH
00141                     ELSE PERFORM ERROR-ROUTINE-2
00142                  ELSE PERFORM ERROR-ROUTINE-2.
00143            PERFORM READ-TRANSACTION-FILE.
00144
00145       ERROR-ROUTINE-1.
00146            PERFORM ERROR-ROUTINE-2.
00147            PERFORM READ-TRANSACTION-FILE.
00148            PERFORM ERROR-ROUTINE-2.
00149
00150       ERROR-ROUTINE-2.
00151            DISPLAY TRANSACTION-FILE-RECORD-1.
00152            WRITE ERROR-FILE-RECORD
00153                FROM TRANSACTION-FILE-RECORD-1.
00154
00155       WRITE-RECORD-TO-NEW-FILE.
00156            IF   MASTER-SWITCH = 'ON'
00157               WRITE NEW-VEHICLE-FILE-RECORD
00158                  FROM WS-VEHICLE-FILE-RECORD
00159               MOVE 'OFF' TO MASTER-SWITCH.
00160
00161       TERMINATION.
00162            CLOSE VEHICLE-FILE TRANSACTION-FILE
00163                  NEW-VEHICLE-FILE ERROR-FILE.
```

Following the conditional execution of the MASTER-ROUTINE, a check is made to see whether or not the TRANSACTION-ROUTINE should be executed. This routine will be executed repeatedly as long as the TRANSACTION-KEY matches the ACTIVE-KEY. On entry to the TRANSACTION-ROUTINE the type of transaction to be processed is determined. Additions are performed before deletions. In the event that the TRANSACTION-CODE is 'ADD', a check is made to see whether or not the MASTER-SWITCH is 'OFF'. This switch will only register 'ON' if a record having the same license number already exists, i.e., if a definite error has occurred. If the switch is off, the transaction record is moved to working storage and the second record of the add pair is read in. This too is moved to working storage. The MASTER-SWITCH is then turned 'ON' to indicate that a record is ready for copying to the NEW-VEHICLE-FILE. In the event that the transaction is a 'DELETE', the procedure is almost the opposite to that for an addition. This time the MASTER-SWITCH should be 'ON', indicating a record is available for copying to the NEW-VEHICLE FILE (otherwise there is no record to delete). All that need be done in this case is to turn the MASTER-SWITCH off, thereby inhibiting its copy.

Following the TRANSACTION-ROUTINE, the record is written to the NEW-VEHICLE-FILE if the MASTER-SWITCH is 'ON'. Finally, a new determination of ACTIVE-KEY is made. Processing will terminate when both the TRANSACTION-FILE and the VEHICLE-FILE have reached an end-of-file.

Note that we have used the Relative I–O file, VEHICLE-FILE, in the sequential access mode. In the next program we shall use it in the random mode.

6.5 PROCESSING RELATIVE I–O FILES RANDOMLY

Once a Relative I–O file has been created in the sequential mode, we can access its records in the random mode. In the random mode, a record is accessed by specifying its relative record number. In order to read or write a specific record, its relative record number must first be stored in the RELATIVE KEY of the file. To illustrate this process, we reconsider the VEHICLE-FILE created in Program 6.1. Suppose now that we wish to write a COBOL program that, given a relative record number, will fetch the record with this number from the file and rewrite it after changing the owner's address, Program 6.3 is created for this purpose.

Program 6.3 Narrative. The random mode allows direct addition and deletion of records. The DELETE instruction can be used for deletions and the WRITE or REWRITE used for additions. A word of caution: Relative I–O file cannot grow in physical size. Additions must replace already existing records. If dummy records are available, this is straightforward. Failing this, a decision must be made to delete records in order to make room for new ones. Changes to existing records do not entail the same complications as additions.

In order to make a change to a record, its relative key must be known beforehand. We assume in Program 6.3 that the relative keys of records to be changed are available and form part of the input data to the program. In the next chapter, we shall study procedures that enable us to determine the relative key of a record given an identifying key, such as the vehicle license number.

The input to Program 6.3 consists of a file labeled INPUT-FILE, a sequential file of records that consists of relative keys and changes to the address field of records in the VEHICLE-FILE. These records are read one by one. The relative key of each record is moved from RECORD-NUMBER in the incoming record to FILE-KEY, the RELATIVE KEY of the VEHICLE-FILE. Next, a READ is executed, bringing in the record to be changed.

The field NEW-ADDRESS of INPUT-FILE-RECORD replaces the PRESENT-ADDRESS in the VEHICLE-FILE-RECORD and a REWRITE is executed. The REWRITE causes the VEHICLE-FILE-RECORD to be written back to the the storage location from which it came. This is only possible because the record has not changed in size during updating. Unlike Program 6.2, processing halts when there are no further records in the INPUT-FILE of record changes. Only those records that are to be changed are actually read and rewritten. Clearly this form of updating is applicable to on-line systems where instantaneous updating is required. More onus is placed, however, on the programmer when using direct access.

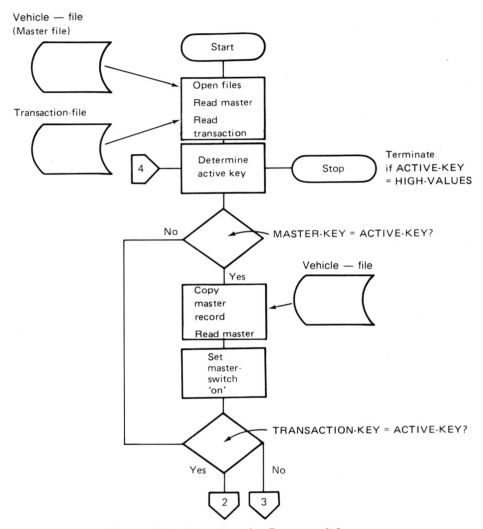

Figure 6.3   Flowchart for Program 6.2.

Changes destroy the current content of the file and adequate backup must be available in the event of error. Direct access provides high speeds, but as with cars, the driver must be more careful.

6.5.1 Input-Output Section

In order to process a Relative I–O file in the random mode, the clause

ACCESS MODE IS RANDOM

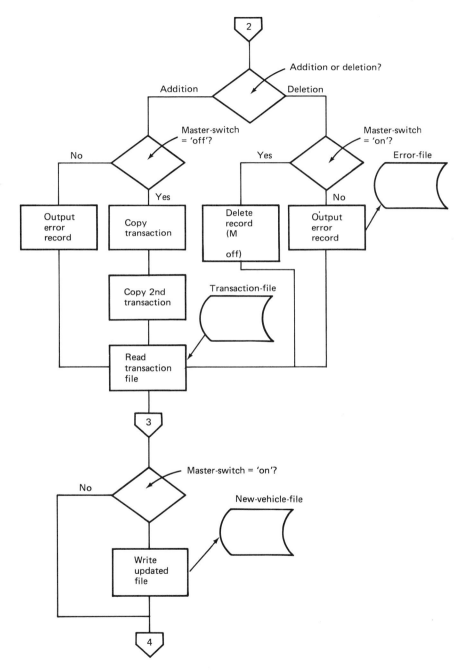

Figure 6.3   (continued)

Program 6.3

```
00008          /    ** UPDATE VEHICLE-FILE AT RANDOM **
00009
00010              INPUT-OUTPUT SECTION.
00011              FILE-CONTROL.
00012
00013                  SELECT INPUT-FILE
00014                      ASSIGN TO CARD-INPUT
00015                      ORGANIZATION IS SEQUENTIAL
00016                      ACCESS MODE IS SEQUENTIAL.
00017                  SELECT VEHICLE-FILE
00018                      ASSIGN TO DISK-VEHICLE
00019                      ORGANIZATION IS RELATIVE
00020                      ACCESS MODE IS RANDOM
00021                      RELATIVE KEY IS FILE-KEY.
00022
00023
00024              DATA DIVISION.
00025              FILE SECTION.
00026
00027              FD   INPUT-FILE
00028                   BLOCK CONTAINS 1 RECORDS
00029                   LABEL RECORDS ARE OMITTED
00030                   RECORD CONTAINS 80 CHARACTERS
00031                   DATA RECORD IS INPUT-FILE-RECORD.
00032              01   INPUT-FILE-RECORD.
00033                   02   RECORD-NUMBER          PIC 999.
00034                   02   NEW-ADDRESS            PIC X(40).
00035                   02   FILLER                 PIC X(37).
00036
00037              FD   VEHICLE-FILE
00038                   BLOCK CONTAINS 1 RECORDS
00039                   RECORD CONTAINS 114 CHARACTERS
00040                   LABEL RECORDS ARE STANDARD
00041                   DATA RECORD IS VEHICLE-FILE-RECORD.
00042              01   VEHICLE-FILE-RECORD.
00043                   02   FILLER                 PIC X(20).
00044                   02   PRESENT-ADDRESS        PIC X(40).
00045                   02   FILLER                 PIC X(54).
00046
00047
00048              WORKING-STORAGE SECTION.
00049
00050              77   FILE-KEY                     PIC S9(8)
00051                       USAGE IS COMP SYNC.
00052              77   INPUT-EOF-FLAG               PIC X(3).
00053                   88   INPUT-EOF        VALUE IS 'ON'.
00054              77   WARNING-FLAG                 PIC X(3).
00055
00056
00057              PROCEDURE DIVISION.
00058
00059                  PERFORM INITIALIZATION.
00060                  PERFORM CHANGE-ADDRESS-ROUTINE
00061                      UNTIL INPUT-EOF.
00062                  PERFORM TERMINATION.
00063                  STOP RUN.
00064
00065              INITIALIZATION.
00066                  OPEN I-O   VEHICLE-FILE
00067                        INPUT INPUT-FILE.
00068                  MOVE 'OFF' TO INPUT-EOF-FLAG.
```

Program 6.3 (cont.)

```
00069                    MOVE 'OFF' TO WARNING-FLAG.
00070                    PERFORM READ-INPUT-FILE.
00071
00072            READ-INPUT-FILE.
00073                    READ INPUT-FILE RECORD
00074                        AT END MOVE 'ON' TO INPUT-EOF-FLAG.
00075
00076            CHANGE-ADDRESS-ROUTINE.
00077                    MOVE RECORD-NUMBER TO FILE-KEY.
00078                    PERFORM READ-VEHICLE-FILE.
00079                    IF WARNING-FLAG = 'OFF'
00080                        MOVE NEW-ADDRESS TO PRESENT-ADDRESS
00081                        REWRITE VEHICLE-FILE-RECORD.
00082                    PERFORM READ-VEHICLE-FILE.
00083                    PERFORM READ-INPUT-FILE.
00084
00085            READ-VEHICLE-FILE.
00086                    READ VEHICLE-FILE RECORD
00087                        INVALID KEY MOVE 'ON' TO WARNING-FLAG.
00088
00089            TERMINATION.
00090                    CLOSE INPUT-FILE
00091                          VEHICLE-FILE.
```

must be added to the SELECT clause associated with this file. The SELECT clause for a Relative I–O file in the random mode has the following format:

```
SELECT file-name
    ASSIGN TO implementor=name
    ORGANIZATION IS RELATIVE
    ACCESS MODE IS RANDOM
    RELATIVE KEY IS data-name
```

This select clause indicates that the file named is a Relative I–O file that is to be processed in the random mode and designates the variable used as the relative key. When the access mode is random, the value of the RELATIVE KEY indicates the record to be accessed.

Defining a File

The FD entry for the file is the same as for file creation. A typical entry:

```
FD file-name
    LABEL RECORDS ARE STANDARD
    BLOCK CONTAINS integer RECORDS
    RECORD CONTAINS integer CHARACTERS
    DATA RECORD IS record-name
```

In some implementations it may not be possible to block records with Relative I–O files.

PROCEDURE DIVISION: Accessing a Relative I–O File Randomly.

The OPEN Statement

If records are to be read but not written, code:

```
OPEN INPUT file-name
```

If the records are to be read and written code:

```
OPEN I-O file-name
```

The READ Statement

The format of the READ statement for Relative I–O files in the random access mode is:

```
READ file-name RECORD [INTO identifier  ]
     INVALID KEY imperative statement
```

This statement causes one record to be read from the file named and transferred to the WORKING-STORAGE SECTION record named as the *identifier* of the optional INTO clause it specifies.

It is assumed that *prior* to the READ statement being executed, the object record's relative record number has been stored in the RELATIVE KEY data item. If the RELATIVE KEY points to a record that is not an element of the file, then the imperative statement following the key words INVALID KEY is invoked. Upon completion of this imperative statement, control returns to the statement following the READ statement.

The WRITE Statement

The format of the WRITE statement to be used with Relative I–O files in the random access mode is:

```
WRITE record-name [FROM identifier ] |
      INVALID KEY imperative statement
```

This statement causes one record stored at *record-name* or at *identifier* (if the optional FROM option is used) to be transferred to the associated Relative I–O file. The optional FROM causes a move of the record at *identifier* in the WORKING STORAGE SECTION to the *record-name* which must be the name of the level 01 record named in the FD associated with the file. It is assumed that the relative record number of the record to be written has been stored in the RELATIVE KEY prior to the execution of the WRITE statment. This statement should only be used to add *new* records to the file or to replace records that have been deleted with the DELETE statement.

The REWRITE Clause

COBOL provides for a second output statement for a Relative I–O file. The REWRITE statement is specifically intended to be used when the user wishes to logically replace a record in the file. A record should not be rewritten to a file unless it has been changed. The general format for a REWRITE statement is:

```
REWRITE record-name [FROM identifier]
     INVALID KEY imperative statement
```

Specifically, the REWRITE statement causes the record named as *record-name* to be rewritten to the file, where *record-name* is the data item named as the level 01 entry for the FD entry of the associated file within the FILE SECTION of the DATA DIVISION. If the optional FROM is included, then the record is first moved to the output buffer from its storage area within the WORKING-STORAGE SECTION called *identifier*.

It is assumed that, prior to rewriting, the relative record number of the record to be rewritten to the file has been stored in the data item named as the RELATIVE KEY of the associated file. In the event that an attempt is made to rewrite a record that does not exist in the file, the *imperative statement* following the key words IN-VALID KEY is invoked. The REWRITE clause may only be used if the file is opened for I–O.

The DELETE Statement

The DELETE statement can be used to delete a record from a Relative I–O file provided the file has been opened in the I–O mode.

The general format of the DELETE statement is

```
DELETE file-name RECORD
     INVALID KEY imperative statement
```

where *file-name* is the name of the associated file.

The relative record number of the record to be removed from the file is assumed to be stored in the RELATIVE KEY data item prior to the execution of the DELETE statement. Once the DELETE statement has been executed, the identified record has been logically removed from the file and can no longer be accessed. The contents of the RELATIVE KEY are not affected by execution of the DELETE statement.

If the file does not contain the record that is to be deleted, the *imperative statement* following the key words INVALID KEY is executed and then control returns to the statement following the DELETE statement.

Sequential Accessing of Records Using Random Access

It is worth noting that even though a file is opened in the random access mode, it can still be treated as though it were a file in the sequential access mode by careful programming. Specifically, the user can set the RELATIVE KEY to 1; read the first record; add 1 to the RELATIVE KEY; read record 2; add 1 to the RELATIVE KEY; read record 3; and so on. It is *not,* however, possible to issue a START statement, because a START statement cannot be issued when the file is opened with ACCESS IS RANDOM. ANSI COBOL allows for intermixing of sequential and random access in the dynamic mode; in this case, ACCESS IS DYNAMIC must be used.

6.6 BLOCKING RELATIVE I–O FILES

IBM OS/VS COBOL does not allow the blocking of Relative I–O records. This is not too surprising, as blocking is generally done to provide for the fetching of a group of sequential records with one READ. This makes most sense with sequential files, as records are then needed one after the other. With Relative I–O files, when access is random, records do not necessarily follow one another. However, there are instances where space saving justifies blocking, and bear in mind that the principle of locality of reference says that retrieval of records tends to occur in the same general area.

There are times, however, when the request for records from a file may well be in sequential order. In an airline reservation system, the requests for information can often be handled sequentially. A traveler wants to know whether there are seats on any of the flights from New York to Dallas on this coming Saturday. Here it might be useful to read a whole series of records at once, rather than fetch each plane's record individually. If an effort to store similar flights in sequential order on the disk were made, blocking would prove useful. Note, that the original request is still random. What flight information is requested? The next user may well be interested in next summer's flights to Mexico. Rather than block these records, perhaps a more appropriate procedure to consider is the storing of the information regarding all flights from city A to city B on a Saturday as one large record. Whenever a user wishes the information, the large record can be brought into memory and there broken up into its various flights. The large record is still a Relative I–O record. This technique is sometimes called *internal blocking.* It is really a matter of carefully deciding in the original design stages what should constitute the contents of a record on the file.

6.7 CONCLUSIONS

In summary, the records of a *relative file* are addressed as integers relative to their position with respect to the first record of the file. The flexibility of direct access to a record is tempered by the disadvantage that the programmer must establish a relationship between the record key and the integer record address. Although a simple relationship may exist that can be exploited; more often, complex programming may be required to establish the relationship. Such considerations are explored in the next chapter.

The COBOL Relative I–O module provides either random or sequential access of a relative file. It is an example of an indexed file organization. As it provides few features, it is fast and has little overhead. Basically, it isolates the programmer from the physical address but requires him to manage space and record assignment.

The relative address acts much like an index of a table. One might view a relative file as a table in external memory and the same uses apply. Of course, they are much slower than tables.

In the sequential access mode, records are processed in ascending order of the relative record numbers. In the random access mode, the programmer must first determine the relative address number. Module level 2 allows mixing of random and sequential access using the dynamic access mode. There are a number of features we have not discussed; they are best learned from the appropriate software manual.

Backup requirements exist as for sequential files rewritten in place. The two major disadvantages of relative files are the need to relate the primary key to the relative address, which may be difficult to do efficiently, and the fact that a file must be completely written when created, which may be before we wish to use the records. Also, when blocking cannot be used, Relative I–O files may be inefficient. They are less efficient than sequential files for sequential access and thus should not be used unless random access is also required.

PROBLEMS

1. What is the main difficulty in addressing a Relative I–O file? Give an example where this difficulty is not a problem. Does your example use all of the file records?

2. Change the ACCOUNT-DIRECTORY file of Program 3.3 to a Relative I–O file.

3. In Problem 2, what difficulties will arise with your solution if new accounts are added? How would you solve these problems? Will you be able to obtain the trial balance order of accounts?

4. In Problem 2, suppose you want to maintain account detail rather than just summary totals. Devise a file layout. (You may make assumptions to obtain a solution.) Discuss the problems with your solution, if any, and comment on your assumptions as they affect the future of Profit Inc.'s accounting system.

5. Discuss the limitations of Relative I–O as you see them.

6. Discuss the advantages of Relative I–O as you see them.

7. Write a program to print the names and addresses of car owners. Use VEHICLE-FILE.

8. It is necessary to mail letters to the owners of 1976 Fords with rust problems. Write a program to produce a list of such owners in alphabetic order. Use VEHICLE-FILE.

7

Record
Addressing
Techniques

In Chapter 6 the concept of a relative file was introduced as one technique for organizing records on a storage device. Each record could be retrieved independently of the others in the file by determining its relative record number. This method requires that the relative position of a record in the file be known before it can be accessed. This is because the logical address used to fetch each record is its position *relative* to the first record of the file. Ignored in Chapter 6 was the burden on the file user of remembering each record's relative address. A user is seldom aware of the relative address of the record he wishes to access. Thus, the basic problem of file addressing is: Given a primary key, how does the program locate the record belonging to this primary key?

7.1 INTRODUCTION

Consider the following scenario: A police officer walking his beat, notices a Ford sedan parked in a No Parking Zone, across the street from the Farmer's Loan and Trust. The officer vaguely recalls a car of this description posted on the bulletin board detailing stolen vehicles. Realizing that he needs confirmation and should summon assistance, he quickly walks to the police call box on the corner and phones the station. To his dispatcher he reports the license number and a brief description of the vehicle.

The duty of the dispatcher is to query a file of stolen vehicles, to determine if this is indeed a stolen vehicle, and, if so, to alert nearby patrol cars. The dispatcher is confronted with several problems. If the vehicle is stolen, its record will be on the file, but where? If it is not stolen, it will not be on the file, but how is he to know? In both cases the answer can be determined by checking sequentially through every record on the file. This defeats the major reason for using relative files which is the direct access of a record or, alternatively, the determination of its absence. Thus the relative address must be known before *direct access* of a record can occur.

In applications programming, determining the relative record number of a given record can be more complex than simple recall. A relative record number is not usually fixed forever like a social security number. It is a function of the storage location of the record rather than its logical content. This address number will change if the record is relocated within the file or if the number of records between the beginning of the file and the record in question is altered during a recreation of the file. In addition, the record may not yet be a member of the file, and in this case there is no relative record number for it.

In this chapter, techniques will be developed to associate a relative record number with the primary key of each file record. We consider techniques that determine the relative key of a record in a file from the record key and determine whether or not a given record is a valid file member. The dynamic nature of a file largely determines the complexity of the method used to determine the relative key. Many methods only allow a limited amount of change and growth in a file; in some cases the file may be reorganized physically in a separate operation. Some techniques adapt better to periodic reorganization than others.

7.2 ADDRESS DETERMINATION

Although our immediate problem is to discover how to adapt relative addressing to more general file organizational problems than those posed in Chapter 6, methods of determining the address of a record have wide and essential uses in file processing. Such techniques are fundamental to data base design, and our discussion is by no means limited to relative files. The user of a file is only interested in the contents of the records and not in their physical locations. Knowledge of the physical location of a record is forced on the programmer, for instance, when he uses a relative file.

Whenever possible, *a user should be relieved of the burden of knowing a record's physical location.*

The essential problem is to provide a mapping from the set of all possible keys, called the *key space,* to the set of all possible addresses, called the *address space.* Although the mappings from key space to address space can be viewed as mathematical functions (recall that a discrete function is a set of ordered pairs), it should be noted that functions do not always have convenient representations such as those we see in algebra. This is further complicated by the fact that it is desirable for these address mappings to be dynamic, and consequently, the definition of a *function may be violated.* Thus, while at a static point in time an address mapping is a function on its key space, we cannot ignore time when considering real files. For convenience we may consider a dynamic address mapping as a parametric set of functions on the key space. If we use α to represent the mapping function at a given point in time, then we have the following:

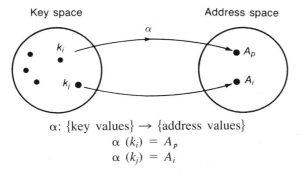

Key space   Address space

$$\alpha: \{\text{key values}\} \rightarrow \{\text{address values}\}$$
$$\alpha\,(k_i) = A_p$$
$$\alpha\,(k_j) = A_i$$

From an abstract view, the addressing problem is one of functional representation. The difficulty is that the functions we desire do not always have convenient and concise representations.

An interesting result from computational theory proves that all sets of strings can be represented by the positive integers. Thus, for our discussion, we can assume that the address space always consists of relative addresses.

There are two basic types of methods for locating a record, given its key: search and calculation. There are many ways to search a file but we only consider some basic methods. The simplest method of locating a file record is to access each record of the file and examine its record key for a match to the given key. Since this requires bringing each record into memory, it is crude and inefficient. It is more usual to keep a separate file of the record keys and associated record addresses. This key file takes less storage space than the file and it can often be stored in memory or in large storage blocks which can be brought into memory as required. This separate file is usually arranged as a table and has various names, such as "directory," "index," or "dictionary," depending on its form.

There are many ways to calculate an address from a key. Calculation attempts to convert a record key into an address by some sort of algorithm. When this can be done, it is faster than searching techniques. Unfortunately, direct conversion is not always possible and considerable complexity can then arise.

Each technique strongly affects the physical organization of data on the file, the speed of retrieval, and the problems of change associated with a dynamic file. The choice of technique is largely dependent on its characteristics and their resulting effect on the efficiency and performance of the file. In this chapter, we examine some of the better-known techniques and their relation to file organization. In particular, we examine in detail the important method of division hashing.

7.3 DIRECTORY TABLE

Conceptually, the most obvious solution to the problem of associating the primary key of each record with its relative record number is to keep a paired list of both. Such a list is shown in Fig 7.1, where the social security number of a citizen is kept alongside the relative record number where his record is stored. The advantage of the list is that it is smaller than the file and can be more efficiently manipulated in memory than the file. As this list takes more than one page, we have shown only a small segment. No doubt the reader has recognized this functional representation as exhaustive enumeration. If a request is made for detailed information on the citizen whose social security number is 400 70 0016, his record can be fetched from the social security file by specifying relative record number 16. This list is called a *directory*.

A directory may be created for an existing file by scanning the entire file and recording the record key (the social security number in the preceding example) of each record fetched, along with the corresponding relative record number. This directory is often kept sorted by the record key (as in Fig 7.1) to enhance searching it, and we then call it a *dictionary*.

KEY Social security number	ADDRESS Relative record number
.	.
.	.
.	.
400 70 0015	204
400 70 0016	16
400 70 0017	2016
400 70 0018	102462
400 70 0019	0
.	.
.	.
.	.

Figure 7.1   Directory table segment.

In the event that a directory is very large, it may be partitioned into smaller segments, a segment being brought into memory only when that segment must be searched. One way of storing such a segment is to make it a record of a relative file. Such segments should be large in order to reduce file accesses. Once a directory has been created, it can be searched to locate the relative record number of a desired record.

The advantages of a directory are as follows:

1. Once the record key is located, the performance is the same as a relative file.
2. Natural file keys can be used, as the mapping function is given by the directory table.
3. The record keys are logically independent of the relative keys and need not change.
4. The file space utilization is good because the mapping is flexible.

The performance of directory lookup depends only on the time to search and the time to reorganize the directory. The main disadvantages are periodic reorganization of the directory because of insertion and deletion, and poor search times compared to hashing methods discussed later. Because of the high file space utilization, this is a good method for relatively static files.

7.4 SEARCHING

An important class of addressing techniques involves searching. Two search techniques are in common use: the *linear search,* which does not require the directory to be sorted on the search key and the *binary search,* which assumes that it is sorted on the search key.

In a search, the value being sought is called the *argument*. When the argument is located within the directory by a search routine, a *match* is said to have occurred. If a directory contains social security numbers and the relative keys of records identified by these social security numbers, one would hunt for a given social security number (the argument of the search) and once it was located (a match), determine from the directory the associated relative key.

7.4.1 Linear Search

In a linear search, the argument is compared against each successive entry of the directory until a match occurs or the directory is exhausted. For every comparison that fails, we must ask: "Are we at the end of the directory?" This test is extremely important when the argument value is not present in the table because then the search would overrun the end of the directory. Thus two tests must normally be made at each step. "Do we have a match?" "Are we at the end of the directory?"

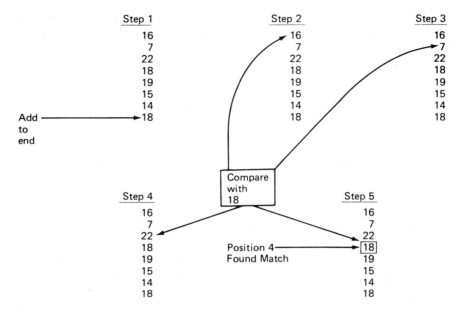

Figure 7.2 Linear search for segment 18.

If, however, we knew that a match for the argument would always occur, it would not be necessary to test for the end of the directory. This leads to a subtle improvement in the algorithm. If we place the argument at the end of the directory before beginning the search (as shown in Fig 7.2), then there will definitely be a match. When a match occurs, it remains to determine if the match has taken place at the end of the table. If so, the argument was not present in the directory; otherwise it has been located.

Figure 7.2 shows five steps in a linear search. Each column shows one stage in searching for the number 18 in an unsorted list. In step 1 the number 18 is added to the bottom of the list. In steps 2-5 the numbers, beginning with the top number 16, are compared sequentially until 18 is located in step 5.

Exercise

If we knew the list was sorted, how could we modify the linear search and the test in order to make the search more efficient when it fails?

7.4.2 Binary Search

In contrast to the linear search, the binary search requires that the directory be sorted, and we now refer to the directory as a *dictionary*. The binary search proceeds in the following manner assuming the dictionary is sorted in ascending order. First, the argument is compared to the entry at the midpoint of the dictionary (if there are an even number of entries in the dictionary, pretend there is one more and take the midpoint). If the argument matches, then the search is finished. If the argument is less than the midpoint, then the entry at the midpoint and all larger entries are ignored and the search is repeated with the half of the table that remains. If the argument is greater than the midpoint, the midpoint and all smaller entries are ignored and the search is repeated on the half of the table that remains. At each successive search, one half of the remaining elements are eliminated. This procedure continues until the match is discovered or all the elements of the dictionary have been eliminated. Binary search is a recursive procedure. Each time a recursive procedure is repeated, something changes, in this case, the number of elements left to search at each step.

The entire routine can be programmed very easily with the use of three integer variables which we shall call FIRST, LAST, and MIDDLE. FIRST always points to the location containing the smallest element and LAST points to the location of the largest element (in that portion of the table left to be searched). At the start of the procedure, FIRST points to the first entry in the dictionary (and therefore the smallest) and LAST to the last entry in the dictionary (and hence the largest). The midpoint is calculated from

$$\frac{FIRST + LAST}{2}$$

If the argument being sought is less than the midpoint entry of the dictionary, then, since the dictionary is sorted, a match to this argument can only occur in the lower half of the dictionary. The midpoint of the lower half of the dictionary is now similarly examined. The new midpoint is obtained by setting LAST to the previous value of MIDPOINT and once more calculating

$$\frac{FIRST + LAST}{2}$$

If, on the other hand, the argument is greater than the midpoint, only the upper half of the dictionary need be considered. FIRST should be reset to the current value of the midpoint and a new midpoint calculated. The algorithm halts when a match is obtained or the dictionary is exhausted.

An example of a binary search is shown in Fig 7.3, which indicates how 25 is located in a list of sorted numbers. The reader is urged to follow each step of the search. Note that the actual arithmetic is performed not on the elements of the array but on the index elements of the array. The reader should also spend a moment deciding how he would terminate the algorithm if 25 were missing from the array.

The binary search proceeds much more rapidly than the linear search because half of the list considered is removed at each step until a match occurs. Since a binary search appears to be more efficient than a linear search and not difficult to program, why is it not always preferred to a linear search?

The main reason is the need to sort the dictionary on the search key and the

```
Find 25 with binary search
     Index        1      2      3      4      5      6      7      8
     Array       16     22     25     26     30     32     33     34
Calculations
1. FIRST = 1, LAST = 8
2. Set quotient = (FIRST + LAST)/2 = (1 + 8)/2 = 4
3. Examine ARRAY(4)
4. Since 25 < 26 reset LAST = 4
5. Set quotient = (FIRST + LAST)/2 = (1 + 4)/2 = 2
6. Examine ARRAY(2)
     Index        1      2      3      4      5      6      7      8
     Array       16     22     25     26     30     32     33     34
7. Since 25 > 22 reset FIRST = 2
8. Set quotient = (FIRST + LAST)/2 = (2 + 4)/2 = 3
9. Examine ARRAY(3)
     Index        1      2      3      4      5      6      7      8
     Array       16     22     25     26     30     32     33     34
```

Figure 7.3 Binary search.

difficulty involved in keeping it sorted in a dynamic environment. Dynamic file situations often exist in which records are continually being added, moved, or deleted; the cost of continually sorting can soon negate any savings realized by a more efficient search. Since the amount of dynamic change can be difficult to predict, it may be simpler to use a linear search.

7.5 ALTERING DICTIONARIES

7.5.1 Linear Insertion

In order to avoid the expense entailed in sorting when a new entry is added to an already sorted dictionary, the programmer may choose a less expensive procedure called *linear insertion*. With this technique, an entry is added at its correct sorted location by moving the following entries down one position, hence avoiding sorting altogether. Let us assume that an entry is to be added to a table sorted in ascending order. The argument is compared first with the *largest* and then successively smaller entries in the dictionary. For each comparison that is greater than the argument, the dictionary value is moved down one position in the array, thereby creating a free slot. When a dictionary entry is located whose value is less than or equal to the argument, the argument is inserted and we are done.

The process is illustrated in the code of Fig 7.4, which compares the argument, data item A, with the elements of an array called DICTIONARY-TABLE whose current length is stored in the elementary item NUMBER-OF-ENTRIES. In this program segment, it has been assumed that the dictionary consists of both social security numbers and relative keys and that both of these items must be moved each

```
WORKING-STORAGE SECTION.
                .

                .

                .

01   DICTIONARY.
     02   NUMBER-OF-ENTRIES PIC9(3).
     02   DICTIONARY-TABLE
               OCCURS 100 TIMES.
          03   SOCIAL-SECURITY-NUMBER
               PIC 9(9).
          03   RELATIVE-KEY
               PIC S9(8)COMP SYNC.

                        .

                        .

                        .

PROCEDURE DIVISION.
          .

          .

          .
     MOVE NUMBER-OF-ENTRIES TO I.
     PERFORM LOCATE-A UNTIL
        A IS GREATER THAN OR EQUAL TO
        SOCIAL-SECURITY-NUMBER (I)
        OR I IS EQUAL TO 0.
     MOVE A TO SOCIAL-SECURITY-NUMBER(I + 1)
     MOVE NEW-RELATIVE-KEY TO
        RELATIVE-KEY(I + 1)
                   .

                   .

                   .

     LOCATE-A.
        MOVE SOCIAL-SECURITY-NUMBER(I)
        TO SOCIAL-SECURITY-NUMBER(I + 1)
        MOVE RELATIVE-KEY(I)
        TO RELATIVE-KEY(I + 1).
        COMPUTE I = I - 1.
                  .

                  .

                  .
```

Figure 7.4   Example of a program for linear insertion.

time an unsuccessful comparison takes place. Upon termination of the routine, both a new social security number and a relative key are inserted into the dictionary.

7.5.2 Deleting Records

Whenever a record is deleted from the file, its corresponding entry must be removed from the dictionary. Physical removal means leaving a gap, which must be compressed by moving all following entries up one table position. An alternative to this technique is simply to leave the dictionary entry present and set a flag that indicates that the record has been deleted. (The reader should determine how this affects the insertions of Fig 7.4.)

This can be effected by setting the corresponding relative key to -1 or by some other manner that is convenient to the user. Using this technique, the programmer can find the entry to be deleted by using a binary search. When this technique is used, a check must be made to ascertain whether the argument of a search, once found, is actually a deleted record. As the dictionary will eventually become dense with deleted entries, the dictionary should be reorganized from time to time to physically remove these elements.

7.6 CALCULATION ADDRESSING

There are numerous methods of converting a key into a file address. Unfortunately, for some methods the resulting record address need not be unique. Surprisingly, the nonunique methods are more useful because the direct methods are either difficult to determine or have inefficient characteristics.

7.6.1 Key-Equals-Address

In some applications the record key is itself the record address. Suppose we assign consecutive account numbers to records beginning with 1. Then, by using a relative file, the account number can be used as the relative address. Thus the record key equals the record address. We have already used this method of direct addressing in Chapter 6.

Unfortunately, in most applications this direct and simple approach is not practical for two main reasons. First, it is not possible to identify each record by an integer in a natural way. Second, when the address space is larger than the file size, many of the physical addresses will not be used. For instance, social security numbers are not suitable as relative addresses of a personnel file. (Why?) If a number is not a natural part of a file, it should not be used. (Why?) The major disadvantage of key-equals-address is that we must reserve a relative address for every potential record key and when these keys are not used, the space reserved is wasted.

The advantage of relative addressing is simplicity; because the address is given by the key value, this is the fastest address method. Because of low software overhead and the simplicity of implementation, it may be desirable to leave a large part of the physical file unused.

Exercise

Discuss vector data structure access with respect to key-equals-addressing.

7.6.2 Key Conversion Algorithm

In the event that the key cannot be used as the record address, it is sometimes possible to transform or map the keys into the record addresses by means of an algorithm, which is often just an algebraic formula. As this is also a form of direct addressing (key-equals-address is really just a special case), it has essentially the same advantages and disadvantages as that of key-equals-address.

Exercise

Discuss a vector data structure with symbolic indices and relate it to key conversion algorithm addressing.

7.6.3 Hashing

At first glance hashing resembles algorithmic conversion. The fundamental difference is that the result of hashing is not unique whereas the result of the algorithm method is. Hashing, in effect, operates like a pseudorandom number generator scattering consecutive keys in the address space and for this reason is often called *randomizing*.

Hashing is sometimes avoided on the grounds that it is too complex. When its advantages are considered, this is not so. Although record access is not as fast or as simple as direct methods, it can handle additions and insertions much more easily; and when properly designed, it generally has a much higher space utilization. With respect to search techniques and tables, it normally finds a record in one or two seeks. A major disadvantage is that sequential ordering of the key is lost.

There have been many techniques proposed for the hash transforms, and they have been studied and compared by many researchers, but a simple division method appears as good as any and better than most.[1] As it is beyond the scope of this text, we do not survey hashing techniques. Rather we concentrate on one specific technique, division hashing, and explore the problems associated with using a hashing transform along with some well-known solutions to them.

7.6.4 Division Hashing

A simple but effective method of hashing is based on the mathematical operation of division. In the following example we consider some of the aspects of division and in so doing develop division hashing.

Suppose we are given a group of 20 records with integer keys in the range of 150 to 200. Using a relative file, we could store each record at the relative address represented by the record key. However, at least 150 file locations will never be

[1]See, for instance, **P. G. Sorenson, J. P. Tremblay,** and **R. F. Deutscher,** "Key-to-Address Transformation Techniques," INFOR, 16, no. 1 (Feb. 1978), 1-33 and the references cited therein.

used and less than half of the remaining will store records. Let us further assume that at most 20 keys of the key space will ever be active.

To conserve space we would prefer to compress the address space of 50 values to 20 values. How can we convert record keys in the range 150–200 into relative addresses 1–20? We must attempt to discover an algorithm that maps a set of large numbers into a set of smaller numbers. One way large numbers are mapped to smaller numbers is through the operation of division. The decimal part of the result is meaningless as an address so we simply ignore it. The COBOL DIVIDE statement, you will recall, provides a quotient and a remainder. Ignoring the decimal result of division, we are left with the quotient.

The first difficulty is the choice of divisor. For a start, try the file size 20.

> DIVIDE KEY BY 20
> GIVING Q REMAINDER R.

Considering quotient $Q(150/20) = 7$, quotient $Q(160/20) = 8$, and quotient $Q(200/20) = 10$, we soon realize that only four quotients are possible. Why? Perhaps the divisor is too large. The smallest divisor that gives a quotient 20 as the maximum address is 10. Try it. Division does not appear to perform the compression of the key space we desire. Before giving up on division, let us tabulate (see Table 7.1) some results of divisor 20 on the key space to better understand what is happening.

As expected, the quotient is not of much use; however, the remainders run from 0 to 19, and by simply adding one we have the relative addresses from 1 to 20 as desired. There is only one problem; the remainders of 160, 180, and 200 are all zero. In fact, many other numbers have common remainders. But this is to be expected since we are mapping 50 numbers into 20 numbers. When two keys transform to the same address, we say a *hash collision* has occurred. The solution to this problem is known as a *hash resolution* technique. It reassigns the hash address when a collision occurs. We discuss several techniques in the following sections.

Our example illustrates the *division hashing* function, which, surprisingly, has survived considerable competition to emerge as the best all-around hashing function.

More formally, the division hashing function is expressed as

$$H(KEY) = KEY \bmod d + 1$$

where H (KEY) is the relative address, KEY the primary key of the record, and d a divisor chosen to give the desired range of relative addresses. If d is not chosen carefully, many hashing collisions can occur and the method then gives poor results. (The reader is urged to experiment on the above example for different choices of d.)

Table 7.1 An Example of Division Hashing

DIVIDE KEY BY 20	GIVING Q	REMAINDER R
150	7	10
151	7	11
152	7	12
153	7	13
154	7	14
155	7	15
156	7	16
157	7	17
158	7	18
159	7	19
160	8	0
161	8	1
162	8	2
.	.	.
.	.	.
.	.	.
170	8	10
.	.	.
.	.	.
.	.	.
180	9	0
.	.	.
.	.	.
.	.	.
190	9	10
.	.	.
.	.	.
.	.	.
200	10	0

7.6.5 Hashing Collisions

The basic problem with hash functions is that they usually are not unique or one-to-one. When $\alpha(k_j)$ is in use and $\alpha(k_i) = \alpha(k_j)$ for $k_i \neq k_j$, there is a hash collision and k_i cannot be stored at $\alpha(k_i)$. A hash resolution method must be available to restore a unique mapping of keys to addresses.

To minimize collisions we always attempt to choose a hash function with a uniform probability distribution of the function values. This is not always possible, so we must settle for a near-uniform function that works well on the most used set of keys. Research has indicated that, on average, division hashing is an excellent method where the divisor d is a prime or is relatively prime to the size of the address space and close to the number of file records. Also, the number of collisions that occur is smallest when there is no apparent ordering on the record keys.

The address space depends on the value of d. Given 20 records, should we actually choose an address space of this size? Choice of a prime d could be 19 or 23. As a general rule, to keep collisions under control, no more than 80% of the address space should be used. Since 20 is a little less than 80% of 29, a prime, an address space of 29 is a good choice.

Exercise

Examine the results of using divisors 29 and 61 in the preceding division hashing example.

The following steps should be used to choose an appropriate address space size as a divisor:

1. Estimate the number of file records; call this N.
2. Find the prime nearest 125% of N.

The basic problem with hashing is that hash collisions can occur and must be somehow resolved. Many good techniques have been developed to handle collisions, and the result is that hashing has become a very useful addressing technique. A hashing algorithm consists of two major parts: a hash function such as we have seen and a collision resolution method. A general rule for controlling hash collisions is that not more than 80% of the address space should be used, therefore this must be larger than the file size. Thus a hashing method will always have a large amount of unused space. In spite of collisions, hashing is very fast and the average number of accesses is generally less than 2; a good method will have 1.2–1.8 accesses on average. Hashing is very flexible in a dynamic file.

7.6.6 Resolving Hash Collisions

The difficulty with hashing, as we have noted, is that collisions are usually inevitable. When a collision occurs, the colliding record, called an *overflow record*, must be stored elsewhere. Two questions naturally arise: where is it to be stored, and once stored how can we retrieve it since hashing the key now gives an incorrect address?

An obvious solution to the first question is to find some free space within the file and to store the overflow record there. Overflow records are then said to be stored in the *prime area*. The problem that arises is that we create *indirect* collisions in two ways. First, in searching for space we have a *secondary* collision each time an examined record location is full. Second, if we store an overflow record in free space, the first record hashed to that space will have a collision. Because of the second problem, a separate overflow area is often created and used only to resolve collisions. This gives a natural classification of solutions into *prime area* and *overflow area* techniques. We next give several important examples of each kind of technique. The reader should be warned that the nature of real files is such that the discussion is necessarily incomplete and provides guideposts rather than a detailed map.

7.6.7 Open Addressing

If a record key is hashed to a record location that is full, a simple resolution strategy is a linear search of the file records until a free location is found. The overflow record is then inserted at this point. To retrieve this record the process is repeated until a match occurs. Such a search as a primary addressing technique would be very inefficient; it can give satisfactory results only because the hashing function varies the initial point of the search. As the number of collisions at a given point increases, the method decreases in efficiency because the following unhashed locations have been used and the search may become very long. This is accentuated as the locations searched are filled by searches that began at other collision points, and we have many secondary collisions. Various search sequences can be used. Since there may be no free space following the collision, the search must, in effect, wrap around to the beginning of the file.

A problem occurs in retrieving records if we previously deleted a record. Then, in searching for a record, we would not know if it were absent from the file until an empty record were found. Therefore, if we delete records, we must be careful not to mark them as empty otherwise the search must be exhaustive.

The advantages of this method are that records are stored in the prime area and that usually only a short seek time is necessary. Simplicity is a major argument that should not be ignored. The major disadvantage is that the adjacent areas may be full and many addresses examined before space is found. Also, multiple collisions will fill adjacent space causing a domino effect when primary collisions occur at the stolen space.

Examples of open addressing are given by Programs 7.1 and 7.2.

Program 7.1 Narrative.   The purpose of Program 7.1 is to build a hash table consisting of the relative record numbers of records in the VEHICLE-FILE. The index of a hash table entry is provided by applying the hashing algorithm to the associated VEHICLE-LICENSE. Hash collisions are resolved by open addressing; the first available slot following a collision is used to store the entry. In order to limit the number of hash collisions, the hash table has been set at size 200 although no more than 100 records are expected to be stored at any time.

If k is the VEHICLE-LICENSE, then n, the value of the index of the hash table entry associated with key k, is defined as

Program 7.1

```
00008          /   ** BUILDS HASH TABLE FOR VEHICLE-FILE **
00009
00010          INPUT-OUTPUT SECTION.
00011          FILE-CONTROL.
00012
00013              SELECT HASH-TABLE
00014                  ASSIGN TO DISK-TABLE
00015                  ORGANIZATION IS SEQUENTIAL
00016                  ACCESS MODE IS SEQUENTIAL.
00017              SELECT VEHICLE-FILE
00018                  ASSIGN TO DISK-LICENSE
00019                  ORGANIZATION IS RELATIVE
00020                  ACCESS MODE IS SEQUENTIAL
00021                  RELATIVE KEY IS VEHICLE-LICENSE-KEY.
00022
00023
00024          DATA DIVISION.
00025          FILE SECTION.
00026
00027          FD  HASH-TABLE
00028              LABEL RECORDS ARE STANDARD
00029              RECORD CONTAINS 400 CHARACTERS
00030              DATA RECORD IS HASH-TABLE-RECORD.
00031          01  HASH-TABLE-RECORD.
00032              02  TABLE-ENTRY              PIC S9(4) COMP SYNC
00033                      OCCURS 200 TIMES.
00034
00035          FD  VEHICLE-FILE
00036              RECORD CONTAINS 114 CHARACTERS
00037              LABEL RECORDS ARE STANDARD
00038              DATA RECORD IS VEHICLE-FILE-RECORD.
00039          01  VEHICLE-FILE-RECORD .
00040              02  FILLER                   PIC X(88).
00041              02  VEHICLE-LICENSE          PIC X(6).
00042              02  FILLER                   PIC X(20).
00043
00044
00045          WORKING-STORAGE SECTION.
00046
00047          77  EOF-FLAG                     PIC X(3).
00048              88  EOF                      VALUE IS 'ON'.
00049          77  I                            PIC S9(8) COMP SYNC.
00050          77  J                            PIC S9(8) COMP SYNC.
00051          77  K                            PIC S9(8) COMP SYNC.
00052          77  NUMBER-OF-TABLE-ENTRIES      PIC S9(8) COMP SYNC.
00053          77  PRIME-NUMBER                 PIC S9(8) COMP SYNC.
00054          77  VEHICLE-LICENSE-KEY          PIC S9(8) COMP SYNC.
00055
00056
00057          PROCEDURE DIVISION.
00058
00059              PERFORM INITIALIZATION.
00060              PERFORM HASHING-ROUTINE UNTIL EOF.
00061              PERFORM TERMINATION.
00062              STOP RUN.
00063
00064          INITIALIZATION.
00065              OPEN  INPUT   VEHICLE-FILE
00066                    OUTPUT HASH-TABLE.
00067              MOVE 197 TO PRIME-NUMBER.
00068              MOVE 200 TO NUMBER-OF-TABLE-ENTRIES.
00069              MOVE 'OFF' TO EOF-FLAG.
```

Program 7.1   (cont.)

```
00070                MOVE 1 TO VEHICLE-LICENSE-KEY.
00071                PERFORM INITIALIZE-TABLE-ENTRY
00072                    VARYING I FROM 1 BY 1
00073                    UNTIL I > NUMBER-OF-TABLE-ENTRIES.
00074                PERFORM READ-VEHICLE-FILE.
00075
00076            INITIALIZE-TABLE-ENTRY.
00077                MOVE -1 TO TABLE-ENTRY (I).
00078
00079            READ-VEHICLE-FILE.
00080                READ VEHICLE-FILE RECORD
00081                    AT END MOVE 'ON' TO EOF-FLAG.
00082
00083            HASHING-ROUTINE.
00084                TRANSFORM VEHICLE-LICENSE CHARACTERS
00085                    FROM 'ABCDEFGHIJKLMNOPQRSTUVWXYZ'
00086                    TO   '012345678901234567889012345'.
00087                MOVE VEHICLE-LICENSE TO K.
00088                DIVIDE K BY PRIME-NUMBER
00089                    GIVING   I
00090                    REMAINDER J.                .
00091                ADD 1 TO J.
00092                IF  TABLE-ENTRY (J) NOT = -1
00093                    PERFORM INCREMENT-COUNTER
00094                        UNTIL TABLE-ENTRY (J) = -1.
00095                MOVE VEHICLE-LICENSE-KEY TO TABLE-ENTRY (J).
00096                ADD 1 TO VEHICLE-LICENSE-KEY.
00097                PERFORM READ-VEHICLE-FILE.
00098
00099            INCREMENT-COUNTER.
00100                ADD 1 TO J.
00101                IF J > NUMBER-OF-TABLE-ENTRIES
00102                    SUBTRACT NUMBER-OF-TABLE-ENTRIES FROM J.
00103
00104            TERMINATION.
00105                WRITE HASH-TABLE-RECORD.
00106                CLOSE VEHICLE-FILE HASH-TABLE.
```

Program 7.2

```
00008            / ** READS VEHICLE-FILE GIVEN RELATIVE KEYS **
00009
00010            INPUT-OUTPUT SECTION.
00011            FILE-CONTROL.
00012
00013                SELECT HASH-TABLE
00014                    ASSIGN TO DISK-TABLE
00015                    ORGANIZATION IS SEQUENTIAL
00016                    ACCESS MODE IS SEQUENTIAL.
00017                SELECT INPUT-FILE
00018                    ASSIGN TO DISK-S-SYSIN
00019                    ORGANIZATION IS SEQUENTIAL
00020                    ACCESS MODE IS SEQUENTIAL.
00021                SELECT OUTPUT-FILE
00022                    ASSIGN TO PRNT-S-SYSOUT
00023                    ORGANIZATION IS SEQUENTIAL
00024                    ACCESS MODE IS SEQUENTIAL.
00025                SELECT VEHICLE-LICENSE-FILE
00026                    ASSIGN TO DISK-LICENSE
00027                    ORGANIZATION IS RELATIVE
00028                    ACCESS MODE IS RANDOM
```

Program 7.2 (cont.)

```
00029                     RELATIVE KEY IS VEHICLE-LICENSE-KEY.
00030
00031
00032           DATA DIVISION.
00033           FILE SECTION.
00034
00035       FD  HASH-TABLE
00036           LABEL RECORDS ARE STANDARD
00037           RECORD CONTAINS 400 CHARACTERS
00038           DATA RECORD IS HASH-TABLE-RECORD.
00039       01  HASH-TABLE-RECORD.
00040           02  TABLE-ENTRY             PIC S9(4) COMP SYNC
00041               OCCURS 200 TIMES.
00042
00043       FD  INPUT-FILE
00044           LABEL RECORDS ARE OMITTED
00045           RECORD CONTAINS 80 CHARACTERS
00046           DATA RECORD IS INPUT-RECORD.
00047       01  INPUT-RECORD.
00048           02  SEARCH-KEY             PIC X(6).
00049           02  FILLER                PIC X(74).
00050
00051       FD  OUTPUT-FILE
00052           LABEL RECORDS ARE OMITTED
00053           RECORD CONTAINS 133 CHARACTERS
00054           DATA RECORD IS OUTPUT-RECORD.
00055       01  CJTPUT-RECORD.
00056           02  FILLER                PIC X.
00057           02  OUTPUT-DATA           PIC X(132).
00058
00059       FD  VEHICLE-LICENSE-FILE
00060           RECORD CONTAINS 114 CHARACTERS
00061           LABEL RECORDS ARE STANDARD
00062           DATA RECORD IS VEHICLE-LICENSE-FILE-RECORD.
00063       01  VEHICLE-LICENSE-FILE-RECORD .
00064           02  FILLER                PIC X(88).
00065           02  VEHICLE-LICENSE       PIC X(6).
00066           02  FILLER                PIC X(20).
00067
00068
00069           WORKING-STORAGE SECTION.
00070
00071       77  END-OF-SEARCH-FLAG         PIC X(3).
00072           88  EOS                   VALUE IS 'ON'.
00073       77  EOF-FLAG                   PIC X(3).
00074           88  EOF                   VALUE IS 'ON'.
00075       77  FOUND-FLAG                 PIC X(3).
00076           88  FOUND                 VALUE IS 'ON'.
00077       77  I                          PIC S9(8) COMP SYNC.
00078       77  J                          PIC S9(8) COMP SYNC.
00079       77  NUMBER-OF-TABLE-ENTRIES    PIC S9(8) COMP SYNC.
00080       77  PRIME-NUMBER               PIC S9(8) COMP SYNC.
00081       77  VEHICLE-LICENSE-KEY        PIC S9(8) COMP SYNC.
00082
00083       01  OUTPUT-LINE.
00084           02  FIRST-PART            PIC X(38).
00085           02  TEMPORARY-KEY         PIC X(6).
00086           02  NUMERIC-KEY REDEFINES TEMPORARY-KEY
00087                                     PIC 9(6).
00088
00089
00090           PROCEDURE DIVISION.
00091
00092               PERFORM INITIALIZATION.
```

Program 7.2 (cont.)

```
00093                    PERFORM SEARCH-ROUTINE UNTIL EOF.
00094                    PERFORM TERMINATION.
00095                    STOP RUN.
00096
00097          INITIALIZATION.
00098                    OPEN   INPUT   INPUT-FILE HASH-TABLE
00099                           OUTPUT OUTPUT-FILE
00100                           I-O    VEHICLE-LICENSE-FILE.
00101                    MOVE 'OFF' TO EOF-FLAG.
00102                    MOVE 197 TO PRIME-NUMBER.
00103                    MOVE 200 TO NUMBER-OF-TABLE-ENTRIES.
00104                    MOVE 'THE GIVEN VEHICLE LICENSE NUMBER IS '
00105                         TO FIRST-PART.
00106                    READ HASH-TABLE RECORD.
00107                    PERFORM READ-INPUT-FILE.
00108
00109          READ-INPUT-FILE.
00110                    READ INPUT-FILE RECORD
00111                         AT END MOVE 'ON' TO EOF-FLAG.
00112
00113          SEARCH-ROUTINE.
00114               MOVE 'OFF' TO END-OF-SEARCH-FLAG FOUND-FLAG.
00115               MOVE SEARCH-KEY TO TEMPORARY-KEY.
00116               MOVE OUTPUT-LINE TO OUTPUT-DATA.
00117               WRITE OUTPUT-RECORD AFTER ADVANCING 2 LINES.
00118               TRANSFORM TEMPORARY-KEY CHARACTERS
00119                    FROM 'ABCDEFGHIJKLMNOPQRSTUVWXYZ'
00120                    TO   '01234567890123456789012345'.
00121               DIVIDE NUMERIC-KEY BY PRIME-NUMBER
00122                    GIVING   I
00123                    REMAINDER J.
00124               ADD 1 TO J.
00125               PERFORM RECORD-RETRIEVAL-ROUTINE.
00126               IF  NOT EOS
00127                    IF  VEHICLE-LICENSE = SEARCH-KEY
00128                         MOVE 'ON' TO END-OF-SEARCH-FLAG FOUND-FLAG
00129                         ELSE
00130                         PERFORM CONTINUE-SEARCH UNTIL EOS.
00131               IF  FOUND
00132                    MOVE VEHICLE-LICENSE-FILE-RECORD TO OUTPUT-DATA
00133                    WRITE OUTPUT-RECORD AFTER ADVANCING 1 LINES
00134                    ELSE
00135                    MOVE '* NOTE * RECORD NOT IN FILE.'
00136                         TO OUTPUT-DATA
00137                    WRITE OUTPUT-RECORD AFTER ADVANCING 1 LINES.
00138               PERFORM READ-INPUT-FILE.
00139
00140          RECORD-RETRIEVAL-ROUTINE.
00141               MOVE TABLE-ENTRY (J) TO VEHICLE-LICENSE-KEY.
00142               READ VEHICLE-LICENSE-FILE RECORD
00143                    INVALID KEY MOVE 'ON' TO END-OF-SEARCH-FLAG.
00144
00145          CONTINUE-SEARCH.
00146               ADD 1 TO J.
00147               IF  J > NUMBER-OF-TABLE-ENTRIES
00148                    SUBTRACT NUMBER-OF-TABLE-ENTRIES FROM J.
00149               PERFORM RECORD-RETRIEVAL-ROUTINE.
00150               IF  NOT EOS
00151                    IF  VEHICLE-LICENSE = SEARCH-KEY
00152                         MOVE 'ON' TO END-OF-SEARCH-FLAG FOUND-FLAG.
00153
00154          TERMINATION.
00155               CLOSE INPUT-FILE HASH-TABLE OUTPUT-FILE
00156                    VEHICLE-LICENSE-FILE.
```

$$n \equiv k \bmod 197 + 1$$

That is, n is the remainder $+1$ when the key k is divided by the prime number 197. We select 197 as a prime less than 200.

During initialization the entire hash table of 200 entries is set to -1. The program reads a record of the VEHICLE-FILE, hashes the VEHICLE-LICENSE, and stores the record's relative key in the hash table. The file is processed sequentially. Processing terminates on end-of-file.

Because each license number consists of alphabetic characters and digits, the alphabetic characters are transformed into digits by means of the non-ANSI standard COBOL verb TRANSFORM available in IBM OS/VS COBOL. If this verb is not available, then a small program segment will need to be written.

Because this program is used for illustration only, error checking has not been provided. The reader should see the problems at the end of the chapter.

Program 7.2 Narrative

The purpose of Program 7.2 is to read vehicle license numbers and retrieve the corresponding records from the VEHICLE-FILE. If the record cannot be found, a message is printed. Processing is terminated when end-of-file is reached.

As each vehicle license number is read, it is hashed using the method described in Program 7.1. When a record is retrieved, its license number is compared with that given. If equal, the record is printed; otherwise, open addressing is used to fetch another record. The search of records halts when the record is found or a -1, denoting an empty entry, forces execution of the INVALID KEY clause on an attempt to read.

Note that the VEHICLE-FILE is processed with ACCESS MODE IS RANDOM.

7.6.8 Chaining

There are numerous chaining techniques. Our discussion is limited to *separate chaining* which places the overflow records in a separate overflow area; this avoids the problem of indirect collisions that occur in open addressing when locations are occupied. Chaining consists of creating a linear list of overflow records for a hash collision. We may regard the hash function as pointing to a list rather than a record. Each record in the prime area represents the head of the list.

As discussed in Chapter 1, a list is connected by pointers and each record must have a pointer field. To indicate the end of the list, a null pointer is used, and the primary records must be created with the null pointer in the pointer field. When an overflow occurs, follow the pointers to reach the record with the null pointer. A free record is obtained from the overflow area by a suitable algorithm and added to the end of the chain by replacing the null pointer with the address of this record. The pointer of the new record must be set to null. We may create the overflow records with null pointers or set the pointers when the records are used; it may be wise to do both.

It is easy to delete a record from the list (in Chapter 13 are detailed instructions, but you should be able to figure it out), and the record location should be made available for future use. To retrieve a record from a chained file, the following steps should be taken:

1. Hash the record key to obtain a relative address.
2. Fetch the record at that relative address. If the search key equals the record key, then stop; the record is in the file. Otherwise, continue.
3. If the pointer field is not null, do step 2 again using the pointer to get the next relative address. Otherwise, stop; the record is not in the file.

Chaining is more complicated than open addressing. Since the overflow area will not be near the original collision, a second disk access is necessary. (Note that there are also chaining methods that embed the overflow areas nearby in the prime area to reduce disk accesses.) However, we should note that in open addressing, clustering can cause nearby records to fill, increasing disk accesses. Since chains can be reordered easily, those records with a high probability of access can be moved to the front of the list. A simple strategy is to move a record up one list position toward the front of the list each time it is accessed.

7.7 ADDITIONAL ADDRESSING TECHNIQUES

7.7.1 The Bucket Concept

Until now we have considered mappings that obtain the desired address directly. In actual practice, hashing methods are not as straightforward, and it is more usual to address a group of records, commonly referred to as a *bucket*. The group of records associated with a single address acts as an adjacent overflow area. The obvious danger in reserving an overflow for each address is unused space when no collisions occur; however, by using consecutive spill addressing, a bucket can receive the overflow of other buckets. We leave the details to the reader. Alternatively, the hashing algorithm can be chosen to ensure ample collisions and pointers to overflow buckets used when the primary bucket is full. This combines spill addressing and chaining. There are indeed many techniques that attempt to handle hash collisions efficiently. Ultimately, the choice of technique depends on the file characteristics and the system design criteria. Analysis of what is best is always difficult.

7.7.2 Directory of Free Space

When many of the buckets are full, unnecessary searching is performed. One method of avoiding further searching is to use a directory of free space, which points to those buckets that have available space. When a bucket with space is found, a pointer to it is placed in the source bucket. The disadvantage of this method is the necessity of updating the directory when additions and deletions change the bucket full status. Also, space is required to store the pointers, and pointer overflow destroys the simplicity of record access. The advantage is that at most two bucket accesses are required for reading. Large bucket sizes are preferred. Why?

As a simple method, we suggest a full flag indicator for each bucket. This avoids a complete search of a full bucket; thus, we spill by bucket rather than record until a free bucket is reached. The flag updating is simple. Again, larger buckets improve the efficiency.

7.7.3 Optimization

Since it is apparent that overflow records take longer to access, frequently accessed records with primary and secondary collisions can seriously degrade file performance. One solution is to load the file in decreasing order of use. However, because of the nature of files, this is not usually possible because either the usage is not known or the file grows, changing the usage patterns. If a usage counter is placed in a record field, then usage statistics can be obtained and the file periodically reorganized. The cost of such statistics should first be related to the cost of using excess space to reduce collisions.

7.8 CONCLUSION

The efficiency of the various hashing methods is highly dependent on the file characteristics. The difficulty in using hashing is in choosing good methods that best exploit the characteristics of the file in use. Many hashing functions have been investigated. Midsquare hashing and hashing by folding can sometimes perform better than division hashing but can also lead to many collisions in some cases. Unless the designer can justify another method, division hashing can be expected to give the best overall performance. Certainly it should always be chosen as a benchmark method.

Indeed, analysis of a dynamic file is difficult and hazardous. In lieu of firm knowledge, we would suggest simple and known techniques. There is a definite danger in being too clever.

When it is clear that the simple techniques are not sufficient, the file can be analyzed empirically, based on usage and structure. We would suggest redesign in the context of the actual computing environment rather than complex analysis of what may well be fictional expectations. There are no hard and fast rules but we believe that it is better to lean to the side of simplicity rather than that of complexity.

REFERENCES FOR FURTHER READING

Lum, V. Y. "General Performance Analysis of Key-to-Address Transformation Methods Using an Abstract File Concept," *CACM* 16 (October 1973): 603–612.

Maurer, W. D., and Lewis, T. G. "Hash Table Methods." *ACM Computing Surveys* 7 (March 1975).

Morris, R. "Scatter-Storage Techniques," *CACM* 11 (January 1968): 38–44.

Scholl, M. "New File Organizations Based on Dynamic Hashing." *ACM T. Database Sy.* (March 1981): 194–211.

Sorenson, P. G.; Trembley, S.P.; and Deutscher, R. F. "Key-to-Address Transformation Techniques," *INFOR* 16 (February 1978).

PROBLEMS

1. We have noted that in studying addressing it can be assumed that the address space consists of integers from 1 to n. Why have we not done this for the key space?

2. (a) What is the disadvantage of a binary search?

(b) Could you overcome this disadvantage by using a linked list as the data structure?

3. Your boss tells you to provide a procedure to assign storage in a vector where the address space is of size 1000. Unfortunately, budget restrictions only permit him to give you a vector of size 99.

(a) How do you reply to this?

(b) Your boss explains as follows, "But only about 50 elements are ever in the address space at any given time." What do you do?

4. Develop an algorithm to perform consecutive spill addressing in the primary area when buckets are used.

5. Develop an algorithm with chaining on buckets.

6. Suppose that the consecutive spill technique was used as the addressing scheme.

(a) For N records in the file, what does the average time to access a record depend on, and what does the average time to store a new record depend on, assuming no deletions? Can you provide a formula?

(b) Compare this method to sequential addressing.

7. Suppose you have an existing sequential file that you wish to change to a direct Relative I–O file with hash addressing. How would you go about it?

8. Devise algorithms for consecutive spill addressing with buckets.

9. Evaluate and compare two transforms on the address space of even numbers from 4000 to 6000, using

$$H(x) = x \bmod m + 1 \quad \text{for } m_1 = 2000 \text{ and } m_2 = 6001$$

10. In order to fetch a record using the open address hash algorithm of Program 7.1, a key must be hashed. Once the key is hashed, the hash value is used as an index into an array that contains record addresses. The record address in the form of a relative record number is used to fetch the record. Once the record is fetched, the key within it is checked against the original key to see whether or not the fetch was successful. An alternative is to keep the record key in the hash table along with the relative address. This way the record need not be fetched unless the keys match, thereby saving I/O time.

(a) Modify Program 7.1 to include this feature.

(b) Modify Program 7.2 to fetch records in accordance with your modification for part (a).

11. Modify Program 7.1 and 7.2 to permit a record on the file to be deleted. Be careful your modification does not interfere with the algorithm's ability to detect a missing record or locate one that is already there.

12. Change your solution to problem 10 to allow for record deletions.

13. Rewrite Programs 7.1 and 7.2 to use chaining of records instead of open addressing to resolve hash collisions.

IBM
Direct File
Organization

The file organization method discussed in this chapter is an IBM-designed file organization that does not conform to the specifications of ANSI COBOL but is available in the IBM OS/VS COBOL compiler. Other manufacturers have provided similar mechanisms for direct access. On the first reading this chapter may be skipped. You would not normally use this file organization because relative files can be used instead. However, the sophisticated file user should be acquainted with it, much as a high-level language user can benefit from an awareness of the machine assembler language.

8.1 INTRODUCTION

In comparison to relative file organization, direct file organization emphasizes the direct access storage device on which the records of a file are stored rather than the order of the records themselves. Any software that provides a file organization on disk must perform the kinds of elementary steps that we discuss here, although they need not be described in COBOL.

Of specific importance is the physical storage unit, called the *track*. A track is that storage section of a disk unit that passes under a Read/Write head when the disk undergoes one revolution. An integral number of tracks are required to store any given file.

On a disk, the tracks assigned to a file are numbered in increasing sequence beginning with zero, and this provides the track address. In order to store a record, a track number must be specified; this number is referred to as the *track identifier*. Most often the physical record size permits more than one record to be stored on a given track, and for this reason each record is also identified by a unique key, called the *record identifier*. A track identifier and a record identifier uniquely determine a physical record of the file on the storage device; consequently, the track identifier and the record identifier are combined to form a unique key designated as the AC-TUAL KEY.

In order to use the direct file organization, it is necessary to determine for the file the track on which each record will be stored and to designate a unique identifier for each record. As this requires at the outset much more involvement with storage details than is required with Relative I–O, it is fair to ask why direct file organization is used at all. First, historically, it preceded relative addressing; that is, the implementation of Relative I–O was completed after direct file organization was already in use. Second, the move from direct to relative addressing was an early move toward the data base concept of isolation from the system hardware. Third, as a programmer you may often run into the problem of looking at someone else's code, in which case an acquaintance with direct addressing may well be necessary. In addition, the current version of the IBM direct file organization *permits* variable-length records, whereas the IBM relative file organization does not. An IBM direct file can be created either sequentially or randomly.

8.2 CREATION OF A DIRECT FILE

8.2.1 The SELECT Clause Entry

A typical SELECT clause for a direct file being created sequentially is

```
SELECT file-name
ASSIGN TO DA-DISK-D-DD1
ACCESS MODE IS SEQUENTIAL
ACTUAL KEY IS data-name
TRACK-LIMIT IS integer.
```

The system name DA-DISK-D-DD1 indicates that this is a direct access (DA) file, stored on a disk (DISK) unit, with the direct file organization (D), and with the name DD1 as the system name of this file.

The ACCESS MODE IS SEQUENTIAL clause specifies that this file will be accessed sequentially. The ACTUAL KEY clause names *data-name* as a data area within the WORKING-STORAGE SECTION that will provide the track and record identifier for each record. The TRACK-LIMIT clause is optional and informs the system that when the file is closed, enough dummy records are to be written to create a file using *integer* tracks. If the file already contains more than this number of tracks, the clause is ignored.

The process of writing the initial data or dummy records onto a track is called *formatting* the track. If the user does not write records on to one or more tracks of the file or force the system to write dummy records for him (by using the TRACK-LIMIT clause), any tracks assigned to the file but not formatted are unusable. For example, suppose a user creates a file of 500 tracks, does not supply a TRACK-LIMIT clause, writes 100 tracks, and then closes the file. Then the 400 leftover tracks allocated to the file remain but might not be usable. If a TRACK-LIMIT clause of the form

```
                    TRACK-LIMIT IS 500
```

is written, all the remaining 400 tracks can be used.

8.2.2 The ACTUAL KEY Entry

The track identifier and the record identifier constitute the ACTUAL KEY of each record. This key is a group item of the WORKING-STORAGE SECTION and might be defined as

```
          01 THE-ACTUAL-KEY
             02 TRACK-IDENTIFIER
                PIC S9(8)
                COMPUTATIONAL
                SYNCHRONIZED.
             02 RECORD-IDENTIFIER
                PIC X(10).
```

The data names shown here are user-defined COBOL words. The first part of the ACTUAL KEY must be reserved for the track identifier and must be described as a PIC S9(8) COMPUTATIONAL SYNCHRONIZED item. The record identifier portion can be defined in any manner by the programmer but must be at least 1 byte in length and not exceed 255.

When a record is to be written to the direct access file during sequential file creation, the track on which the record is to be written must be moved to the track identifier portion of the actual key and its unique distinguishing key placed in the record identifier portion. The record identifier need not also be stored within the logical record itself as the record identifier is placed alongside the record within the file automatically by the operating system. Placing it within the logical content of the record will cause two copies of the record identifier to be kept on the file. When a record is written to the file, its track identifier is returned in the ACTUAL KEY on the completion of a successful WRITE. On sequential output, the system automatically increments the track identifier whenever it is forced to advance to another track in order to store a record. The user need not advance it manually.

If a user wished to place some intervening dummy records between two records on the file, say records A and B, he should first write record A and then advance the ACTUAL KEY by the desired number of intervening tracks of dummy records and then write record B. For example, suppose record A is written as a record on track 10. If the user increments the track identifier to 20 and then writes record B, the system will first write dummy records to fill track 10, write dummy records onto tracks 11 through 19, and then write record B as the first record on track 20.

A dummy record for files with fixed-length records has undefined content, but the first byte of the record identifier is HIGH-VALUES. When the user is writing variable-length records and requests the insertion of dummy records by the method indicated above, no actual record is written to the file by the system; however, some control information is placed on each track to indicate the capacity that remains to store data. This "capacity record" is updated whenever the user writes data to a given track.

Program 8.1 Narrative. The purpose of Program 8.1 is to read input data and to store it on a *direct access* file. Two data records supply the information for

Program 8.1

```
00008          / ** LOADS A DIRECT ACCESS FILE **
00009
00010             INPUT-OUTPUT SECTION.
00011             FILE-CONTROL.
00012
00013                 SELECT INPUT-FILE
00014                     ASSIGN TO CARD-SYSIN
00015                     ACCESS MODE IS SEQUENTIAL
00016                     ORGANIZATION IS SEQUENTIAL.
00017                 SELECT OUTPUT-FILE
00018                     ASSIGN TO DA-DISK-D-DD1
00019                     ACCESS IS RANDOM
00020                     TRACK-LIMIT IS 12
00021                     ACTUAL KEY IS THE-ACTUAL-KEY.
00022
00023
00024             DATA DIVISION.
00025             FILE SECTION.
00026
00027             FD  INPUT-FILE
00028                     BLOCK CONTAINS 1 RECORDS
00029                     LABEL RECORDS ARE OMITTED
00030                     RECORD CONTAINS 80 CHARACTERS
00031                     DATA RECORD IS INPUT-FILE-RECORD.
00032             01  INPUT-FILE-RECORD.
00033                 02  FILLER                      PIC X(80).
00034
00035             FD  OUTPUT-FILE
00036                     LABEL RECORDS ARE STANDARD
00037                     RECORD CONTAINS 100 CHARACTERS
```

Program 8.1   (cont.)

```
00038                    DATA RECORD IS OUTPUT-FILE-RECORD.
00039            01   OUTPUT-FILE-RECORD.
00040                 02   LICENSE-NUMBER            PIC 9(6).
00041                 02   MAKE-OF-VEHICLE           PIC X(15).
00042                 02   YEAR-OF-MODEL             PIC 9(2).
00043                 02   COLOUR                    PIC X(9).
00044                 02   TYPE-OF-CAR               PIC X(6).
00045                 02   DATE-STOLEN               PIC 9(6).
00046                 02   OWNER-ADDRESS             PIC X(18).
00047                 02   CITY                      PIC X(10).
00048                 02   STATE-OR-PROVINCE         PIC X(7).
00049                 02   OWNER                     PIC X(16).
00050                 02   FILLER                    PIC X(5).
00051
00052
00053        WORKING-STORAGE SECTION.
00054
00055            77   HASH-QUOTIENT             PIC S9(8) COMP SYNC.
00056            77   HASH-REMAINDER            PIC S9(8) COMP SYNC.
00057            77   INPUT-FILE-EOF            PIC X(3).
00058                 88   END-OF-FILE-IF VALUE IS 'ON'.
00059            77   OVERFLOW-RECORD-FULL-FLAG   PIC X(3).
00060                 88 OVERFLOW-RECORD-FULL VALUE IS 'ON'.
00061            77   OVERFLOW-TRACK-NO         PIC S9(5) COMP SYNC
00062                    VALUE IS +11.
00063
00064            01   CARD-IN-FORMAT-1.
00065                 02   MAKE-OF-VEHICLE           PIC X(15).
00066                 02   YEAR-OF-MODEL             PIC 9(2).
00067                 02   OWNER                     PIC X(16).
00068                 02   LICENSE-NUMBER            PIC 9(6).
00069                 02   DATE-REPORTED             PIC 9(6).
00070                 02   OWNER-ADDRESS             PIC X(18).
00071                 02   CITY                      PIC X(10).
00072                 02   STATE-OR-PROVINCE         PIC X(7).
00073
00074            01   CARD-IN-FORMAT-2.
00075                 02   COLOUR                    PIC X(9).
00076                 02   TYPE-OF-CAR               PIC X(6).
00077                 02   FILLER                    PIC X(65).
00078
00079            01   THE-ACTUAL-KEY.
00080                 02   TRACK-IDENTIFIER          PIC S9(5) COMP SYNC.
00081                 02   KEY-OF-RECORD             PIC X(6).
00082
00083
00084        PROCEDURE DIVISION.
00085
00086                PERFORM INITIALIZATION.
00087                PERFORM READ-AND-STORE-RECORD
00088                    UNTIL END-OF-FILE-IF OR
00089                        OVERFLOW-RECORD-FULL.
00090                PERFORM TERMINATION.
00091                STOP RUN.
00092
00093        INITIALIZATION.
00094            MOVE 'OFF' TO OVERFLOW-RECORD-FULL-FLAG.
00095            MOVE 'OFF' TO INPUT-FILE-EOF.
00096            OPEN INPUT INPUT-FILE.
00097            OPEN OUTPUT OUTPUT-FILE.
00098            PERFORM READ-ROUTINE.
00099
00100        READ-ROUTINE.
```

Program 8.1 (cont.)

```
00101                    READ INPUT-FILE RECORD
00102                        INTO CARD-IN-FORMAT-1
00103                        AT END MOVE 'ON' TO INPUT-FILE-EOF.
00104                    IF NOT END-OF-FILE-IF THEN
00105                        READ INPUT-FILE RECORD
00106                            INTO CARD-IN-FORMAT-2
00107                            AT END MOVE 'ON' TO INPUT-FILE-EOF.
00108
00109            READ-AND-STORE-RECORD.
00110                MOVE CORRESPONDING CARD-IN-FORMAT-1
00111                        TO OUTPUT-FILE-RECORD.
00112                MOVE CORRESPONDING CARD-IN-FORMAT-2
00113                        TO OUTPUT-FILE-RECORD.
00114                PERFORM HASH-ROUTINE.
00115
00116            HASH-ROUTINE.
00117                DIVIDE 11 INTO LICENSE-NUMBER
00118                    OF OUTPUT-FILE-RECORD
00119                    GIVING HASH-QUOTIENT
00120                    REMAINDER HASH-REMAINDER.
00121                MOVE HASH-REMAINDER TO TRACK-IDENTIFIER.
00122                MOVE LICENSE-NUMBER OF OUTPUT-FILE-RECORD
00123                    TO KEY-OF-RECORD.
00124                WRITE OUTPUT-FILE-RECORD
00125                    INVALID KEY PERFORM OVERFLOW-ROUTINE.
00126                PERFORM READ-ROUTINE.
00127
00128            OVERFLOW-ROUTINE.
00129                MOVE OVERFLOW-TRACK-NO TO TRACK-IDENTIFIER.
00130                WRITE OUTPUT-FILE-RECORD
00131                    INVALID KEY DISPLAY 'OVERFLOW RECORD FULL'
00132                    MOVE 'ON' TO OVERFLOW-RECORD-FULL-FLAG.
00133
00134            TERMINATION.
00135                CLOSE INPUT-FILE
00136                      OUTPUT-FILE.
```

one 100-byte record on the file called OUTPUT-FILE. It is created in the random access mode. The ACTUAL KEY is called THE-ACTUAL-KEY and contains a full word TRACK-IDENTIFIER declared as a computational synchronized item and a record identifier called KEY-OF-RECORD declared as a 6-byte display item.

TRACK-LIMIT IS 12 has been specified asking the operating system to format 12 tracks when the file is opened for output. These tracks are labeled 0 through 11. It has been decided that track 11 will be used to store overflow records caused by hash collisions.

Since each record of the file requires a track identifier from 0 to 10, the record key is divided by 11 and the remainder used as the track identifier. If a record cannot be stored on its designated track, an attempt is made to store it on track 11. Failing this, an ''OVERFLOW RECORD FULL'' message is printed and processing is terminated.

Note that this is a simplified version of the hashing algorithm used in Chapter 7. No hash table has been included. Here a bucket (track 11) has been used to store all overflow records. In Chapter 7, hashing collisions were resolved by storing their relative keys at open locations in the hash table.

8.2.3 The FD Entry: Defining the File

An IBM direct access file can support variable-length or fixed-length records, but records cannot be blocked. FD entries have either of two forms:

Fixed-Length Records

```
FD file-name
    LABEL RECORDS ARE STANDARD
    RECORD CONTAINS integer CHARACTERS
    DATA RECORD IS record-name.
01 record-name.
    02 etc.
```

Variable-Length Records

```
FD file-name
  LABEL RECORDS ARE STANDARD
  RECORD CONTAINS integer1 TO integer2 CHARACTERS
  DATA RECORDS ARE record-name1, record-name2, . . . .
01 record-name1.
    02 etc.
01 record-name2.
    02 etc.
01   . . .
```

It is assumed for variable-length records that at least two of the records described have different lengths or that an OCCURS DEPENDING ON clause is used within at least one of the record descriptions. (Refer to Chapter 3, where variable-length records are discussed in detail.)

8.2.4 Procedure Division Statements

The OPEN Statement

The OPEN statement for reading a sequentially accessed direct file is

```
OPEN INPUT file-name
```

and for writing is

```
OPEN OUTPUT file-name
```

The READ Statement

The general format of the READ statement for sequential access is

```
READ file-name [INTO data-name]
    AT END imperative statement
```

Here *file-name* is the name of the file, and *data-name* names a data area within the WORKING-STORAGE SECTION to which the record read from the file is to be moved with a group MOVE if this optional INTO statement is employed.

The *imperative statement* following the AT END clause is invoked whenever an attempt is made to read beyond end-of-file.

The WRITE Statement

The standard form of the WRITE statement is

```
WRITE record-name [FROM data-name]
    INVALID KEY imperative statement.
```

where *record-name* is the name of the level 01 entry within the FD describing the file, and *data-name* is the name of an area within the WORKING-STORAGE SECTION that is to undergo a group MOVE to the FD or buffer area of the file. The FROM clause is optional.

The *imperative statement* following the INVALID KEY clause is invoked if an attempt is made to write a record beyond the physical boundary of the file. Note very carefully that this clause is not invoked if an attempt is made to write a record to the file with the same record identifier as one already written on the current track or on any other. During random access processing the software is only capable of retrieving the first record on a track with a given record identifier thus making other records with the same record identifier on that track not retrievable. They can, however, be retrieved when the file is read sequentially.

The CLOSE Statement

```
CLOSE file-name
```

This statement causes an end-of-file marker to be placed on the file after formatting any tracks as required by a TRACK-LIMIT clause.

8.3 RANDOM ACCESS OF A DIRECT FILE

Creating a direct file in the random access mode is quite different from creating one in the sequential mode. The major difference is that the tracks must be first formatted, this process being accomplished as part of the OPEN routine rather than during the CLOSE as is the case with sequential creation. For this reason the presence of the TRACK-LIMIT clause takes on greater importance. If the TRACK-

LIMIT clause is present, the number of tracks specified is automatically formatted (that is, either dummy or capacity records are written onto the file). If the clause is not present, only the primary allocation is formatted. Unused tracks specified as secondary allocation are not formatted. Once the tracks are formatted, the user is free to write data records onto the track locations of his choice.

8.3.1.The SELECT Clause Entry

The general format of the SELECT clause entry is

```
SELECT file-name
ASSIGN TO DA-DISK-D-DD1
ACCESS MODE IS RANDOM
ACTUAL KEY IS data-name.
```

The file access is now stated as random by ACCESS MODE IS RANDOM.

When the file is opened for I–O, the system name may optionally be written as DA-DISK-W-DD1 with a "W" replacing the "D". The W allows the use of the REWRITE statement and shall be discussed presently.

8.3.2 The ACTUAL KEY Entry

A typical ACTUAL KEY entry is:

```
01 THE-ACTUAL-KEY.
   02 TRACK-IDENTIFIER
   PIC S9(8)
   COMPUTATIONAL
   SYNCHRONIZED.
   02 RECORD-IDENTIFIER
   PIC X(255).
```

This is set up exactly the same as for ACCESS MODE IS SEQUENTIAL.

To write a record in random access mode, it is necessary to first store the track identifier and the record identifier in the ACTUAL KEY. The user may specify the track identifier of his choice, and provided there is room on the named track, the record will be written. Once the record is written, the ACTUAL KEY will still contain the corresponding record and track identifiers. An example of the ACTUAL KEY entry in the random access mode is shown in Program 8.2.

Program 8.2

```
00008         /  ** RETRIEVES RECORDS GIVEN RECORD KEYS **
00009
00010            INPUT-OUTPUT SECTION.
00011            FILE-CONTROL.
00012
```

Program 8.2 (cont.)

```
00013                    SELECT CARD-READER
00014                        ASSIGN TO UT-CARD-S-SYSIN
00015                        ORGANIZATION IS SEQUENTIAL
00016                        ACCESS MODE IS SEQUENTIAL.
00017                    SELECT INPUT-FILE
00018                        ASSIGN TO DA-DISK-D-DD1
00019                        ACCESS IS RANDOM
00020                        ACTUAL KEY IS THE-ACTUAL-KEY.
00021                    SELECT OUTPUT-FILE
00022                        ASSIGN TO UT-PRNT-S-SYSPRINT
00023                        ACCESS MODE IS SEQUENTIAL
00024                        ORGANIZATION IS SEQUENTIAL.
00025
00026
00027            DATA DIVISION.
00028            FILE SECTION.
00029
00030            FD   CARD-READER
00031                     LABEL RECORDS ARE OMITTED
00032                     RECORD CONTAINS 80 CHARACTERS
00033                     DATA RECORD IS CARD-READER-RECORD.
00034            01   CARD-READER-RECORD.
00035                     02  LICENSE-NUMBER          PIC 9(6).
00036                     02  FILLER                  PIC X(74).
00037
00038            FD   INPUT-FILE
00039                     LABEL RECORDS ARE STANDARD
00040                     RECORD CONTAINS 100 CHARACTERS
00041                     DATA RECORD IS INPUT-FILE-RECORD.
00042            01   INPUT-FILE-RECORD.
00043                     02  LICENSE-NUMBER          PIC X(6).
00044                     02  MAKE-OF-VEHICLE         PIC X(15).
00045                     02  YEAR-OF-MODEL           PIC 9(2).
00046                     02  COLOUR                  PIC X(9).
00047                     02  TYPE-OF-CAR             PIC X(6).
00048                     02  DATE-STOLEN             PIC 9(6).
00049                     02  OWNER-ADDRESS           PIC X(18).
00050                     02  CITY                    PIC X(10).
00051                     02  STATE-OR-PROVINCE       PIC X(7).
00052                     02  OWNER                   PIC X(16).
00053                     02  FILLER                  PIC X(5).
00054
00055            FD   OUTPUT-FILE
00056                     LABEL RECORDS ARE OMITTED
00057                     RECORD CONTAINS 133 CHARACTERS
00058                     DATA RECORD IS OUTPUT-FILE-RECORD.
00059            01   OUTPUT-FILE-RECORD.
00060                     02  FILLER                  PIC X.
00061                     02  FILLER                  PIC X(5).
00062                     02  LICENSE-NUMBER          PIC X(6).
00063                     02  FILLER                  PIC X(8).
00064                     02  MAKE-OF-VEHICLE         PIC X(15).
00065                     02  FILLER                  PIC X(5).
00066                     02  COLOUR                  PIC X(9).
00067                     02  FILLER                  PIC X(84).
00068            01   TITLE-LINE.
00069                     02  FILLER                  PIC X.
00070                     02  FILLER                  PIC X(5).
00071                     02  LICENSE-NUMBER          PIC X(11).
00072                     02  FILLER                  PIC X(3).
00073                     02  MAKE                    PIC X(5).
00074                     02  FILLER                  PIC X(15).
00075                     02  VEHICLE-COLOUR          PIC X(6).
```

Program 8.2 (cont.)

```
00076                02  FILLER                    PIC X(87).
00077            01  MESSAGE-LINE.
00078                02  FILLER                    PIC X.
00079                02  INVALID-LICENSE-NUMBER    PIC X(6).
00080                02  FILLER                    PIC X(3).
00081                02  MESSAGE-DESCRIPTOR        PIC X(18).
00082                02  FILLER                    PIC X(105).
00083
00084
00085        WORKING-STORAGE SECTION.
00086
00087            77  CARD-READER-EOF              PIC X(3).
00088                    88  END-OF-INPUT-CR
00089                        VALUE IS  'ON'.
00090            77  HASH-QUOTIENT                PIC S9(8)
00091                        COMPUTATIONAL SYNCHRONIZED.
00092            77  HASH-REMAINDER               PIC S9(8)
00093                        COMPUTATIONAL SYNCHRONIZED.
00094            77  OVERFLOW-TRACK-NO            PIC S9(5)
00095                        COMPUTATIONAL SYNCHRONIZED
00096                                    VALUE IS +11.
00097
00098            01  THE-ACTUAL-KEY.
00099                02  TRACK-IDENTIFIER         PIC S9(5)
00100                        COMPUTATIONAL SYNCHRONIZED.
00101                02  KEY-OF-RECORD            PIC X(6).
00102
00103            01  RECORD-NOT-LOCATED.
00104                02  FILLER                    PIC X(3).
00105                    88  INVALID-READ VALUE IS 'ON'.
00106                    88  SEARCH-FAIL VALUE IS 'ON'.
00107                    88  SEARCH-POSITIVE VALUE IS 'OFF'.
00108
00109
00110        PROCEDURE DIVISION.
00111
00112            PERFORM INITIALIZATION.
00113            PERFORM READ-KEY-FETCH-RECORD
00114                UNTIL END-OF-INPUT-CR.
00115            PERFORM TERMINATION.
00116            STOP RUN.
00117
00118        INITIALIZATION.
00119            MOVE 'OFF' TO CARD-READER-EOF.
00120            OPEN INPUT INPUT-FILE
00121                        CARD-READER.
00122            OPEN OUTPUT OUTPUT-FILE.
00123            PERFORM PRINT-TITLE.
00124            READ CARD-READER RECORD
00125            AT END MOVE 'ON' TO CARD-READER-EOF.
00126
00127        TERMINATION.
00128            CLOSE CARD-READER
00129                    OUTPUT-FILE
00130                    INPUT-FILE.
00131
00132        READ-KEY-FETCH-RECORD.
00133            PERFORM HASH-ROUTINE.
00134            PERFORM FETCH-RECORD.
00135            IF INVALID-READ THEN
00136                PERFORM OVERFLOW-SEARCH.
00137            IF SEARCH-POSITIVE THEN
00138                PERFORM PRINT-RECORD.
```

Program 8.2 (cont.)

```
00139                    IF SEARCH-FAIL THEN
00140                        PERFORM PRINT-NO-RECORD-FOUND.
00141                    READ CARD-READER RECORD
00142                        AT END MOVE 'ON' TO CARD-READER-EOF.
00143
00144               HASH-ROUTINE.
00145                    DIVIDE 11 INTO LICENSE-NUMBER OF CARD-READER
00146                        GIVING HASH-QUOTIENT
00147                        REMAINDER HASH-REMAINDER.
00148
00149               FETCH-RECORD.
00150                    MOVE HASH-REMAINDER TO TRACK-IDENTIFIER.
00151                    MOVE LICENSE-NUMBER OF CARD-READER
00152                    TO KEY-OF-RECORD.
00153                    MOVE 'OFF' TO RECORD-NOT-LOCATED.
00154                    READ INPUT-FILE RECORD
00155                        INVALID KEY MOVE 'ON' TO RECORD-NOT-LOCATED.
00156
00157               OVERFLOW-SEARCH.
00158                    MOVE OVERFLOW-TRACK-NO TO TRACK-IDENTIFIER.
00159                    MOVE 'OFF' TO RECORD-NOT-LOCATED.
00160                    READ INPUT-FILE RECORD
00161                        INVALID KEY MOVE 'ON' TO RECORD-NOT-LOCATED.
00162
00163               PRINT-RECORD.
00164                    MOVE SPACES TO OUTPUT-FILE-RECORD.
00165                    MOVE CORRESPONDING INPUT-FILE-RECORD
00166                        TO OUTPUT-FILE-RECORD.
00167                    WRITE OUTPUT-FILE-RECORD
00168                        AFTER POSITIONING 1 LINES.
00169
00170               PRINT-NO-RECORD-FOUND.
00171                    MOVE SPACES TO MESSAGE-LINE.
00172                    MOVE LICENSE-NUMBER OF CARD-READER
00173                        TO INVALID-LICENSE-NUMBER.
00174                    MOVE 'RECORD NOT LOCATED' TO MESSAGE-DESCRIPTOR.
00175                    WRITE OUTPUT-FILE-RECORD
00176                        AFTER POSITIONING 1 LINES.
00177
00178               PRINT-TITLE.
00179                    MOVE SPACES TO TITLE-LINE.
00180                    MOVE 'LICENSE-NO' TO LICENSE-NUMBER
00181                        OF TITLE-LINE.
00182                    MOVE 'MAKE' TO MAKE.
00183                    MOVE 'COLOUR' TO VEHICLE-COLOUR.
00184                    WRITE TITLE-LINE AFTER POSITIONING 0 LINES.
```

8.3.3 The FD Entry: Describing the File

Fixed-Length Records

For fixed-length records, a typical entry is:

```
FD file-name
    LABEL RECORDS ARE STANDARD
    RECORD CONTAINS integer CHARACTERS
    DATA RECORD IS record-name.
01 record-name.
```

where *file-name* is the name of the file, *integer* specifies the number of characters in each fixed length record, and *record-name* names the record in the following level 01 entry.

More than one level 01 entry may be present but each group item must have the same length. Multiple level 01 entries are treated as automatic redefinitions of the record. These additional record names may be named by the optional DATA RECORDS ARE clause as

```
DATA RECORDS ARE
record-name1
record-name2...
```

Variable-Length Records

A typical variable-length entry is:

```
FD file-name
   LABEL RECORDS ARE STANDARD
   RECORD CONTAINS integer1 TO integer2 CHARACTERS
   RECORDING MODE IS V
   DATA RECORD IS record-name.
01 record-name.
   02 etc.
```

where *file-name* is the file being described.

The RECORD CONTAINS clause specifies the number of characters (*integer1*) in the minimum-sized, variable-length record and the number of characters (*integer2*) in the largest variable-length record. RECORDING MODE IS V indicates that this is a variable-length record file. The DATA RECORD clause indicates the name (names) of succeeding level 01 entry (entries).

Presumably (since this is a variable-length record file), there are present either multiple level 01 record descriptions of various sizes and/or one or more level 01 entries containing the OCCURS DEPENDING ON clause.

Before a record may be written to the file, the data portion of the record must be transmitted to the FD buffer area and its actual key specified.

As a reminder, we reiterate that the records of a direct file may *not* be blocked.

8.3.4 Procedure Division Statements

The OPEN Statement

Random access permits a direct access file to be opened in one of three modes: INPUT, OUTPUT, and I–O. The corresponding OPEN statements are

```
OPEN INPUT file-name
OPEN OUTPUT file-name
OPEN I-O file-name
```

In the INPUT mode, file records can only be read; in the OUTPUT mode, file records can only be written. In the I–O mode, records can be both read and written.

The READ Statement

The general format of the READ statement in all three modes of the OPEN verb is

```
READ file-name RECORD [INTO identifier]
     INVALID KEY imperative-statement
```

where *file-name* is the name of the associated file. This statement causes one logical record to be made available in the buffer area or moved with a group MOVE to the data name *identifier* within the WORKING-STORAGE SECTION if the optional INTO clause is used. The *imperative statement* following the INVALID KEY is invoked if the record is not found or if the track address specified is not within the limits of the file.

Before a READ statement is issued, the ACTUAL KEY data item must be set to the track and record identifier of the desired record.

The WRITE Statement

The general format of the WRITE statement is

```
WRITE record-name [FROM identifier]
      INVALID KEY imperative-statement
```

where *record-name* is the name of the level 01 entry within the associated FD for the file. The record to be written to the file must be moved to this entry by the user or automatically from the data area named *identifier* by a group MOVE if the optional FROM clause is invoked.

The track and record identifiers of the record to be written must be placed in the ACTUAL KEY data item before the record is written.

If the ASSIGN clause contains a D in the system name entry, as in DA-DISK-D-DD1, the WRITE statement will only write a record to the file to replace a file record already in existence if

(a) the record to be replaced has an ACTUAL KEY identical to the one in the record to be added and

(b) if the record to be replaced was read by the last READ statement executed.

The programmer should always read and check a record before he replaces it to be sure it is eligible for replacement.

If a READ statement is not executed prior to writing, the record will not replace any record on the file but will be added as a new file record whether or not it duplicates the record key of another record on the file.

The INVALID KEY clause is invoked if an attempt is made to write a record with HIGH-VALUES in the first character position of the record identifier (you cannot create dummy records this way with ACCESS IS RANDOM) or if the ACTUAL KEY is outside the physical limits of the file.

The REWRITE Statement

Some users prefer to use the REWRITE verb when they wish to replace an already existing file record. This statement can only be used if a W is placed in the system name of the SELECT clause for the file as in DA-DISK-W-DD1. The general format of the REWRITE clause is

```
REWRITE record-name [FROM identifier]
        INVALID KEY imperative-statement
```

where *record-name* is the name of the level 01 entry within the FD of the file to which the record to be written must first be moved. The record can be moved there automatically by a group MOVE from the data area named *identifier* if the optional FROM clause is used.

In order to use the REWRITE statement, the following steps should be taken:

1. MOVE the record's track and record identifier to the ACTUAL KEY data item.
2. READ the record and check, now that you have read it, that it is eligible for replacement.
3. Issue the REWRITE statement before you issue another READ.

The INVALID KEY clause will be invoked if an attempt is made to replace a record that does not exist or if the record identifier is outside the limits of the file.

The REWRITE statement can only be used if the OPEN mode is I–O.

A WRITE statement used with a W in the system name of the SELECT clause will automatically add a new record to the file whether or not a duplicate exists. Files are closed by the normal use of a CLOSE statement.

Program 8.2 Narrative.   The purpose of Program 8.2 is to retrieve records from the file created in Program 8.1. The record keys are read and then divided by 11. The remainder on division is used as the track identifier to fetch the record. If the record cannot be located, an effort is made to locate the record on overflow track number 11. If the record is not located on track 11, it is considered to be missing from the file and an appropriate error message is printed. Processing halts when end-of-file is encountered.

8.4 CONCLUSION

The foremost difficulty with IBM direct access is record addressing. The address consisting of two parts is more complex than the simple relative address of Chapter 6. Unlike relative addressing, knowledge of the storage device is essential to direct addressing. However, in any system direct physical addressing must be done somewhere. It need not be done in COBOL but the general problems remain the same.

The advantage of direct access is that it is fast, since there is no layer of software control between the program and the device. The disadvantage is that since there is no software control, all control, addressing, and data management must be performed by the programmer with device-dependent considerations. Direct access, as described in this chapter, should normally be avoided as a file access method. However, requirements of speed and flexibility could make it necessary, but the programmer should be prepared to demonstrate such necessity.

9

COBOL
Indexed I-O
Files

A COBOL Indexed I–O file is a file in which data records may be accessed by the *value* of a key. It is characterized by the fact that the physical relation of the records corresponds to the logical order of the file key values in so far as this can be maintained in a dynamic environment. Thus an Indexed I–O file allows records to be efficiently accessed in sequential as well as random order. For this reason a COBOL Indexed I–O file is an example of *indexed sequential* file organization and we sometimes refer to it by this general name. You will recall, however, that a Relative I–O file also allows such access. What then is the difference?

9.1 INTRODUCTION

A major feature of the Indexed I–O file organization is that each record address is *uniquely* named by the *value* of one or more keys that are part of the record. This is

in contrast to a Relative I–O file which requires knowledge of the sequential ordering of records within the file (and thus their relative addresses) or the direct access
file which requires both track addresses and record keys in order to locate a record.
Recall that in a Relative I–O file the programmer was required to provide the relationship between the record key and the relative address at which the record was to
be stored. Indexed I–O solves the addressing problem for the programmer.

Just as important, it is possible to add new records to an Indexed I–O file and
place them between sequentially adjacent records without recreating the file. The
sorted order of the file, by key, is thus not destroyed. Not only can additional records be added easily but they can also be deleted to make room for new records.
Indexed I–O files provide system solutions to the problems the programmer encounters with relative files. As always, the system solution in relieving the programmer
of tedious detail isolates the programmer from the mechanism of device access.
Moreover, the solution to the problems encountered may not be suitable to the use
the programmer intends. It is necessary then for the programmer to understand the
particular method by which an Indexed I–O file is implemented and its characteristics. Many IBM systems implement indexed files with ISAM or VSAM, and their
general concepts are explained in Chapters 10 and 11. One can use indexed files
without knowing how they are implemented, but such use can be quite inefficient.

In this chapter the Indexed I–O module of ANSI COBOL will be discussed; it
provides the most advanced file handling facilities of the COBOL language. With
Indexed I–O, unlike Relative I–O, the programmer can create files with fixed- or
variable-length records. In addition, many data retrieval and updating functions are
automatically provided as COBOL language features. As examples:

- Additional records can be added long after initial file creation with no
  significant deterioration in accessing speed.
- Specific records can be deleted.
- More than one key can be established for purposes of record retrieval.

A thorough grasp of this particular module will enable the COBOL programmer to
code quickly and effortlessly many complex data processing applications.

9.1.1 The Primary Key

When an Indexed I–O file is used, data records must be accessed by specifying the value of a key. The record layout or description of the file may contain one
or more key data items. Each of these key data items is associated with a directory
or index that links each key to the physical address of the record. Only one key,
however, may be specified when records are to be added, deleted, or changed. This
key is called the RECORD KEY of the file and may not be changed when a record is
updated. Other data items used as keys are called ALTERNATE RECORD KEYs.
These keys may provide alternate access paths for the retrieval of records and are
not required to be unique.

Indexed I–O provides for both sequential and random access to records and permits the program to change from one form of access to the other, once the file has been opened. When accessed sequentially, records are retrieved in ascending order of the RECORD KEY values. When accessed by ALTERNATE RECORD KEYs, records having duplicate keys are accessed in the order in which the records were written into the file.

When records are accessed in the random access mode, the order of retrieval is at the discretion of the programmer. Each record is accessed by specifying one of its record keys.

9.2 CASE STUDY: LEAKEY VALVE CREDIT UNION

The employees of the J. L. Leakey and Sons Valve Company have formed a small credit union. Each member is given a passbook; deposits and withdrawals are made in person. Check privileges are not possible. The accounts of the credit union members are kept on a disk and accounts are updated when transactions are made. A monthly statement of account is also prepared.

9.2.1 Logical Analysis: Leakey Valve Credit Union

Each account is given a unique number that serves to identify it. It was decided to use an Indexed I–O file for this application for the following reasons:

1. Each account has a unique identifier.
2. Customer transactions occur at random.
3. Account statements are prepared monthly.
4. The number of transactions per customer is variable.

Monthly accounts can be produced by listing the month's transactions for each customer. This can be done by sequentially processing the records of the file.

Direct random accessing is necessary so that tellers can enter transactions immediately.

For each customer the account will contain the following fields:

1. credit account number
2. customer name
3. customer address
4. credit rating
5. current amount borrowed from credit union
6. loan account number if applicable

7. current credit balance in savings account plus any number of transactions of the form
   - date
   - amount
   - transaction code

The possibilities for transaction code are D for deposit, W for withdrawal, S for service charge, L for loan payment, and B for amount loaned.

In view of the fact that the monthly transactions must be kept on the file and because the number of these entries is variable, the Indexed I–O file is created with variable-length records.

9.2.2 Indexed File Processing: Leakey Valve Credit Union

If records are added to the file in the sequential access mode, they must be sorted in ascending order on their primary keys. Records need not be sorted if they are added to the file in the random access mode.

Program 9.1 adds the initial records to the credit union file. The reader should familiarize himself with this program.

Program 9.1

```
00010        /  ** LOADS INDEXED I-O FILE **
00011
00012        INPUT-OUTPUT SECTION.
00013        FILE-CONTROL.
00014
00015            SELECT INPUT-FILE
00016                ASSIGN TO CARD-SYSIN.
00017            SELECT OUTPUT-FILE
00018                ASSIGN TO DISK-DD1
00019                ORGANIZATION IS INDEXED
00020                ACCESS MODE IS SEQUENTIAL
00021                RECORD KEY IS CREDIT-ACCOUNT-NUMBER
00022                OF OUTPUT-FILE
00023                FILE STATUS IS STATUS-VARIABLE.
00024
00025
00026        DATA DIVISION.
00027        FILE SECTION.
00028
00029        FD  INPUT-FILE
00030                LABEL RECORDS ARE OMITTED
00031                RECORD CONTAINS 80 CHARACTERS
00032                DATA RECORD IS INPUT-FILE-RECORD.
00033        01  INPUT-FILE-RECORD.
00034            02  CREDIT-ACCOUNT-NUMBER     PIC 9(4).
00035            02  CUSTOMER-NAME             PIC X(20).
00036            02  CUSTOMER-ADDRESS          PIC X(20).
00037            02  CREDIT-RATING             PIC 9.
00038            02  AMOUNT-BORROWED           PIC 9(7).
00039            02  LOAN-ACCOUNT-NUMBER       PIC 9(4).
00040            02  CURRENT-BALANCE           PIC 9(7).
```

Program 9.1   (cont.)

```
00041              02  FILLER                   PIC X(17).
00042
00043       FD  OUTPUT-FILE
00044              BLOCK CONTAINS 1 RECORDS
00045              LABEL RECORDS ARE STANDARD
00046              RECORD CONTAINS 70 TO 1159 CHARACTERS
00047              DATA RECORD IS OUTPUT-FILE-RECORD.
00048       01  OUTPUT-FILE-RECORD.
00049              02  CREDIT-ACCOUNT-NUMBER    PIC 9(4).
00050              02  CUSTOMER-NAME            PIC X(20).
00051              02  CUSTOMER-ADDRESS         PIC X(20).
00052              02  CREDIT-RATING            PIC 9.
00053              02  AMOUNT-BORROWED          PIC 9(8)
00054                  USAGE IS COMP.
00055              02  LOAN-ACCOUNT-NUMBER      PIC 9(4).
00056              02  CURRENT-BALANCE          PIC 9(8)
00057                  USAGE IS COMP.
00058              02  NUMBER-OF-TRANSACTIONS   PIC 9(4)
00059                  USAGE IS COMP.
00060              02  TRANSACTIONS
00061                  OCCURS 1 TO 100 TIMES
00062                  DEPENDING ON NUMBER-OF-TRANSACTIONS.
00063                  03  TRANSACTION-DATE     PIC 9(6).
00064                  03  TRANSACTION-AMOUNT   PIC 9(8)
00065                      USAGE IS COMP.
00066                  03  TRANSACTION-CODE     PIC X.
00067
00068
00069       WORKING-STORAGE SECTION.
00070
00071       77  INPUT-FILE-EOF               PIC X(3).
00072              88  NO-MORE-DATA-CARDS
00073                  VALUE IS 'ON'.
00074       77  OUTPUT-FILE-EOF              PIC X(3).
00075              88  END-OF-FILE-OF VALUE IS 'ON'.
00076       77  STATUS-VARIABLE             PIC 99.
00077
00078
00079       PROCEDURE DIVISION.
00080
00081           PERFORM INITIALIZATION.
00082           PERFORM BUILD-FILE
00083              UNTIL NO-MORE-DATA-CARDS.
00084           PERFORM TERMINATION.
00085           STOP RUN.
00086
00087       INITIALIZATION.
00088           MOVE 'OFF' TO INPUT-FILE-EOF.
00089           OPEN INPUT INPUT-FILE.
00090           OPEN OUTPUT OUTPUT-FILE.
00091           READ INPUT-FILE RECORD
00092              AT END MOVE 'ON' TO INPUT-FILE-EOF.
00093
00094       BUILD-FILE.
00095           MOVE CORRESPONDING INPUT-FILE-RECORD
00096              TO OUTPUT-FILE-RECORD.
00097           MOVE 1 TO NUMBER-OF-TRANSACTIONS.
00098           WRITE OUTPUT-FILE-RECORD.
00099           IF STATUS-VARIABLE NOT EQUAL ZERO
00100              PERFORM ERROR-ROUTINE.
00101           READ INPUT-FILE RECORD
00102              AT END MOVE 'ON' TO INPUT-FILE-EOF.
00103
```

Program 9.1 (cont.)

```
00104       * **** SUPPLY ERROR ROUTINE FOR PRODUCTION RUNS ****
00105         ERROR-ROUTINE.
00106             DISPLAY 'FATAL ERROR'.
00107             DISPLAY STATUS-VARIABLE.
00108             DISPLAY OUTPUT-FILE-RECORD.
00109
00110         TERMINATION.
00111             CLOSE INPUT-FILE
00112                   OUTPUT-FILE.
00113             PERFORM VERIFY.
00114
00115         VERIFY.
00116             OPEN INPUT OUTPUT-FILE.
00117             READ OUTPUT-FILE RECORD
00118                 AT END MOVE 'ON' TO OUTPUT-FILE-EOF.
00119             PERFORM READ-AND-DISPLAY
00120                 UNTIL END-OF-FILE-OF.
00121             CLOSE OUTPUT-FILE.
00122
00123         READ-AND-DISPLAY.
00124             DISPLAY OUTPUT-FILE-RECORD.
00125             READ OUTPUT-FILE RECORD
00126                 AT END MOVE 'ON' TO OUTPUT-FILE-EOF.
```

Program 9.1 Narrative. The purpose of this program is to load the credit union file with initial customer records.

The file is called OUTPUT-FILE, and the record key for this file is called CREDIT-ACCOUNT-NUMBER. Note that the file consists of variable length records; the variable part is described under the level 02 entry TRANSACTIONS within OUTPUT-FILE-RECORD.

The OCCURS clause for this file states

```
        02 TRANSACTIONS
           OCCURS 1 TO 100 TIMES
           DEPENDING ON NUMBER-OF-TRANSACTIONS.
```

The data item NUMBER-OF-TRANSACTIONS is stored above the data item TRANSACTIONS in the fixed part of the record as required.

Since the OCCURS clause ranges from 1 to 100 times the data item NUMBER-OF-TRANSACTIONS is given the value 1 in the paragraph BUILD-FILE even though there is no data as yet for this part of the record.

9.3 INDEXED I–O MODULE

9.3.1 The Record Key

For access, the record key must be placed in a data item designated as the RECORD KEY. In IBM OS/VS COBOL, the RECORD KEY may be any fixed-length item within the record. It must be less than 256 bytes in length.

If more than one description of a record is provided within the FD of the file the RECORD KEY must have the same description and must appear at the same location within each record definition relative to the start of the record. It is not, however, required that the same data name be used in each instance.

It is suggested that, when using IBM OS/VS COBOL, this data item be defined to exclude the first byte of each record, because it is used to mark deletions. In particular, it *must exclude* the first byte in the following cases:

1. The file contains records that *may be deleted.*
2. The file contains *unblocked* records.
3. The file contains one or more records whose primary key has HIGH-VALUES in the first byte position.

With these exceptions, the primary key may occur anywhere within the record.

9.3.2 Environment Division: Defining the Indexed I–O File

The Indexed I–O file is defined by a SELECT clause within the INPUT-OUTPUT section of the environment division.

```
SELECT file-name
ASSIGN TO implementor-name
ORGANIZATION IS INDEXED
                 ⎡ SEQUENTIAL ⎤
ACCESS MODE IS ⎨ RANDOM      ⎬
                 ⎣ DYNAMIC    ⎦
RECORD KEY IS data-name-1
ALTERNATE RECORD KEY IS data-name-2
FILE STATUS IS data-name-3.
```

The clause ORGANIZATION IS INDEXED specifies that this is an Indexed I–O file.

ANSI COBOL permits one of three access modes for Indexed I–O files. ACCESS MODE IS SEQUENTIAL indicates that access is sequential. This is assumed if the ACCESS clause is omitted. For sequential access, the records in the file are retrieved or stored in sequential order by ascending order of the RECORD KEY. *If records are to be stored in the sequential access mode, the records must be sorted in ascending order by primary key before they are written to the storage device.*

When ACCESS MODE IS RANDOM is specified, records may be stored or retrieved in any order. The order is determined by the programmer, and any record to be stored or retrieved is designated by its RECORD or ALTERNATE RECORD KEY. To retrieve records from the file, this key should be placed in a data item named as part of the READ statement. To store records, the user must ensure that the primary key of the record is stored within the record.

ANSI COBOL permits switching from the sequential access mode to the random access mode or vice versa any number of times during one OPEN of the file provided ACCESS MODE IS DYNAMIC is specified.

The RECORD KEY clause specifies the name of the data item, i.e., *data-name-1*, that locates the record key of the file within the record description of the file FD.

The ALTERNATE RECORD KEY clause names one or more data items that may be used as alternate keys instead of the RECORD KEY to locate a record within the file. These ALTERNATE KEYs need not be unique, as is the case with the RECORD KEY of the file, and they can only be used to retrieve records. The following format should be used to specify that duplicates on the file may exist:

```
ALTERNATE RECORD KEY IS data-name-2 WITH DUPLICATES
```

Any number of alternate keys may be specified. As previously mentioned, ALTERNATE RECORD KEYs are not used to add, change, or delete records. They can only be used for record retrieval.

The FILE STATUS clause names a data item, *data-name-3*, that is updated by the operating system after every operation that references the file to indicate the execution result of the statement. Programmers wishing to check the success status of an operation should consult the manual for the appropriate return codes. This should always be done in production programs.

9.3.3 Data Division: The FD Entry for an Indexed I–O File

```
FD file-name
      BLOCK CONTAINS integer-1 TO integer-2 RECORDS
      RECORD CONTAINS integer-3 TO integer-4 CHARACTERS
      LABEL RECORDS ARE     { STANDARD }
                            { OMITTED  }
      DATA RECORDS ARE record-name-1
                       record-name-2
                            .
                            .
                            .
```

At least one record description must contain the primary key and secondary keys named in the RECORD KEY and ALTERNATE RECORD KEY clauses of the file.

The BLOCK CONTAINS clause denotes the size of a physical record. This clause is not required if one logical record is to constitute the block or if the hardware device has only one physical record size. Respectively, *integer-1* and *integer-2* specify the minimum and maximum physical record sizes. If only *integer-2* is given, the physical record is a fixed-length record; otherwise, it is a variable-length record.

The RECORD CONTAINS clause is optional and specifies the length of a logical record. Respectively, *integer-3* and *integer-4* designate the minimum and maximum record lengths of file records. If only *integer-4* is specified as in

RECORD CONTAINS *integer-4* CHARACTERS

the logical records are considered to be fixed-length records. When the RECORD CONTAINS clause is omitted, the logical record size(s) is determined from the level 01 record descriptions which follow the FD. Variable-length records are assumed if these record descriptions have different lengths or if they contain one or more OCCURS clauses with the DEPENDING ON option.

9.3.4 Procedure Division: Indexed I–O Files

There are several formats of the read, write, and open statements available in the Indexed I–O module of ANSI COBOL, and care must be exercised in using them. This is especially true when updating records or using secondary keys. Moreover, changes in the access mode affect the nature of the statements and alter the conditions that abnormally terminate their execution.

Before discussing the exact format of each I–O statement and its action, a warning is necessary. Earlier in the text, methods were presented that allowed a user to map record keys to physical addresses when using IBM Direct Access or relative files. There was a hidden advantage in using these methods. The programmer was forced to think carefully through the process of adding a record to a file or updating one already present. User routines should reject the obvious errors such as trying to add already existing records or deleting records not present. User routines to maintain secondary keys should detect incorrectly duplicated record key values or branch to user-defined error routines when unable to carry out retrieval requests. *This is not true of Indexed I–O files where the key mappings are provided.* Errors are trapped and flagged, but processing flow is not necessarily altered. It is essential that the user learn to check the file status variable after every I–O operation and alter the program flow appropriately if the result is not acceptable. It is quite possible for a program to set an error condition in the file status variable for 50 consecutive write statements following a failed open that was also ignored. If it then commences an expensive reporting phase and wastes a box of 2000 forms costing $5.00 each, then the error will be obvious and everyone will be wise. If the set of writes, on the other hand, are supposed to update accounts receivable by $250,000.00 but are not followed by a reporting phase, no one may be the wiser until an audit takes place. Then someone is sure to be!

Checking the file status variable clause is only one of many requirements. On-lineup dating in random access mode requires extremely careful programming.

- A record must never be updated until it has been read first and the correctness of the change verified.

- A record must never be added to a file if a record already on the file has the same record key.
- A record must never be added to the file if its addition would destroy the uniqueness of an alternate key that is not permitted to have duplicates.

Modes of Access

There are three modes of access with Indexed I–O files:

1. ACCESS MODE IS SEQUENTIAL
2. ACCESS MODE IS RANDOM
3. ACCESS MODE IS DYNAMIC

ACCESS MODE IS SEQUENTIAL is the default. It should be used when initially loading the Indexed I–O file or when retrieving records sequentially. Records must be stored in sorted order by record key with this mode and are also retrieved in sorted order.

ACCESS MODE IS RANDOM should be used for random retrieval or storage of records after initial file loading.

ACCESS MODE IS DYNAMIC allows intermixing of random and sequential modes. It should be used for record retrieval on secondary keys or for skipping over records by using a random read to jump over records during sequential reading of a file.

OPEN Statements

There are three formats of the OPEN statement:

1. OPEN INPUT *file-name*
2. OPEN I-O *file-name*
3. OPEN OUTPUT *file-name*

OPEN INPUT and OPEN OUTPUT are normally used with sequential processing. OPEN OUTPUT is used to load a file initially or for adding records in sorted sequence to the end of a file. OPEN I-O is used for file updating.

READ Statements

There are two formats of the READ statement:

1. READ *file-name* RECORD [INTO *identifier*]
   AT END *imperative statement*

2. READ *file-name* RECORD [INTO *identifier*]
   KEY IS *data-name*
   INVALID KEY *imperative statement*

The first of these formats is used for sequential reading of the file. It is also used to read records with secondary keys after the first record with a given key value has been retrieved. The second format is used for random retrieval by record or secondary key. The KEY IS clause names the key to be used for retrieval. The value of the key must be placed in the data-name specified prior to the read being issued. When using a secondary key with duplicates, this read is only used to fetch the first record. Subsequent records with the same secondary key value are then obtained with the first format. The imperative statement following the INVALID KEY clause is invoked if no record exists on the file with the specified key value.

WRITE Statement

There are two types of write statement WRITE and REWRITE. The formats are as follows:

```
1. WRITE record-name [FROM identifier]
   INVALID KEY imperative statement

2. REWRITE record-name [FROM identifier]
   INVALID KEY imperative statement
```

The WRITE statement is used to write records to the file during initial file creation or for adding records in sorted sequence to the end of the file after initial loading. It is used in the random access mode to write records to the file that do not already exist. The REWRITE statement is used for updating existing records. A READ statement should be issued on any record to be updated prior to the REWRITE being issued, and no other I/O statements to the file should intervene. Verify the validity of any record prior to update. The INVALID KEY clause is invoked with the WRITE statement if a record with the same primary key already exists, if there is not enough physical room in the file for the record to be written, or if a record in the file has the same secondary key value and this secondary key is not permitted to have duplicates. The INVALID KEY clause on the REWRITE statement will be invoked if a READ has not preceded the REWRITE statement for the record or if a DELETE command for the record has been issued prior to REWRITE. Always check the file status variable following use of WRITE or REWRITE.

The DELETE Statement

The format of the DELETE statement is

```
DELETE file-name RECORD
   INVALID KEY imperative statement
```

The DELETE statement is used to remove a record logically from a file. A READ of the record must be issued prior to deletion. The INVALID KEY clause should only be used with ACCESS MODE IS RANDOM. The imperative statement following INVALID KEY is invoked if a record with the record key cannot be found. This should not happen, as a successful read and verification for deletion should proceed its use in normal practice.

The START Statement

Often in sequential processing, it is desirable to start somewhere in the file other than at the beginning or to skip over records during the processing of the file. The START statement is provided for this purpose. The general format of the START statement is

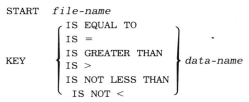

The START statement is used to position the current record pointer to any specified record. The OPEN statement automatically positions this pointer at the start of the file. Sequential reading of records will begin from whichever record is pointed to by the START statement.

Each record is located within the file by its record key. The *data-name* is the name of a data item that contains a record key. The START statement will locate this key within the file or the first one following depending on whether the programmer specifies IS EQUAL TO or IS GREATER THAN, respectively. If the programmer specifies IS NOT LESS THAN, he is indicating that he wants the current record pointer set at the value of *data-name* or, if a record with that primary key is missing, at the first record with a primary key greater than *data-name*.

The INVALID KEY clause is invoked if a record that satisfies the KEY IS condition cannot be found. Thus, there are three conditions that will trigger an INVALID KEY clause:

1. KEY IS EQUAL TO is specified and no key with this exact value found.

2. KEY IS GREATER THAN is specified and no key with a value greater than the given key can be found.

3. KEY IS NOT LESS THAN is specified and no key can be found either equal to the key specified or larger than it.

If the INVALID KEY clause is invoked, the current record pointer is not changed.

In summary, records can be changed or updated sequentially by using a combination of READ and REWRITE statements interspersed with one or more START statements. As the condition value that a START statement relies on is stored in *data-name,* the START statement can be inserted between a REWRITE statement and the following READ. It can then be executed conditionally whenever the difference between the key of the record to be added and the value of the current record pointer is large, thereby skipping over many records. For example, if the current record pointer points to key 600, the record to be added is 900, and there is a high probability that there are many records in between, then it would make sense to use a START statement prior to the next READ to skip records.

9.4 CASE STUDY: LAKESIDE GENERAL HOSPITAL

This case study treats secondary keys in detail and uses variable-length records. It can be skipped on a first reading of the chapter. For those not familiar with data structures it may be advisable to read Chapters 13 and 14 before beginning this example.

Lakeside General Hospital is a small hospital in northern Wyoming which serves surrounding ranch country. It has a medium-sized staff and caters to an average of from 300 to 700 patients at any one time.

Procedures concerning admittance are well established. When a patient is admitted, he is given an admitting identifier, which is unique to each separate admittance. This identifier is 5 characters long, a letter of the alphabet followed by four digits. Additional information is taken from the patient: name, address, telephone number, state Medicaid number, social security number, and the name of the referring physician. This information is entered on an admissions form. The patient is then assigned to a ward, a room, and a specific bed. A diagnostic code specifying the nature of the problem is given by the supervisory physician, whose name is also recorded along with the current date. The supervisory physician may, at this time or shortly thereafter, schedule one or more tests. Each of these tests has a designated procedure number, a consulting physician, and a scheduled date and time.

9.4.1 Logical Analysis: Lakeside General Hospital

A hospital is a complicated organization in a constant state of flux. It requires accurate management to utilize its scarce resources fully. Typical requirements are the following:

1. Patients must be scheduled for the various services of the hospital with due regard to their state of health, the health of others, and the current availability of services.

2. Hospital services must be fully utilized owing to their enormous cost and high demand.

3. Hospital employees must be mobilized to perform numerous tasks in concert with others.

4. Supplies must be ordered.

5. Operational costs must be accounted for.

We shall examine some of the programs necessary to handle patient admitting.

The first program needed to handle patient admissions is a program to store the data of each admission form. Since information on individual patients is required by other programs in the overall system, a random access file is chosen. There are three choices for such a file: a direct file, a Relative I–O file, or an Indexed I–O file. It will be simplest to choose an Indexed I–O file, although, with some programming effort, we could build the system with either of the other two file types.

To build an Indexed I–O file, it is first necessary to designate a record key. Each patient is identified by an admitting identifier which is unique to each separate admittance. This record field is therefore designated as the record key of the Indexed I–O file. The social security number or the state Medicaid number could not be chosen for this application, as they are not unique identifiers regarding patient admittance. A patient may enter the hospital many times, but the social security number will remain the same.

Each patient record will contain the following information:

- patient name and address
- admitting identifier
- social security number
- state Medicaid number
- assigned ward number (there are 20 wards)
- a room number (there are 300 rooms)
- a unique bed number
- name of referring physician
- name of supervisory physician (which may be the same as the referring physician)
- preliminary diagnostic code

In addition up to 30 scheduled tests may be performed on admission, each of which has recorded

- procedure number
- consulting physician
- date and time when the test or procedure is scheduled

The need for these variable portions of a patient record is a further incentive for using an Indexed I–O file. Relative files do not permit variable-length records.

9.4.2 *Indexed I–O File Processing: Lakeside General Hospital*

There are two stages in the creation of an Indexed I–O file. In the first stage the file is allocated space by the computer operating system. Many computer systems support the file environment for Indexed I–O files. On IBM machines the file can be supported by the VSAM access method. Some installations may help the user set up the necessary environment, and the programmer is advised to consult them for advice. Those readers using VSAM will find advice in Chapter 12, "VSAM Applied."

In the second stage the file is loaded, and this is the responsibility of the COBOL programmer. In this stage the initial file records are placed on the file. The records must be entered in ascending order by record key. We shall assume that the admissions data has been transcribed from the original forms to tape by a remote device in a local mode or some form of document reader.

Program 9.2 adds the initial records to the Indexed I–O file called the ADMITTING-DATA-FILE. The reader should become familiar with this program.

Program 9.2 Narrative.   The purpose of this program is to load the admitting data file with a set of initial records. The data records are currently stored as a sequential file on tape (the INPUT-FILE). They have been *presorted* by the record key called ADMITTING-IDENTIFIER in ascending sequence.

Program 9.2   Creating the admission data file.

```
00009        /  ** THIS PROGRAM LOADS PATIENT DATA INTO THE    **
00010        *  ** ADMITTING-DATA-FILE FROM A SEQUENTIAL FILE **
00011
00012           INPUT-OUTPUT SECTION.
00013           FILE-CONTROL.
00014
00015              SELECT INPUT-FILE
00016                  ASSIGN TO DISK-DD2
00017                  ACCESS MODE IS SEQUENTIAL
00018                  ORGANIZATION IS SEQUENTIAL.
00019              SELECT ADMITTING-DATA-FILE
00020                  ASSIGN TO DISK-DD1
00021                  ORGANIZATION IS INDEXED
00022                  ACCESS MODE IS SEQUENTIAL
00023                  FILE STATUS IS FILE-STATUS
00024                  RECORD KEY IS ADMITTING-IDENTIFIER
00025                      OF ADMITTING-DATA-FILE.
00026
00027
00028           DATA DIVISION.
00029           FILE SECTION.
00030
00031           FD  INPUT-FILE
00032               LABEL RECORDS ARE STANDARD
00033               BLOCK CONTAINS 30 RECORDS
00034               RECORD CONTAINS 140 CHARACTERS
00035               DATA RECORD IS PATIENT-DATA.
00036           01  INPUT-DATA.
00037               02  PATIENT-NAME.
```

Program 9.2 (cont.)

```
00038                          03    LAST-NAME              PIC X(15).
00039                          03    INITIALS               PIC X(4).
00040                   02  PATIENT-ADDRESS.
00041                          03    STREET-ADDRESS         PIC X(20).
00042                          03    CITY                   PIC X(15).
00043                   02  PHONE-NUMBER                    PIC 9(7).
00044                   02  ADMITTING-IDENTIFIER
00045                                                        PIC X(5).
00046                   02  ADMISSION-DATE                  PIC 9(6).
00047                   02  SOCIAL-SECURITY-NUMBER
00048                                                        PIC X(11).
00049                   02  STATE-MEDICAID-NUMBER
00050                                                        PIC X(8).
00051                   02  WARD-NUMBER                     PIC 9(2).
00052                   02  ROOM-NUMBER                     PIC 9(3).
00053                   02  BED-NUMBER                      PIC 9(4).
00054                   02  REFERRING-PHYSICIAN.
00055                          03    LAST-NAME              PIC X(15).
00056                          03    INITIALS               PIC X(4).
00057                   02  SUPERVISORY-PHYSICIAN.
00058                          03    LAST-NAME              PIC X(15).
00059                          03    INITIALS               PIC X(4).
00060                   02  PRELIMINARY-DIAGNOSIS
00061                                                        PIC 9(2).
00062
00063         FD   ADMITTING-DATA-FILE
00064              LABEL RECORDS ARE STANDARD
00065              BLOCK CONTAINS 1 RECORDS
00066              RECORD CONTAINS 173 TO 1072 CHARACTERS
00067              DATA RECORD IS ADMITTING-DATA-RECORD.
00068         01   ADMITTING-DATA-RECORD.
00069                   02  PATIENT-NAME.
00070                          03    LAST-NAME              PIC X(15).
00071                          03    INITIALS               PIC X(4).
00072                   02  PATIENT-ADDRESS.
00073                          03    STREET-ADDRESS         PIC X(20).
00074                          03    CITY                   PIC X(15).
00075                   02  PHONE-NUMBER                    PIC 9(7).
00076                   02  ADMITTING-IDENTIFIER
00077                                                        PIC X(5).
00078                   02  ADMISSION-DATE                  PIC 9(6).
00079
00080                   02  SOCIAL-SECURITY-NUMBER
00081                                                        PIC X(11).
00082                   02  STATE-MEDICAID-NUMBER
00083                                                        PIC X(8).
00084                   02  WARD-NUMBER                     PIC 9(2).
00085                   02  ROOM-NUMBER                     PIC 9(3).
00086                   02  BED-NUMBER                      PIC 9(4).
00087                   02  REFERRING-PHYSICIAN.
00088                          03    LAST-NAME              PIC X(15).
00089                          03    INITIALS               PIC X(4).
00090                   02  SUPERVISORY-PHYSICIAN.
00091                          03    LAST-NAME              PIC X(15).
00092                          03    INITIALS               PIC X(4).
00093                   02  PRELIMINARY-DIAGNOSIS.
00094                          03    DIAGNOSIS-CODE         PIC 99.
00095                   02  PROCEDURE-NUMBER                PIC 99.
00096                   02  PROCEDURE-OR-TEST-SCHEDULED
00097                          OCCURS 1 TO 30 TIMES
00098                          DEPENDING ON PROCEDURE-NUMBER.
00099                          03    PROCEDURE-TYPE         PIC 99.
00100                          03    DATE-SCHEDULED         PIC 9(6).
00101                          03    TIME-SCHEDULED         PIC 9(4).
```

Program 9.2 (cont.)

```
00102                     03   CONSULTING-PHYSICIAN.
00103                          04   LAST-NAME        PIC X(15).
00104                     '    04   INITIALS         PIC X(4).
00105
00106
00107          WORKING-STORAGE SECTION.
00108
00109          77  FILE-STATUS                    PIC 99.
00110          77  INPUT-FILE-EOF                 PIC X(3).
00111          88  END-OF-FILE-IF
00112                  VALUE IS 'ON'.
00113          77  TYPE-COUNTER                   PIC S9(4)
00114                  USAGE IS COMPUTATIONAL SYNCHRONIZED.
00115
00116
00117          PROCEDURE DIVISION.
00118
00119              PERFORM INITIALIZATION.
00120              PERFORM COPY-DISK-TO-DISK
00121                  UNTIL END-OF-FILE-IF.
00122              PERFORM TERMINATION.
00123              STOP RUN.
00124
00125          INITIALIZATION.
00126              MOVE 'OFF' TO INPUT-FILE-EOF.
00127              OPEN INPUT   INPUT-FILE
00128                  OUTPUT ADMITTING-DATA-FILE.
00129              READ INPUT-FILE RECORD
00130                  AT END MOVE 'ON' TO INPUT-FILE-EOF.
00131
00132          COPY-DISK-TO-DISK.
00133              PERFORM MOVE-INPUT-TO-OUTPUT.
00134              PERFORM WRITE-ADMITTING-DATA-FILE.
00135              DISPLAY ADMITTING-DATA-RECORD OF
00136                  ADMITTING-DATA-FILE.
00137              DISPLAY 'FILE STATUS IS ----> ' FILE-STATUS.
00138              READ INPUT-FILE RECORD
00139                  AT END MOVE 'ON' TO INPUT-FILE-EOF.
00140
00141          MOVE-INPUT-TO-OUTPUT.
00142              MOVE 1 TO PROCEDURE-NUMBER.
00143              MOVE SPACES TO ADMITTING-DATA-RECORD
00144                  OF ADMITTING-DATA-FILE.
00145              MOVE INPUT-DATA
00146                  TO ADMITTING-DATA-RECORD.
00147              MOVE 1 TO PROCEDURE-NUMBER.
00148
00149          WRITE-ADMITTING-DATA-FILE.
00150              WRITE ADMITTING-DATA-RECORD
00151                  OF ADMITTING-DATA-FILE.
00152
00153          TERMINATION.
00154              CLOSE INPUT-FILE
00155                  ADMITTING-DATA-FILE.
```

The SELECT clause for the ADMITTING-DATA-FILE specifies it as an Indexed I–O file and that it is to be accessed in the sequential access mode. The record key is the field ADMITTING-IDENTIFIER in the 01 record description following the FD for the ADMITTING-DATA-FILE.

Since the records in the Indexed I–O file are variable length, the RECORD

CONTAINS clause in the FD for ADMITTING-DATA-FILE specifies from 173 to 1072 characters. These figures are arrived at in the following manner. First, the bytes of storage specified in all the PICTURE clauses in the 01 record description under the FD for the ADMITTING-DATA-FILE are added together except those following the field called PROCEDURE-OR-TEST-SCHEDULED (which contains the OCCURS DEPENDING ON clause and hence the variable portion of the record). This sum is 142 bytes. This is the number of bytes that will be occupied by the fixed portion of the variable-length record. The number of bytes grouped together under the field PROCEDURE-OR-TEST-SCHEDULED is 31 bytes. Each time a variable portion is added to the record, it will take up 31 bytes. The sum 142 + 31 = 173 is thus the smallest size of the variable-length record. Remember that at least one occurrence of the variable portion of a record is always present in each variable-length record in COBOL. It is *incorrect* to specify OCCURS 0 TO 30 TIMES DEPENDING ON. It must always be OCCURS 1 (or more) to 30 TIMES DEPENDING ON. The maximum size record is 142 + 30 (the maximum number of variable portions) × 31 = 1072.

The PROCEDURE DIVISION is straightforward. It merely copies the record from the input file buffer to the output file buffer and writes the record to the Indexed I–O file. Note that, prior to the first move being issued, a 1 is first moved to the field PROCEDURE-NUMBER in the ADMITTING-DATA record. This field is the subject of the OCCURS DEPENDING ON field and thus makes the record the minimum possible size. The data-name that is the subject of DEPENDING ON must have a value.

9.4.3 The Indexed I–O Module: Record Update And Retrieval

Updating the Admission Data File

Each patient admitted must be scheduled for one or more tests. In order to do this, the admitting identifier is required.

Logical Analysis: Record Retrieval and Update

In order to add information concerning the scheduled tests for any particular patient, the unique record key is needed. Using this key, a record can be retrieved from the admission data file and updated if necessary. Program 9.3 is used to update the ADMISSION-DATA-FILE.

Program 9.3 Updating the admitting-data-file

```
00009        / ** UPDATE OF ADMITTING-DATA-FILE **
00010        * **      FROM A SEQUENTIAL FILE      **
00011
00012          INPUT-OUTPUT SECTION.
00013          FILE-CONTROL.
```

Program 9.3   (cont.)

```
00014
00015                    SELECT INPUT-FILE
00016                        ASSIGN TO DISK-DD1
00017                        ACCESS MODE IS SEQUENTIAL
00018                        ORGANIZATION IS SEQUENTIAL.
00019                    SELECT ADMITTING-DATA-FILE
00020                        ASSIGN TO DISK-DD2
00021                        ORGANIZATION IS INDEXED
00022                        ACCESS MODE IS RANDOM
00023                        FILE STATUS IS FILE-STATUS
00024                        RECORD KEY IS ADMITTING-IDENTIFIER
00025                            OF ADMITTING-DATA-FILE.
00026
00027
00028            DATA DIVISION.
00029            FILE SECTION.
00030
00031            FD   INPUT-FILE
00032                    LABEL RECORDS ARE STANDARD
00033                    BLOCK CONTAINS 0 RECORDS
00034                    RECORD CONTAINS 141 CHARACTERS
00035                    DATA RECORDS ARE
00036                        NEW-PATIENT-RECORD
00037                        SCHEDULED-TEST-INFORMATION.
00038            01   NEW-PATIENT-RECORD.
00039                 02   PATIENT-NAME.
00040                      03    LAST-NAME-PN          PIC X(15).
00041                      03    INITIALS-PN           PIC X(4).
00042                 02   PATIENT-ADDRESS.
00043                      03    STREET-ADDRESS        PIC X(20).
00044                      03    CITY                  PIC X(15).
00045                 02   PHONE-NUMBER               PIC 9(7).
00046                 02   ADMITTING-IDENTIFIER
00047                                                  PIC X(5).
00048                 02   ADMISSION-DATE              PIC 9(6).
00049                 02   SOCIAL-SECURITY-NUMBER
00050                                                  PIC X(11).
00051                 02   STATE-MEDICAID-NUMBER
00052                                                  PIC X(8).
00053                 02   WARD-NUMBER                 PIC 9(2).
00054                 02   ROOM-NUMBER                 PIC 9(3).
00055                 02   BED-NUMBER                  PIC 9(4).
00056                 02   REFERRING-PHYSICIAN.
00057                      03    LAST-NAME-RP          PIC X(15).
00058                      03    INITIALS-RP           PIC X(4).
00059                 02   SUPERVISORY-PHYSICIAN.
00060                      03    LAST-NAME-SP          PIC X(15).
00061                      03    INITIALS-SP           PIC X(4).
00062                 02   PRELIMINARY-DIAGNOSIS
00063                                                  PIC 9(2).
00064                 02   TRANSACTION-CODE            PIC X.
00065
00066            01   SCHEDULED-TEST-INFORMATION.
00067                 02   ADMITTING-IDENTIFIER       PIC X(5).
00068                 02   PROCEDURE-OR-TEST-SCHEDULED.
00069                      03    PROCEDURE-TYPE        PIC 99.
00070                      03    DATE-SCHEDULED        PIC 9(6).
00071                      03    TIME-SCHEDULED        PIC 9(4).
00072                      03    CONSULTING-PHYSICIAN.
00073                           04    LAST-NAME        PIC X(15).
00074                           04    INITIALS         PIC X(4).
00075                 02   FILLER                      PIC X(104).
```

Program 9.3 (cont.)

```
00076                    02  TRANSACTION-CODE          PIC X.
00077
00078          FD   ADMITTING-DATA-FILE
00079               LABEL RECORDS ARE STANDARD
00080               BLOCK CONTAINS 1 RECORDS
00081               RECORD CONTAINS 173 TO 1072 CHARACTERS
00082               DATA RECORD IS ADMITTING-DATA-RECORD.
00083          01   ADMITTING-DATA-RECORD.
00084               02  PATIENT-NAME.
00085                    03   LAST-NAME-PN           PIC X(15).
00086                    03   INITIALS-PN            PIC X(4).
00087               02  PATIENT-ADDRESS.
00088                    03   STREET-ADDRESS         PIC X(20).
00089                    03   CITY                   PIC X(15).
00090               02  PHONE-NUMBER                 PIC 9(7).
00091               02  ADMITTING-IDENTIFIER
00092                                                PIC X(5).
00093               02  ADMISSION-DATE               PIC 9(6).
00094
00095               02  SOCIAL-SECURITY-NUMBER
00096                                                PIC X(11).
00097               02  STATE-MEDICAID-NUMBER
00098                                                PIC X(8).
00099               02  WARD-NUMBER                  PIC 9(2).
00100               02  ROOM-NUMBER                  PIC 9(3).
00101               02  BED-NUMBER                   PIC 9(4).
00102               02  REFERRING-PHYSICIAN.
00103                    03   LAST-NAME-RP           PIC X(15).
00104                    03   INITIALS-RP            PIC X(4).
00105               02  SUPERVISORY-PHYSICIAN.
00106                    03   LAST-NAME-SP           PIC X(15).
00107                    03   INITIALS-SP            PIC X(4).
00108               02  PRELIMINARY-DIAGNOSIS.
00109                    03   DIAGNOSIS-CODE         PIC 99.
00110               02  PROCEDURE-NUMBER             PIC 99.
00111               02  PROCEDURE-OR-TEST-SCHEDULED
00112                        OCCURS 1 TO 30 TIMES
00113                        DEPENDING ON PROCEDURE-NUMBER.
00114                    03   PROCEDURE-TYPE         PIC 99.
00115                    03   DATE-SCHEDULED         PIC 9(6).
00116                    03   TIME-SCHEDULED         PIC 9(4).
00117                    03   CONSULTING-PHYSICIAN.
00118                         04   LAST-NAME    PIC X(15).
00119                         04   INITIALS     PIC X(4).
00120
00121
00122
00123          WORKING-STORAGE SECTION.
00124
00125          77  FILE-STATUS                      PIC 99.
00126          77  END-OF-FILE-IF                   PIC X(3).
00127               88  NO-MORE-INPUT
00128                   VALUE IS 'ON'.
00129          77  TYPE-SWITCH                      PIC X(6).
00130               88  NEW-RECORD
00131                   VALUE IS 'NEW'.
00132               88  UPDATE-RECORD
00133                   VALUE IS 'UPDATE'.
00134          77  RECORD-ON-FILE-SWITCH            PIC X(3).
00135               88  VALID-RECORD
00136                   VALUE IS 'OFF'.
00137               88  INVALID-RECORD
```

Program 9.3   (cont.)

```
00138                         VALUE IS 'ON'.
00139              77  TRANSACTION-CODE-ERROR-FLAG  PIC X(3).
00140                  88  NOT-ERROR
00141                         VALUE IS 'OFF'.
00142                  88  ERROR-EXISTS
00143                         VALUE IS 'ON'.
00144
00145
00146              PROCEDURE DIVISION.
00147
00148                  PERFORM INITIALIZATION.
00149                  PERFORM UPDATE-ADMITTING-DATA-FILE
00150                  UNTIL NO-MORE-INPUT.
00151                  PERFORM TERMINATION.
00152                  STOP RUN.
00153
00154              INITIALIZATION.
00155                  DISPLAY 'INITIALIZATION'.
00156                  OPEN INPUT  INPUT-FILE
00157                       I-O    ADMITTING-DATA-FILE.
00158                  MOVE 'OFF' TO END-OF-FILE-IF.
00159                  PERFORM READ-INPUT-FILE.
00160
00161              READ-INPUT-FILE.
00162                  READ INPUT-FILE RECORD
00163                       AT END MOVE 'ON' TO END-OF-FILE-IF.
00164
00165              UPDATE-ADMITTING-DATA-FILE.
00166                  MOVE 'OFF' TO TRANSACTION-CODE-ERROR-FLAG.
00167                  MOVE 'OFF' TO RECORD-ON-FILE-SWITCH.
00168                  PERFORM DETERMINE-UPDATE-TYPE.
00169                  DISPLAY 'TCEF--> ' TRANSACTION-CODE-ERROR-FLAG.
00170                  DISPLAY 'TYPE-SWITCH---> ' TYPE-SWITCH.
00171                  IF NOT-ERROR
00172                  THEN
00173                       IF NEW-RECORD
00174                       THEN
00175                            PERFORM ADD-RECORD-TO-FILE
00176                       ELSE
00177                          IF UPDATE-RECORD
00178                          THEN
00179                          PERFORM MAKE-CHANGE-TO-FILE.
00180                  PERFORM READ-INPUT-FILE.
00181
00182              DETERMINE-UPDATE-TYPE.
00183                  IF TRANSACTION-CODE
00184                     OF SCHEDULED-TEST-INFORMATION
00185                     EQUAL '1'
00186                  THEN
00187                       MOVE 'NEW' TO TYPE-SWITCH
00188                  ELSE
00189                       IF TRANSACTION-CODE
00190                          OF SCHEDULED-TEST-INFORMATION
00191                          EQUAL '2'
00192                       THEN
00193                          MOVE 'UPDATE' TO TYPE-SWITCH
00194                       ELSE
00195                          PERFORM ILLEGAL-TYPE-ERROR-ROUTINE.
00196
00197              ILLEGAL-TYPE-ERROR-ROUTINE.
00198                  MOVE 'ON' TO TRANSACTION-CODE-ERROR-FLAG.
```

Program 9.3 (cont.)

```
00199
00200              ADD-RECORD-TO-FILE.
00201                  MOVE 1 TO PROCEDURE-NUMBER.
00202                  MOVE CORRESPONDING
00203                  NEW-PATIENT-RECORD
00204                  TO ADMITTING-DATA-RECORD.
00205                  DISPLAY 'WRITE---> ' ADMITTING-IDENTIFIER
00206                  OF ADMITTING-DATA-RECORD.
00207                  WRITE ADMITTING-DATA-RECORD
00208                  INVALID KEY
00209                  PERFORM ERROR-IN-NEW-PATIENT-RECORD.
00210
00211              ERROR-IN-NEW-PATIENT-RECORD.
00212                  DISPLAY '****ERROR****'.
00213                  DISPLAY 'UNABLE TO WRITE'.
00214                  DISPLAY 'THE NEW PATIENT RECORD TO FILE'.
00215                  DISPLAY 'POSSIBLY FILE FULL'.
00216                  DISPLAY 'OR RECORD WITH ADMITTING-IDENTIFIER'.
00217                  DISPLAY 'ALREADY IN EXISTENCE'.
00218                  DISPLAY 'ADMITTING-IDENTIFIER---->  '
00219                      ADMITTING-IDENTIFIER
00220                      OF ADMITTING-DATA-RECORD.
00221
00222              MAKE-CHANGE-TO-FILE.
00223                  PERFORM READ-ADMITTING-DATA-FILE.
00224                  IF VALID-RECORD
00225                  THEN
00226                      PERFORM UPDATE-RECORD-ROUTINE
00227                  ELSE
00228                      PERFORM ILLEGAL-TRANSACTION-ROUTINE.
00229
00230              ILLEGAL-TRANSACTION-ROUTINE.
00231                  DISPLAY '****ERROR****'.
00232                  DISPLAY 'UNABLE TO READ RECORD'.
00233                  DISPLAY 'WITH GIVEN ADMITTING-IDENTIFIER'.
00234                  DISPLAY 'ADMITTING-IDENTIFIER---->'
00235                      ADMITTING-IDENTIFIER OF
00236                      SCHEDULED-TEST-INFORMATION.
00237
00238              READ-ADMITTING-DATA-FILE.
00239                  MOVE ADMITTING-IDENTIFIER
00240                  OF SCHEDULED-TEST-INFORMATION
00241                  TO ADMITTING-IDENTIFIER
00242                  OF ADMITTING-DATA-RECORD.
00243                  READ ADMITTING-DATA-FILE RECORD
00244                  KEY IS ADMITTING-IDENTIFIER
00245                  OF ADMITTING-DATA-RECORD
00246                  INVALID KEY
00247                  MOVE 'ON' TO RECORD-ON-FILE-SWITCH.
00248
00249              UPDATE-RECORD-ROUTINE.
00250                  DISPLAY 'PROCEDURE-NUMBER---> ' PROCEDURE-NUMBER.
00251                  IF PROCEDURE-NUMBER EQUAL 1
00252                  THEN
00253                      MOVE CORRESPONDING
00254                      PROCEDURE-OR-TEST-SCHEDULED
00255                      OF SCHEDULED-TEST-INFORMATION
00256                      TO PROCEDURE-OR-TEST-SCHEDULED
00257                      OF ADMITTING-DATA-RECORD(1)
00258                      ADD 1 TO PROCEDURE-NUMBER
00259                  ELSE
00260                      DISPLAY 'PROCEDURE-NUMBER---> '
```

Program 9.3   (cont.)

```
00261                        PROCEDURE-NUMBER
00262                    MOVE CORRESPONDING
00263                    PROCEDURE-OR-TEST-SCHEDULED
00264                    OF SCHEDULED-TEST-INFORMATION
00265                    TO PROCEDURE-OR-TEST-SCHEDULED
00266                    OF ADMITTING-DATA-RECORD
00267                    (PROCEDURE-NUMBER)
00268                    ADD 1 TO PROCEDURE-NUMBER.
00269                DISPLAY 'REWRITE---> ' ADMITTING-IDENTIFIER
00270                OF ADMITTING-DATA-RECORD.
00271                REWRITE ADMITTING-DATA-RECORD
00272                    INVALID KEY
00273                    PERFORM ERROR-IN-UPDATE-RECORD-ROUTINE.
00274
00275           ERROR-IN-UPDATE-RECORD-ROUTINE.
00276                DISPLAY '****ERROR*****'.
00277                DISPLAY 'UNABLE TO REWRITE RECORD'.
00278                DISPLAY 'WITH ADMITTING-IDENTIFIER ---->'
00279                ADMITTING-IDENTIFIER
00280                OF ADMITTING-DATA-RECORD.
00281
00282           TERMINATION.
00283                CLOSE ADMITTING-DATA-FILE
00284                    INPUT-FILE.
00285
```

Program   9.3   Narrative.   Program   9.3   fetches   records   from   the ADMITTING-DATA-FILE, reads update records from a sequential input file (which is in random order), and adds the update material to the appropriate patient record. The patient record is then rewritten to the file. Sometimes the INPUT-FILE contains new patient records, in which case the records are simply written directly to the file.

Note that the clause ACCESS MODE IS RANDOM is used in the SELECT statement for the ADMITTING-DATA-FILE. Once an Indexed I–O file has been created in the sequential access mode, it may always be referred to in the random access mode.

In the PROCEDURE DIVISION the Indexed I–O file is opened with the statement OPEN I–O ADMITTING-DATA-FILE. This form of the OPEN statement is used because it is necessary both to read and to write records to the file.

In the PROCEDURE DIVISION there are two types of records that can be added to the Indexed I–O file. One type, called NEW-PATIENT-RECORD, consists of a new patient record not already entered in the ADMITTING-DATA-FILE. These records are written to the ADMITTING-DATA-FILE with a WRITE statement. The WRITE statement is always used when it is necessary to add extra records to an Indexed I–O file. This should be contrasted with the second type of record, called in the program SCHEDULED-TEST-INFORMATION. This is a record containing information about tests scheduled for the patient. This information is appended to the variable part of a PATIENT-RECORD and then written to the file with a REWRITE command. The REWRITE command is necessary because we want the updated record to replace an existing file record. Had we used the WRITE command, an error would have resulted, since an attempt to add a record that already exists to a file is not permitted. This is such a dangerous happenstance that the programmer would probably appreciate the error message. Destroying valuable data is a possibility the programmer should always guard against. The examples here are for illustrative purposes. Production programs should always contain software tests to prevent such accidents.

In this program it was the logic that made it necessary to read the file record before the REWRITE statement was executed (because the record itself had to be updated). If the record is not updated, it need not be rewritten back to the file. A READ from a file only makes a copy of a record in the buffer area. It does not physically remove it from the file.

9.5 INDEXED I–O MODULE: MULTIPLE KEYS

9.5.1 Retrieving Records on Other Keys

Very often it is convenient to be able to retrieve records on keys other than the record key. For billing purposes it is convenient to be able to fetch a record by state Medicaid number. Of course, if the patient has a history of visits to Lakeside General, there may be more than one record under a single Medicaid number. The same would be true of the social security number. The actual record required could be determined exactly by fetching all of the records that are stored with the same social security number and selecting the one with the most recent admission date. Other fields have similar properties. The admission date itself is a useful retrieval field. It might, for example, be convenient to print a list of all patients admitted on a particular date. Then each of these fields, social security number, Medicaid number, and admission date, are useful keys for record retrieval. Keys such as these are called *secondary keys*. Sometimes secondary keys are always unique and sometimes they are not. All the keys mentioned for Lakeside General hospital may or may not have duplicates; it depends on circumstances. If no patient is ever admitted more than once, there will obviously be no duplicate social security number or duplicate Medicaid number on the file; but even then an admission date and a ward number will still refer to more than one patient. Only *retrieval* is ever allowed on a secondary key. All updating, the deleting of records and the adding of new records, requires specification of the record key. Secondary keys can still be useful in such cases. Suppose only a person's social security number is known and the doctor wishes to change the patient record. In this case the social security number can be used as a secondary key in order to fetch the record. Once fetched, the admitting identifier is available and the record can be modified.

At regular intervals the hospital needs a report of the patients assigned to the various wards within the hospital. Each ward has a two-digit number, and this is an assigned field within each record of the ADMITTING-DATA-FILE. In order to obtain this output, it is necessary to consider the ward number a secondary key. Program 9.4 prints out patients by ward.

Program 9.4   Listing patients by ward.

```
00009          /   ** LIST PATIENTS BY WARD **
00010
00011          INPUT-OUTPUT SECTION.
00012          FILE-CONTROL.
00013
00014              SELECT INPUT-FILE
00015                  ASSIGN TO DISK-DD2
00016                  ACCESS MODE IS SEQUENTIAL
00017                  ORGANIZATION IS SEQUENTIAL.
00018              SELECT PATIENT-PROCEDURE-FILE
00019                  ASSIGN TO DISK-DD1
00020                  ORGANIZATION IS INDEXED
00021                  ACCESS MODE IS DYNAMIC
00022                  FILE STATUS IS FILE-STATUS
00023                  RECORD KEY IS ADMITTING-IDENTIFIER
00024                      OF PATIENT-PROCEDURE-FILE
00025                  ALTERNATE RECORD KEY IS WARD-NUMBER
00026                      OF PATIENT-PROCEDURE-FILE
00027                      WITH DUPLICATES.
00028
00029
00030          DATA DIVISION.
00031          FILE SECTION.
00032
00033          FD  INPUT-FILE
00034              LABEL RECORDS ARE STANDARD
00035              BLOCK CONTAINS 1 RECORDS
00036              RECORD CONTAINS 80 CHARACTERS
00037              DATA RECORD IS PATIENT-DATA.
00038          01  INPUT-DATA.
00039              02  WARD-NUMBER-ON-CARD        PIC X(2).
00040              02  FILLER                     PIC X(78).
00041
00042          FD  PATIENT-PROCEDURE-FILE
00043              LABEL RECORDS ARE STANDARD
00044              BLOCK CONTAINS 1 RECORDS
00045              RECORD CONTAINS 173 TO 1072 CHARACTERS
00046              DATA RECORD IS HOSPITAL-RECORD.
00047          01  HOSPITAL-RECORD.
00048              02  PATIENT-NAME.
00049                  03  LAST-NAME             PIC X(15).
00050                  03  INITIALS              PIC X(4).
00051              02  PATIENT-ADDRESS.
00052                  03  STREET-ADDRESS        PIC X(20).
00053                  03  CITY                  PIC X(15).
00054              02  PHONE-NUMBER              PIC 9(7).
00055              02  ADMITTING-IDENTIFIER
00056                                            PIC X(5).
00057              02  ADMISSION-DATE            PIC 9(6).
00058
00059              02  SOCIAL-SECURITY-NUMBER
00060                                            PIC X(11).
00061              02  STATE-MEDICAID-NUMBER
00062                                            PIC X(8).
00063              02  WARD-NUMBER               PIC 9(2).
00064              02  ROOM-NUMBER               PIC 9(3).
00065              02  BED-NUMBER                PIC 9(4).
00066              02  REFERRING-PHYSICIAN.
00067                  03  LAST-NAME             PIC X(15).
00068                  03  INITIALS              PIC X(4).
00069              02  SUPERVISORY-PHYSICIAN.
00070                  03  LAST-NAME             PIC X(15).
00071                  03  INITIALS              PIC X(4).
```

Program 9.4   (cont.)

```
00072                02  PRELIMINARY-DIAGNOSIS.
00073                    03  DIAGNOSIS-CODE        PIC 99.
00074                02  PROCEDURE-NUMBER          PIC 99.
00075                02  PROCEDURE-OR-TEST-SCHEDULED
00076                    OCCURS 1 TO 30 TIMES
00077                    DEPENDING ON PROCEDURE-NUMBER.
00078                    03  PROCEDURE-TYPE         PIC 99.
00079                    03  DATE-SCHEDULED         PIC 9(6).
00080                    03  TIME-SCHEDULED         PIC 9(4).
00081                    03  CONSULTING-PHYSICIAN.
00082                        04  LAST-NAME          PIC X(15).
00083                        04  INITIALS           PIC X(4).
00084
00085
00086            WORKING-STORAGE SECTION.
00087
00088            01  FILE-STATUS.
00089                02  FILE-STATUS-KEY-1          PIC 9.
00090                02  FILE-STATUS-KEY-2          PIC 9.
00091                88  VALID-DUPLICATE
00092                    VALUE IS 2.
00093            77  INPUT-FILE-EOF                 PIC X(3).
00094                88  END-OF-FILE-IF
00095                    VALUE IS 'ON'.
00096            01  ERROR-FLAG-1                   PIC X(3).
00097                88  ERROR-1
00098                    VALUE IS 'ON'.
00099            01  END-OF-ALTERNATE-INDEX         PIC X(3).
00100                88  END-OF-LIST
00101                    VALUE IS 'ON'.
00102                88  MORE-OF-LIST
00103                    VALUE IS 'OFF'.
00104
00105
00106            PROCEDURE DIVISION.
00107
00108                PERFORM INITIALIZATION.
00109                PERFORM GET-PATIENTS-ON-WARD
00110                    UNTIL END-OF-FILE-IF.
00111                PERFORM TERMINATION.
00112                STOP RUN.
00113
00114            INITIALIZATION.
00115                MOVE 'OFF' TO INPUT-FILE-EOF.
00116                OPEN INPUT  INPUT-FILE
00117                     I-O PATIENT-PROCEDURE-FILE.
00118                READ INPUT-FILE RECORD
00119                    AT END MOVE 'ON' TO INPUT-FILE-EOF.
00120                IF NOT END-OF-FILE-IF THEN
00121                    DISPLAY 'WARD NUMBER ON INPUT CARD ---> ',
00122                        WARD-NUMBER-ON-CARD.
00123
00124            GET-PATIENTS-ON-WARD.
00125                MOVE 'OFF' TO ERROR-FLAG-1.
00126                MOVE 'OFF' TO END-OF-ALTERNATE-INDEX.
00127                MOVE WARD-NUMBER-ON-CARD
00128                TO WARD-NUMBER
00129                OF PATIENT-PROCEDURE-FILE.
00130                READ PATIENT-PROCEDURE-FILE RECORD
00131                    KEY IS WARD-NUMBER
00132                    INVALID KEY PERFORM ERROR-ROUTINE-1.
00133                DISPLAY FILE-STATUS.
```

Program 9.4   (cont.)

```
00134                    IF NOT ERROR-1 THEN
00135                        DISPLAY 'NAME OF PATIENT ----> ',
00136                        LAST-NAME OF PATIENT-NAME
00137                        OF HOSPITAL-RECORD
00138                        DISPLAY 'ADMITTING-IDENTIFIER --->  ',
00139                        ADMITTING-IDENTIFIER OF
00140                        HOSPITAL-RECORD
00141                        DISPLAY 'WARD NUMBER----> ',
00142                        WARD-NUMBER OF
00143                        HOSPITAL-RECORD
00144                        PERFORM GET-SIMILAR-KEYED-RECORDS
00145                        UNTIL NOT VALID-DUPLICATE
00146                        OR END-OF-LIST.
00147                    READ INPUT-FILE RECORD
00148                        AT END MOVE 'ON' TO INPUT-FILE-EOF.
00149                    IF NOT END-OF-FILE-IF THEN
00150                        DISPLAY 'WARD NUMBER ON INPUT CARD ---> ',
```

Program 9.4 Narrative.   Program 9.4 is a program that uses the secondary key, ward number, to fetch records on a particular ward and print out the patient names and admitting identifiers.

There are two stages involved in making a particular field of a set of records into a secondary key. In the first stage the operating system access methods must be told of the existence of the secondary key, its location in each record, and the maximum number of records likely ever to have this particular key. This is done independently of the COBOL language and may require the programmer to seek the aid of computing center personnel at the installation in question. The access methods will read the Indexed I–O file and build a directory which maps each secondary key value to every record that contains it. This directory will then be available to the COBOL program for processing.

VSAM is one of the access methods used by IBM to implement the secondary key feature, and the reader will find more information on this in Chapter 12.

The second stage involves accessing the Indexed I–O file with the COBOL language.

In Program 9.4 the SELECT clause is modified to include the clause

```
ALTERNATE RECORD KEY IS WARD-NUMBER
    OF ADMITTING-DATA-FILE
    WITH DUPLICATES
```

This informs the COBOL processor that WARD-NUMBER is a secondary key and that more than one record in the file may share a common secondary key value. Many patients may be found on any given ward. The WITH DUPLICATES portion of the clause may be omitted only if there is no possibility that two or more records could be found with the same secondary key. The programmer is urged to include this clause even if the file currently contains no duplicates but might do so later. Updating may be inhibited during production runs if care is not employed.

The clause ACCESS MODE IS DYNAMIC indicates that two forms of the read statement are needed to fetch records using a secondary key. The first record with a particular secondary key value is fetched with a READ having the KEY IS format. Other records with the same key value are retrieved with the sequential access form of the READ. The file status clause is set to 02 to indicate that a valid duplicate has been retrieved by a sequential read. Interrogate the file status variable after each read. It should also be noted that the conditions under which the AT END clause of the sequential read is invoked seem to be implementation dependent; the manual of the manufacturer should be consulted.

9.5.2 Summary of Statements

Within the procedure division we have examined five language verbs in their various formats, namely the READ, WRITE, REWRITE, DELETE, and START verbs. Each of these verbs performs a specific task and is subject to various rules depending on the access mode and the format of the OPEN verb employed. For quick review and reference, the rules for the use of these verbs are summarized in the Tables 9.1 and 9.2. Table 9.1 summarizes the various statement formats for each verb, and Table 9.2 keys the use of these formats to the access mode and the OPEN format. Table 9.3 gives the return codes for the file status clause.

Table 9.1   Verb Formats for Indexed I–O

Verb	Format	Statements
READ	1	READ file-name RECORD [INTO identifier] AT END imperative statement
	2	READ file-name RECORD [INTO identifier] KEY IS data-name INVALID KEY imperative statement
WRITE		WRITE record-name [FROM identifier] INVALID KEY imperative statement
REWRITE		REWRITE record-name [FROM identifier] INVALID KEY imperative statement
DELETE	1	DELETE file-name RECORD
	2	DELETE file-name RECORD INVALID KEY imperative statement
START		START file-name KEY {IS EQUAL TO / IS = / IS GREATER THAN / IS > / IS NOT LESS THAN / IS NOT <} data-name INVALID KEY imperative statement

Table 9.2   Summary of Formats from Table 9.1 and Access Modes

Access	Input	Output	I-0
Sequential	READ format 1 START	WRITE	READ format 1 REWRITE DELETE format 1 START
Random	READ format 1	WRITE	READ format 2 WRITE REWRITE DELETE format 2

Table 9.3   Valid FILE-STATUS Values

Status Key 1	Status Key 2	Meaning
0	0	Successful completion
0	2	Successful completion—duplicate key
1	0	At end
2	1	Sequence error
2	2	Invalid key duplicate key
2	3	No record found
2	4	Boundary violation
3	0	Permanent error
3	4	Boundary violation
9	—	Implementor defined, check manufacturer's manual

9.6 SUMMARY

An Indexed I–O file consists of records sequentially ordered in ascending sequence by a record key. Records can be accessed randomly by specification of the record key or by any record field designated as a secondary key. The record key must be unique; secondary keys are permitted to have duplicates. Record updates, deletions, and additions require specification of the record key. An indexed I–O file must be loaded in sorted sequence in the sequential access mode. Variable-length records and secondary keys are a feature of the standard but are not supported in all implementations.

9.7 CONCLUSION

It should be realized at the outset that Indexed I–O files are a convenience. The programmer willing to do some programming on his own can implement equivalences to Indexed I–O files with a combination of relative files and data structures. This is very difficult to do, and we would not recommend it unless the reasons are compelling. A very important difference between the two file types is that each Indexed I–O file record must contain a specially designated and uniquely valued field, called the *record key*.

The reader is cautioned that the use of Indexed I–O requires a fair amount of system overhead. There is a price to be paid for all the bookkeeping provided by the access method used. Whether the price is worthwhile depends on the value received as compared to the costs of programming, run time, maintenance, and delayed operation because the programmer chooses to write more code.

REFERENCES FOR FURTHER READING

Bradley, J. *File and Data Base Techniques.* New York: Holt, Rinehart and Winston, 1981.

Behymer, S. A., et al. ''Analysis of Indexed Sequential and Direct Access File Organizations.'' In *Proceedings of 1974 ACM SIGMOD Workshop,* pp. 389–417.

PROBLEMS

1. Use Program 9.1 to create a credit union file. Do not forget that you will have to run an Access Method Services Procedure to allocate the file.

2. Prepare some transactions for the credit union file and write a program to update it.

3. Delete and add some records to the credit union file.

4. Set up an index file of the students in your class or of the people with whom you work. Employ at least two secondary keys and fetch records using these secondary keys.

5. Upon admission to the emergency room of the local hospital, a patient is required to give the information described in COBOL below.

```
01 ADMITTING-RECORD
   02 MEDICAID-NUMBER    PIC X(10).
   02 NAME-LAST          PIC X(15).
   02 NAME-FIRST         PIC X(15).
   02 ADDRESS-OF-PATIENT
      03 STREET          PIC X(16).
      03 CITY            PIC X(10).
   02 MILITARY-IDENT-NUMBER
                         PIC x(10).
```

Other information is also taken but will be ignored for this example.

Write a COBOL program that creates an index sequential file on primary key MEDICAID-NUMBER for these admitting records. Keypunch and store at least ten such records.

6. Write a COBOL program that reads in a deck of data cards each containing a ten digit MEDICAID-NUMBER. Access the file you created in question 5 and print out the records corresponding to the MEDICAID-NUMBER read in. Print an appropriate warning message if no admitting record corresponds to a particular MEDICAID-NUMBER read in.

7. Below is a partial description in COBOL of a military record keyed on the MILITARY-IDENT-NUMBER. Create an index sequential file of these records as you did in question 5. In addition modify the program from question 5 so that MILITARY-IDENT-NUMBER can be a secondary key for the admitting records file (no duplicates allowed). If your system does not allow for secondary keys, create a directory of MILITARY-IDENT-NUMBERs and corresponding MEDICAID-NUMBERs. It will now be possible to read a record from the military file, then to read the corresponding record from the admitting file. Try this in a COBOL program.

When files are linked together this way, we call the admitting record file an index coordinated file. This technique is very useful in data base technology because it allows information needed in one file application to be stored in a separate file, perhaps in a file updated by another party.

Do you see any connection between index coordinated files and variable length records? Index coordinated files can be used to store information that would normally be stored in the variable length portion of a record in situations where the use of fixed length records is preferable.

```
01 MILITARY-RECORD.
   02 MILITARY-IDENT-NUMBER PIC X(10).
   02 SERVICE-UNIT          PIC X(10).
   02 RANK                  PIC X(10).
   02 YRS-IN-SERVICE        PIC X(2).
```

10

Physical Organization of Indexed Sequential Files

This chapter and the two following provide insight into two file access methods used by IBM to implement the Indexed I–O module, which we discussed in the previous chapter. As such, neither this chapter nor the next two are strictly necessary, and the reader may skip to Chapter 13. However, the Indexed I–O module is easier to understand if one has a grasp of the kind of physical organization that underlies it.

10.1 INTRODUCTION

A well-known implementation of a file structure for indexed sequential files is the IBM indexed sequential access method (ISAM). Unfortunately, a generic name was used for a system implementation, and much more than *access* is intended. Because this method does not give total support of the Indexed I–O module of COBOL, certain features, such as the DELETE statement, ACCESS MODE IS DYNAMIC, and ALTERNATE KEY, are not available. While ISAM is gradually being replaced with VSAM by IBM, it remains in wide use and is an interesting example of an implementation of the indexed sequential file organization. Although ISAM is a file access method available to a host of different languages on IBM machines, other manufacturers have provided similar forms of file structures for their computers.

When COBOL is the language to be used, we often speak of the Indexed Sequential method of file organization in preference to Indexed I–O. The COBOL compiler contains routines that link the Indexed Sequential language features into the ISAM system. It is *not* our purpose to give a detailed description of ISAM but rather to examine the physical organization of the records in storage and to see how the sequential nature of the file is maintained. The purpose is to give the programmer insight into the advantages and limitations of the Indexed I–O module and to see how its use is system dependent.

10.2 A BASIS FOR AN INDEXED SEQUENTIAL ORGANIZATION

Suppose we want the records of a file to be organized sequentially by ascending key order and yet at the same time want to be able to fetch records directly. One solution is to sort the records before creating a relative file. Let us complicate the issue a little further by imagining that the file is to contain in excess of a million records. Most medium-sized credit card companies have file systems much larger than this. As we are using a relative file, we must either create a directory or invent a good hashing algorithm. We can, if we wish, create a directory containing 1 million entries. The directory will therefore need to be stored on disk or on some other storage device. Parts of the directory can be read into memory in small segments and table lookup performed there. If the binary search is being used for table lookup, keeping the dictionary sorted will be a nightmare, because as records are added to the file, their keys and relative addresses need to be placed in the directory at the correct locations to maintain sorted key order. Similar problems apply to hashing. This could mean large linked chains in the file and a consequent increase in the I/O time for record retrieval as these long chains of hash colliding records are searched. None of our options are very attractive.

There is, however, an alternate solution. Suppose we logically block the records into groups and maintain a pointer to the first record in each group. We could arbitrarily let each group consist of 100 records with a dictionary entry for the first record in each of these groups. As there are 10,000 of these groups (1,000,000 ÷ 100 = 10,000), the directory will have 10,000 entries and can remain in memory. To search for any given record, we first determine which group it is in. Then we sequentially fetch each record in the group until we find the required record. To illustrate the ideas involved, we shall consider a very small file. The reader should keep in mind, however, that with small files practically any method will do.

Consider the file of Fig. 10.1, which consists of four groups of three records

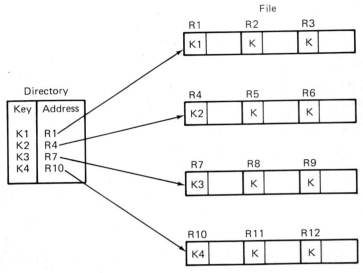

Figure 10.1   Indexing block records.

each and a directory which is used to provide the pointers to the groups. Each record contains a unique key. Only the key of the first record in each group is placed in the directory along with a pointer to its record. The records are stored sequentially in order of the key. Note how this keeps the directory much smaller than the size of the file.

To locate a record, we first find (from the directory) the group to which it belongs. This is done by locating the two adjacent directory key entries that bracket the desired key. We then go to the group pointed to by the lower-valued key and search this group sequentially for the desired key.

For example, in Fig. 10.2, to find record K38, we check the directory and find that keys K31 and K78 bracket this value. The record must be in the group whose leading record is K31. Since this has address 7 in the directory, we start sequentially searching this group for the record we want. We examine records 7, 8, and 9 in turn. Record 9 is the one we want.

It is an idea like this for file organization which forms the basis of the ISAM method. ISAM elaborates and extends this method by utilizing some of the physical characteristics of a disk.

The disk unit in Fig. 10.3 has a movable arm, resembling a comb, with read/write heads mounted on it for each platter surface. This arm moves laterally in and out of the space between the platters seeking a track. To reach any point on the surface of any platter, the following three steps take place. First, the unit moves inward toward the central spindle (or away from it, depending on its position relative to the track sought). Then one of the heads is selected by the hardware. Finally, a waiting period takes place until the rotation of the drive mechanism brings the desired location on the track under the head, at which time it is then read.

Directory

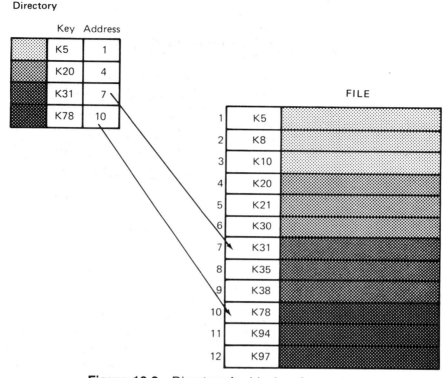

Figure 10.2   Directory for blocks of records.

There are as many tracks on a platter as there are fixed stops for the access arm in its movement from rim to spindle. When the arm is in position at one of these stops, it can select either of the surfaces on any platter. The set of tracks that can be selected when the arm is stopped is called a cylinder. If the movement of the arm is much slower than the rotation of the disk, then sequential processing should proceed by cylinder rather than by platter. This was true at the time ISAM was designed, and it is this feature that ISAM is designed to exploit.

10.3 PHYSICAL DATA ORGANIZATION UNDER ISAM

When a record is stored by ISAM, its record key must be one of the fields in the record. (This is not a requirement of Relative I–O.) The records themselves are first sorted by record key into ascending order before they are stored on one or more disk drives. ISAM will always maintain the records in this sorted order. Each record is stored on one of the tracks of a disk. Those records that follow it in sorted sequence are placed directly after it on the same track or, if room does not permit, are spilled over onto the next track in the same cylinder. In other words, they are dropped

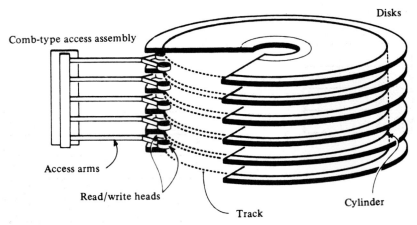

Figure 10.3 Disk pack unit.

down to the next platter surface. The arm does not move; looking downward, the next head is selected electronically. Since the tracks on a cylinder are labeled 0, 1, 2, . . . , the records that follow those on track 1 are placed on track 2. Track 0 is reserved. Records that follow those on the last track of a cylinder are moved over to the next file cylinder. The cylinders are also labeled 0, 1, 2, ...

Figure 10.4 shows two cylinders of records, but only their keys are shown. Note that the keys are in ascending sequence throughout their storage on both cylinders. We have not shown record 0 on either cylinder, as this is used by ISAM for control. Of course, the number of tracks on each cylinder is a function of the size of the disk pack.

When ISAM retrieves a record, it needs to know the cylinder, the track address, and the record key. These are the components that must make up the directory entries for the ISAM file. In ISAM a directory is called an *index*. For example, if a directory entry for record 1500 gave cylinder 9 and track 3, then ISAM would select cylinder 9. The read head associated with track 3 would then be activated. The bottom side of the top platter is usually track 0 because the top being exposed is subject to damage; therefore, the read head selected would be that for the top side of the third platter, as shown in Fig. 10.5. Of course, the required record might be one of the many records stored on track 3. Rotation of the drive would eventually bring the required record under the read head. The desired record is identified by its record key.

Because the records in an ISAM file are kept in sorted order by record key, it is not necessary to have a directory entry for every single record. *It is sufficient to know the largest record key on every track of the file*. For example, suppose the largest key on track 3 is 100 and the largest on track 4 is 200. A record with key 175, if it exists in the file at all, must be on track 4. It cannot be on track 3 as the largest key on that track is 100.

The most obvious place to keep the directory for each cylinder on the file is,

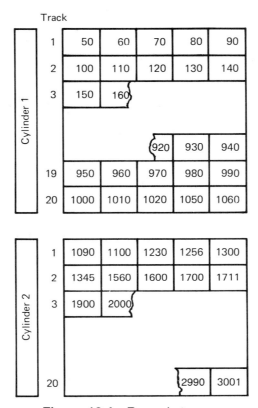

Figure 10.4   Record storage

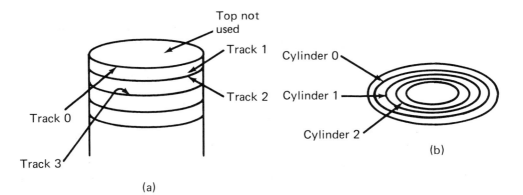

Figure 10.5   Disk organization: (a) disk; (b) top view of platter.

Figure 10.6 Track index.

of course, on the cylinder itself, and it is on track 0 of each cylinder that ISAM keeps its directory. This directory is known as a *track index;* it contains the largest key on every track and the hardware address of that track. Figure 10.6 shows a typical track index for one cylinder of a file. In this cylinder, for example, 400 is shown to be the largest key on track 3 and 700 the largest key on the cylinder. Later we will see that this directory is slightly more complicated. This will be clarified when we discuss how ISAM keeps track of records that are added to the file after its original creation. For the moment, this simplified version of the directory is more than sufficient.

How does ISAM use this directory to find a record on the file? First it positions the read/write mechanism over the appropriate cylinder and selects track 0. Let us suppose that the index on track 0 has the entries shown below in Fig. 10.6 and the system seeks the key 350. The entry

indicates that the record, if it is to be found, will be on track 3. The read head for track 3 is selected and the rotation of the drive will eventually bring the record with key 350, if it exists, under this read head. The fact that the index for this cylinder is on the cylinder itself means that no additional movement of the read/write mechanism is necessary.

When an ISAM file is spread over several cylinders, there is more than one track index. A track index is placed on track 0 of each cylinder used by the file. There remains then in this case a further problem. When a record is being sought, which track index should be examined? Not surprisingly, ISAM keeps a cylinder index with an entry for each of its track indexes. Each entry in this index specifies the address of every track index and the largest entry in each track index. In other words, the cylinder index has an entry for each cylinder of the file and the largest entry on that cylinder. The following is a typical cylinder index:

13	1650	14	1750	15	2000	16	3000	· · ·
cyl	key	cyl	key	cyl	key	cyl	key	

This cylinder index shows that on cylinder 15 the largest key that will be found is 2000. If ISAM is seeking record 1886, an examination of this cylinder index reveals that the record, if it exists, can be found on cylinder 15. The read/write mechanism moves to cylinder 15, selects track 0, and consults the track index. If that track index is

1	1800	2	1890	3	1900	$\cdots$

track   key   track   key   track   key

then track 2 is selected.

The cylinder index is not associated with any particular cylinder of the file and is stored in a separate area or on another disk altogether. This area is referred to as the *cylinder area*. The file itself along with the track indexes is called the *prime area*.

Sometimes a file may be very large, even extending across several disk drives. In this case hundreds of cylinders may be involved causing the cylinder index itself to be several tracks or cylinders in size. In this eventuality, ISAM may even create an index of the cylinder index. Such an index is called a *master index*. Each entry of the master index then points to a track of the cylinder index and specifies the largest key given on this track of the cylinder index. Even another master index might be made of this index. Perhaps now the reader can appreciate why the name "Indexed" is the first word in ISAM.

Figure 10.7 shows segments of each of the three types of indexes. The reader should try to follow the search algorithm, beginning at the master index, for the location of record 45. Only two tracks of both the master index and cylinder index are shown. The first entry in the master index says that the largest key mentioned in track 1 of the cylinder index is 211. The first entry on track 1 of the cylinder index shows that 95 is the largest key on the track index on cylinder 6. Checking the track index of cylinder 6 shows that record 45 is located on track 2. Record 45 also happens to be the largest record key on track 2.

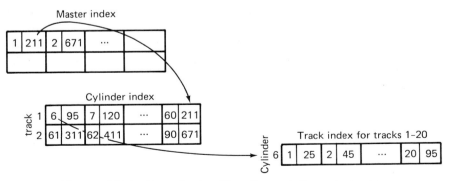

Figure 10.7 Search algorithm through three indexes.

10.4 OVERFLOW RECORDS IN ISAM

Unlike Relative I–O, which does not permit the addition of a new record to a file unless an empty slot is available, ISAM allows any number of new records to be added to an existing file. The number is limited by the availability of sufficient storage space. As mentioned earlier, ISAM also maintains the original ordering of the sorted file. Any record to be added is inserted into the file at an appropriate place. To accomplish this insertion, room must be made available for the record on its track by shifting each record *that logically follows the one to be added* forward on the track and dropping the last record on the track off the end. For example, if the records at the end of a track are

· · ·	26	28	30	31	33	35	37

and record 34 is to be added, then the track will be changed to

· · ·	26	28	30	31	33	34	35

and record 37 will be dropped off the end. The track's highest key is now 35 and the track index is changed accordingly. The question, of course, is what to do with record 37 that was dropped. If it is added to the next track, it will cause the record at the end of that track to be dropped off the end and a domino effect will cascade through all the records on the file. In each case, the track index will need to be changed as will the cylinder index when the last record on the cylinder is forced off. To avoid this problem, the record dropped off the original track is removed from the file and placed in an overflow area. This overflow area may be on another disk unit, elsewhere on the same disk unit, or even perhaps on the same cylinder if several tracks on each cylinder are set aside and designated for overflow use. The exact placement of the overflow area is determined when space for the file is requested from the operating system.

Earlier, it was noted that a simplified version of the track index had been presented. This version can now be upgraded. In actual fact, there are two entries for each track on a given cylinder. We shall designate them as "N" and "O" entries, where "N" denotes a normal entry and "O" an overflow entry. Before overflow records are added to the file, both entries are the same. For example, the track index for cylinder 6 of a file might appear as

N		O		N		O		N		
1	120	1	120	2	200	2	200	3	250	· · ·

In this case, both the N and O entries for track 2 designate that 200 is the largest key on this track. Suppose, in fact, that track 2 contains the following records (only the keys shown):

130	145	150	$\cdots$	180	190	200

As indicated by the track index, the largest key to be found on track 2 is 200. Now suppose record 185 is to be added to this track forcing record 200 off the end into the overflow area. Track 2 now becomes

130	145	150	$\cdots$	180	185	190

As the largest key on track 2 is now 190, the N entry for this track in the index must be changed to 190 as follows:

N		O		N		O		N		
1	120	1	120	2	190	2	200	3	250	$\cdots$

Suppose further that record 200 is placed in an overflow area on track 10 and is the first record on this overflow track. If this is designated as 10:1, the overflow area should be changed as follows:

N		O		N		O		N		
1	120	1	120	2	190	10:1	200	3	250	$\cdots$

In effect, then, record 200 has become the first of many possible records in the overflow area.

If record 186 is added to track 2, forcing 190 off the end into the overflow area leaving track 2 as

130	145	150	$\cdots$	180	185	186

then record 190 will be added as the second record in the overflow area, namely 10:2, and the overflow entry on the track index will be replaced by 10:2 so that the track index becomes

N		O		N		O		N		
1	120	1	120	2	186	10:2	200	3	250	$\cdots$

Note that in the O entry the 200 is not changed as it still represents the largest record key in the overflow area. In fact the previous entry 10:1 is added to the latest record to be added to the overflow area, record 190, so that it is not lost. The overflow area now looks like

#	200	10:1	190	$\cdots$

with record 190 pointing to record 200. The symbol "#" indicates that record 200 does not point to another record. The overflow entry always contains two values:

one represents the largest key value in the overflow area that has been moved there from an individual track (200 in the above example) and the other contains a pointer to the smallest key in the overflow area (190 in the above example). If record 194 is now spilled to the overflow area, the O entry will not be changed as 190 is still the smallest record key value in the overflow area. As the record with key 194 comes after 190, record 190 is adjusted to point to record 194 and 194 to 200. The sorted order is maintained in the overflow area, which now appears as

#	200	10:3	190	10:1	194	· · ·

It is not necessary that the records stored on a track in the overflow area be associated with only one track of the prime area. This is only the case here because we have assumed that all the overflow records on track 10 come from track 2. This is not always so. It is quite possible to have overflow records from many other tracks so that we could well imagine an overflow area as follows:

#	200	10:4	190	#	216	10:1	194	10:3	214	· · ·

where records 214 and 216 have arrived from track 4. Record 214 is the second overflow record from track 4 and points to the first from track 4, namely 216, at location 10:3.

The algorithm to be employed in adding a record to the overflow area can now be stated:

ALGORITHM: OVERFLOW ADDITIONS

1: Find the first available position in the overflow area.

2: Move the record to this position.

3: If this record is the record of lowest key in the overflow area, place the pointer to this record in the overflow entry of the track index and move the old value in the track index to the pointer field of the newly added record. If this is not the case, move the address of the new record to the pointer field of the record in the overflow area that precedes it in sorted sequence and place the old value of the pointer into the pointer field of the new record.

10.4.1 Overflow Considerations

If a record is in the prime area of a file, its retrieval is straightforward. The master, cylinder, and track indexes are examined; the appropriate track selected; and finally, after rotational delay of the drive, the record is retrieved. This is not true if the record is in the overflow area.

If the record is in the overflow area, its retrieval can take a long time. Suppose, for example, that record 16,000 is the first record moved to an overflow area and later followed by 60 more such records. As these 60 later records are chained together in key sequence order by pointers, all 60 records will have to be read before record 16,000 can be located. As each read is a time-consuming process, this can take a long time. The efficiency of ISAM is defeated by allowing large numbers of records to overflow from a single track.

This problem can be overcome by writing a "clean-up" program which reads all the records on the file, including those in the overflow areas and creates a larger file. This can be done whenever the time taken to retrieve records has become unacceptable. *The time taken for retrieval is the dominant criterion here as it is acceptable to have a large overflow area if the records in it are seldom retrieved.*

The other possibility is, as with relative files to create dummy records. In ISAM a dummy record is a record that contains HIGH-VALUES in the first character position but must, as with all records in ISAM, also contain a unique key. During file creation these records are sorted along with all the other file records and scattered wherever desired within the file.

Dummy records prevent growth in the overflow area in two ways. First, if a record to be added to an ISAM file has the same key as a dummy record, it merely replaces the dummy record. This is the ideal situation as no records are shifted along a given track and none of the indexes are changed. The second feature of dummy records is that they are not moved to the overflow area if they are forced off the end of the track by the insertion of a new record. They are simply ignored. The N entry in the track index is changed to reflect the fact that a different record now holds the last position on the track. If both the O and N keys are the same before the addition takes place, then they are both changed. Suppose, for example, that the N and O entries for track 7 of a certain cylinder are given as

N		O	
7	100	7	100

and that track 7 has the keys

50	60	70	· · ·	90	100

with record 100 being a dummy record. The addition of record 55 would change track 7 as follows:

50	55	60	70	· · ·	90

and since record 100 is a dummy record (and therefore not transferred to the overflow area), the N and O entries become

N		O	
7	90	7	90

10.5 CREATING AN ISAM FILE

An ISAM file must be loaded sequentially in sorted order by record key. ISAM will detect a record out of order. Any dummy records to be added to the file should be placed in the input data stream in sequence. These records are best added where record additions are expected to take place. For instance, a credit card company may expect in the near future to add records whose keys range between 416–250–000 and 416–275–000 as a new district of credit card holders is opened up. In this case, dummy records with these keys can be created and added to the file during file creation. Another possibility is simply to scatter a certain percentage of dummy records throughout the file. This is not nearly as effective nor always possible (there may be no unused keys in the file). Recall that a dummy record is only ignored if it is at the end of a track. It will stay on a track until it is replaced by a valid record with the same key or pushed off the end by a new insertion.

Once the file is in use, any record whose deletion is desired can be turned into a dummy record by writing HIGH-VALUES in its first character position. This is a useful feature, especially in a credit card situation or phone number list where inactive customers can be replaced.

10.6 CONCLUSION

In this chapter we have superficially explored ISAM an access method that has enabled one manufacturer, IBM, to implement the Indexed I–O module of COBOL. Other manufacturers will link this module to their hardware in other ways. These other approaches must be explored as necessary; it is our firm belief that this effort will be worthwhile. This sort of knowledge helps in providing an educated guess to such questions as "Can it be done?" and "How much can easily be done?" The latter question is one of the many ways people have of asking the real question, "How much will it cost?"

REFERENCES FOR FURTHER READING

Larson, P. A. "Analysis of Indexed-Sequential Files with Overflow Chaining." *ACM T. Database Sy.* 6 (December 1981): 671–680.

Wagner, R. E. "Indexing Design Considerations." *IBM Sys. J.* 12 (1973): 351–67.

PROBLEMS

1. What access method does your installation use for handling indexed se-

quential files? If yours is a non-IBM installation, prepare a short description of the access method used.

2. Ask a system programmer or consult your job control language manual to determine the job control statements for creating an IBM ISAM file (or do this for the index access method at your installation). Learn the meanings of the keywords involved and relate these meanings to the physical implementation of an indexed file.

3. Discuss what would happen in ISAM if a portion of the file containing 10% of the file records increased fourfold.

4. What does overflow do to sequential search performance in ISAM?

11

VSAM Concepts

This chapter examines the concept of dynamic physical file storage as implemented in the Virtual Storage Access Method (VSAM). It also describes the basic concepts of the VSAM file structures and provides insight into the intelligent use of VSAM. However, the reader can skip this chapter and proceed directly to the use of VSAM in Chapter 12.

11.1 INTRODUCTION

The Indexed Sequential Access Method (ISAM) system used by IBM to manage data on direct access storage devices has a number of disadvantages, but we will only briefly mention three. Primarily, ISAM's handling of addition and deletion of indexed sequential records by means of overflow areas is static. Thus, ISAM either tends to run out of space at a local point or seriously degrades access times by sequentially searching overflow areas. As a result of this, a complete file reorganization, which is costly and temporarily prevents file access, must be done periodically. Secondly, ISAM tends to be device dependent, restricting its flexibility in locating files in the system storage structure and increasing the user's difficulty in managing ISAM files. Finally, ISAM does not implement all COBOL file features (see Section 10.1 for details).

The introduction of IBM's System/370 virtual memory architecture set the stage for a new approach to file storage that would take advantage of the virtual memory concept. With the release of VSAM in 1973, IBM dealt directly with many of the problems of ISAM. The VSAM approach implemented a new IBM philosophy to file storage based on dynamic assignment of storage space, device independence, centralized system control of storage, and more efficient manipulation of files by the VSAM user.

VSAM is a complete file handling package. It includes programs for creating and deleting files, printing file contents, building indexes, creating inverted lists, and handling record overflows. Its services can be invoked indirectly by statements in COBOL and directly by writing commands in a language referred to as Access Method Services (AMS). VSAM shares memory with the operating system whenever COBOL programs that use it are running, or when Access Method Services is being used independently. It services all the input and output requests when a READ, WRITE, REWRITE, DELETE, OPEN, or CLOSE statement is executed in a COBOL program. Figure 11.1 shows this interaction.

VSAM allows the user to create three different kinds of physical files: Entry-Sequenced Data Sets (ESDS), Relative Record Data Sets (RRDS), and Key-Sequenced Data Sets (KSDS). These VSAM data sets support the language statements that are found in the Sequential I–O module, the Relative I–O module, and the Indexed I–O module of COBOL. For example, if you want to create a COBOL indexed sequential file when the file structures are supported by VSAM, it is necessary to create a KSDS for the COBOL program to reference. The commands necessary to create VSAM data sets are described in Chapter 12.

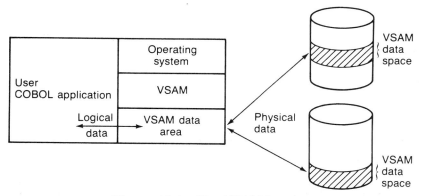

Figure 11.1 The VSAM interface.

The VSAM data structure is conceptually more sophisticated than that of ISAM. It introduces a number of new and radically different concepts. The purpose of this chapter is to examine the underlying concepts and the basic theoretical approach of VSAM. While the basis of VSAM is the main concern in this chapter, it is hoped that the reader will also obtain insight into the design of solutions to dynamic physical file storage problems and derive some general conclusions about such designs. In this sense, VSAM is simply an example of an abstract process of dynamically allocating storage space. We have chosen VSAM and its terminology as a useful example, relevant to all readers, rather than construct an abstract model. This is because VSAM is in wide use as IBM's primary access method and is intended by IBM to replace all other access methods.

11.2 DATA FORMAT IN VSAM

All file structures share one data unit in common, which is the block, and this provides a useful comparative starting point in the examination of any file structure. Conceptually, all file structures move a block of file data to and from memory as the minimum unit transferred. The internal structure of these blocks may vary from system to system and be called by various names, but they form the essential building block of any file structure.

Control Interval

In VSAM a block is called a control interval, and it is of fixed size for a given file. A *control interval* is a contiguous area of storage containing logical records along with control information describing the records. In addition, a control interval may contain unused space, called free space, for the future addition of logical records within the control interval. The general format of a control interval is given in Fig. 11.2. Note that there may be no free space within a control interval; an RRDS control interval, for example, contains no free space.

The *size* of a control interval (Fig. 11.2) is initially determined b y either the user or VSAM (by default) but is then fixed for a given data set. VSAM chooses the control-interval size as a function of the logical record size, the buffer size, the amount of free space requested, and the characteristics of the storage device to be used. The size is always a multiple of 512 bytes; the maximum length is 32,768 bytes. Typical sizes are 512, 1024, 2048, and 4096 bytes.

R1	R2	R3	Free space	Control information

Figure 11.2 Control interval.

Whenever a COBOL program asks for a logical record, VSAM searches storage for the control interval that contains the requested record, brings that control interval into a memory buffer, and then releases the record to the COBOL program. A file contains one or more control intervals. To the user a file is a collection of logical records. To VSAM a file is a collection of control intervals.

Control Area

A *control area* is a group of control intervals. It is the unit that VSAM preformats for the reception of control intervals, and it can contain free space at the end until filled with control intervals. The size of a control area (in number of control intervals) is determined by VSAM and fixed for a given file. The control area concept is most significant for a Key-Sequenced Data Set (KSDS), and it will be discussed further in that context.

With respect to ISAM, a control interval would be a track and a control area would be a cylinder.

11.2.1. Relative Byte Address

The VSAM address of a logical record is independent of the record's actual physical address on the storage device. A VSAM record is addressed by its displacement, in bytes, from the beginning of the file. This is essentially a relative address called a Relative Byte Address (RBA) and assumes that the control intervals of the file are all contiguous beginning at RBA zero. The first record in the first control interval has an RBA of zero; the second has an RBA of 0 + the length of the first logical record; the third an RBA of 0 + the length of the first logical record + the length of the second logical record and so on. The second control interval, if there is one, has an RBA equal to 0 + the length of the first control interval.

Though the RBA is the basis of VSAM's address access, fortunately, it need not concern the COBOL programmer. However, it is possible through assembler to access RBAs and thus directly manipulate some VSAM files. For instance, you can randomly access an ESDS from assembler language if you know the RBA of the desired record.

11.3 FILE TYPES: VSAM DATA SETS

The IBM name for a physical file (the logical file with associated control descriptors) on a storage device is *data set*. VSAM provides three types of data sets for storing files which functionally correspond to the fundamental generic types: sequential, relative, and indexed sequential. The three VSAM data sets—Entry-Sequenced, Relative Record, and Key-Sequenced—provide corresponding physical storage for these generic types and any other type we can map into these data sets. These VSAM types are actually more flexible than the pure generic files.

A VSAM data set is a collection of control intervals and, thus, made up of one or more control areas. The different types of VSAM data sets format the control intervals and provide modes of access in different ways to obtain their different characteristics.

11.3.1 Entry-Sequenced Data Set: The Sequential File

An *Entry-sequenced Data Set* (ESDS) consists of control intervals that are serially loaded with records; thus, new records are always loaded to the end of the file because free space always occurs after the last record. It can contain either fixed-length or variable-length records.

The record sequence is determined only by the order of entry into the file; thus, it is an efficient way to implement the sequential I–O module of COBOL. An ESDS can only be accessed sequentially from COBOL.

Logical records are added to a control interval (see Fig. 11.2) beginning at the far left-hand side and moving toward the right. For each logical record added, a corresponding Record Definition Field (RDF) is added to the right-hand side of the control interval. The RDF for each record tells the system where each record begins and ends. As record additions continue, the free space available is gradually consumed until a new control interval is needed and made available by VSAM. A record cannot be deleted from a control interval in an ESDS, but it is possible to replace an existing one with a record of exactly the same length provided the RE-WRITE statement is used and the file is opened in the I–O mode. Normally this is not attempted by the programmer. The *standard* method of updating a sequential file is to make a new copy of it using the balance line algorithm.

When a record is added, VSAM returns its RBA, which can then be used to access the record directly. This means that an ESDS can be used as a direct file and the programmer, who has access to the RBAs, can build a file structure using addressing techniques to determine RBAs.

11.3.2 Relative Record Data Set: The Relative File

A *Relative Record Data Set* (RRDS) consists of a string of N predefined, fixed-length slots for logical records. Each control interval has the same number of slots, and overflow space is only provided by unused slots.

The fixed nature of the slots means that they can be assigned relative address numbers within the control intervals when the file is created. Slots are numbered, beginning at 1, at the far left-hand side of the first control interval. The second slot is numbered 2, the third 3, and so on. The last slot in the last control interval has the highest slot number. The process of actually writing logical records to these slots in a COBOL program is referred to as loading. The COBOL programmer has the option of loading a relative file sequentially, or, if desired, since the slot numbers are available once the file has been allocated, the programmer can load the file with ACCESS MODE IS RANDOM with the file opened in the I–O mode. Each slot number corresponds to the relative key.

Records can be replaced, added, or deleted both sequentially and directly by relative address. An RRDS corresponds directly to the relative file concept, and it is used to implement the Relative I–O module of COBOL.

11.3.3 Key Sequenced Data Set: The Indexed Sequential File

A *Key-sequenced Data Set* (KSDS) consists of a set of control intervals ordered by primary record key and always has a prime index that relates a primary key value to the control interval that should contain the keyed record. Only KSDSs have free space *distributed* throughout the control intervals and control areas, which can be specified at file creation by the programmer or by VSAM. KSDS files generalize access and space management at the cost of time and space overhead. Fig. 11.3 shows the KSDS *data* control interval format.

Because the control intervals must be ordered by primary key, a KSDS is initially loaded in sequential mode with the records already ordered by primary key. Records can then be replaced, added, or deleted sequentially or randomly by primary key, and they may be either fixed-length or variable-length. Because the physical position of records may change, their RBAs can change. This is completely different from RRDS and ESDS files, in which records are stored either in slots or as they arrive in sequential order during creation and for which RBAs *never* change.

The Key-Sequenced Data Set is the most complicated but useful file organization in VSAM. Correct use of this file organization will save the programmer a lot of extra programming, keep programs efficient, and provide powerful file handling capabilities. This file organization supports the entire Indexed I–O module of COBOL, unlike ISAM.

The programmer will normally choose a KSDS unless it can be shown that either an ESDS or an RRDS is more appropriate for an application. A sequential file

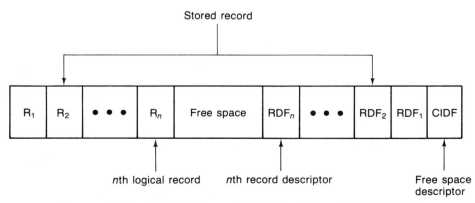

Figure 11.3   KSDS data control interval for variable-length records.

stored as an ESDS will be more efficient in time and space than if it were stored as a KSDS. A direct file that does not require sequential access may be more efficient as an RRDS than as a KSDS, but the programmer must arrange for indexing and space management.

11.4 THE VSAM DATA STRUCTURE

In essence, neither sequential files nor relative file structures are difficult to implement; in fact, relative files (through RRDSs) were not implemented in the original release of VSAM. It is only indexed files that pose difficulties in efficient access and space management for insertions and deletions.

A KSDS requires the VSAM data structure and is managed by VSAM. An ESDS provides the programmer with a device-independent, direct access file through knowledge of the RBAs and must be managed by the programmer except when used as a sequential file. An RRDS provides the most efficient representation of a relative file in VSAM. These types of data sets are provided for efficiency because the advantages of a KSDS are obtained at the cost of system overhead to manage a complex data structure and are not efficient for pure sequential and relative files.

In the remainder of this chapter, we discuss the representation of a KSDS, and the reader should bear firmly in mind that the data structure we discuss is that used by a KSDS. The ESDS and RRDS use a much simplified subset of this data structure to reduce system overhead, and most of the following discussion does *not* apply.

11.4.1 Index Structure

Previously, we discussed methods for retrieving records given their key. Many of these used the concept of an indexed file. ISAM stores records on tracks in ascending sequence by key and uses a series of indexes to locate the track containing the desired record. In VSAM, a record is in a control interval so the question becomes one of deciding which control interval a particular record is in. VSAM accomplishes this by creating an index data structure called an *index component*, consisting of control intervals. An example of an index component is shown in Figure 11.4. To avoid confusion with the index component, the group of control intervals containing data records is referred to as the *data component*.

An index component consists of two groups of control intervals: an *index set*, which points to other indexes, and a *sequence set*, which points to data control areas and the individual control intervals. Sequence set indexes contain index entries consisting of two data items referred to as a pair. The pair consists of the address of a control interval and the largest primary key that can be found in that control interval in the data component. For each control interval in the data component, there is

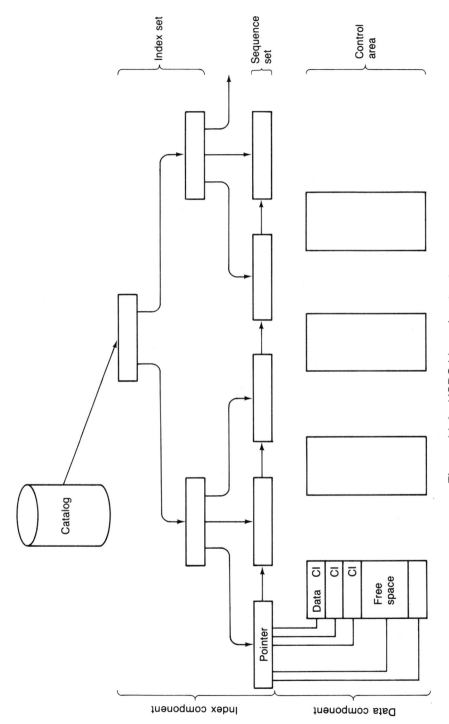

Figure 11.4 KSDS hierarchy structure.

thus a corresponding record in one of the control intervals of the sequence set containing its largest primary key.

Each control area is indexed directly from a sequence index, and this forms the simplest KSDS. Since records are added in key-sequence order, each control interval has a maximum key value. To locate a record, its control interval is first located by an ordered sequential search of the sequence index until the record key or the first key greater is found; this determines the index entry that points to the required control interval. This control interval is then moved to memory, and an ordered sequential search locates the requested record or its insertion position.

As the file grows, we could increase the size of the control area and its sequence index, but in essence this index is a sequential index. The solution for large files is to have many control areas; then the index problem is to select first the required sequence index from the sequence set. The first step is to provide a higher level index set to select the sequence index that points to the required control area. This is illustrated in Fig. 11.4 and is the simplest index structure for files of more than one control area. This index is again sequentially searched for a key to locate the pointer to the next required lower level index. To keep the index size within reason, a higher level index is used to select indexes of the level below. The highest level always contains *exactly one index*. There is a hierarchy of control intervals, index control intervals pointing down to index control intervals, sequence sets pointing down to control areas, and control areas containing control intervals. Thus we have created a tree structure.

The index structure gives direct access. To process in sequential order, it is only necessary to process the sequence set in order and the index set is not used. The sequence set has horizontal pointers that order the sequence set for sequential search.

The records of the sequence set are sorted in ascending order by their largest primary keys. In order to locate a given logical record sequentially, VSAM scans the sequence set (bypassing the index set), looking for a key equal to or greater than its primary key. Once it is found, the control interval address paired with it is used to fetch the required control interval as before.

11.4.2 . Storage Reorganization

Insertion and deletion of records in an indexed file requires some form of space management and file reorganization. An important advantage of VSAM is the dynamic insertion of records by reorganization of space through the movement of data records. This is superior to the static insertion of records in overflow space by ISAM through chaining overflow pointers. Rather than separate overflow areas, VSAM distributes free space throughout control intervals and control areas at data set creation. The distribution of free space can be specified by the programmer or allocated by VSAM as a default.

Control Interval Insertion

When a record is to be added, the insertion point is located by the index. The higher order key records of the selected control interval are then moved to the right (into the free space) and the new record inserted in the free position just created. Similarly, the corresponding RDF records are moved to the left (into the free space) and an RDF inserted for the new record.

VSAM can also recover space whenever a record is deleted. This is done by performing the reverse of record insertion and recovering free space in the control interval.

Control Interval Split

As records are added to a control interval, the free space is displaced by data. When a control interval runs out of free space, VSAM responds by having the control interval divide into two control intervals; this process is called a *control interval split*. Approximately one half of the records and their associated RDFs are moved to the new control interval, thus recreating free space in the original control interval and only half filling the new one. The new record, which caused the control interval split to occur, is then inserted in the appropriate control interval. The new control interval is obtained from the control area's free space, and the index is adjusted to reflect the change. Since the sequence set has already indexed the free control interval, the index item need only be moved from free to data status; however, because the control intervals are not moved, eventually they will not be ordered on keys. Nevertheless, records are still accessed in order by the sequence set even though individual CIs are out of physical order.

Control Area Split

Just as a control interval can run out of free space for a record insertion, a control area can eventually run out of free space for a control interval split. When this occurs, VSAM establishes a new control area and performs a *control area split* by moving approximately one half of the control intervals of the full control area to the new control area, modifying the indexes to reflect the changed locations. New records are then inserted in the appropriate control area, as before.

The dynamic control of free space by VSAM is not without cost. Deletion and insertion of records means that time-consuming moves must take place. In particular, sufficient free space should be defined at data set creation in order to make splitting an infrequent operation; nevertheless, as a file fills, a complete data set reorganization will be required at some point in order to maintain efficiency. Even so, the advantage of splitting is that complete file reorganizations are infrequent in comparison to those required by ISAM. Moreover, the indexing method ensures that indexed access remains efficient; whereas, in ISAM, overflow access rapidly degrades in efficiency.

While control intervals and control areas gradually lose physical order, the records of control intervals never do, and this is where physical order is most important.

11.5 MULTIPLE KEYS: THE ALTERNATE INDEX FEATURE

It is often necessary in the solution to data processing problems to have more than one key. A student record file will be accessed by student ID number most of the time, and this should be chosen as the primary key. Government uses social security numbers, by which they might also like to access the file. One might even like to be able to access the file by the last name of the student. All file keys other than the primary key are called *secondary keys*. VSAM supports secondary keys as well as primary keys for KSDS and ESDS files.

There are two types of secondary keys: those which are unique and those for which there are duplicates. In the above example, the student ID number would be unique but the same last name could be shared by many students. VSAM supports both types of secondary keys.

VSAM provides access to records via secondary keys by creating, for each secondary key, a special type of data set called an *alternate index cluster*. This is a KSDS, with a data component and an index component. To avoid confusion, the original data set to which an alternate index cluster points is called a *base cluster*. An alternate index cluster in no way affects the manner in which records are stored in the base cluster. An alternate index cluster is a file created after the KSDS base cluster has been created and loaded. Since it is a special data set, it is created by a special set of commands called DEFINE ALTERNATEINDEX, BLDINDEX, and DEFINE PATH (these are discussed in the next chapter).

An alternate index cluster is shown in Figure 11.5. The data component, as you can see, consists of records stored in control intervals. These records consist of a header, a secondary key value, and a set of primary keys. For each value of the given secondary key in the base cluster, there is a corresponding data record in the data component of the alternate index cluster. These records in the data component are stored in ascending sequence by the values of the secondary key. Thus, the alternate index is a KSDS whose primary key is the secondary key of another KSDS, the base cluster.

A record in the alternate index cluster is fetched in exactly the same manner in which a record in the base cluster is fetched, using a primary key value. Given a secondary key value, VSAM searches the index set and the sequence set of the alternate index cluster in order to locate the control interval in the data component where the alternate index data record is stored. Each such data record contains all the primary keys (in the base cluster) associated with the particular alternate key value.

For example, the student name BROWN would have associated with it a record, in the data component of an alternate index cluster created for the secondary key LAST-NAME, having a key of BROWN. This record would contain the pri-

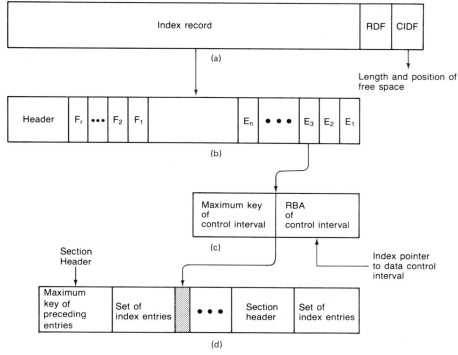

Figure 11.5   Index control interval format; (a) index control interval; (b) index record; (c) index entry; (d) grouping index entries by section (for block-sequential search).

mary key of every record in the base cluster containing the secondary key BROWN. All students with the name BROWN could be fetched from the base cluster because VSAM can find all their associated primary keys in the data component of the alternate index cluster.

The advantage of an alternate index cluster is that VSAM is then responsible for all the modifications to the alternate index cluster that are necessitated as a result of changes being made to the base cluster. Whenever a new record is added to a base cluster, VSAM adds its primary key to each alternate index cluster of that file. One word of warning, however. The first time an alternate index is created for a base cluster, all of the primary keys stored in the data component records of the alternate index cluster are in sequence within the record. This sequence is *not* maintained as new records are added to the base cluster. The primary keys of these records are added to the *end* of the appropriate records in the alternate index data component. When using COBOL to retrieve records by means of a secondary key, the records are retrieved one by one from the base cluster in the order their primary keys are stored in the corresponding record in the alternate index cluster. This will make the alternate index clusters somewhat unsuitable for the creation of inverted lists needed in the file query system to be created in Chapter 18, "File Implementation."

11.6 DATA PATHS IN VSAM

There is one last type of data cluster to mention. A *path* cluster is a special type of data structure that links an alternate index cluster with its associated base cluster. Once the programmer creates an alternate index, an associated path must be created. Nothing more need be said.

11.7 DATA SPACES IN VSAM

Eventually, control intervals must be stored on the tracks of a mass storage device. As the control of mass storage space is generally the responsibility of the computing center involved, the programmer will have to approach the systems personnel at the installation to arrange to be given disk space for the data sets. This is generally a straightforward procedure. The systems consultant will create a user catalog for the user and allot data space. Data space is set aside with a DEFINE SPACE command. This data space may be set aside when the user applies for space and then SUBALLOCATED as data sets are created; or the user may simply be given permission to create data spaces, in which case the user will employ the word UNIQUE in the commands needed to create the files involved.

11.8 CONCLUSION

The conceptual information of this chapter should assist the programmer in using VSAM intelligently and efficiently. Fortunately, VSAM seems to default to the most reasonable parameters when the programmer does not want to set the sizes of control intervals, decide how much space should be left free within control intervals or control areas, or decide how large index components should be. Thus, VSAM can be used without a full understanding or appreciation of how it performs its tasks. Nevertheless, the programmer who is willing to get into the system and tinker with the options, which Access Method Services makes so easy to do, will be well rewarded. Chapter 12 explains simple applications of VSAM and provides sufficient background to understand the use of VSAM files in practice.

REFERENCES FOR FURTHER READING

IBM. *OS/VS2 Virtual Storage Access Method (VSAM) Logic.* Order Form SY26-3825.

PROBLEMS

1. Discuss why control areas are a useful concept. What problems would arise if the control area concept was removed from VSAM? Can you suggest another concept?

2. Since VSAM dynamically manages space, why should it ever be necessary to recreate a VSAM data set? Discuss the use of free space in each type of VSAM data set.

3. Discuss the cost of direct file access to a KSDS file.

4. Compare the cost of direct access to each VSAM file type.

12

VSAM Applied

12.1 INTRODUCTION

Data must be physically organized on a storage medium, and conceptually there are many ways to do this, some of which we explored in Chapter 10. The design of a *file access method* selects a set of consistent concepts to represent and access files in physical storage; the techniques developed from the concepts are then implemented as a software utility package that can be used to manage data. Virtual Storage Access Method (VSAM) is a widely used IBM file access method, and the underlying concepts of its design are explored in Chapter 11. VSAM can organize and manage the data of many users; however, in this chapter we examine VSAM from a single user's viewpoint. Our starting question is: What must the programmer know about the basics of VSAM in order to have the operating system, through VSAM, set aside physical storage space on I/O devices for sequential, relative, and indexed sequential files and to relate relative, primary, and secondary keys to physical storage addresses?

After reading this chapter, the user will be able to create, delete, and access Entry-Sequenced Data Sets (sequential files), Relative Record Data Sets (relative files), and Key-Sequenced Data Sets (indexed sequential files). This chapter can be read and VSAM used without reference to Chapters 10 and 11 even though they form a basis for a more informed view of VSAM use.

The direct purpose of this chapter is to examine the use of some basic utility programs provided by the VSAM Access Method Services (AMS) package. AMS is the file user's interface with VSAM files. While this chapter is intended as a hands-on introduction to applying VSAM, it is hoped that the reader will indirectly derive some general conclusions about the design and use of a file access method by actually using VSAM.

12.2 ACCESS METHOD SERVICES

AMS is a service program that is used with VSAM to create and maintain data sets and catalogs. A user invokes AMS by issuing commands as input to the program IDCAMS. This program scans the commands for errors before executing them.

Access Method Services Commands have the general format

```
command parameter-list terminator
```

Parameters are either positional or key word. As a group, positional parameters must precede key word parameters. A key word parameter may have a set of subparameters. We suggest that command parameters be placed on separate lines for readability. To continue a command line, end the line with one or more blanks followed by a hyphen. Command separators are blanks, commas, and comments. Comments are of the form

```
/*  character string  */
```

A simple example is

```
PRINT   INDATASET   (CARS)
```

which requests that VSAM locate a file named "CARS" and then print a formatted copy of it. The command is "PRINT," and the parameter "INDATASET (filename)" is a key word parameter.

The number of parameters differs from command to command and with use. Fortunately, most parameters need not be specified; there are default values for almost all parameters, and these satisfy the majority of uses encountered. In this chapter we discuss only a few basic parameters, relying on VSAM to default as required.

For effective use of VSAM, the reader should consult the IBM reference manuals listed in the chapter references.

In this chapter, the commands and parameters used at the authors' installation to create the file environments for the programs in this book are illustrated. At minimum, a knowledge of this chapter will make you an intelligent questioner should you run into difficulties at your own installation. Although, for later reference, it should be sufficient to read each individual section, it is recommended that Sections 12.3, 12.4, and 12.5 be read first in sequence.

12.3 ENTRY-SEQUENCED DATA SETS

VSAM Entry-Sequenced Data Sets (ESDS) correspond functionally to sequential files. Records are loaded in the order they are written to the data set; thus the term "entry-sequenced." Obviously, a new record is stored at the end of the data set, if there is room.

An Entry-Sequenced Data Set defines an area where we can store a COBOL sequential file, and of course this data set must physically exist before a COBOL program reference. To define the existence of a VSAM data set, we run a creation program of AMS.

12.3.1 Defining an Entry-Sequenced Data Set

In order to allocate space for an ESDS, several items of information must be known: the name of the data set to be created, the record type (fixed or variable), the average and maximum length of each record (the same length if fixed-length records), and the disk volume on which the file is to be stored. Other information can be provided by the user, but VSAM will default to its own preferred values unless overridden. For the moment only those parameters that VSAM requires will be discussed. Some parameter values that can be overriden will be discussed later in this chapter.

AMS, the program which provides all the utility services for VSAM, is invoked with the minimum JCL shown in Fig. 12.1. The accounting information, of course, will differ from installation to installation.

```
//JOBNAME JOB 'accounting information'
//    EXEC  PGM=IDCAMS,REGION=512K
//SYSPRINT DD SYSOUT=A
//SYSIN    DD *
```

Figure 12.1 JCL to invoke access method service.

The commands needed to create a sequential file follow the JCL statement

```
//SYSIN DD *
```

as will all subsequent commands to be described.

Figure 12.2 is the program which created the music log that was accessed in Program 3.1. A clear distinction must be made between creating (or defining) and loading a file. A file is created by AMS. Specifically, this causes physical space on an I/O device to be reserved for the actual records of the file. The file is loaded later by a COBOL program or other means. Loading, of course, means that records are stored in the reserved file space. Programmers often do not distinguish between creating and loading a file and tend to interchange the terminology. The important thing is to remember that there are two parts to the process: use AMS commands to set aside the physical storage and use COBOL or IDCAMS to place the records in the file.

The DEFINE CLUSTER command is used to create a data set or *cluster,* as it is known in VSAM. The RECORDS parameter specifies the number of records the cluster is to contain. The first number in the RECORDS parameter, 1000 in Fig. 12.2, specifies the primary number of records in the cluster. The *primary number* is the number of records the user expects to have in his cluster or at least a good first approximation. The second parameter, 100 in this example, is the number of records in a secondary extent. A *secondary extent* is the amount of disk space (in this case that which is needed to store 100 records) that will be made available as extra space for file records when the primary allocation is not enough. When the UNIQUE parameter is used, 15 of these extents will be made available to the user,

```
//JOBNAME JOB 'accounting information'
//     EXEC   PGM=IDCAMS,REGION=512K
//SYSPRINT DD SYSOUT=A
//SYSIN     DD *
      DEFINE CLUSTER -
         (NAME (MUSIC.LOG) -
          RECORDS (1000 100) -
          VOLUMES (USER11) -
          NONINDEXED -
          RECORDSIZE (149 149) -
          UNIQUE ) -
        CATALOG (YOUR.CATALOG)
/*
//
```

Figure 12.2 Program to reserve space in VSAM for the music log of Program 3.1.

one at a time as needed. For instance, in this example, the file could grow to hold a maximum of 2500 (1000 + 15 × 100) records. If more than 15 extents are necessary, the user will have to recreate the file with a more appropriate primary record specification.

The VOLUME parameter names the disk pack that is to be used for storage. In the preceeding example, the disk pack is "USER11," which is the six-letter designation of a disk pack at the authors' installation. Consult your computing center to obtain the designation of an available disk pack.

The NAME parameter specifies the VSAM file name. This name can be up to 44 alphanumeric characters (A through Z and 0 through 9) made up of segments 8 characters or less in length separated by periods, each segment of which begins with a letter. The so-called national characters (@, # $) can also be used throughout, even as the starting characters of a segment. We strongly suggest that names be invented that are sensible in length and meaningful to the programmer and the user. Some installations require the use of a user prefix for all that user's files. This allows the system to distinguish between users.

Do not confuse this VSAM name with the name of the file in your COBOL program. This is the system name of the VSAM file where your program file is stored, and it is independent of the program file name used in your program. This VSAM file could in fact be accessed through VSAM by other languages, such as PL/1.

The keyword NONINDEXED specifies that the file is an ESDS.

The key word UNIQUE specifies that the components of the cluster are allocated space separately.

The CATALOG parameter is used to locate the VSAM file address within the VSAM catalog and assumes that YOUR.CATALOG is a previously defined user catalog.

12.3.2 The CATALOG Key Word

It is not unusual for an installation to have thousands of files on its computer system spread over many storage devices. For processing purposes, the operating system requires a list of all the file names along with associated device and storage addresses and some technical data describing each file. This information is stored in a directory called a *catalog*.

In older systems there was no such main catalog; but in VSAM there is a hierarchy of catalogs. Some catalogs point to other catalogs, and some point to files. The general idea is that each user group should have its own catalog. This is useful for accounting, billing, and management purposes, and also for security. These catalogs should be created for you by the VSAM administrator at your installation.

In all the AMS commands, in this chapter, where the CATALOG parameter is required, we shall supply the catalog named "YOUR.CATALOG".

12.3.3 Deleting an Entry-Sequenced Data Set

In order to delete an ESDS, it is necessary to supply the command statement DELETE to the AMS program called IDCAMS. The program to delete the music log VSAM file is shown in Fig. 12.3.

```
//JOBNAME JOB 'accounting information'
//     EXEC   PGM=IDCAMS,REGION=512K
//SYSPRINT DD SYSOUT=A
//SYSIN     DD *
       DELETE -
          (MUSIC.LOG)  -
          CLUSTER -
          ERASE -
          CATALOG (YOUR.CATALOG)
/*
//
```

Figure 12.3   Program to delete music log VSAM file of Program 3.1 from VSAM.

The DELETE CLUSTER command deletes the named data set. It is necessary to supply the name of the data set and the name of the catalog. The ERASE statement is optional. It has the effect of replacing the entire contents of the named data set with binary zeros. This is a very useful security feature, although it should be used only when warranted.

12.3.4 Printing an Entry-Sequenced Data Set

The PRINT command is used to print a VSAM data set in a combination format, character and hexadecimal, which is very easy to read.

```
//JOBNAME JOB 'accounting information'
//JOBCAT DD DSN=YOUR.CATALOG,DISP=SHR
//     EXEC PGM=IDCAMS,REGION=512K
//SYSPRINT DD SYSOUT=A
//SYSIN     DD *
       PRINT -
          INDATASET  (MUSIC.LOG)
/*
//
```

Figure 12.4   Program to print music log VSAM file of Program 3.1.

Note the addition of the //JOBCAT statement added to the IDCAMS program in Fig. 12.4. The JOBCAT statement is required to identify the catalog that VSAM is to access in order to discover the physical location of the file, because there is no CATALOG key word with the PRINT command.

12.4 RELATIVE RECORD DATA SETS

Relative Record Data Sets (RRDS) correspond functionally to COBOL Relative I–O files, where records are added in relative number sequence. To insert a record, the user specifies a relative record number, or VSAM can assign the next available record number in the sequence. Essentially an RRDS is a file that consists of a string of fixed-length slots each of which has an ordinal number according to its relative position in the file, the ordinal number of the first record being set at 1.

12.4.1 Defining a Relative Record Data Set

Figure 12.5 shows the DEFINE CLUSTER command required to allocate space for the Relative I–O file called VEHICLE-FILE used in Program 6.1.

The user will note that the only major difference between this DEFINE CLUSTER and that shown for sequential files previously is that the key word NONINDEXED has been replaced by the key word NUMBERED. The key word NUMBERED designates a relative record data set. The RECORDSIZE parameter indicates that VEHICLE.FILE contains records that are 114 characters in length. The integer 114 appears twice because AMS requires that the first integer represent the average record length and the second specify the maximum record length expected for the file. Since an RRDS can only contain fixed-length records, these numbers are both the same.

```
//JOBNAME JOB 'accounting information'
//    EXEC  PGM=IDCAMS,REGION=512K
//SYSPRINT DD SYSOUT=A
//SYSIN    DD *
       DEFINE CLUSTER -
         ( NAME (VEHICLE.FILE) -
           RECORDS (1000 100) -
           VOLUMES (USER11) -
           RECORDSIZE (114 114) -
           NUMBERED -
           UNIQUE ) -
         CATALOG (YOUR.CATALOG)
/*
//
```

Figure 12.5 Program to define a relative record data set.

Programs to delete and print an RRDS are identical to those needed to delete and print an ESDS previously described in this chapter.

12.5 KEY-SEQUENCED DATA SETS

Key-Sequenced Data Sets (KSDS) correspond functionally to COBOL Indexed I–O files. Each record of a KSDS has a unique primary key, and records may be of fixed or variable length. Records are loaded in key sequence; thus, the resulting file is sequentially ordered by its key. Additional records may be added in sequence once the file is created. The commands necessary to create a KSDS will be described in two versions. The first will describe the *minimal* commands necessary to create a KSDS and will suffice for most users. Multiple key features and control over system options will be left to a more detailed second description.

12.5.1 Defining a Key-Sequenced Data Set: The Simple Version

Figure 12.6 shows the commands necessary to allocate space for a KSDS.

```
//JOBNAME  JOB 'accounting information'
//    EXEC   PGM=IDCAMS,REGION=512K
//SYSPRINT DD SYSOUT=A
//SYSIN    DD *
      DEFINE CLUSTER -
         ( NAME (OUTPUT.FILE) -
           RECORDS(500 500) -
           RECORDSIZE(452 1072) -
           VOLUMES(USER11) -
           INDEXED -
           KEYS (5 61) -
           UNIQUE ) -
        CATALOG(YOUR.CATALOG)
/*
//
```

Figure 12.6 Program to define a key-sequenced data set.

This program creates the KSDS called OUTPUT.FILE required by Program 8.1. The parameter INDEXED causes VSAM to create a KSDS. The KEYS parameter specifies two integers. The first integer, 5 in the example, specifies the length of the unique primary key of the KSDS. This key is the ADMITTING-IDENTIFIER field specified in the ADMITTING-DATA-RECORD of the file called ADMITTING-DATA-FILE of Program 8.1. The second integer is the offset in bytes showing where the key in each record begins. Because the key is at byte position 62 in the ADMITTING-DATA-RECORD, the offset is set to 61 and indicates the number of bytes in the record that precede the key. If the key started at the tenth byte in the record, the offset would be 9. As before, the RECORDSIZE parameter designates the average and maximum length of each record in the data set. In Program 8.1 the file ADMITTING-DATA-FILE contained variable-length records. Each of these records contained a minimum of 173 bytes and a maximum of 1072 bytes as shown by the OCCURS DEPENDING ON clause in that program. Note carefully that while COBOL uses the OCCURS DEPENDING ON clause to specify the *minimum* and maximum record size, VSAM requires the *average* and maximum record size. For purposes of this program it was assumed that the average record would contain 10 of the variable components. As the variable components are 31 bytes long and the fixed portion of the record is 142 bytes long, we have assumed an average record size of 452 bytes. The reader is urged to review these calculations. Note especially that those variables whose usage is specified as COMPUTATIONAL in Program 8.1 are not synchronized. Thus, there are no slack bytes in these records. Should the user design a record that contains slack bytes, it becomes necessary to include them in calculating the parameters for the key word RECORDSIZE.

12.5.2 Deleting a Key-Sequenced Data Set

The DELETE command is the same as that shown for an ESDS.

12.5.3 Printing a Key-Sequenced Data Set

In order to print the entire contents of a KSDS, the PRINT command for a n ESDS can be used. Sometimes, however, it is useful to print a subset o f a file. In this case, the FROMKEY keyword and the TOKEY keyword can be used, as shown in Fig. 12.7.

```
//JOBNAME JOB 'accounting information'
//JOBCAT DD DSN=YOUR.CATALOG,DISP=SHR
//    EXEC  PGM=IDCAMS,REGION=512K
//SYSPRINT DD SYSOUT=A
//SYSIN    DD *
      PRINT -
        INDATASET (OUTPUT.FILE) -
        FROMKEY ('A1234') -
        TOKEY ('C8888')
/*
//
```

Figure 12.7 Program to print a key-sequenced data set.

The FROMKEY parameter specifies the key of the record that is to be the first record printed. If the record is not available in the data set, the first record with a higher key is printed. The TOKEY parameter specifies the primary key of the last record that is to be printed. The user should note that if the data set has primary keys that are characters rather than integers the keys in these two keywords should be enclosed in single quotes.

12.5.4 Creating a Key-Sequenced Data Set with a Secondary Key

In this section we shall describe the AMS commands necessary to create a KSDS that has a secondary key. In addition, many new parameters of the DEFINE CLUSTER command will be introduced. The user may discover on consulting the AMS manual that some of these parameters may be also available when defining an ESDS or an RRDS.

There are several steps involved in creating a KSDS with a secondary key. First the user must create the KSDS and designate the primary key, as we did in Program 12.6. Once this file is created, it is referred to as the *base cluster* of the data set. At this point, it can be loaded with records by a COBOL program and used for record retrieval as shown in Program 8.2. In order to create a secondary key, it is necessary to create two kinds of data sets. The first data set is known as an Alternate-Index Data Set. The operating system will load this data set with pointers that map secondary keys into primary keys. This is similar to the idea of a *directory* as discussed in Chapter 7. The second data set that needs to be created is called a Path-Entry Data Set. This data set is used by the operating system to link an alternate index to its base cluster making both available to the COBOL program. It should be noted that an Alternate-Index Data Set and a Path-Entry Data Set must be created for each secondary key.

```
//JOBNAME JOB 'accounting information'
//JOBCAT DD DSN=YOUR.CATALOG,DISP=SHR
//    EXEC  PGM=IDCAMS,REGION=512K
//DD1    DD   VOL=SER=SCS001,UNIT=M3330,DISP=OLD
//SYSIN  DD *
  DEFINE ALTERNATEINDEX  (NAME(BOOK.ALTWARD)  -
              RELATE(OUTPUT.FILE)  -
              RECORDS(20 20)  -
              VOLUMES(SCS001)  -
              FILE(DD1)  -
              KEYS(2 91)  -
              RECORDSIZE(507 507)  -
              NONUNIQUEKEY)  -
           CATALOG(YOUR.CATALOG)
/*
//
```

Figure 12.8 Program to define an alternate-index data set.

Figure 12.8 shows the IDCAMS statements necessary to create an Alternate-Index Data Set.

The DEFINE ALTERNATEINDEX statement names the Alternate-Index Data Set. The RELATE key word specifies the name of the associated base cluster. The RECORDS key word, as before, specifies a primary and secondary number of records that are to be reserved for storing the alternate-index records. There will be one alternate-index record for each of the possible secondary keys. The records themselves will consist of the primary keys in the base cluster that have the same secondary key value. The Alternate-Index Data Set created above is that needed in order to specify the secondary key WARD-NUMBER used in Program 8.3. At the moment, there are twenty wards in LAKESIDE GENERAL HOSPITAL, and thus we have asked for a primary allocation of twenty records. The RECORDSIZE key word, as before, specifies the average and maximum lengths of these records. When an alternate index supports a key-sequenced base cluster, the following formula can be used to calculate the record size:

$$RECSZ = 5 + AIXKL + (n \times BCKL)$$

where RECSZ is the average record size, AIXKL is the alternate key length, and BCKL is the primary key length in the base cluster. If the secondary key is unique, $n = 1$; otherwise, n equals the largest number of records in the base cluster that can have the same secondary key value. In the example shown, it was assumed that there might be as many as 100 patients on the same ward. Thus, $n = 100$ in this example, BCKL = 5 (the length of ADMITTING-IDENTIFIER), and AIXKL = 2 (the length of the field WARD-NUMBER). This yields

$$RECSZ = 5 + 2 + (100 \times 5) = 507$$

The key word NONUNIQUEKEY specifies that the secondary key WARD-NUMBER is a secondary key with duplicates. The key word FILE names a JCL dd-card that directs IDCAMS to a mass-storage device where the alternate–index will be physically allocated. In this example, a mass-storage device labeled SCS001, which is a mountable IBM 3330 (UNIT=M3330) disk pack, has been designated. This is the name of a pack at the authors' installation. Consult your own computing center for the name of a mass-storage device at that location.

The Path-Entry Data Set needed for the secondary key WARD-NUMBER of Program 8.3 is shown in Fig. 12.9.

There are two key words that name data sets for a DEFINE PATH command: The key word NAME names the path data set for the secondary key, and PATHENTRY the associated alternate-index. Note that it is the *path* that the COBOL programmer uses to access the base cluster data with an alternate key.

An alternate index is normally created after the base cluster has been loaded with an initial set of records. Once this has been done, the path data set is created

```
//JOBNAME JOB 'accounting information'
//JOBCAT DD DSN=YOUR.CATALOG,DISP=SHR
//      EXEC  PGM=IDCAMS,REGION=512K
//SYSPRINT  DD  SYSOUT=*
//DD2    DD   UNIT=M3330,VOL=SER=SCS001,DISP=OLD
//SYSIN  DD *
          DEFINE PATH (NAME(BOOK.WARDPATH) -
               PATHENTRY (BOOK.ALTWARD) -
               FILE(DD2) -
             CATALOG(YOUR.CATALOG)
/*
//
```

Figure 12.9   Program to define a path-entry data set.

and a BLDINDEX command is executed. The BLDINDEX command causes loading of the alternate index with the appropriate pointers. The program to do this is shown in Fig. 12.10.

The BLDINDEX command has two new key words, INFILE and OUTFILE. INFILE names the base cluster containing the records for which the secondary key is to be created and OUTFILE names the path-entry data set of the associated Alternate-Index Data set. Upon execution of this job the KSDS base cluster is scanned and the alternate index filled with pointers (actually primary keys) to records that share the same secondary key.

If later the decision is made to add new records to an already loaded base cluster, the BLDINDEX command should not be executed again. The VSAM access method will automatically update any alternate indexes that exist provided that an ALTERNATE RECORD KEY clause is present in the COBOL program for each secondary key and that a BLDINDEX command for each associated alternate index has been executed.

```
//JOBNAME JOB 'accounting information'
//JOBCAT DD DSN=YOUR.CATALOG,DISP=SHR
//      EXEC  PGM=IDCAMS,REGION=512K
//SYSPRINT  DD  SYSOUT=*
//DD1    DD   DSN=OUTPUT.FILE,DISP=OLD
//DD2    DD   DSN=BOOK.WARDPATH,DISP=OLD
//SYSIN  DD *
          BLDINDEX  INFILE(DD1) -
               OUTFILE(DD2) -
             CATALOG(YOUR.CATALOG)
/*
//
```

Figure 12.10   Program to load alternate-index.

12.6 CONCLUSION

We have illustrated some simple uses of Access Method Services for allocating and deleting space in VSAM. Table 12.1 indicates some of the kinds of things that can be done by AMS. Reference to the IBM manuals is the ultimate definition of the VSAM system.

Table 12.1 Functional Commands of Access Method Services

ALTER	used to alter previously defined catalog entries
BLDINDEX	constructs alternate indexes for existing data sets
CHKLIST	used to identify tape volumes mounted when a checkpoint was taken
CNVTCAT	used to convert entries in an OS CVOL (control volume) into entries in a VSAM catalog
DEFINE	used to create catalog entries for data sets, catalogs, and space that VSAM is to allocate from
DELETE	used to delete catalog entries
EXPORT	used to create a copy of a VSAM data set for backup or to make a data set or user catalog portable so that it can be used on another system
EXPORTA	retrieves VSAM data sets and catalog entries that are no longer accessible from a VSAM catalog
IMPORT	used to read a backup copy of a VSAM data set or to make a data set or catalog that was previously exported from one system available for use in another system
IMPORTA	returns VSAM data sets and catalog entries to an accessible condition
LISTCAT	used to list catalog entries
LISTCRA	used to diagnose suspected problems in VSAM catalogs
PRINT	used to print VSAM, ISAM, or SAM data sets
REPRO	used to copy data sets, to convert sequential and indexed-sequential data sets to VSAM format, to convert VSAM and indexed-sequential data sets to sequential format, to back up a VSAM catalog, to read a back-up copy of a VSAM catalog, and to copy VSAM catalogs
RESETCAT	synchronizes a catalog to the level of its owned volumes
VERIFY	is used to cause a catalog to reflect correctly the end of a data set after an error occurred in closing a VSAM data set that may have invalidated the catalog entry

REFERENCES for FURTHER READING

Atkinson, J.W., and **DeSanctis, P.A.** *Introduction to VSAM.* Rochelle Park, N.J.: Hayden, 1980.

IBM. *OS/VS2 Access Method Services.* Order Form GC26-3841.

IBM. *OS/VS Virtual Storage Access Method (VSAM) Programmer's Guide.* Order Form GC26-3838.

IBM. *Planning for Enhanced VSAM Under OS/VS.* Order Form GC26-3842.

IBM. *VSAM Primer.* Order Form G320-5774.

PROBLEMS

1. Write the AMS command necessary to reserve space, on the disk pack designated PACK05, for an ESDS named MY.DATA.FILE. The file will initially contain 1500 records and should be allowed to grow to contain a maximum of 4500 records. Each record will contain 253 bytes of information. Assume that a user catalog, named MY.VSAM.USER.CATALOG, has been defined for your use.

2. You want to define a KSDS named ACCOUNT.DATA.FILE on volume VOL003. The file is to have a primary allocation of 1000 records and a secondary extent of 250 records. Each record is 512 bytes in length and contains a 9-character primary key beginning in the fortieth byte. Assuming the user catalog named in the previous question has been set up, show the command you would issue to AMS to define this data set.

3. Assuming records had been loaded (using either a COBOL or PL/1 program) to the KSDS defined in the previous question, write the AMS command to print out all of the records having a primary key between 'AATM-0067' and 'XCLT-0389', inclusive. Also show the command to print out all of the records in the data set.

4. Write the AMS command to define an RRDS named MY.SECOND.DATA.FILE on volume USER33. The data set is to have a primary allocation of 1200 records and a secondary extent of 300 records, with each record being 80 bytes in length. Establish COOPER as the master password, and JOHNSON as the read password, for the data set. The master password will allow you full access to the data set; the read password may be used to allow other people read-only access to your data set. Assume the existence of a user catalog named USER.CATALOG.TWO that has an update password CATPASS. The catalog is password protected because data set passwords are contained in the catalog entries for those data sets which are password protected.

Note: Refer to OS/VS2 Access Method Services for a description of the DEFINE CLUSTER parameters necessary for establishing data set passwords.

13

Data Structures

So far we have mainly considered how to store and access records in COBOL. The COBOL file structures we have examined have been in many respects quite limited and far from ideal. Nevertheless, a programmer can use these file structures to devise a wide variety of logical structures, a much more complicated procedure. Indeed, an examination of the limitations posed by COBOL illustrates the problems that occur in the external physical storage of data.

There are two major difficulties that arise when the programmer superimposes another structure on a file structure: he must devise an often-complex set of programs to create and manipulate the new structure via the physical file structure, and the performance of his creation may be extremely poor because the organization of the underlying COBOL language file may be unsuitable to his purpose and, therefore, inefficient in terms of the operations required. Even so, the programmer is never limited to the forms of data organization provided by a programming language. The trick is to determine when it is worthwhile to program a more complicated organization for data.

As a rule of thumb, data should be organized to reflect the manner in which we perceive it. To do this, we must often go beyond the simple file structures of COBOL. In fact, we should actually think of COBOL files as host organizations that store the logical organizations we impose on our data.

It is desirable, then, to study the relationships that occur among data, independently of COBOL or any programming language for that matter. The theory of the structural relationships of data and of the manipulation of these relationships is called *data structures*. When we consider the abstract relationships of physical records and their contents, we see that certain fundamental types of structure are recognizable and reoccur so frequently that they are worthy of close study, independently of any programming language. This can be done because the study of data structures ignores the physical realities of storage and discusses only logical properties and relationships. Such a simplification of the detail necessary to a physical organization of data can be important in determining the kind of data base organization desired, since it is useful first to consider the best way to organize data independently of how it will be organized in an implementation. It may well be that, in order to implement a data base, the ultimate form of data organization chosen will be compromised by the available file structures and the characteristics of the system used. Nevertheless, only by considering an ideal structure can we determine the degree of compromise in effect and thus determine the degree of efficiency gained by such compromise.

Data structures are the subject of intense mathematical analysis; however, this need not concern us greatly here. Our intent is a *practical* consideration of data structures as the underlying logical theory for file organization. As such, we provide some abstract tools for the programmer that will release him from the confines of a particular computer language.

In Chapter 1 we briefly considered several data structures: stack, queue, linear list, and tree. This was necessary because reference to the data structure concept was required in the intervening chapters. Vectors, arrays, and tables are also data structures with which the reader is no doubt more familiar. Now we are concerned with four important aspects of a data structure: how it is described or represented, how it is organized, how it is accessed, and how the organization is changed. Since the last does not always apply, we may classify data structures as static or dynamic.

13.1 STATIC DATA STRUCTURES

If we think of a data structure as consisting of a number of storage cells that can contain data, then a static data structure is one with a fixed number of cells whose relationship to each other does not change, where the relationship refers to the cell organization not the cell content. Vectors and their generalization, arrays, are static.

Usually, as in vector algebra for example, they are of fixed size, but some programming languages allow dynamic size definition. In an array, all elements are homogeneous (i.e., of the same type and size). When the elements of an array are not homogeneous, then we have a table.

The data structures available in most languages are static. This is because static data structures having efficient addressing schemes are easy to implement. A serious drawback is the difficulty involved in logical reorganization; because of the static structure, we must move the contents of cells rather than change the relationships of the cells which are fixed. Ideally, the structure of the data we perceive should directly correspond to the structure of the cells. We can, of course, devise complicated mappings to obtain the desired correspondence, but it is more fruitful to attempt to obtain a cell structure that directly corresponds to the structure of the data.

13.2 DYNAMIC DATA STRUCTURES

Our intent here is to introduce several fundamental data structures and to highlight some of their important aspects. In the space allotted, we can do no more. The reader is referred to a rich and growing theory of data structures. (See the References section at the end of the book.) However, for practical programming, much of the theory is not relevant. We defer the actual form of operations on these data structures to the section on linked lists as this form is very dependent on the representation chosen.

13.2.1 Strings

Generalizing from the idea that the letters in a word constitute a string of symbols, we could state the following primitive definition: a string is a linearly ordered collection of homogeneous elements. If we consider a sentence as a string of words, then clearly the elements need not be homogeneous. This definition is too restrictive.

We will consider the concept of a string as follows: *A string is a finite sequential collection of elements.* These elements are representations of some entity; they may, in fact, be strings. If the elements are not homogeneous or single symbols, (a list could be a list or a sentence, for example) then they must be separated by delimiters that can be recognized, and no decomposition is allowed within the delimiters. A string does not have a fixed length. We do not consider it to be indexed as is a vector, although in many representations (such as a vector) this is possible. The definition of a string poses some difficulty, in part, because it is often represented as a vector and appears to have the characteristics of a linear list. On the other hand, the operations we perform on a string appear to differentiate it from a list.

A fundamental requirement is that string operations are not restricted to elements but operate on substrings of strings. A *substring* of a string is any contiguous collection of elements of that string. Figure 13.1 gives an example of string S and substring S′. We should point out that the prime symbol (′) is a commonly used delimiter for strings. There are many interesting operations on substrings, but since they are not pertinent to this book, we refer the reader to the string language of SNOBOL[1] for an interesting example of an implementation of the string concept.

```
         String     S   'abcde'
      Substring S'       'bc'
Concatenation of S and S'      S•S'='abcdebc'
```

Figure 13.1   String examples.

13.2.2 Lists

A *linear list* is a sequential set of elements that are accessed from *logically* adjacent elements. Any element may be added or deleted. Elements are stored in cells; therefore we will often use the term *cell* rather than *element*. The physical list consists of its storage cells. The representation of a linear list takes many forms, but the linked list form, as indicated in Chapter 1, is most commonly used in computing. The concept of a list is not new to the reader. For instance, if you write the first five names of people that occur to you one after the other, you have a linear list. When written on a single page, this is a static list and not easy to modify. This single page list can be considered as a model of a sequential file. However the elements need be neither physically adjacent nor homogeneous. Vectors and tables are also examples of lists.

The simplest way to represent a list is to order it by physical location, as we do when we write a list on a sheet of paper. Then, as shown in Figure 13.2, to insert C following B we must first move the contents of cells 3 and 4 into cells 4 and 5. In

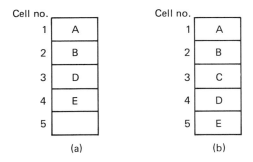

Figure 13.2   Insertion of "C" in list: (a) before; (b) after.

[1]R.E. Griswold, J.F. Poage, and I.P. Polonsky, *The SNOBOL 4 Programming Language* (Englewood Cliffs, N.J.: Prentice-Hall, 1971).

a dynamic list this form of representation causes a great deal of work. Later we introduce a more flexible representation, known as a "linked list."

Henceforth, we shall refer to linear lists simply as *lists*. Lists have a beginning, called the *head*, and an end, called the *tail*. The tail cell must be somehow marked, and normally it contains an indicator, such as the symbol ø, that no cells follow in the list. In a *one-way list*, a cell is only accessed from the preceding cell. In a *two-way list*, a cell is accessed from either the preceding or following cell. A two-way list is not logically more powerful than a single list. For instance, while it is easy to find the preceding cell in a two-way list, this can still be done in a one-way list by beginning at the head and locating the current cell by always remembering the preceding cell location. Pictorially, list structures are usually represented as in Fig. 13.3.

Stack

A *stack* is a list in which additions and deletions are restricted to the head of the list. As an example of a stack, consider empty railroad cars placed on a dead-end

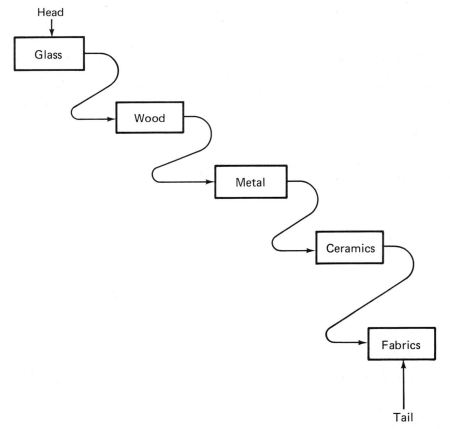

Figure 13.3   Linear linked list of materials sold by Profit, Inc.

siding. As shown in Fig. 13.4, car G is the tail and A is the head. We can only move a car onto or off of one end of the stack, namely the head. Therefore, the first car removed must always be removed from position 1. After car A is removed, then car B can be removed, and so on. Similarly, new cars can be added only at one end of the track.

Queue

A *queue* is a list in which additions are restricted to the tail and deletions are restricted to the head. As an example of a queue, or a "first-come-first-served" linked list not in physical order, consider the example of customers waiting to be served at a bakery, as shown in Fig. 13.5. In order to serve customers in their order of arrival, suppose a set of consecutive numbers are available on tags. On arrival customers take the top tag from a stack of available tags arranged in ascending order. There may be several tags out awaiting service. When a person's number is called, that person is served and his or her tag is placed on another stack of tags belonging to previously served customers. Then the next tag to be served is determined as the lowest number among the unserved tags.

Deque

A *deque* is a list in which additions and deletions are restricted to the head or the tail. As an example of a deque, suppose that we wish to store empty boxcars at a given position along a north-south railroad line. For this purpose the stack cited in Fig. 13.4 is not a good organization. In the stack example only a train bound in a

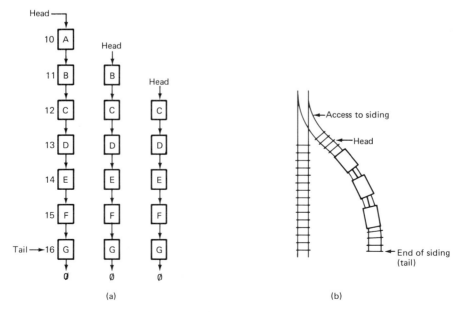

(a)   (b)

Figure 13.4   Dead end siding as an example of a stack.

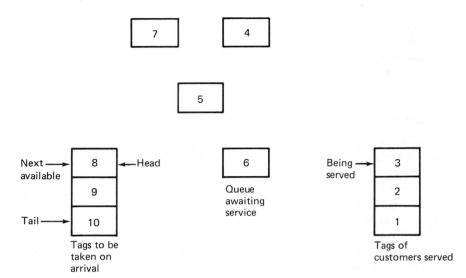

Figure 13.5 Serving queue.

single direction (either north or south) can properly access a dead-end siding because a boxcar must couple behind the engine of a regular train. If we use a shunt siding, as shown in Fig. 13.6, then a north-bound train can access the siding when coming from the north junction, while a south-bound train can access the siding from the south junction. Boxcars are bidirectional, so they can be accessed from either junction. This shunt siding is equivalent to a deque.

The reader should be aware that although the preceding restrictions are placed on additions and deletions, we have not restricted the operation of access, as some authors do. We feel that for programming purposes this is unnecessarily restrictive.

13.2.3 Trees

Most people have an intuitive concept of a hierarchical structure: the familiar family tree is a convenient illustration. The command structure of the military or the administrative organization chart of a business is also a hierarchical structure. An important property of the definition of a hierarchical structure is that there are no circles or cycles in the structure; that is, once leaving an element in the structure there is no return to that element following the structure.

A *tree* is simply an abstract model for a structure that has a hierarchical form. It is difficult to overstate the importance of trees; they occur everywhere; and in computing they are indispensable. Because trees occur in so many guises, they have been independently discovered many times by theorists.

Trees are a special class of discrete structures known as *graphs* for which there is now a vast and interesting mathematical theory. While in our view graph theory is fundamental to the foundations of computer science and should be familiar

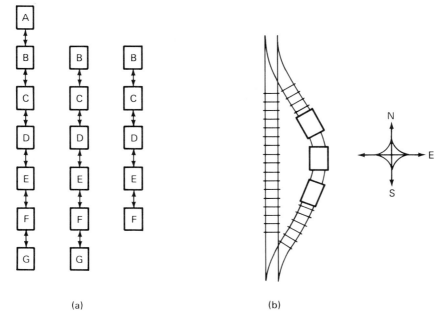

(a)   (b)

Figure 13.6   Shunt siding as an example of a deque.

to any serious programmer, we shall treat trees in a simple descriptive manner, which is sufficient for our purposes.

A *tree* is a set of related *nodes,* or hierarchical elements such that no node is indirectly related to itself. That is, no circle of related nodes can exist. Pictorially we indicate the direct relationship of two nodes (represented by points) by a line, called an *edge,* joining each node as shown in Fig. 13.7.

In a hierarchical structure, the relationship of two entities is not symmetric. In a business, commands flow down the organization chart and information up the

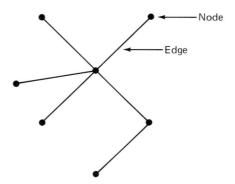

Figure 13.7   A tree.

chart. Thus a tree is not a complete model for all aspects of the organization of people in an enterprise. When the relation between nodes is asymmetric, a tree is directed or called a *ditree*. This is indicated, as shown in Fig. 13.8, by an arrow, called an *arc*, that is added to the lines between nodes to show the asymmetry of the relations.

The trees discussed most often in computer science are special cases of the ditree just defined and are actually called "ditrees" in graph theory. The relationships depicted by these trees are not symmetric but directed, and the nodes are thus ordered. Pictorially, the direction implied is down, and two joined or *adjacent* nodes are always pictured at different vertical positions. In addition, the nodes are ordered. That is, a node to the left of a node at the same level cannot be moved to

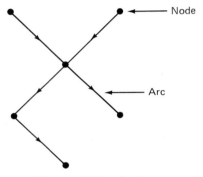

Figure 13.8   A ditree.

the right of that node. Such directed and ordered trees are called *oriented trees* and are represented by Fig. 13.9.

In an oriented tree, there is a unique node that cannot be reached from any other node; pictorially, it is the highest node and is called the *root*. Given two related nodes, the higher of the two is the *father* and the lower is the *son*. A root then is fatherless. By definition each node with the exception of the root has exactly one father. Nodes with no sons are called *terminals*.

A tree is an important example of a nonlinear data structure. The reader

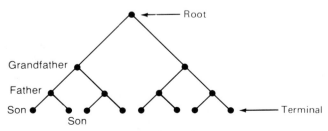

Figure 13.9   An oriented tree.

should observe that a list may be considered as a special oriented tree where each father has at most one son and the head is the root and the tail the only terminal.

Tree Analysis

In order to analyze the properties of trees that are important to file processing, we introduce a few numerical concepts. The distance of a node from the root is a fundamental concept in rooted trees. Because of the way rooted trees are normally represented, all nodes of a tree that are the same distance from the root are drawn at the same level. Thus the *level* of a node is its distance from the root measured as the number of edges in the path from the root to the node. It is often convenient to have a function LEVEL on the tree nodes that gives their level. The level of the root LEVEL(R) is then zero and the level of any node v is $1 + $ LEVEL(FATHER(v)).

An important characteristic of a tree is the length of the longest path from the root to a terminal node, and this is called the *height* of the tree, $H(T)$.

$$H(T) = \max \text{LEVEL}(v) \quad \text{for all } v \in T$$

13.2.4 Plexes

Often data relationships are too complex to be represented as trees. Certainly, circular relationships are common: the highway network is an obvious example if we think of the nodes as cities. By removing the "no-cycle" restriction from trees, we obtain a network structure, and this generalization of a tree is then a *graph*. In computer science, the graphs have node labels (or are cells), and these structures are called *plexes*.

A plex is a general nonlinear data structure. Two representations of plexes are shown in Fig. 13.10. There are, however, other structures which have more than one relationship between two nodes, so a plex is not the most general form of structure.

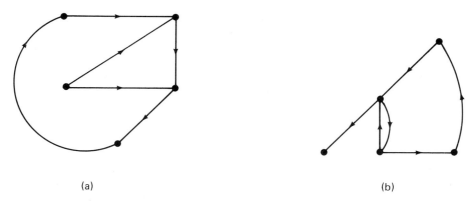

(a)   (b)

Figure 13.10   Plex structures.

13.3 LINKED LISTS

Our discussion so far has made no reference as to how these data structures are to be stored or represented within a computer. In the representations chosen for the data structures we have discussed, the logical and physical relationships of data have agreed. Certainly, this is visually convenient, and indeed we always attempt to find a physical structure that directly represents the logical structure of the data. Visually, this allows us to view directly the logical structure; storagewise, this correspondence can also be invaluable. Unfortunately, a subtle difficulty arises when we realize that this direct correspondence is not always possible nor is it even desirable when using storage. The problem is how conveniently to divorce the logical structure from that of the physical representation when it is appropriate to do so.

Fortunately, this can be done. We have a powerful and flexible tool for structural representation using a concept based on the idea of storing structural information within the elements of the structure itself. This concept, the *linked list,* is simply a set of data elements where each element contains its directed relationship to the other elements; the receiving element need not explicitly store its relationship with the sender. Previously, we found it convenient to view a directed relationship as a pointing arrow between related cells. Obviously, within the computer we cannot draw pointed arrows; however, we certainly can represent pointers. To do so the following steps should be taken:

1. Assume a single list.
2. Assign to each data cell an address and add to a data cell a cell address field which we call a *link*.
3. Then in the address link of a cell store the address of the cell that is related.

This address then effectively points to the related cell, and we call the address a *pointer.*

It is important to note that we consider the linked list concept as a powerful representational tool for data structures not, as some authors do, as just another data structure. We feel that the latter is not only misleading but confuses a data structure model with a particular representation. To do so unnecessarily restricts the process of generalization and inhibits insight into the study of structure.

Let us now use linked lists to reexamine the data structures of the last sections and to consider reorganization operations on them.

13.3.1 Linked List Stack

The stack of Fig. 13.4 is implemented in Fig. 13.11. As can be seen, the pointers are replaced by adding a link field to each list data cell and making the cells addressable. Pictorially there is no great advantage, and in fact it is harder to follow.

It is still not obvious how to describe a linked list in a computer. Let us sup-

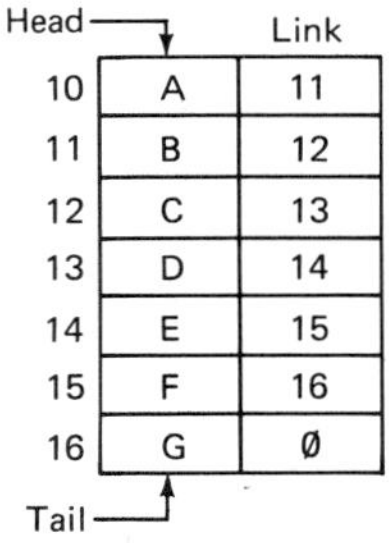

	Head ⟶	Link
10	A	11
11	B	12
12	C	13
13	D	14
14	E	15
15	F	16
16	G	Ø

Tail ⟶

Figure 13.11   Linked list stack.

pose that the cells are rows of a table; the data fields of the cells are the first element and the link fields the second element. We may now define the cells of a linked list in COBOL as follows:

```
WORKING-STORAGE SECTION.
       .
       .
       .
01 LINKED-LIST.
    02 CELL OCCURS 100 TIMES.
       03 DATA PIC X(30).
       03 LINK PIC 99.
```

To determine the head of the stack, we must know the index that points to the head. We will use the data name HEAD as the location in which this head index value is stored. The tail indicator is chosen as zero: thus, initially LINK(HEAD) = 0.

To add a new cell to the stack that has address NEW and that contains data, we add to the head of the list as

```
MOVE HEAD TO LINK (NEW).
MOVE NEW TO HEAD.
```

Of course, we must now update NEW:

```
MOVE free cell name TO NEW.
```

To delete a cell from the stack is simpler:

```
MOVE LINK (HEAD) TO HEAD.
```

The former head cell is then lost. If we want the data, we must refer to DATA (HEAD) before HEAD is changed. The add and delete operations for queues and deques are similar, and we leave them to the reader.

13.3.2 Algorithms

Let us examine several operations on a linked list. We shall consider them as general algorithms rather than as COBOL programs and leave it as an exercise for the reader to make the necessary translations.

Operation NEXT

First suppose we are at cell x as indicated by POINTER and wish to obtain the next cell.

ALGORITHM: NEXT(POINTER)
1: POINTER ← LINK(POINTER)
2: RETURN

This is the basic operation by which we move to the next cell.

Operation ACCESS

More generally, suppose we wish to move to the cell that contains the value KEY.

ALGORITHM:ACCESS(KEY,HEAD,POINTER)
1: POINTER←HEAD
2: WHILE (POINTER≠0) DO
   IF KEY = VALUE (POINTER)THEN RETURN
   ELSE POINTER←LINK(POINTER)
3: RETURN

Note that the variable HEAD and step 1 can be moved outside the algorithm but this is not a good idea if we always start at the head of the list. Why? On the other hand, if we do not always need to start at the head of the list, is there a disadvantage to the preceding algorithm?

Operation DELETE

To delete cell x we must know the address of the preceding cell. Suppose the preceding cell is pointed to by POINTER.

ALGORITHM:DELETE(POINTER)
1: LINK(POINTER)←(LINK(POINTER))
2: RETURN

Operation ADD

To add a cell pointed to by NEW we must know the address of the cell that precedes the new cell.

ALGORITHM: ADD(POINTER,NEW)
 1: LINK(NEW)←LINK(POINTER)
 2: LINK(POINTER)←NEW
 3: RETURN

To determine the appropriate cell that precedes an addition or deletion, we can use the algorithm ACCESS. These algorithms have only dealt with the organization of a single linked list, and the operations on the data contained have been purposely omitted. From these algorithms we can see that there is an increased flexibility of cell organization but this is at the cost of increased access time and storage.

A two-way list requires that two pointers must be reset for addition and deletion. Multilinked lists require increasing storage as the number of pointers per cell grows.

The advantage of a two-way list is that it is as easy to find the predecessor as it is the successor cell. Two-way lists also provide some protection against the possible loss of a single cell when external storage is used. If a tail pointer is kept as well as a head pointer the list on either side of the lost cell can be found.

Because of the possibility of losing a cell in writing to external storage, the sequence of writing is chosen to allow recovery. The pointer to a new cell is written first and if successful then the data to that cell. If we wish to insert an existing record X in between records A and B, first point X to B and then point A to Z. Then by saving the location of X or X itself, we can recover if A fails to point to X and B will not be lost.

Two advantages of linked lists over physical lists are that insertion and deletion are easy and that by adding more pointers to a cell we are no longer restricted to linear lists but can represent any complex relationship we wish. Two disadvantages are the extra storage required for the pointers and the cost of traversing pointers to locate a cell. Pointer traversal is essentially a linear search and thus random retrieval can be slow.

We have glossed over the fact that to add an element to a list a free cell must be available. Where does it come from? There are various techniques for obtaining a free cell. One method is to keep them in a stack. Then to acquire a free cell, you obtain the stack head and to delete a cell, you return it to the stack head. Initially all cells are placed in the free cell stack. In the linked list concept, the pointer is considered part of the cell. When a linked list is stored on external memory, a long search through embedded pointers can require many record fetches. Another technique is to remove the pointers and place them in separate directories that can be searched more efficiently.

13.4 INVERTED LISTS

If the record keys are organized in lists by attributes, with one list for each attribute to be ordered on that attribute, then structure is stored outside the file and it is called an *inverted file*. We can now access a record by attribute rather than by primary key if we examine the appropriate inverted list (the attribute list). Addition and deletion of a record can become quite complicated, as each attribute list is affected. This type of organization can take many forms and is particularly useful for information retrieval; we examine inverted files in more detail in the next chapter.

13.5 BINARY TREES

There is one special class of tree graphs that appears to grow in almost every area of computing because of its ability to represent ordered binary relations. A *binary tree* is a special case of an oriented tree with at most two descendants.

We allow a binary tree to be empty, and this turns out to be convenient in the following recursive definition of a binary tree, which is very useful in a computing context. Knuth and others claim that a binary tree is not a special case of a tree, but if we apply constraints to a class of trees to obtain a new, more restricted class, then we can quite naturally think of the result as a special case of the more general class.

Definition

> A *binary tree* is a finite set of nodes that is either empty or consists of a root node that has left and right subtrees which are themselves binary trees.

Noting that the right and left subtrees can be empty, we observe that a node of a binary tree has one of the following distinct possibilities: no descendants, a left descendant, a right descendant, or both left and right descendants. Thus our original definition of at most two descendants holds.

In the case where all nodes except one have exactly one descendant, a binary tree degenerates into essentially a linear list, although the left–right orientation of descendants may in fact carry additional information not possible in a linear list.

Traversal

A frequent operation on any set is to examine each member exactly once; this is often called *enumeration,* and one method is an intelligent search based on some structure of the set. Because "search" has a special meaning for us, we will use the term *traversal* to mean a systematic search of a tree so that the data at each node is examined exactly once.

A complete traversal of a tree orders the nodes linearly in the order of the visits. Any derived order is a traversal; there are very many ways to do this, but three methods are basic in computing: preorder, inorder, and postorder.

Procedure: Preorder Traversal
   Visit the root.
   Traverse the left subtree.
   Traverse the right subtree.

Procedure: Inorder Traversal
   Traverse the left subtree.
   Visit the root.
   Traverse the right subtree.

Procedure: Postorder Traversal
   Traverse the left subtree.
   Traverse the right subtree.
   Visit the root.

13.6 FILE STRUCTURES

Data structures are generally considered memory-based structures. This is because consideration of the pure structure is simplified by ignoring the physical details required of an implementation in physical media. Implementation in memory is fairly straightforward, and efficient access to all memory cells allows us to ignore address determination as a problem.

A file structure of a programming language is a data structure on the set of physical records of a file defined by that file structure. Moreover, the logical organization of a logical record is a data structure. Ideally, the logical and physical organization of a file should coincide. Since the appropriate file structure may not exist in the language used, this is not always possible.

It should now be apparent to the reader that data structures provide important concepts that can be used in the creation of useful file techniques and in the understanding of these techniques. Also, data structures provide a formal way of looking at a data base organization independent of the contents of the data base.

The prime problem in the physical and logical organization of records on external storage is that record access is much more complicated than in memory. The prime consideration is not the representation of structure but rather the manner in which a structure can be appropriately manipulated. It must be possible to efficiently traverse both the physical and logical records of a file structure and to keep the physical size of the file related to the logical size.

REFERENCES FOR FURTHER READING

Adel'son-Vel'skii, G.M., and **Landis, E.M.** "An Algorithm for the Organization of Information." *Dokl. Acad. Nauk. SSR Math.* 146 (1962): 263–266.

Baer, S.L., and **Schwab, B.** "A Comparison of Tree Balancing Algorithms." *CACM* 20 (1977): 322–330.

Nievergett, J. "Binary Search Trees and File Organizations." *ACM Computing Surveys* 6 (September 1974): 195–207.

PROBLEMS

1. Devise an algorithm to insert a cell in a physical list stored in consecutive addresses within memory.

2. Devise an algorithm to delete a cell from the list in Problem 1. Use the simplest method possible. What is the disadvantage of your simple method?

3. Give a COBOL definition of a storage structure capable of representing a binary tree of up to 200 cells where each cell has elements key, data, and appropriate pointers.

4. Investigate the storing of file record keys and record addresses in a binary tree form rather than as a table. To locate a key some form of searching the binary tree must be devised. Some methods are exhaustive, but if the tree is properly constructed only one path from the root to a terminal need be examined to see if a key is present.

5. Implement your solution to Problem 4 in COBOL.

14

Index
Organization

There are two important aspects to files: record access and file reorganization of records. File organizations are chosen to suit the characteristics of access and reorganization required by intended file use with regard to selected criteria of efficiency. Access is a problem of determining a record address, some aspects of which we investigated in Chapter 7. A widely used solution to address determination is to provide an index that can be efficiently searched and reorganized. Some authors allow an index to be contained in the structure of the file records, but the usual approach is to separate the index from the file. We define an *index* to be a set of record pointers *external* to the file records. Since an index must contain a key for every record, it is usually too large to be contained in memory and, thus, the index itself is usually a file.

When a file has several indexes, a master index can be used to select the required index to search. When we have indexes of indexes, the top index is called a *directory*. In order to search a directory quickly, it is usually designed so that it can reside in memory.

In this chapter, we consider several basic techniques for index organization of single and multiple key files. There are three main considerations in the design of an index structure: its size, its search length, and its dynamic reorganization characteristics. Reorganization is a consequence of insertion and deletion. It is important that insertion and deletion of records not degrade the original access aspect of a file organization. The three considerations mentioned ultimately control the cost of using the file structure.

14.1 FLAT INDEX

A *flat index* is a linear list of record descriptors, usually a record key and record access pointer. A common organization is to arrange the pairs as a table. Access is simple in a flat index. There are four basic search techniques that can be used: linear search, ordered linear search, block search, and binary search. When a flat index is so large that it cannot reside in memory, none of these are efficient.

Reorganization is straightforward for tables but can be time consuming if the keys are ordered. If the index is stored as a pointer list, then reorganization is simple and efficient, but searching is slower.

If the index is stored indirectly as a hash function, then the search length is good (close to 1) but the file cannot be searched sequentially. Sequential access to a host file can be obtained by storing the index as a hash table (or linked list) ordered on the key, but the random nature of record storage location makes sequential access very inefficient. For large indexes the standard solution is a hierarchical index.

14.2 HIERARCHICAL INDEX

A *hierarchical index* is a tree structure, in which the nodes contain indexing information. Although this structure is more complex than a linear list, tree search techniques are inherently faster than linear list searches. If the index is resident in memory, it can be organized as a binary tree structure. If the index does not fit into memory, a binary search tree is generally not the most efficient method because of the cost of storage accesses.

The number of storage accesses is reduced by lowering the length of search. We can lower the height of a tree (the maximum search length) by increasing the number of descendants of each node, and a generalization of the binary tree, the *m*-way tree, has become the main approach to hierarchical organization of large indexes.

14.2.1 *m*-WAY TREE

Although binary trees are one of the most important and useful classes of trees, they are too constrained for many purposes. However, general trees are so unconstrained that they do not have sufficient structural properties of particular use in index design. A useful compromise between too much and too little constraint is the *m-way tree,* which limits the maximum number of descendants of a node to a constant *m*.

A binary tree is then a special case, a 2-way tree; and a single pointer list another, a 1-way tree. (We wanted to follow Knuth and use the term *m*-ary, but how does one say 7-ary without a talent for poetary.) For the *m*-way concept to be efficient, additonal constraints are devised to obtain desirable properties. For instance, Landouer [see Knuth (1973)] suggested in 1963 that level *L* should be nearly full before level *L* + 1 is created.

There are many ways to organize an *m*-way index, but we examine only two that are sufficient to illustrate the approach and meet most design needs. The two most widely used variants of the *m*-way tree are the B-tree and the B+tree; they provide the underlying theoretical basis of VSAM, and the reader should reexamine Chapter 11 following their descriptions.

14.2.2 B-Tree

An important concept in maintaining good search performance in a tree is that of balance. A fully balanced tree fills all nodes of a level before adding a new level. This is difficult to do in a dynamically changing tree and requires major and costly reorganization. A compromise is usually chosen that leads to a semibalanced tree.

A *B-tree* of order *m* is a semibalanced *m*-way tree with growth constraints.

B-Tree Constraints

1. The root has at least two sons, unless it is a terminal node.
2. Each internal node has at least *m*/2 sons.
3. All terminals are on the same level.

B-trees [Bayer & McCreight, Knuth] seems to be one of those ideas whose time has come; however, Bayer appears to be the father as he is the main author of a number of the early papers. A B-tree (Fig. 14.1) becomes a data structure when we restrict insertion and deletion to the procedures B-insertion and B-deletion, which preserve the definition of a B-tree. The value of B-trees as an index is that search length can be made very short and a good degree of balance is relatively easy to maintain in a dynamic index.

B-Insertion

If a *find* fails to locate the query key, then it ends at a leaf-fail. If the leaf can accommodate the query key, it is inserted and B-balance is maintained (Fig. 14.2). If a key cannot be inserted in a node, then a *node split* occurs. The midpoint key is moved to the parent node of the node being split and the lower keys placed in the original node while the upper keys are placed in the new node. A node split maintains B-balance. If the parent node is full, then it must be split to obtain room for the

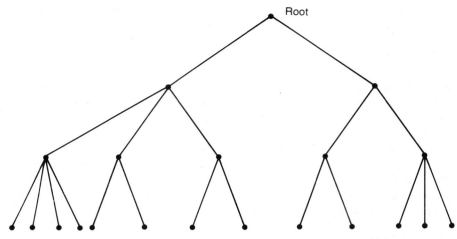

Figure 14.1   B-tree for $m = 4$.

midpoint key of the previous split. This can continue until the root is split; then, of course, room will be formed in the new root. In the worst case, a root split, the tree increases in height by one level.

A B-tree fills from the bottom up and grows in height from the top up through a root split. This insertion process preserves the properties of a B-tree, and that is why we call it B-insertion.

B-Deletion

When we have found the key to be deleted, it is either in a leaf or in a node. If it is in a leaf, then it is removed and the higher value keys are shifted down one position. If there are then fewer than $m/2$ keys, reorganization is necessary among the children of the parent node. If there are insufficient keys among the children, then node concatenation is performed; this is the inverse of a node split combining two nodes into one.

If the key to be deleted is in a node, then it is replaced with a key from the child of the deleted key. Thus the key to be deleted moves down to a leaf and we have the previous case of a leaf deletion (Fig. 14.3).

Discussion

The efficiency of a B-tree arises from the fact that access to storage is the major component of manipulation in the B-tree and by making m large we keep the height of the tree low. For $m = 10$, 1010 keys only require $h = 2$ in a full tree; thus, at most two node accesses are required to find any key. Since nodes begin only half full, there is considerable room to insert keys before a node split is required.

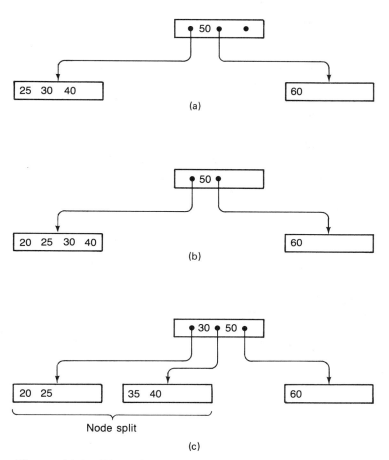

Figure 14.2   B-tree insertion: (a) before insertion of 20; (b) after insertion of 20 but before insertion of 35; (c) after insertion of 35 by performing a node split.

14.2.3 B+tree

Sequential search is poor in a B-tree. By reorganizing a B-tree so that all keys reside in the terminal nodes, a sequential search of the terminal nodes becomes a sequential search of the file. The terminal nodes have an additional pointer to the next terminal node in the sequence. The set of terminal nodes is then a linear list called the *sequence set*.

The general performance of a B+tree is similar to that of a B-tree except that all searches now terminate at a terminal; thus, search length is always the height of the tree, but this is not much worse than the average search in a B-tree. B+trees are used to implement indexed sequential organizations (see Chapter 11).

14.3 MULTIPLE-INDEXED FILES

In the general case, we would like to be able to process a file on more than one key. Alternate keys have many uses, and there are many ways to implement alternate keys. In a sequential file, for instance, we need only sort the file on the alternate key field and then use it as the processing key. The obvious approach for an indexed file is to provide an alternate index for each alternate key; however, the method of organizing the alternate indexes is not obvious.

The first problem of an alternate index is to decide how it accesses file records: directly or indirectly (Fig. 14.4). An *indirect index* is an alternate index that points to the prime key, not to the address of the record. An indirect index has the advantages that it need not be updated because records are physically moved and that queries based solely on the index attributes need not access the records if we only want the record name as its prime key. The disadvantage is that the search is slower because the prime index must always be searched.

14.3.1 Inverted Files

Multiple-indexed files are sometimes referred to as inverted files. The basic idea of inversion is that individual records can be located by content rather than by name without direct reference to the actual records. This basic concept leads to

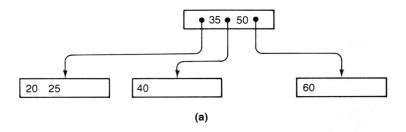

(a)

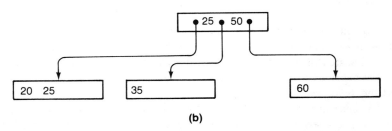

(b)

Figure 14.3 B-tree deletion: (a) after deletion of 30 from Fig. 14.2 (c); (b) after deletion of 40 from (a).

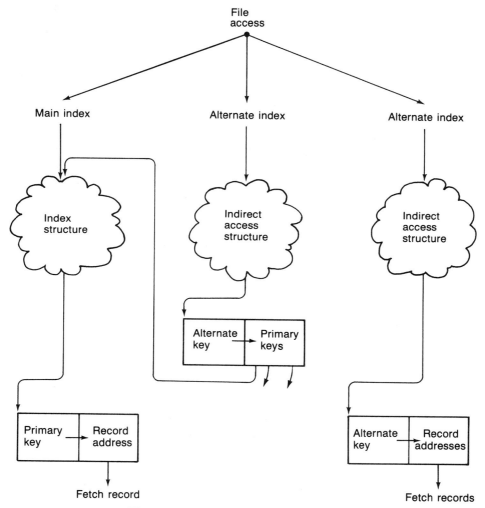

Figure 14.4   Multiple index structure.

many forms of inverted files, and because of this not only do inverted files not have a well-defined structure but their definition varies from author to author. Trying to discover exactly what an inverted file organization means can be confusing to say the least.

We define an *inverted list* to be an ordered list of those records of a file that possess an attribute, which is the name of the list. An inverted list is, thus, an index to a set of records that have an attribute in common. The list records are named by their access pointers. For simplicity we assume indirect indexes, and the record pointers are then their primary keys. We define an *inverted file* to be an indexed file with inverted lists. (Figure 14.5 shows an example, in which each ID number is the record address of an engineer in the personnel file. No other IDs belong to engineers.)

The major advantages of using inverted lists are that they can be combined to select records that satisfy Boolean functions of the attributes and, futhermore, that queries based on the inverted attributes can be answered without access to the data records themselves. This can make query very fast, and inversion is the most popular technique used to organize files for information retrieval. This we investigate in the next chapter.

The major disadvantage is the size of the resulting index, which can be larger than the data record set. The ordered nature of an inverted list complicates insertion and deletion of records, so that reorganization of inverted files is costly. They are best used when frequent, fast, unstructured queries are required of a file.

Engineers

ID-record key
10
22
30
35
75
101

Figure 14.5   Inverted list.

14.3.2 MULTILIST INDEX

A *multilist* file organization (Fig. 14.6) imbeds lists within the data records; the index locates an attribute value, which then has an associated pointer to the first record in a list of records containing that attribute, but this list is contained within the records themselves by means of pointers imbedded within each record. Thus the multilist index is used to select the first record, and that record selects the next, and so on. Usually the attribute value also has an associated list size to predict the size of the list to be examined.

There are two main advantages: the index records are of fixed size, and reorganization is simple (insert and delete on a linear list). The main disadvantage is that pointer traversal is inefficient because records are unlikely to be in the same block, and query performance is poor compared to inverted lists.

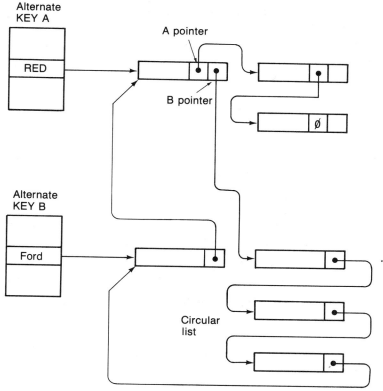

Figure 14.6   Multilist on two alternate keys.

14.4 CONCLUSION

Index organization is a complex problem and a subject in itself; we can only hope that research will lead to the discovery of better techniques. The types of index organizations known are not clearly distinguished in the literature because of their hybrid nature, mixing many fundamental concepts. There is a need for a general theory of index organization.

Fortunately for the file designer, B-trees, B+trees, and inverted lists not only form the basis of most index organizations in use but are sufficient for most design purposes.

REFERENCES FOR FURTHER READING

Bayer, R., and **McCreight, E.** "Organization and Maintenance of Large Ordered Indexes." *Acta Informatica* 1 (1972): 173–189.

Cardenas, A.F. "Analysis and Performance of Inverted Database Structures," *CACM* 18 (May 1975): 253–263.

Comer, D. "The Ubiquitous B-Tree." *ACM Computing Surveys* 11 (June 1979).

Lefkovitz, D. *File Structures for On-Line Systems.* New York: Spartan Books, 1969.

PROBLEMS

1. Describe three files that require at least three retrieval keys. Select one as the primary key, giving reasons for your choice.

2. An inventory record contains part name, supplier, cost, stock limits, quantity, daily sales rate, location, description.
(a) If you can only have two keys, what should they be and why?
(b) If you were to invert the file, on which items would you do this?

3. Design a system that maintains four inverted lists. Assume there are 10,000 records of 512 bytes and that the attribute lists vary from 1 to 3000 records.

4. Design a system with multiple pointers on four alternate keys.

15

File Query

In the previous two chapters, we studied data structures that could be used to organize the fields and records of a file into networks of interlocking relationships. The structures studied were internal as opposed to external; that is, the paths that linked data items together were located within the file itself, either through the use of stored pointers or indirectly by means of language data structures used to store fields or records. In this chapter, we shall study techniques that impose structure on a file by organizing a logical adjacency of records and storing information concerning this organization external to the file.

15.1 CASE STUDY: ICTL CAR LEASING AGENCY

The ICTL (It's Cheaper to Lease) Car Leasing Agency offers automobiles for rental on a daily, weekly, monthly, or annual basis. Each rental office has an on-line terminal to a data file that describes the automobiles available at that location. This file can be examined by an agent in order to choose a car that best suits the needs and price range of a prospective client.

15.1.1 Logical Analysis: ICTL Car Leasing Agency

The basic component of ICTL's computer information system is a file of information about each company automobile. Random accessing is required because many rental customers request an automobile on the spot. A good choice of record key is state vehicle license number. For simplicity, the file can be created as an index sequential file. Thus our attention need only focus on how to obtain a list of the license numbers of those cars a client might wish to lease. Once this is done, these license numbers can be used to fetch each automobile's record from the index sequential file and the client can base his decision on the descriptions that these records provide.

The problem of selecting a vehicle is a complex issue because it depends on the individual whim of the customer. The list cannot be predetermined until the client has made his wishes known. In order to design a system that can produce the list required, some restrictions must be imposed on the nature of the description the customer provides. We could not do much with a description such as: ''I want a car my wife would like but I don't want one of those chrome-plated lemons like my mother-in-law has.'' Rather, the descripion must be restricted to a list of attributes possessed by the company's automobiles. It might be possible, for example, to locate a car that is ''blue,'' ''four-door,'' ''air-conditioned,'' ''with a V-8 engine.'' One way of viewing such a request is to see it as describing a subset that contains blue cars. Among these blue cars there is a possibly smaller set of cars that have V-8 engines,and among these a set of cars that have four doors. The request is ultimately the intersection of the set of blue cars, with the sets of air-conditoned cars, four-door cars, and cars with V-8 engines. The first technique that we describe in this chapter, inverted lists, is based on this observation.

We refer to a request to locate a group of records having certain characteristics in a file as a *file query*. If a query is regarded as a request to locate a set of records that is derived from the intersection of sets of records that share one attribute in common, such as blueness or air-conditioned, then the license numbers pertaining to these common attribute sets must be readily available. A list of the record keys that share one attribute in common is called an *inverted list*. In order to process the query, it is necessary to have inverted lists of blue cars, cars with V-8 engines, air-conditioned cars, and four-door cars. The cars that the customer is interested in are those cars whose record keys appear on each of these inverted lists.

The inverted lists are not part of the data file but are data structures that are stored outside the data file, either in memory or in storage. Normally, inverted lists are stored in ascending order by key. If AAA 111, SUE 425, COB 162, TOM 645, and WIN 219 are the only license numbers on the file of blue cars, the inverted list of blue cars is simply

> AAA 111
> COB 162
> SUE 425
> TOM 645
> WIN 219

An inverted list for a particular attribute such as color may be created by opening a file, extracting and examining each record, and adding the key to an inverted list whenever the record matches the inverted list attribute. Afterwards, the inverted list is sorted. When an index sequential file is used, the inverted list created will already be sorted. Why? Remember that records in an index sequential file are stored in order of record key.

In some files, the inverted lists for particular attributes may be very large (as, for example, the inverted list that points to verses in the Bible that contain the word "Jesus"). As new records are added to a file and old records are deleted, the inverted lists must be updated to reflect current status. The problems faced here are very similar to those encountered in maintaining dictionaries.

Given that the inverted lists have been created, it remains to process a query. Let us suppose that the customer presents a request for a blue air-conditioned car. We may denote this request as

> Q (BLUE $\wedge$ AIR-CONDITIONED)

using the symbol $\wedge$ for the Boolean operator AND. The codes BLUE and AIR-CONDITIONED are the names of two inverted lists. These lists are brought into memory for examination. Because these lists are sorted in ascending order they resemble two sequentially ordered files. We seek those record keys that occur in both lists. If we regard the lists as sequential files, this is very much like a request to update a master file from a transaction file. (In sequential file processing we update only those records whose keys appear on both the transaction and master files; here we want only those keys on both inverted lists.) The balance line algorithm discussed in Chapter 3 can be modified to do the task. Instead of issuing a read instruction to advance along a file as we would when processing records with the balance line algorithm, we merely advance a *pointer* along the list in question. When the pointers for each list match an active key, the record pointed to is fetched. Processing is continued until one of the inverted lists is exhausted. Why? Clearly the $\wedge$ operation requires the record key to be on both lists.

Sometimes the queries can be longer, such as

> Q(BLUE $\wedge$ AIR-CONDITIONED $\wedge$ V-8 $\wedge$ FOUR-DOOR)

but the basic algorithm does not change. Each attribute entry in the query is called an *operand* of the query and the inverted list for each operand is fetched. The active key of the balance line algorithm is initially set to the smallest vehicle license number that appears at the front of the lists. The pointers on each list are advanced and compared with the active key which is always updated to point to the smallest key of those at the head of the lists. If at any point in the process all five keys pointed to match the active key, that record is fetched because it satisfies the query. Processing is halted whenever one inverted list is exhausted. The basic algorithm is

ALGORITHM: ANDQUERY

1: Fetch each inverted list that appears as an operand in the body of the query.

2: Set a pointer to the head of each list. If any list is empty, stop.

3: Set the active key to the smallest value pointed to by the inverted list pointers.

4: Compare the key pointed to on each inverted list with the active key. If every key matches the active key, fetch the record whose key is the active key.

5: Advance each list pointer whose current value matches the active key one position. If any list is exhausted, stop. Otherwise, return to Step 3.

It is often very useful to allow the Boolean OR operator $\lor$ to be used in a query. A client may wish either a blue or red car that has air conditioning. Such a query could be represented as

$$Q [(BLUE \lor RED) \land AIR-CONDITIONED]$$

Parentheses have been added to indicate the priority of operations. The car must be either blue or red and in addition it must be air-conditioned. If the parentheses were omitted, the query could mistakenly be read as a request for either a blue car or an air-conditioned red car.

The balance line algorithm can easily be modified to handle the OR operator. This is simply a request for a key that is on at least one of several lists. Let us consider a query such as

$$Q (RED \lor YELLOW \lor BLUE \lor GREEN)$$

Such a query is very easy to process. *A record is fetched for every value the active key assumes during the execution of the balance line algorithm.* The balance line algorithm for a series of OR operators is

ALGORITHM: ORQUERY

1: Fetch each inverted list that appears as an operand in the body of the query.

2: Set a pointer to the head of each list. If all lists are empty, stop.

3: Set the active key to the smallest value pointed to by the inverted list pointers.

4. Fetch the record whose key is the value of the active key.

5: Advance each list pointer that matches the active key by one position. If all lists are exhausted, stop. Otherwise, return to Step 3.

The reader would be wise to compare this algorithm with the one for the Boolean operator $\wedge$.

The real difficulty arises in processing a query that contains both types of operator, $\wedge$ and $\vee$.

15.2 THE HSIAO–HARARY ALGORITHM

Suppose we have a *compound* query, which is a query consisting of both the OR and AND operators, such as

$$Q[(L_1 \wedge L_2 \wedge L_3) \vee (L_4 \wedge L_5)]$$

where each L_i represents the name of an inverted list. From the preceding discussion we could apply the modified balance line algorithm on $L_1 \wedge L_2 \wedge L_3$ and instead of fetching each record when the primary keys on L_1, L_2, and L_3 match, we could instead store the matching keys in a new inverted list, say L_6. We could then perform a similar process on $L_4 \wedge L_5$, creating another new inverted list L_7, which would be a list of keys on both lists L_4 and L_5. Then we could use the OR version of the modified balance line algorithm on lists L_6 and L_7. The records whose keys are on either of L_6 or L_7 should be fetched.

ALGORITHM: COMPOUNDQUERY

1: Fetch each inverted list that appears as an operand in the body of the query.

2: For each set of operands bracketed together and joined by $\wedge$ operators, create a new inverted list by using the ANDQUERY routine suitably modified to output an inverted list rather than a series of file records.

3: Employ the ORQUERY routine on all the inverted lists that remain after the completion of Step 2.

The Hsiao–Harary algorithm is a modification of this idea. Consider once again the query

$$Q[(L_1 \wedge L_2 \wedge L_3) \vee (L_4 \wedge L_5)]$$

It is clear that any record that is on all three lists, L_1, L_2, and L_3, is certainly on the smallest of these three lists. Suppose this list is L_3. Similarly, records whose primary keys are on both L_4 and L_5 are on the shortest of these, say L_5. Clearly, the records desired by this query are a subset of the records on L_3 and L_5. Using the ORQUERY version of the balance line algorithm, fetch all the records of L_3 and L_5. As each record is fetched, it is examined to see whether or not it satisfies the original query. Those that do can be processed. As an example, consider the following query:

Q [(CONVERTIBLE $\wedge$ BUCKET SEATS $\wedge$ AUTOMATIC TRANSMISSION)
$\vee$ (LUXURY CAR $\wedge$ AIR-CONDITIONING) $\vee$ (FOREIGN $\wedge$ SPORTS CAR)]

Suppose that Table 15.1 gives the number of keys on each inverted list. From the part of the query (CONVERTIBLE $\wedge$ BUCKET SEATS $\wedge$ AUTOMATIC TRANSMISSION), we select the smallest list, the one for bucket seats. Similarly, we select the lists of luxury car and foreign car as the smallest lists from their respective parts of the query.

Using the ORQUERY algorithm, we fetch all the records whose keys are on these three lists. As each record is fetched, it is examined

Table 15.1   Primary Keys

Name of List	Size of List
Convertible	60
Bucket seats	10
Automatic transmission	100
Luxury car	4
Air conditioning	75
Foreign car	20
Sports car	40

to see whether or not it satisfies the given query. Remember, in the example, that although a car occurs on the short list of cars with bucket seats, the query required it to be a convertible with an automatic transmisson. Of course, any car that appears on more than one of those three lists is only fetched once. Thus, in all, the maximum number of records fetched is 10 (bucket seats) + 4(luxury cars) + 20(foreign) or 34 cars. The figure will be less if any car shares two or more of these characteristics. Many of the foreign cars, for instance, may have bucket seats.

As an alternative to fetching the records to determine whether or not they satisfy the given query, the balance line algorithm can be further modified. Normally in the balance line algorithm, the active key is set to the value of the smallest record key at the head of all the inverted lists; alternatively, it can be set as follows: Suppose the query to be given is

Q [(L_1 $\wedge$ L_2 $\wedge$ L_3) $\vee$ (L_4 $\wedge$ L_5)]

where each of L_1, L_2, L_3, L_4, and L_5 are the names of inverted lists. Let L_3 be the shortest list of L_1, L_2, and L_3, and let L_5 be shortest of L_4 and L_5 as before. The balance line algorithm then becomes the Hsiao-Harary algorithm.

METHOD: HSIAO–HARARY

1: Set the active key to the smallest record key selected from L_3 and L_5. If both lists are empty, stop.

2: Advance the pointers on all lists until they point to keys larger than or equal to the active key. If the keys pointed to on L_1, L_2, and L_3 are the same as the active key or if those on L_4 and L_5 are the same as the active key, fetch the record.

3: Move all pointers ahead one position on their respective lists if they have just matched the active key. If lists L_3 and L_5 are exhausted, stop. Otherwise reset the active key to the smallest of the keys now pointed to on lists L_3 and L_5 and return to Step 2.

The advantage gained is in using the smaller inverted lists. This method can easily be generalized to handle any given query. Rather than use an inverted list on a single attribute, we can create a list on a set of attributes. For example, we might agree to put all blue, air-conditioned, V-8 cars into one bin or bucket. This makes the process of finding records satisfying a given query extremely fast. Unfortunately, it leads to a lot of storage redundancy because many of the blue, air-conditioned, V-8 cars may also be stored in the bucket pertaining to luxury four-door cars with automatic transmissions. A file that has a separate bucket for every possible query is called a *query-inverted* file. It has minimum look-up time and maximum redundancy. The methods studied in this chapter have minimum redundancy but maximum *search times*.

15.3 THE TRACE ALGORITHM

An alternative to the Hsiao–Harary algorithm is the trace algorithm of Welch and Graham. This algorithm requires the recursive calculation of a value called the trace, which helps to maximize the movement of the pointers along the inverted lists in satisfying a query.

Let $P(L)$ be the pointer associated with a given list L. The *trace* $T(L)$ of a list L is defined as the value of $P(L)$. The trace of a query on two lists, L_1 and L_2, ANDed together as $L_1 \wedge L_2$ is defined as

$$T(L_1 \wedge L_2) = \max[T(L_1), T(L_2)]$$

The trace of a query on two lists, L_1 and L_2, ORed together is defined as

$$T(L_1 \vee L_2) = \min[T(L_1), T(L_2)]$$

The trace function is defined recursively so that

$$T((L_1 \wedge L_2) \vee (L_1 \wedge L_3 \wedge L_5)) = \min\{T(L_1 \wedge L_2), T(L_1 \wedge L_3 \wedge L_5)\}$$

but

$$\begin{aligned} T(L_1 \wedge L_2) &= \max\{T(L_1), T(L_2)\} \\ &= \max\{P(L_1), P(L_2)\} \end{aligned}$$

and

$$\begin{aligned} T(L_1 \wedge L_3 \wedge L_5) &= \max\{T(L_1 \wedge L_3), T(L_5)\} \\ &= \max\{\max\{T(L_1), T(L_3)\}, T(L_5)\} \\ &= \max\{P(L_1), P(L_3), P(L_5)\} \end{aligned}$$

So the original expression gives

$$\begin{aligned} & T((L_1 \wedge L_2) \vee (L_1 \wedge L_3 \wedge L_5)) \\ &= \min\{\max\{P(L_1), P(L_2)\}, \max\{P(L_1), P(L_3), P(L_5)\}\} \end{aligned}$$

Thus the trace algorithm can be used to modify the balance line algorithm:

ALGORITHM: TRACE

1: Let $P(L_i)$ be the pointer to inverted list L_i, for all inverted lists, L_1, $L_2, L_3, \ldots, L_i, \ldots, L_k$, given in the query for $i = 1, 2, 3, \ldots,$ k. If list L_j is an empty set, $P(L_j) = \infty$ (HIGH-VALUES in COBOL).

2: Set the active key to the trace of the query Q. Stop if $T(Q) = \infty$.

3: Advance all inverted list pointers until the value of each pointer is greater than or equal to the current value of the trace function. If the record whose primary key is the value of the active key satisfies the query (that is, its primary key is a member of the appropriate combination of lists), fetch the record.

4: Advance the pointers of all inverted lists whose pointer values match the current value of the active key. Set the value of any pointer that now points to an empty list to ∞ or HIGH-VALUES. Return to Step 2.

As an example, suppose we are given the query $Q((L_1 \wedge L_2) \vee L_3)$ on three lists, L_1, L_2, and L_3. The value of the trace function by definition is

$$\begin{aligned} T((L_1 \wedge L_2) \vee (L_3)) &= \min\{T(L_1 \wedge L_2), P(L_3)\} \\ &= \min\{\max\{P(L_1), P(L_2)\}, P(L_3)\} \end{aligned}$$

Suppose the following inverted lists were given:

L_1	L_2	L_3
11	6	9
9	5	4
7	4	
2	3	

The first value of the trace function is

$$\min\{\max \{2, 3\}, 4\} = 3$$

Record 3 does not satisfy the query; it is not fetched. The inverted lists become

L_1	L_2	L_3
11	6	9
9	5	4
7	4	

The trace function is now

$$\min\{\max \{7, 4\}, 4\} = 4$$

Record 4 satisfies the query (since it is on L_3); it is fetched. The inverted lists become

L_1	L_2	L_3
11	6	9
9	5	
7		

The trace function is now

$$\min\{\max\{7, 5\}, 9\} = 7$$

Record 7 does not satisfy the query; therefore it is not fetched. The lists become

L_1	L_2	L_3
11		9
9		

The trace function is now

$$\min\{\max\{9, \infty\}, 9\} = 9$$

Record 9 satisfies the query; it is fetched. The inverted lists become

$$\underline{L_1} \qquad \underline{L_2} \qquad \underline{L_3}$$
$$11$$

The trace function becomes

$$\min\{\max\{11, \infty\}, \infty\} = \infty$$

The algorithm terminates.

15.4 BINARY TABLES

The methods just presented require a scanning algorithm to dissect the query into its basic components, to locate imbedded brackets, and to inform the overall program which operands (lists) are associated with which operators. If the number of operators is small, there is a simple technique that can be used which avoids using brackets and allows the user to give priority to either $\wedge$ or $\vee$. It is best illustrated by example. Suppose the following query is given:

BLUE AND TWO-DOOR OR GREEN

using the character strings AND and OR as the operators $\wedge$ and $\vee$. Let us examine this query. BLUE, TWO-DOOR, and GREEN are the names of inverted lists. One inverted list is like any other; all it contains is a list of record keys. Presumably the program has a directory of inverted lists. If a Relative I-O file is used, the directory might look something like:

BLUE	2
BROWN	6
GREY	3
GREEN	14
.	
.	
.	

This is a list of the names of inverted lists and their relative record numbers. Each list involved in the query is fetched from disk.

Suppose, in the above query, we are restricted to two operators. For any query there are four possibilities:

$$
\begin{array}{cc}
\text{OR} & \text{OR} \\
\text{OR} & \text{AND} \\
\text{AND} & \text{OR} \\
\text{AND} & \text{AND}
\end{array}
$$

If there are two operators, then there are three inverted lists, say, L_1, L_2, and L_3. The central question is: Given that a record key satisfies a query, on which lists will its record key be found?

For example, if we are given the query

$$L_1 \quad \text{AND} \quad L_2 \quad \text{OR} \quad L_3$$

and AND is given precedence over OR, any record key that is on

    (a) both L_1 and L_2
    (b) only on L_3
    (c) on L_1, L_2, and L_3

is a key that satisfies the query. There are two possibilities for each list: either a key is on it or it is not. Since there are three lists, there are 2^3 possibilities for any given key.

Let us label these eight possibilities with the binary numbers 0 through 7:

$$
\begin{array}{c}
000 \\
001 \\
010 \\
011 \\
100 \\
101 \\
110 \\
111
\end{array}
$$

and make the following correspondence. A 0 in the first column means a given key is not on list L_1; a 1 means it is. A 0 in the second column means a given key is not on list L_2; a 1 means it is. A 0 in the third column means a given key is not on list L_3, a 1 means it is. Thus 011 means a given key is not on list L_1, but is on both L_2 and L_3. For each of these eight possibilities it is for the user to decide whether or not it satisfies the query. With the query

$$L_1 \quad \text{AND} \quad L_2 \quad \text{OR} \quad L_3$$

we have the results shown in Table 15.2, which gives us all the information we need to know. If a key is found only on list L_2 (thus the case 010), the table tells us that it does not satisfy the query.

Usually column three of Table 15.2 is shown as a row in a *binary table* of eight columns as in

AND OR	0	1	0	1	0	1	1	1

The complete binary table as the reader should verify is

OR	OR	0	1	1	1	1	1	1	1
OR	AND	0	0	0	1	1	1	1	1
AND	OR	0	1	0	1	0	1	1	1
AND	AND	0	0	0	0	0	0	0	1

As an example, suppose we are given the query

$$Q (L_1 \text{ OR } L_2 \text{ AND } L_3)$$

Table 5.2   Summary of AND OR Results

Base 10	Base 2	Query Satisfied (1 is Yes, 0 is No)
0	000	0
1	001	1
2	010	0
3	011	1
4	100	0
5	101	1
6	110	1
7	111	1

The operators involved are OR AND. Thus we consult row 2 of the table. Suppose the keys at the head of each list at some point during processing are

L_1	L_2	L_3
5	4	4

The active key will, of course, be set to 4 (always set to the smallest). Does record 4 satisfy the query? Since 4 is not on L_1, but is on L_2, and on L_3, the binary number generated is 011. This is 3 in base 10, so we consult column 4 of row 2 (the first column is labelled 0). Since it contains a 1, record 4 does indeed satisfy the query. Binary tables for any number of operators can be created. If three operators are involved, there will be 2^3 rows, and since there are now four operands, there will be 2^4 columns.

It should be remembered that since the user initializes the binary table, he can decide what each operator means and the order of precedence of the operators.

The following algorithm can be employed to process queries using a binary table.

ALGORITHM: BINARY TABLE QUERY

1: Fetch each inverted list that appears as an operand in the body of the query.

2: Set a pointer to the head of each list. If any list is empty, set the pointer to ∞ (HIGH-VALUES in COBOL).

3: Set the active key to the smallest value pointed to by the inverted list pointers.

4: Generate a binary number by assigning a 0 digit (working from left to right in the order in which lists are given in the query) if the active key does not match a given pointer and a 1 digit otherwise. Use the binary number thus formed as the column index into the binary table whose row is given by the operators present in the query. Fetch the record whose key is the same as the active key if a 1 is found in the table; otherwise ignore the active key.

5: Advance each list pointer whose current value matches the active key one position. If all lists are exhausted, stop. Otherwise, return to Step 3.

15.5 SUMMARY

The reader may sense that a lot has been left unsaid. Designing techniques and algorithms that permit a file to be queried bring us to an area of ongoing research in computer science. Storing data is one problem but retrieving the information from it is quite another. The brief overview presented in this chapter should suggest the following requirements for file query:

1. Analysis of the nature of file queries should come early in design.
2. Techniques for file queries depend very heavily on the type of query.
3. Efficient general browsing of a file would be very difficult to implement.
4. *Efficient* retrieval algorithms for all cases will be very difficult to design.

The greatest information retrieval system that has ever been developed is the human brain. Some information there is certainly very well indexed. Think of the names of four Presidents of the United States. Any four. How did you accomplish the retrieval of information? You were not prepared for the query. Does your brain contain a partial inverted list of Presidents? Was it an exhaustive search or did the brain use an algorithm for retrieval beyond the scope of our current knowledge? Students often use the word "cram" when they talk of studying as though the purpose was only to store material, stuff it in so to speak. How often the student learns that getting it in is easy; it's getting it out that is the hard part.

REFERENCE FOR FURTHER READING

Salton, G., and **McGill, M.J.** *Introduction to Modern Information Retrieval,* New York: McGraw-Hill, 1983.

PROBLEMS

1. Baseball fans love to collect statistics of baseball players. They keep track of the following information:

(**a**) name of player

(**b**) names of teams played on

(**c**) number of times at bat

(**d**) number of hits

(**e**) number of hits to 1st base

(**f**) number of hits to 2nd base

(**g**) number of hits to 3rd base

(**h**) number of home runs

(**i**) number of strikeouts

(**j**) number of times walked

(**k**) batting average (number of hits per number of times at bat)

(**l**) positions played by player when team is not at bat.

You have just been hired by the New York Yankees to design an information retrieval system for them about baseball players. Discuss how you would do this with emphasis on record layout, file organization, the inverted list(s) employed, and query processing.

2. Obtain a copy of *Gone With the Wind*. Suppose the entire text of the novel were entered into the computer. Suppose further that you had to write a COBOL program that reads in a keyword such as RHETT and returns the passages printed in the novel. How would you use the techniques of this chapter to carry out such a task? Give some consideration in your reply to the record layout you would use and the natue of any key(s) you would establish.

Security
and Integrity

In this chapter we shall be concerned with two problems: What reasonable precautions can be taken to ensure that the data stored in files is accurate and what measures can be taken to protect against the unauthorized disclosure or loss of stored information? Data *integrity* refers to the accuracy of stored data, whereas data *security* refers to the privacy of stored data. As data integrity is of fundamental importance (there is after all no point in trying to keep data secure if it is garbage to begin with) we shall consider it first.

16.1 DATA INTEGRITY

Occasionally we read in the newspapers that a computer has incorrectly issued a check for an exorbitant amount of money. On the other occasions, not nearly as enjoyable to the recipient, someone is sent an incorrect bill for a ridiculous amount.

In the early days of computing, such events provided comic relief and quickly faded as the favorite story at cocktail hour. Today they are viewed by most people as symbols of gross incompetence, and their occurrence can often be enough to terminate an otherwise brilliant career. The real problem, aside from any embarrassment that occurs, is the fact that such errors tend to cast serious doubts on the reliability of the system and the files involved. It is, after all, a truism that usually only the large mistakes are discovered. The question then becomes ''Just what other things are going wrong?''

Somewhere in the internal workings of the system inconsistent information lies at the heart of the difficulty. Like a malignant tumor, it may creep into otherwise healthy computations, get added into record fields, grow across record boundaries, and spread into other files. All too often warning signs are diagnosed during the funeral. A credit card customer discovers to her delight that her monthly bills do not reflect her purchases. She continues to spend long after her credit limit is reached and when the mistake is finally discovered, she cannot pay her debts. Such accounts are often never reconciled. Litigation is expensive and civil court action, viewed by many as brush fires in the war against the individual in society, loses more customers than the effort is worth.

There may even be a deliberate attempt to destroy the integrity of a system. A bank manager opens an account for a fictitious individual and lends him some money. Later, when a payment comes due, another individual is invented, a new loan is made, the orginal payment is met, and any extra money is spent. As the payments become heavier and heavier, more and more loans are made. The data, however, is never in error. Accounts balance nicely, loan payments are made on time, and there is genuine cash flow. For a limited time the individual may even be praised for her aggressive and dynamic business sense. When the bubble collapses, it is far too late for correction. Confidence in the institution is destroyed, and widespread public knowledge can cause a significant loss of business.

Clearly, no system can afford to ignore the integrity of its data. Prevention and early detection of errors are as important in this respect as they are with human diseases. There are no clearcut solutions to the problem of ensuring data integrity but some techniques have been learned, often through bitter experience.

16.1.1 External Validation

Every effort should be made to correct bad data before it is entered into a system. Errors in data input are caused in one of two ways: either the source documents that describe the data are in error or an error is made in transcribing data from source documents into machine-readable form.

Verification is a test of the correct transcription of data. The weakness in verification is that some transcription errors are easy to repeat and may not be caught. In the case of numbers, control totals provided on the source document can be compared against machine computed totals to test for correct transcription. When using batch entry, batch totals will test for missing records and correct transcription.

A far more serious error, is that introduced by a source document. Only quality control on the part of the users and good system design that expects human error can prevent this. Our consulting work has indicated that employees who introduce errors into source documents have often been brainwashed into believing they need not be careful as "the computer will catch their mistakes." They are consequently less careful. A frequent contributor to carelessness is the individual who works in a large department where it has been made impossible to single out who actually produced a given source document. People are more cautious when the mistakes they make can be traced back to them. Our own experience suggests that effective liasion should be created between the computer personnel and the department in charge of source documents. Most people are not anxious to create a lot of work for others, particularly, when they have met the possible victims. A little psychology, a dash of education, and the personal touch are the only ways to really make progress in solving this type of problem.

When documents are entered at a terminal, local editing of errors can take place but unfortunately clerks tend to rely on this fact and sometimes are less concerned about making errors. A much safer approach is to design the terminal system to require the reentry of data by a verifier operator to warn of any discrepancy. The terminal only makes it easier to correct errors not to eliminate them. Computer programmers can take a lesson from accounting. Double entry accounting is an error detection system that can be applied. For instance, enter hand totals to be checked against machine totals.

16.1.2 Internal Validation

Once the data has been placed in a record, every effort should be made to ascertain its accuracy before it is applied as an update to a master file. The process of verifying records is called *edit checking* and, as suggestions, fields of records can be checked with the following tests in mind:

1. If the field is alphabetic, a test can be made to ascertain if it contains only alphabetic characters. Always describe purely alphabetic fields in COBOL with the "A" designation as in

   ```
   77 ITEM PICTURE A(20)
   ```

   rather than as

   ```
   77 ITEM PICTURE X(20)
   ```

   The COBOL language provides an alphabetic test to be used with the IF statement:

   ```
   IF ITEM NOT ALPHABETIC
         THEN imperative statement
   ```

2. If the field is numeric, it should contain only integers. Always describe purely numeric fields with the ''9'' designation as in

```
77 PART-NO PIC 9(6)
```

rather than as

```
77 PART-NO PIC X(6)
```

The COBOL language also provides a test for numbers:

```
IF PART-NO NOT NUMERIC
   THEN imperative statement
```

3. If the field is numeric, is the value reasonable? Verification should be required for excessively small or large amounts. If a bank teller, for instance, enters a $100,000 deposit, he should be asked to verify that he indeed intends to do that.

4. A reasonable value check can be made by comparing against previous entries. For instance, a monthly gas meter reading can be checked against last month's reading. A large discrepancy can be noted.

5. If the field is limited to specific values, such as an airline flight number, a check can be made against a table of valid entries.

6. Occasionally a field cannot take on one or more specific values, such as a purchase order for $0.00 of merchandise or a request for 30.5 cars, and appropriate arithmetic checking can be made to detect this.

7. An entry in one field of a record may invalidate another field of the same record. This should be checked. For example, an American citizen is not permitted to vote for both the Republican and Democratic candidate for president.

8. Some numeric fields, such as a bank account number, contain critical values. If a single digit is incorrectly entered, the results may be catastrophic; and yet a one-digit slip may leave a value that passes all the validation tests. If a 2 is typed instead of a 3 in a credit card account number, for example, the account number may remain a valid account number but it will be someone else's. In these instances check digits should be added to the number. One such method for forming check digits is as follows:

  • Working from right to left, write the successive digits 2,3,4,5,6,7,8,9,2,3,4, . . . one at a time under each digit of the given number.

  • Multiply each digit in the given number by the number just written below it.

  • Add together all the products developed in step 2.

  • Divide the sum by 11 and subtract the remainder on division from 11. This

```
Given:
  An Account Number          416 247 819

Step 1:
  Write the digits 2,3,4,..  416 247 819
  Under the Account Number   234 567 892

Step 2:
  MULTIPLY                       4    1    6    2
                             ×  2 × 3 × 4 × 5
                               ---  ---  ---  ---
                                8    3   24   10

Step 3:
  ADD                        8 + 3 + 24 + 10 + 24 + 49 + 64 + 9 + 18
                             = 209

Step 4:
  DIVIDE by 11               209 = 19 × 11 + 0
  AND TAKE REMAINDER

Step 5:
  SUBTRACT REMAINDER         11-0 = 11
  FROM 11

This is
  CHECK DIGIT                11

Step 6:
  REWRITE NUMBER GIVEN AS    416 247 819 11
```

Figure 16.1 Check digit.

last number, referred to as P, is the check digit. An example is given in Fig. 16.1.

Validation is a test of the completeness of a set of data. Information generated from an entire batch of records may prove useful in validation checking. Random samples of records can be printed for hand verification. Subtotals from various fields of all the records can be useful because estimates of the range of their values can often be made. For example, the number of requests for new credit cards may appear unusually high. A large batch of customer transactions that include only payments but never purchases may be highly improbable. A large batch of transactions that have invalid fields probably signals a catastrophic situation as would information that a batch of transactions was about to delete an enormous number of master records. Transaction records should be checked for duplication. A source document may be processed more than once or an error left in the system even if it was corrected.

In data processing a large portion of most programs is concerned with testing and maintaining integrity. We have discussed entering correct data. A second major problem is maintaining integrity. There are three major hazards: hardware failures, software failures, and operational errors. It is important then that the integrity of data be tested beyond its point of orginal entry. Many of the ideas we discussed for testing at entry can still be used.

Designing for integrity is very much an art. It requires considerable foresight as to what could go wrong. A very useful idea is to have an audit of a program performed by another programmer to test for integrity weaknesses.

The ideas that can be considered to eliminate errors are endless. We have found that a group of users is a rich growth medium for ideas to track down the elusive and destructive error. Design audits will catch many software weaknesses and expose potential operational errors. Any idea that has a reasonable likelihood of detecting an error should be considered. The determining factor in which ideas are chosen, apart from the obvious ones, is the cost of error detection weighed against the cost of that error.

The costs of achieving integrity will be high and difficult decisions are necessary to determine the degree of integrity checking that should be done as the costs of integrity failure may be difficult to calculate.

16.2 DATA SECURITY

As the true cost and value of data have become widely recognized, the protection of data against unauthorized access has become a major problem and, indeed, a major design criteria that, along with integrity, can make or break a system. The problem extends beyond the enterprise. We do not treat here the ethical and social implications of an invasion of privacy nor the political aspects of multinational firms. Although we limit our discussion to some basic technical aspects of security and their relations to file design, this should not in any way be considered a measure of the relative importance of data security in system design.[1]

Data security involves the protection of data against unauthorized disclosure, modification, or destruction. Security also provides protection against accidental modification or destruction and thus cannot be separated from the problem of data integrity. Security can be divided into two aspects: *internal,* having to do with file access and machine form, and *external,* having to do with the operational procedures and printed material.

16.2.1 Internal Security

An important basis for the protection of machine-stored data is text encryption. This involves a *cipher,* which is a mapping that transforms data (the plaintext) into an unreadable or unintelligible form (the ciphertext).[2] The transform must have an inverse if we wish to decipher the ciphertext; that is, it must be possible to change the ciphertext back to the plaintext.

---

[1]Our techniques are secret, and we have decided not to publish them.

[2]The study of ciphers and secret writing known as cryptography, is an ancient art. Computers now assist in cryptanalysis, or the breaking of ciphers, by reducing the human work factor and by the application of statistical methods.

Cryptography is a rapidly developing discipline with a large literature. Its use in the military has clouded it in secrecy, but the advent of data base technology has brought it into the open. We cannot do justice to it in a short chapter such as this; all we can do is make the reader aware of its existence. The real danger to the systems designer is a naive belief that an untried and untested cryptographic technique can provide true security. A security expert must be consulted when confidentiality is a serious design consideration.

There are three distinct approaches used to encrypt data.

1. Transposition

One approach to text encryption, called *transposition,* involves permuting the letters of the original plaintext message. Since this method involves no change to the frequency of occurrence of letters, only their rearrangement, cryptanalytic attack methods rely on discovering patterns in the permutations.

2. Substitution

A second approach, called *substitution,* involves the actual replacement of symbols in the plaintext with those of one or more other alphabets. The letter A, for example, may be coded by the letter X at one point and by the letter T at another.

3. Polygraphics

The third, and probably the most fruitful approach, is to map large groups of letters onto other groups. Such methods, called *polygraphic* ciphers, are a derivative of substitution ciphers. In such methods the letter combination FINANCE, for example, may be mapped to the letter combination XTMZNFI. Any other grouping of seven letters is mapped to an entirely different set. These methods have been discussed in recent literature.[3] These methods are not easily broken by statistical techniques but involve complex mathematical sophistication for their employment.

Passwords

There are a number of cases where high school students have used a computer to breach the security of timesharing companies, much to their embarrassment. It is now common practice to assume that any ciphering method used will not be kept secret since it is part of the data base. For this reason, ciphers that require a key or *password* to be provided in order to perform the correct transformation are used to provide security.

Since the password is critical to security, the following procedures are recommended for the creation and use of passwords:

1. Do not use short passwords such as your initials.

2. Avoid single English words; use a sentence instead.

3. Commit passwords to memory; do not leave them written in unsecure areas.

[3]See, for example, Cooper (1973) and Diffie and Hillman (1976).

4. Change passwords frequently.

5. Destroy hard copy containing passwords (i.e. back space and overstrike).

6. Allow the user to invent the passwords.

Access

While it is not always necessary to encrypt data, file access should be controlled and limited to authorized users. Data access should consist of identification and authentication of authorized users. For instance, the employee number followed by a password could be used. This process may be repeated, consisting of a dialogue between computer and user:

ENTER ACCOUNT NUMBER

2001

WHAT IS YOUR ID

LFJ-007

YEAR OF EMPLOYMENT

1971

PASSWORD

SUPER AUTHOR

PROCEED

It is a good idea to log invalid attempts at authentication. However, since many valid users require more than one attempt, we might wish only to log, say, five or more invalid attempts. Exception reporting could be used to detect a serious attempt to penetrate security. Logging users is a good way to discourage browsers who may penetrate security. If a user knows that security breach detection methods are watching, he is less likely to browse. Also, the less he knows about how the system is watching, the better. The use of terminals can make it difficult to detect illegal use. Call back for hardware terminal identification can increase the difficulty of illegal access and discourage the casual offender.

Although a measure of security is cheaply obtained by using a cipher only to control access to the file (in this case an inverse need not exist but do not lose the password), the data should also be encrypted if important. If not, an easy way to bypass access control where data is not encrypted is to steal a tape copy of the data.

The design of a good cipher is a difficult problem. Because of the computing cost of encrypting data, cipher systems have been implemented in hardware. Such systems are based on the password concept, since the cipher method can hardly be secret. The United States government has approved a standard for computer encryption, called the Data Encryption Standard. However, the method has been under criticism by cryptographers who claim that the government may know a secret method of decryption.

Although many proponents of cipher systems claim that their system is virtually unbreakable, new mathematical discoveries can quickly invalidate such claims.

A breach of machine security can occur in many ways. For instance, in a terminal system, wire tapping can directly bypass an otherwise sophisticated system. The solution, of course, is encryption at the terminal, but that is expensive. Cheap hardware cipher devices at the terminal are necessary to control cost.

One of the major problems in a data base is that different levels of security must be present that correspond to the degree of authorization a user has to access and alter data. Such flexible security must be incorporated into the data base design and adds to system overhead. Security is an installation and enterprise problem and should not be left to the individual programmer.

16.2.2 External Security

Although a great deal of security concern has involved the protection of data within the computer, perhaps the greater danger and weakness lie outside the file access mechanisms. There are a number of external points that can lead to a security breach: improper handling, defective procedures, and uncontrolled dissemination of data.

Improper handling is treated by rigid internal procedures that are well supervised. The accounting profession has developed many good techniques to deal with the improper handling of money, and these can be applied. Procedures for physical security are also well known. It is pointless to design a highly sophisticated security system if sensitive computer printouts are left lying on a desk for unauthorized eyes. Prevention of *defective procedures* is more a matter of hindsight, but design review and audit by consultants can decrease the risk of the unforeseen. Unfortunately, even when data is properly controlled, collation of that data may lead to *unauthorized disclosure*. Public data, for instance, can be used to crack encrypted files.

Security does not necessarily require great expense or total encryption of data. Physical isolation can give a fair degree of security. For instance, controlled access to machine rooms and external memory devices is cheap. The tape library should also have controlled access. Librarians and operators should clearly understand that they are guardians of data and a breach of trust will cost them their job.

Any system that is designed to protect data is vulnerable to a determined attack. Nevertheless, such an attack is not without cost for the perpetrator. A good security system should increase the cost for penetration sufficiently to discourage penetration. As the cost for penetration approaches the value of the data, penetration is discouraged. Although many techniques for data security can be attacked by other computers or by your own, the cost of the attack may not be worth the value of the information.

Similarly, the cost of losing data determines how much we should pay to protect it. The value of the data being protected should be clearly understood. It is not enough to realize that the loss of data is bad but rather how bad. There is no point in going to great expense to secure data that is superficially confidential. It may be enough for management to take reasonable precautions and to be seen as having done so.

Data should only be protected in the system if it is not otherwise available. Although this may seem obvious, such assumptions are dangerous. As an example, consider the data processing manager who informed us that the payroll file had been scrambled to prevent disclosure of salaries. To circumvent the security, we phoned the payroll office, impersonated the manager, and indignantly claimed an overpayment of salary had been made. A breathless clerk, on obtaining the manager's file, verified the error giving the correct amount. When we told the manager what his salary was and how we had obtained the information, the payroll office procedure was subsequently changed. Information on salaries is now only given in person after suitable identification. It is most important to realize that as data must flow throughout an organization, often beyond control of the data base, so too must security precautions flow through the organization.

A breach of security concerns people not machines, and it is wise to locate potential sources of a breach rather than attempt to detect that a breach has occurred. Potential sources generally fall into three classes: careless employees, dishonest employees, and disgruntled employees. If you fire a programmer, prudence dictates that you take precautions to prevent him from destroying data or taking it with him when he leaves. Above all, the seriousness of such offences must be made clear to employees.

16.3 CONCLUSION

The degree of security achieved is directly related to the cost of providing it. The costs can be difficult to determine and arise, for example, from increases in design time, implementation complications, access time, user frustration, and system overhead. It must be stressed that no system can be made secure; all that can be done is to increase the cost of penetration so that unauthorized access is effectively discouraged.

If we think of system security as a chain of entry points, a system is only as strong as its weakest link. Thus in designing security for a data system, optimization requires a balanced approach to the possible entry points. The problems of integrity and security as well as the solutions are intermingled. If we can give warning for integrity failure, then we can also give warning of security breaches. A major drawback to the data base concept is that multiple and concurrent users of data vastly increase the magnitude of the problems of integrity and security.

REFERENCES FOR FURTHER READING

Denning, D. E., and **Denning, P. J.,** "Data Security." *ACM Computing Surveys* 11 (September 1979).

Diffie, W., and **Hellman, M. E.,** "A Critique of the Proposed Data Encryption Standard." *Communications of the ACM* 19 (March 1976): 164–65.

Konheim, A. G., *Cryptography: A Primer.* New York: Wiley, 1981.

Lempel, A. "Cryptology in Transition." *ACM Computing Surveys* 11 (December 1979).

Meyer, C. H., and **Matyr, S. M.** *Cryptography: A New Dimension in Computer Data Security.* New York: Wiley, 1982.

PROBLEMS

1. The Canadian postal code consists of six alphanumeric symbols ldl dld, where l is a letter and d a digit. Compare it to the American integer zip code with respect to integrity.

2. Examine and report on the security of your computer installation.

3. If you are a student, examine the integrity of your grades. Are they really a correct assessment of your performance? If not, where does the problem(s) lie?

4. In this chapter we discussed error detection. Correcting an error is called *recovery.* What would happen if you dropped a deck of 500 cards on the floor? How would you recover? Should error recovery be designed into a system as well as error detection?

17

File Design

Now that we have dealt in some detail with basic techniques for data base design, a consideration of when to use or not to use various access methods and, in particular, which file organization to use is now appropriate. File design is difficult, and often many compromises are necessary. It is the choice and degree of compromise, necessitated by conflicting requirements, that make good file design both frustrating and challenging. Our approach is top down as in the programming methods that we have used. So, first, we consider just what constitutes good design, keeping in mind that our ultimate interest is file design in a data base context. Then, we review the main attributes of various general file organizations. With this preparation, we attack the problems of how to *design* and *implement* files and consider their place in a data base.

17.1 AN APPROACH TO DESIGN

So far we have assembled some basic tools for file design that have been specifically related to COBOL but are also generally applicable to any programming language. It should be noted that the file capability of COBOL has increased over the years with successive standards.

Suffice it to say that the problems of definition and access encountered in COBOL resemble those of other high-level languages such as PL/1. There is considerable advantage to be gained from a comparison of file organizations of different languages; unfortunately, this must be left to another book.

When it comes to technical work, the facts are all important. Details are the nuts and bolts that hold the structure firmly together. These nuts and bolts stare us rudely in the eye and cannot be avoided; the concepts, on the other hand, are hidden and elusive. It would be remiss of us, indeed, if we did not stop to consider in the design process what it is we are building, why we are building it, and, moreover, why we choose to build it in a particular way. Good design begins with a conceptual view of how to satisfy the user's needs.

It cannot be overemphasized that the nuts and bolts of a system are but the means to an end—*not* the purpose of the system. There are many types of nuts and bolts, all of which are useful to a degree in their many properties. It is usually the case that no one type is the best. We may agonize over the choice of nut and bolt to use in a particular case; however, once the choice is made, it must be used.

Within a system be *consistent;* should your choice be less than perfect, change it in the next *system* that you design; otherwise, you will never complete a design, never meet schedules, never be recognized as a good designer. Remember, design is an iterative process but *do* restrict the number of iterations so that the end result is achievable within the constraints of the given problem.

It does happen that some design decisions can only be made after the user has received initial output from the system. Although this is to be expected, it is not always easy to predict what will be affected. For example, in a system we had designed for job accounting, an upper limit on the number of jobs was required. The client was asked to analyze the number of jobs he had active and to give an upper limit on future growth. It is a good approach to let the user design his system and we were earnestly trying to employ this technique. The end result was that the client provided us with an average figure based on past accounting records. It was agreed to double this figure for future growth. In addition, we thought we would be clever and added 50% more to be safe. After testing, the system was turned over to the client. Surprisingly, only two bugs occurred: an update function did not work properly and—you guessed it—the client had more jobs than we had allowed for, and redesign was required. What happened? The client had three kinds of jobs: those that were on his mind, small jobs that were not important and consequently had not been counted, and jobs that were not very active but not dead either. This problem might have been avoided if we had more vigorously analyzed the number of jobs, but at the time we were trying to build a relationship of trust and cooperation. Surely the client should know his business and how many jobs he had.

A second factor that was not predicted was that the client decided to view other activities as jobs by adding them to the system. Also, the convenience of the computer system led him to break jobs into subjobs for more detailed information. Not only was the job estimate incorrect, but a clever programmer took advantage of the low value for the number of jobs and simplified the design. Thus, the correction of the problem, although not too serious, was nontrivial.

To be successful in making continuous progress, major and measurable milestones of a design should last no longer than three months. Why three months? The human factor dictates that a person's enthusiasm and progress deteriorate into discouragement and vacillation without frequent and regular success. We feel that three months is long enough to wait for a major success and yet sufficient time in which to achieve one. Others may find different time spans more attuned to their nature. The main point is that progress is based on success and both must be seen to happen to keep a project on target. Planning, measurement, and success are essential to continuous forward progress.

In the analyst's approach to file design, two essential and overriding points must be kept firmly in mind: people and communications. But what about the details, protests the keen analyst who wishes to proceed to the real problems of design? The details are *not* the real problems of design; the designer knows all too well the need for details, and since after all, it is design not basic research that is required, the details are available without great difficulty.

People have needs and desires that give purpose to their life. If a project is not seen to be consistent with these needs and desires, not only may you lose their cooperation but you may be faced with an active, resourceful, and powerful enemy. That the enemy is at work may not become clear until after your system has failed or been degraded. The politics of the design may well be more important to success than the actual technical choices.

The user may well feel that he is losing control of a part of his operations and sabotage may be seen as protection of his interests. Members of a design team may be more interested in promotion at the expense of others and the project. Communication failure while not malicious may be as destructive. It is difficult, if not impossible, to achieve good results on misinterpreted information. When the left hand does not know what the right hand is up to there is bound to be confusion and conflict. Minor changes in specifications can cause major changes in the design and, consequently, massive and costly modifications. It is surprising how a major change can ripple through a design building into a wave of modifications. Ideally, designs should be easy to modify, but this is difficult to achieve overall since we must anticipate the unexpected. Good communication should decrease occurrences of the unexpected.

File design, or any design for that matter, has two important aspects we choose to call the *metatechnical,* which is the main subject of this chapter, and the *technical,* which is the main subject of the next chapter. The metatechnical aspect is the *why* of file design. By this we mean the reasons for the existence of the file, its record structure, and its content. Why does it contain this particular information, what use is it put to, and what use will it be put to for a given period, say, five years? The answers lie in a thorough analysis of the problem that is to be solved. There must be sufficient understanding of an application before a solution is proposed in order that the solution be suitable. The metatechnical aspects of design are difficult and frustrating, make no mistake about this. It is for these very reasons that they are scandalously neglected. In contrast, the technical aspects are the *how* of file design and are more immediately satisfying. This will be discussed later.

The fundamental question of design is: What does the user need? The fundamental problem of design is that most often these needs are not explicitly known. Unfortunately, they may only be discovered after the system is up. The human aspect of the design question is: What does the user want? The cardinal sin of design is to give the user what *you* think is *best* for him. It may well be that the user does not know what he requires. Then, it is the analyst's or designer's job to *uncover* the user's requirement and to demonstrate this requirement to the user. Note that we did not say *convince;* it is not the analyst's job to score debating points or sell his personal beliefs. Rational arguments are sometimes set aside in favor of intimidation. A statement such as "this is the *logical* way to do it" implies that the listener does not understand the *correct* solution; "the truly professional way would be this" implies that the listener does not know anything about the solution and should leave the judgment to the speaker, who is of course the expert.

The designer considers a system that does what he intended and provides what he desires to be a good system, if not an excellent one; however, the user considers a system that does not fulfill his needs (not his desires but his needs) to be a bad system. Thus, depending on the individual's viewpoint, a system can be considered both good and bad, both workable and unworkable. The *mature* designer will realize that, given such a contradiction, the user's view must prevail. Unfortunately, all too often the designer's *ego* takes charge and the user's wishes are ignored. Examples of bad design abound; to the uninitiated, the extremes of good and bad design are often confused. Good design requires clearly stated and achievable objectives; objectives that the design judiciously attains. Overdesign is bad design; avoid it.

Although good design has been discussed, the details for achieving it have not been explicitly expressed. That is beyond the scope of any one book. We can, however, list the following criteria for good design:

- simplicity
- meeting specifications
- user acceptability
- cost effectiveness
- adaptability to change
- maintainability

The design process is best approached in an orderly manner through several stages. In Table 17.1 we give a suitable sequence of stages applicable to any system design along with typical activities at the end stage. A similar table should be used to describe any proposed system; this table should result from the design proposal and describes the key system activities up to actual operation.

Table 17.1   Activities in System Development

Stage	Activity
Planning	Problem analysis
	Problem definitions
	Interviews
	Plan attack
	Feasibility study, general system requirements, solution proposal
Development	System requirements
	General system design
	Sign off, design freeze, system manual
Solution	Design
	Program specifications
	Programming
	System testing, software manual
Implementation	Installation plan
	User training, user's manual
	System installation, maintenance manual
	Review and complete all documentation
Follow-up	Audit evaluation and report
	Maintenance

Systems are not eternal. Table 17.2 describes a basic life cycle common to all systems that reach the operational stage. The rate of flow through the various stages is unpredictable and will vary from system to system, but estimates are useful as design parameters.

We hope the reader will appreciate the importance of the approach to design, for it is all too often the weak link in the design chain. The methodology of design has been considered by many authors whose works the reader is advised to study (see the References section at the end of this book). A good source to the literature is Brooks (1975). Above all, think of good design as a problem to be solved. *Work at it* steadily until it is solved; there is always room for improvement.

17.1.1 Design Quality

Overdesign is the design of features that are not required by the application. One of its main causes is the designer's need for artistic reward from his work; the need to feel that he is good at his job. It is designing a cable to withstand a tension of

Table 17.2 System Life Cycle

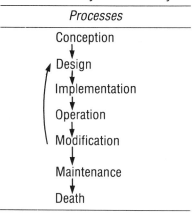

Processes
Conception
↓
Design
↓
Implementation
↓
Operation
↓
Modification
↓
Maintenance
↓
Death

1000 pounds when the required use cannot possibly exceed 50 pounds. It stems from neglecting the consideration of cost, if not function, as a design criterion.

Primarily, overdesign results from a lack of appreciation of cost as a major factor to be considered in any design and a lack of management control. In many people's minds, economy is confused with cheapness, which in turn implies inferiority. No designer would want to be considered a purveyor of inferior designs. Thus the tendency to overdesign is a natural one, but this insidious people problem of design can often be solved by the communication of upper bounds on specifications that must not be exceeded as well as the usual lower bounds that must be exceeded. Often the absence of management control results from a lack of technical knowledge. The first level of management should contain sufficient technical expertise to maintain control of products. One solution to control at the design process is the *design review*. A design is subjected to critical evaluation *before* it is executed, and, when necessary, appropriate changes are made.

That overdesign is serious is evident from the fact that a branch of engineering, known as *value engineering,* has arisen in an attempt to deal with the problem. It is not our purpose, nor is it possible, to treat this question here. However, we can give a framework that will ensure that the problem is not neglected by default.

Let us choose the degree of *luxury* as a measure of the quality of a design so that we can discuss the positive limits that a design should not exceed. Remember it is essential to use neutral terms since people respond in undesirable ways to the emotional content of words. It is convenient and instructive to divide the level of design luxury into three groups: Volkswagens, station wagons, and Cadillacs.

After people problems the subordinate problems of communication rank next in elusive difficulty. Misunderstanding the required luxury of a design is common and generally due to lack of *effective* communication. This results from the use of vague generalities when measurable specifics are required, or more often simply the failure of the designer to listen to requests. The failure to specify the luxury level required of a design results in the designer doing his best design, his Cadillac. But Cadillacs cost money, and if the user wants to buy only a Volkswagen, he does not want to pay for a Cadillac. Money may not even be the prime consideration. For instance, if the user wants a unique and expensive sports car, he will find a Cadillac equally unsuitable.

Mixed with the problem of overdesign is the coproblem of underdesign. Here the problem is a failure to analyze and solve the metatechnical problems we have mentioned. This largely results from a confusion of the interests of the designer with the requirements of the design solution. Programmers are notorius for their interest in programming detail and neat tricks that lead to bad design. The result is all too often a cheap imitation of a Cadillac that is outperformed by a Volkswagen. A number of programming disciplines, such as structured programming, have been created to force the programmer to behave in the prescribed manner. Unfortunately, good tools do not a craftsman make.

The luxury level of a design must be clearly discussed, agreed to, and written down in specific terms that can be measured. This will protect both the designer and the user. Another term for "luxury" might be level of "sophistication." *Never, never,* under any circumstances, mistake unnecessarily complicated design for sophistication and quality. Always remember, when in doubt, make it simple, simple, simple.

17.1.2 Documentation

An essential part of any design and its quality is the documentation of the design process and the operational procedures for the completed system. Any design should start with a *feasibility study* or proposal, which will contain the reasons why the system should be built and the general specifications of the system and its objectives. From this, the *system description* is generated through the design process. The system description can take many forms. It should be such that new people can take over the project when others unexpectedly leave, as they invariably do. Although never up-to-date, it must be sufficiently current to achieve this. When a system is completed, the original designers are not apt to be available for solving bugs that arise, changing requirements, and generally maintaining the system; thus the description must be complete enough that the system can be modified without undue effort.

Although it may seem a management function, the designers must be aware of the *schedules* and *budget* if they are to create a system within the time and cost constraints of the system objectives. Too often analysts and programmers are kept in the dark concerning time and cost. Consequently, they can hardly be blamed if the system is late and costly. *Time* and *cost* are parameters of a design as much or more so than the technical objectives. Time is mainly a function of the availability of manpower and skills to design, implement, and operate the system. Cost is mainly a function of the failure to have the required manpower and the lost opportunity to the enterprise as a system is debugged. We like to believe that if you give designers and programmers the proper objectives to optimize, they will do so. Bringing a system in on time under budget can be as gratifying as developing an obscure programming trick. But it must be realized that people optimize on their own reward structure. It is the job of management to see that the individual's reward structures correspond with the enterprise's reward structure and its objectives. Moreover, this correspondence *must* be perceived by the designer or the programmer for it to be effective.

It seems that program documentation must be more difficult than programming, since most programmers are unable to document effectively. Documentation of a program is, without doubt, a learned skill, and to do it well requires a lot of thought and hard work, as does programming itself. Many programmers (coders) do not find documentation rewarding, so they ignore it or produce at best a feeble attempt. It is difficult to understand why, if the programmer is truly proud of his work, he does not wish to publicize it through good documentation. One might conclude that the programmer knows what a rotten job he did and does not want anyone else to know; thus, his documentation is obscure at best.

In terms of technique, it is best to document a program within that program as it is easier to keep the documentation current and to spot errors. External program documentation may be necessary, but since it is difficult to keep current, it should be designed as an overview and functional specification leaving detail to the program. For simplicity, installation standards should be adhered to. Documenting files separately from programs can be advantageous, particularly when they are used in more than one program.

Documentation per se is not the subject of this book and we can do no more than emphasize its importance in successful file design. The reader will note that we have not taken great care to document our programs or our files; this is because our examples would become unwieldy and would obscure the points we wish to make. Our programs are for illustration; they are not production programs.

Obvious as it may seem, it is important to date every document and to date every revision. Every page should indicate its revision status. Obsolete documents can cause significant problems. Any project of more than two people requires assigned responsibility for documentation control.

17.2 FILE ORGANIZATIONS

File structures are data structure systems on which the physical world poses additional design constraints of time and space because files are incorporated in a programming language and resident on external storage. When a data structure is discussed abstractly or stored in memory, neither addressing nor access are a particular problem, since memory cells are indexed by their address. For instance, memory is organized as a vector. Programming languages provide structured access for traversing their data structures. While we tend to classify data structures by form, file structures are more often classified by address technique. (This is not strictly true; for instance, compare a stack to a list.)

We refer to a file class as a *file organization*. After we have encountered several types of file organizations, the reader will recognize the COBOL file structures we have so far studied as examples of these general types. There are some terminology difficulties in doing this since the terms used to describe programming language files and file structures overlap with and are inconsistent with those describing file organizations. For instance, an Indexed I–O file is not an example of an indexed file but rather an indexed sequential file. The differences will, we are sure, be appreciated when the reader examines the file structures of more than one programming language.

Some major types of file organizations are: pile, sequential, direct, indexed, indexed sequential, inverted, and pointer lists. We briefly examine their defining features and design attributes.

17.2.1 Pile

Perhaps the most primitive file structure is the pile. A *pile* is a group of records with no restrictions on individual records except that the record consists of related items. For instance, in preparing this book, the data on the top of our desks most often was organized as a pile. In a pile the records may be quite unrelated other than the fact that they belong to the same pile. However, as a file structure, we need a few restrictions.

The pile records are arranged sequentially in order of arrival. Since the records differ, each record contains identification of the meaning of its elements. Since there may not be an item common to all records, it is not always possible to order a pile on its contents. In COBOL, some sequential files can be constructed as piles by declaring alternate record formats. Thus we could consider a pile as a sequential file. Nevertheless, the distinction appears worthwhile.

17.2.2 Sequential File

As we have noted, records in a sequential file can only be addressed by moving from one logically adjacent record to the next. The records are most often identical in format and length. In COBOL, provision is made for alternate record formats and variable-length records.

Use

The most common use for sequential files is when cost is the prime consideration and large volumes of data are accessed sequentially. Their use is restricted to batch processing operations, such as data back-up, archival purposes, and the physical transmission of data.

Advantages

Sequential files can provide the best utilization of space and are fast when the records are accessed sequentially. In addition, with sequential files the record address is implicit in the file and is invulnerable (i.e., it is not lost) to system failure.

Also, the system overhead is low and operation is inexpensive when tape drives are used with large files.

Disadvantages

Single record access time is poor, bordering on disastrous, and random access is impractical.

17.2.3 Direct File

When the location of a file record is known, either because a record key value is the location or can be used to calculate the location, we have a *direct* file. Relative I–O files (and the files of Chapter 6) are direct files when key-equals-address or hashing is used to determine the relative address.

Use

The primary use of direct files is when fast access is important and sequential ordering is not important. It is best used where the file is relatively stable, such as for tables, or where the need to reorganize the data between capture and use is not significant.

Advantages

The direct file has the fastest access: one access for key-equals-address and algorithm addressing and, on the average, less than two accesses for a well-designed hashing algorithm. Also, by using direct files, the knowledge of a record location is invulnerable to system failure.

Disadvantages

The direct file is difficult to reorganize or expand because of the fixed binding of addresses to locations. A second disadvantage is the poor utilization of space because unused addresses can reserve space. Also, records are sequentially organized by a key attribute whose order may be of little use. Therefore, records cannot be ordered within the file except on the access key, and they may require separate sorting.

17.2.4 Indexed File

We say a file is *indexed* when record keys and record addresses are stored in a table, called an *index table* or a *directory*. To retrieve a record, search the index table until the desired key is found and then use the key address to locate the record. To insert a record, simply enter the key and an available record address in the table. To delete a record, erase the desired entries.

We can create an index table for each record key. The key need not be unique if we allow more than one address for a key entry. COBOL Relative I–O files or direct files (as in Chapter 7) can be used to create indexed files.

Use

While indexed files may or may not be fast depending on the level of indexes, they are very popular in software and application programs because they provide the most suitable solution to the demands of dynamic files and multiple key files.

Advantages

Indexed files provide fast access for single-level tables, assuming that they are not too large. Excellent space utilization is another advantage, although some space is required for the index tables. In addition, indexed files are easy to reorganize and allow multiple key access since we can order the tables on the keys. In short, indexed files are the most flexible organization and can coexist with any one of the direct addressing techniques.

Disadvantages

An important disadvantage is that indexed files are vulnerable to system failure when a table is lost in main memory. To remedy this either a back-up table can be kept (except for the problem with updates) or, preferably, each record should contain a self-identifying item that can be used to reconstruct the index table. Another disadvantage is the time required to maintain the index tables in a dynamic file, particularly if several keys are used.

17.2.5 Indexed Sequential File

An indexed sequential file orders the records sequentially on a principal primary key and provides an index for direct access. (Normally a bucket is located and then searched sequentially.) Thus an indexed sequential file is a compromise combination of sequential and index organizations. Sometimes secondary index keys are provided. COBOL Indexed I–O is an example of indexed sequential organization.

Use

Indexed sequential files are best used where random access is required and where significant sequential processing of the file will occur. Also, when primary key addressing is handled by the file structure, indexed sequential files are efficient to program. They may be used where processing inefficiency is acceptable.

Advantages

Indexed sequential processing is efficient as compared to nonsequential files.

Other advantages are that addressing can be done by primary key and records can be added in sequence without reorganizing the entire file.

Disadvantages

Because of its compromise nature, the processing of indexed sequential files is not as efficient as the processing of sequential, direct, or indexed files, and more information must be read to locate a record (see Chapter 10). Another disadvantage is that when records are added, they are placed in overflow areas and a very active file can soon become very inefficient to process. However, this can be corrected by periodic reorganization.

17.2.6 Inverted File

If we think of a file stored on rows of records in a table, we may consider an inverted file as those same records accessed by columns of the table. Each column represents some attribute of the record. To access, an index of attribute values for a particular attribute is kept and each attribute value is associated with all the records that contain it. If the attribute values are ordered, then the index can be searched efficiently.

Use

This organization should be used when fast access on multiple keys is required, where a general query on record attributes is required, for on-line systems where file search would be too slow, and for text retrieval systems. Because inverted files have poor characteristics for general processing, they are restricted to specialized uses.

Advantages

Inverted files allow random access on multiple keys, are suitable for queries on file attributes, and provide fast location of records.

Disadvantages

The principle disadvantage is the cost of storing and maintaining inverted indexes (a fully inverted file requires more space for indexes than the file data). In addition, inverted files are difficult to update, and it is necessary to update and index to accommodate a change in record attribute value of that index.

17.2.7 Pointer File

A pointer file interconnects records by means of pointers embedded in the records. Thus, addressing is contained in the records. This organization is based on the concept of the linked list. Chains, rings, trees, and plexes can all be implemented as pointer files. While in many structures one-way pointers will logically suffice, it is often advisable to use two-way pointers.

Use

Pointer files are used primarily where other file organizations cannot as conveniently provide the flexibility of structure provided by embedded pointers.

Advantages

This extreme flexibility of structure, which results in freedom of organization such as variable-length records obtained by using overflow pointers, is the primary advantage of pointer files.

Disadvantages

When linked records span many blocks, many READs will be required to traverse a path through the records; consequently, search time is slow. In addition, traversing a path of records treats records as logically sequential, so the drawbacks of sequential organization apply. Also a pointer file is vulnerable to the loss of a record, since it may contain the addresses of other records. More storage for pointers is required in each record. There is a considerable increase in processing overhead because of the pointers.

17.2.8 File Classification by Content and Use

There are other ways to classify files, such as by content and by use. In particular, system files will be classified by the actual file structures provided. The content classification of files will consist of the following types of files:

- master
- transaction
- dictionary
- table
- work

The use classification of files will consist of the following types of files:

- current
- backup
- archival

Ultimately, a major criterion of any file organization is its cost. The costs arise from many factors of the file such as creation, processing, maintenance, media, and, in particular, installation limitations of equipment as well as available expertise. It may be desirable to increase costs in order to enhance user requirements such as immediate, on-line, low-volume transactions rather than delayed, high-volume, batch transactions. It may even be that because of the firm's overhead costs, on-line is actually cheaper than batch. Remember, there are rules of thumb that usually hold, but blind application in the exceptional situation can be disastrous.

17.2.9 Selection of File Media

Ideally, the use of memory for file storage would simplify file processing. Although it is possible to store files for use in memory, the cost of doing so makes it impractical. There are times, however, when performance can be greatly enhanced by using memory when it is available; thus, while we associate files with external storage, memory should be considered as a possible medium.

Figure 17.1 indicates some of the possible media for storage. On large systems the choice is usually between magnetic tape reels and magnetic disk. In Chapter 2 we discussed their properties. In many cases, the choice is dictated by the hardware configuration or installation standards. Of course, the choice should only be made by the analyst when he thoroughly understands the advantages and disadvantages of the various media and the local constraints of hardware and cost. These depend in turn on the file size, file organization, and type of processing required.

17.3 PRACTICAL CONSIDERATIONS

The effective use of any software system involves a number of practical considerations and these are often ignored or neglected by the programmer and designer swamped with the problem of finding a solution and creating it in code. This bias is

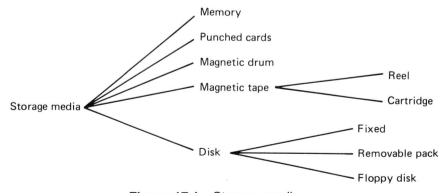

Figure 17.1   Storage media.

aptly illustrated by the programmer who declares his system to work because it happens to run error-free on his test data. Certainly, this is necessary, but to the user a system works because it runs on real data over a significant period of time.

We must first assume that there will always be errors. Since specific errors are unexpected, a general error recovery must be planned and built into a file system. Errors occur from three sources: people, bugs, and installation generation. (*Bugs* is a euphemism for programmer errors that are not fatal.) Second, we must assume that the system will require change and that files are dynamic.

Security, integrity, backup, recovery, maintenance, and future uses and requirements are important factors in a practical system. Security and integrity as discussed in Chapter 16 are essential considerations in the original design. The other practical factors are a function of the operational environment. What factors are most important and how they are to be provided for requires careful consideration based on experience and foresight.

17.3.1 Backup

Although it is widely recognized that copies of programs and data should always be kept, it is not as widely recognized that current master copies should be kept in a fireproof vault with controlled access, with "current" being defined by the cost of recovery. There are several stages of backup ranging from transaction logging on an on-line system to vault storage.

At the first level, errors undetected by edit will occur. They arise from program errors or deficiency, hardware failure, and operational errors. Such errors may cause loss of a file or serious modification of a file. Since loss of file data cannot be permitted, it must be possible to recover such data and restart processing properly.

A transaction file can be recreated by reprocessing the input transaction. This can be difficult on an on-line system and so transactions should have a backup log. Backup of master files can be by an old master or by making periodic copies. In order to recover, all transactions processed against the master file since backup must be rerun.

The frequency of backup is determined by balancing the cost of backup against the cost of backup recovery. Some estimate of the frequency of recovery is required. It may be best to use a safe frequency of backup and decrease it as experience with the system is acquired.

As we continue to make backup copies, we must decide what to do with previous backup files. File retention depends on the backup cycle and the successful creation of new master files. If a batch processing cycle occurs every week, then the backup for the previous week could be destroyed on successful completion, but it would be wise to wait one more accounting cycle. What normally happens is that a safe number of backup copies for several periods are maintained and the oldest file is overwritten by creation of the current backup file.

Some files must be retained after they cease to be updated. This may be to provide historical data or because of legal requirements for retention. Any information that determines taxes must usually be retained for a fixed period.

17.3.2 File Reorganization

The process of adding and deleting records causes a file to lose the original structure it had when initialized. At some point a file may overflow or be largely empty, and reorganization is required. Overflow will become apparent when the file fails to store a new record. In a complicated file organization, the processing of a file may slowly become very inefficient. The designer must take this into account and provide some means of determining disorganization in a file. This can be done by accumulating statistics on the file processing time or by regularly scheduled reorganizations. For instance, a COBOL Indexed I–O file can lose physical sequentiality of the logical sequence of the records. Some compilers will indicate this condition.

17.3.3 Audit Trails

When we think of errors in a system, we tend to think of programming errors and neglect data errors. In large systems it may not be feasible to scratch data and start again. Therefore, it is important to understand and control the flow of data generated by an initial input transaction. The logical path of data in the system is called an *audit trail,* and it is important to be able to examine and verify that proper actions are taking place. Certainly, in a computer accounting system, auditors want to verify that correct accounting procedures are taking place. The concept of audit should be extended to other computer systems. In particular, it should be possible to independently audit the computer data of an enterprise.

17.3.4 Data Compaction

Files consume a great deal of space, but many methods of compacting files are available. Even the simple method of suppressing blanks may give considerable savings on some files. The less frequently a record is used, the more suitable it is for compaction because the cost of space saved must be balanced against the additional processing cost. The possibility of file compaction should be considered during the design stage.

17.3.5 Portability

The portability of software refers to its degree of machine independence. If software is portable, we can expect it to run correctly at a new installation with only minor bookkeeping changes. COBOL is intended to be portable and the bookkeeping changes should be confined to the ENVIRONMENT DIVISION and the external job control language.

Portability is enhanced by late binding of addresses to physical storage. The system designed can achieve portability by interfacing with standard software rather than the machine. While at some point software must be machine dependent, interfaces can and should be machine independent. Where the designer must interface with the physical machine, for instance in a mini, where full software support is not available, careful isolation of the machine dependencies into modules will buffer their effects from the main software of the designer's system.

While it is useful to be able to transfer software from installation to installation, the most important need for portability is within an installation. The continual upgrading of hardware will play havoc with machine-dependent programs and create a nightmare of program maintenance that will devour program development time and machine resources.

17.4 FILE DESIGN CRITERIA

Files have two important sets of characteristics, which provide the operational criteria that a designer can use to make design choices. *File use characteristics* are determined by the file data and the manner in which the file is used. The file designer has little or no control over the user's objectives; his job is to discover what the user characteristics are, keeping in mind that neither the data interrelationships nor the user's requirements may be readily apparent. *File design characteristics* are determined by the designer with due regard to use characteristics, and here the designer has complete control—he may even make the wrong choices. It is the file designer who chooses record content, record format, file organization, and storage mechanism.

In order to choose a file organization, a file structure for program implementation, and a storage medium, knowledge concerning the use and nature of the file must be acquired. Those factors that are the most important to consider are

- file access
- file activity
- file capacity
- file processing speed
- cost of a file design

File access, suggested by use, can be sequential, direct, or mixed (such as indexed sequential). The nature and frequency of queries will indicate the complexity of the access organization required.

File activity is defined as the number of transactions processed against a file for a specified period of processing time. The period of time must be chosen to reflect the average activity expected of the file. For files with high activity, sequential organization is very efficient. Other organizations should be considered for low-activity files.

File capacity is the maximum size of the physical storage required and is the record size times the number of records plus the filler space required by the system. While both tape and disk can store files of any size, nonsequential files require that the whole file be mounted, and the hardware configuration may not have the capacity to do this. Thus large files may require segmentation and sequential organization, since only a single disk or tape providing the required group of records need be mounted at any one time. In such an event, batch processing is required.

File processing speed is influenced both by the file techniques used and by the hardware configuration. The time performance of a file organization is measured in terms of the expected mean number of block accesses required to locate a record. Minimum and maximum access times are often easier to calculate than the expected or average access time. The hardware configuration will determine the file performance once the file organization is selected. Device access speed is the hardware limiting factor, but nonavailability of a device due to system lockout will seriously degrade response time.

File design costs have three main components: the design manpower costs, the cost to process a record, and system maintenance costs. The objective is to minimize the total of these costs over the lifetime of the file; this is a nontrivial problem.

We should quantify operational parameters where possible. When choice of a single number is not practical, range bounds should be chosen. Values may be obtained by various calculations based on a thorough analysis of the expected file operations or, as often happens, simply based on assumptions arising from the best guesses and experience of an analyst. Calculations are based on three methods:

- empirical formulas based on experience and common sense
- simulation
- mathematical models

File Measures

The following are some useful general parameters for files. These measures are stated in terms of the base file at the beginning of the period chosen.

File Activity. Invariably some records are used more than others. While we may not know which records are processed, we can measure file activity in general. The number of records processed per run (in batch) or per period (in on-line) indicates the usage of a file. If we assume that a run is a time period, then we can define *file activity* to be the percentage of file records that are processed in a given period.

$$\text{File activity} = \frac{\text{Number of records processed per period}}{\text{Number of records at the start of the period}} \times 100$$

Sequential files are efficient for high values of file activity, whereas direct files are efficient for low values of file activity. Transaction files have high activity values. In a payroll file where 10% are laid off, 10% have left employment, and 10% are on vacation, we would expect file activity to be less than 70%.

File Volatility.   We have referred at times to files being static or dynamic in their need for reorganization. *File volatility* is a measure of the percent change of file record organization:

$$\text{File volatility} = \frac{\begin{array}{c}\text{Number of inserts} \quad + \quad \text{Number of deletions} \\ \text{per period} \qquad\qquad \text{per period}\end{array}}{\text{Number of file records at the start of the period}} \times 100$$

Given a highly volatile file, it may be unwise to base design on perceived characteristics of the interrelationships of file records, as these may change drastically with time. It can be rather difficult to estimate file volatility beforehand, but the designer should attempt to estimate its magnitude. Sequential processing easily deals with volatile files. Indexed files that are based on B-trees also have good performance on volatile files. Other types of file organizations must be evaluated on their reorganization characteristics.

Growth Rate.   When reserving space for a file, the designer must have not only an estimate of the size of the file but also an estimate of the future need for space.

$$\text{File growth} = \frac{\begin{array}{c}\text{Number of inserts} \quad - \quad \text{Number of deletions} \\ \text{per period} \qquad\qquad \text{per period}\end{array}}{\text{Number of file records at start of period}} \times 100$$

File growth has important effects on the capacity of the computer hardware required to service the file and the costs of doing so.

File Load Factor.   The *load factor* times the capacity, C, gives the capacity actually used at any point in time.

$$\text{Load factor} = \frac{\text{Number of records in file}}{\text{Number of record spaces reserved for file}} = \frac{N_R \times R}{\hat{C}_F}$$

$$C_F = \frac{1}{\text{File utilization factor}} \times \frac{N_R \times R}{\text{Load factor}} = \frac{1}{\hat{U}_F} \times \hat{C}_F$$

A load factor is chosen on the basis of anticipated file growth, the type of file organization, and the time desired before file reorganization must be done. The amount of space reserved, C_F, is determined by the current size of the file and the initial load factor.

$$C_F = \frac{\text{File size}}{\text{Load factor}}$$

The performance of a file (or any system, for that matter) must be measured in terms of criteria determined by the design goals. The following are suggested file organization performance measures:

- read time
    arbitrary record/next record
- write time
    arbitrary record/next record
- update time
    insert record/delete record
- file processing time
- file reorganization time
- storage required by a record

17.5 STEPS IN FILE DESIGN

A common error in designing files is to determine quickly what the input will be and then to decide on the file layouts to contain this input. The importance of the creation and processing costs as well as the difficulty in changing files demand that considerable thought be given to the purpose of the file and what the enterprise can obtain from it before layout. Ultimately a file exists for one purpose only, *output*. The contents, layout, and file organization are determined by the nature of the information to be obtained from a file. The user must participate in the design of the output, and the final approval is a management function.

There are three aspects to adding a file to a data base that determines its ultimate value to an enterprise, and the design of every file must be tested against these. First, what is the cost to the enterprise of this file? The file cost consists of data capture, processing, and maintenance. These costs should be balanced against the cost of lack of information from the file. Second, what new information will be made available to the enterprise? Third, will it be timely, that is, will the information be available when required?

In short, we must first determine the value of the proposed file to the enterprise. This can be a difficult question, and for this reason it is often ignored in the rush to get on with the job. We propose a checklist of five general steps to use in file design.

1. Determine the objectives of the enterprise.
2. Determine the objectives of the proposed system.
3. Determine what output we want to provide, based on the file.
4. Decide what the logical aspects of the enterprise operation to be modeled are and what data is necessary to obtain the output of Step 3.

5. Design the file repeating the preceding steps as necessary.

Like all checklists this can and should be modified to suit the application. Steps 1 and 2 are crucial in deciding Step 3 and in deciding if a file should be created at all.
As part of Step 2, the following four file objectives must be considered:

- to minimize file accesses
- to minimize file space
- to minimize data migration
- to maximize file system integrity

When we have decided on the output required and the transformation process that will be used to obtain this output, then we can decide what data the file should contain. Programming does not enter at this stage, only a good knowledge of the file organizations available and the application. It is important that files be defined and structured by a *senior* person. The user should have considerable input and be asked to approve the file design.

Step 5 in the checklist requires a good technical understanding of file techniques and should be done by an analyst. It is not necessary that he do the programming of the file description, but he should do the system file description. Also, the analyst should be familiar with the other files of the organization. *Never, never* consider a file in isolation, but strive for integration of all data files.

To effectively define a file, the analyst goes, roughly, through the following processes, revising his answers as new information is provided:

1. How much do we wish to spend?
2. What are the data base goals?
3. What kinds of application programs are required?
4. What is the dynamic nature of the file?
5. How should the data be processed?
6. What file organization should be used?
7. What is the difficulty of implementation?
8. What is the system overhead?
9. How much will these choices cost?
10. How much should we spend?
11. What are the data base goals realized and what alternatives are there?
12. Reiterate until answers are satisfactory.
13. Generate system description of file.

A word of caution is in order about the design of a file processing system. Among programmers there is often a great concern for efficiency. Unfortunately they tend to concentrate on local efficiency and thereby neglect and even degrade global efficiency. Any attempt to obtain efficiency must be balanced against the cost of doing so which involves the *total costs* of a system. In our view it is better to take the approach that a system be tunable. It is often not clear where the bottlenecks in processing or execution time will occur until the system is in operation. For instance, sorts can be tuned later when they become a problem and more knowledge of the structure of the files to be sorted is available. If sorts consume insignificant resources, why optimize them? Where possible and when the solution is not well understood by the designer, we would advise incremental design of the system —build usable parts of the system and get the user involved with computer-assisted manual procedures. It can be too much to expect a complex system to function smoothly without some trial-and-error development.

PROBLEM

You have been asked to head a research group to investigate drug use among high school students. You are to prepare a plan for carrying out a study of this problem and submit it to a committee of the state legislature.

As a start you decide to prepare a questionnaire.

Write up this plan, paying attention to the appropriate steps in the design process. Remember that you are not required to implement the study, but you are responsible for detailing exactly how it is to be carried out. Your plan must convince members of the legislature review board that you have thought through the design steps carefully. You will not be called in person, and you will not be given a second chance.

Ask your professor or a colleague to read your plan and offer constructive criticism.

18

File
Implementation

The ultimate requirement of data processing is to implement design—to translate blueprint into production. The previous chapters, through discussion of file organizations, data structures, query techniques, and design considerations, have filled the workshop with programming tools. Implementation involves choice: choosing the tools that will do the job effectively subject to the constraints of time, money, personnel, availability of storage, CPU cycles, security requirements, data integrity, and end use. In this chapter we shall illustrate by example the process of choosing tools.

18.1 CASE STUDY: THE STOLEN VEHICLE FILE

The data bases used to keep track of crimes are extensive, complex in design, international in scope, and extremely expensive. If we restrict our interest, however, solely to the crime of auto theft, we can build with what we have learned in this book a small version of such a data base. The design is straightforward, and the reader should be able to easily modify the design and the programs to create a similar system for another purpose.

18.1.1 Logical Analysis: The Stolen Vehicle File

Let us suppose that we are to create a data base of stolen vehicle information for use in a midwestern state. Each record in the data base is to be kept active until the automobile it represents is located, or for five years, after which the vehicle is assumed unrecoverable and the associated record removed from the data base to an archive file. We shall assume the data base has at any time approximately 20,000 active records.

Design of a data base system normally begins with an understanding of its use and its content—output and input. In this case there is already some knowledge of the content; it is stolen vehicle data. Knowledge of its use will determine the manner in which this data base is to be organized and place constraints on the programs to be developed.

The primary function of any data base is to supply information of value to its users, in this case the officer at risk in the field, helping him to determine whether or not he is dealing with a stolen vehicle. The data stored must therefore be timely, accurate, and immediately available. A batch environment is obviously ruled out. The ability to handle random query is essential. The data need not be exhaustive, but it must be sufficient—enough to provide warning to an officer, though not necessarily replete with all the available details concerning the theft. It is known that the data base will be used for statistical reporting, possibly in a batch mode. Some information will have to be carried that is not of immediate value to a police officer. As with most data bases there will be a host of end users, some of whom will not be initially known, nor as immediately affected as others.

As many end users as possible must always be consulted in the determination of a data base's reporting facility. Often the end users will not be able to specify clearly the exact details nor the nature of every report they will expect a system to produce. They will, however, be able to provide distinct guidelines regarding what they want. Later, when they see the first reports produced, they will probably suggest changes and require slightly different format and information. The programmer's responsibility is to produce a system flexible enough to adapt to changing needs.

Discussion with end users of the stolen vehicle data base suggests a reporting facility capable of supporting the current manual system. The following facts are known about this system:

1. Each patrol car is given, at the start of a six-hour shift, a list of those vehicles stolen in the past two weeks. (This is what T. J. Hooker calls "a hot sheet.")

2. If a car is reported stolen during one particular six-hour shift, its description is radioed at once to all vehicles in the field and later entered manually on filing cards.

3. When an officer requests information by radio regarding a particular vehicle and its occupants (a routine procedure that takes place any time a vehicle is stopped for a traffic or other violation), every effort is made to determine whether or not the automobile involved is stolen. This is a manual process and subject to significant error.

All users are convinced the data base must be capable of responding to broad searches. Knowledge of the combined characteristics of a vehicle such as its make, color, and year must be sufficient to permit retrieval of information from the data base. Criminals often change license plates shortly after stealing a vehicle, so the license plate number alone will not be sufficient for vehicle identification in all circumstances.

It is thus apparent that the data base must be supported by a file organization with the following properties:

1. Access to the records is available by license plate number.

2. Access to the records is available through one or more vehicle characteristics such as color, make, date stolen, or year of model.

3. Access is usually in a non-batch environment, though for statistical purposes a batch environment is sufficient.

4. It must be possible to add records immediately as vehicles are reported stolen.

5. It must be possible to delete records soon after a vehicle is recovered (in order to avoid a legitimate owner being continually harassed after the car is located).

Once the output requirements are made known, the data base designer usually asks the following question: Which of the known file types best provides an organization of records capable of fulfilling the reporting and updating requirements with a minimum of programming effort—the sequential, direct, relative, or indexed?

The necessity for random retrieval immediately precludes the choice of sequential processing. Unfortunately none of the other three types perfectly matches the requirements. However, the Indexed I–O file almost meets the requirements. Records in such a file can be added and deleted at random, a record key can easily be established, and Indexed I–O files provide for secondary keys (in this case color, make, state, year of model, etc.) by means of which records can be retrieved. Regrettably, Indexed I–O files are not organized to retrieve records given a combination of secondary keys. COBOL is not equipped with a READ statement capable of responding to a request for information such as

Are there any stolen, blue, two-door, 1983 Cadillacs with Wyoming license plates?

In this request a combination of secondary keys is specified: blue, two-door, Cadillac, 1983, and Wyoming. Even if color, number of doors, make, year of model, and state were established secondary keys, it would be up to the programmer to combine the keys, using one of the methods discussed in Chapter 15 on file query. This is the normal state of affairs in designing a data base. The output requirements and the nature of the input determine the file organization type. The organizations available are not normally sufficient to do the job at hand, but the user must choose one of those available and combine it with data structures and algorithms to complete the task. Normally the file organization that most closely corresponds to the end requirements is chosen. In this case we choose Indexed I–O. Relative I–O files do not provide a secondary key capability nor an automatic record key. In all fairness, however, it must be pointed out that implementations of Indexed I–O files are sometimes not as fast as Relative I–O files and a programmer willing to implement a hashing algorithm to link record keys with record addresses may produce a system having more rapid retrieval.

Once it has been decided what kind of file organization is required, it is time to design the record layout. This is an important decision because the record length determines the eventual file size. In our case there are 20,000 records, so each byte added to or deleted from the record length represents 20,000 bytes of storage.

The following information is recorded for each stolen vehicle:

1. license number

2. type of car

3. number of doors

4. make of car

5. model year

6. color

7. date reported stolen

8. owner

9. owner's address

The following is the COBOL record layout:

```
01 INDEXED-FILE-RECORD.
   02 LICENSE-NUMBER    PICTURE 9(6).
   02 TYPE-OF-VEHICLE   PICTURE 9(1).
   02 NOS-DOORS         PICTURE 9(1).
   02 MAKE              PICTURE X(15).
   02 YEAR              PICTURE 9(2).
   02 COLOR             PICTURE X(6).
   02 DATE-STOLEN       PICTURE 9(6).
   02 OWNER             PICTURE X(10).
   02 FIRST-INITIAL     PICTURE X(1).
```

```
02  SECOND-INITIAL    PICTURE  X(1).
02  STREET-NO         PICTURE  9(3).
02  STREET            PICTURE  X(19).
02  CITY              PICTURE  X(14).
02  STATE             PICTURE  X(13).
```

The entry TYPE-OF-VEHICLE represents the eight possibilities

```
COMPACT
FOREIGN
LUXURY
NORMAL
SPORTS CAR
STATION WAGON
TRUCK
4-WHEEL DRIVE
```

Note that the PICTURE clause for this field allows for only a 1-digit number. Whenever a field of a record in a data base has a fixed number of possible values, the programmer should consider replacing the original value of the field (for example, the value 'STATION WAGON' above) by a number. When the record field value is to be printed, the program can look the number up in a dictionary, called a *translation table,* and replace the number by its associated value. This saves a great deal of storage space. In this example the associated field, if left in the original format, would have to be designated as PICTURE X(13) to accommodate the entry '4-WHEEL DRIVE'. Using the translation table has therefore saved 20,000 x 12 = 240,000 bytes. This should not be done if there is a large number of possible values because table lookup becomes unduly time consuming. In this chapter only the type of vehicle is *coded.* The translation table for type of vehicle is shown in Fig. 18.1.

In this example we might also choose to code color and state. Street addresses could not be coded, and there are far too many cities.

Since each record is 98 bytes long, after reduction with the translation table, the amount of storage needed can be approximated. This is clearly the number of records times the record size, 20,000 x 98 = 1,960,000 bytes. The disk packs at the

COMPACT	1
FOREIGN	2
LUXURY	3
NORMAL	4
SPORTS CAR	5
STATION WAGON	6
TRUCK	7
4 WHEEL DRIVE	8

Figure 18.1

authors' installation, IBM 3380s, store some 47,476 bytes per track with 15 tracks per cylinder, so roughly 42 tracks, or almost 3 cylinders, are required. VSAM allows specification of disk space in records; but it is always useful to have a good estimate of the storage requirements, as you may have to request more space from your local computer center. Many installations with large central mainframes have a policy of granting users' requests for space as needed during program execution. On a frequent basis, however, they "clean up" the system, and users who have surpassed their current space allocation for storage suddenly find some of their older data sets have been quietly moved to backup facilities.

18.2 ALLOCATING STORAGE SPACE: THE STOLEN VEHICLE FILE

There are two stages in the creation of an Indexed I–O file: allocating space on a storage device and loading the initial records.

Program 18.1 allocates, using IDCAMS, the storage space needed for the Stolen Vehicle File.

Program 18.1

```
//COOPER JOB '***your accounting information***'
//JOBCAT DD DSN=***your VSAM catalog***,DISP=OLD
//    EXEC PGM=IDCAMS,REGION=512K
//DD1 DD UNIT=M3350,VOL=SER=***your disk address***,DISP=SHR
//SYSPRINT DD SYSOUT=*
//SYSIN DD *
  DEFINE CLUSTER-
          (NAME(COOPER.STOLEN)  -
          RECORDS(200001000)  -
          FILE(DD1)  -
          VOLUMES (***your disk address***)  -
          INDEXED -
          KEYS(6 0)  -
          RECORDSIZE(98 98))  -
          CATALOG(***your VSAM catalog***)
//
```

18.2.1 Program 18.1 Narrative

The purpose of Program 18.1 is to allocate, using IDCAMS, the file space necessary to store the approximately 20,000 records of the stolen vehicle file. For a complete description of the language statements see Chapter 12. Information surrounded by '***' will differ from installation to installation. Notice that the RECORDS key word specifies a primary allocation of 20,000 records with up to 15 extents of 1,000 records. Usually you will not know the exact size of a file and will have to estimate.

18.3 PROGRAM 18.2: LOADING THE DATA BASE

Now that the space has been allocated for the data base, it is necessary to load it with records. This is accomplished by Program 18.2. For purposes of the example we shall assume the data base records come initially from a magnetic tape supplied by the Federal Bureau of Investigation in Washington, D. C. It should be remembered that this tape file will have to be sorted by the record key before the records can be loaded into the Indexed I–O file. Read through the program carefully.

Program 18.2

```
00001              IDENTIFICATION DIVISION.
00002              PROGRAM-ID. PROG18P2.
00003              DATE-WRITTEN. 85/05/31.
00004              ENVIRONMENT DIVISION.
00005              CONFIGURATION SECTION.
00006              SOURCE-COMPUTER. IBM-3081.
00007              OBJECT-COMPUTER. IBM-3081.
00008          /   ** BUILDS AN INDEXED I-O FILE **
00009
00010              INPUT-OUTPUT SECTIQN.
00011              FILE-CONTROL.
00012
00013                  SELECT INPUT-FILE
00014                      ASSIGN TO TAPE-DD1
00015                      ORGANIZATION IS SEQUENTIAL
00016                      ACCESS MODE IS SEQUENTIAL.
00017                  SELECT OUTPUT-FILE
00018                      ASSIGN TO DISK-DD2
00019                      ORGANIZATION IS INDEXED
00020                      ACCESS MODE IS SEQUENTIAL
00021                      RECORD KEY IS LIÇENSE-NUMBER
00022                          OF OUTPUT-FILE-RECORD.
00023                  SELECT INTERNAL-SORT-FILE
00024                      ASSIGN TO DISK-SORTWK01
00025                      ORGANIZATION IS SEQUENTIAL
00026                      ACCESS MODE IS SEQUENTIAL.
00027                  SELECT INDEXED-FILE
00028                      ASSIGN TO DISK-DD2
00029                      ORGANIZATION IS INDEXED
00030                      ACCESS MODE IS RANDOM
00031                      RECORD KEY IS LICENSE-NUMBER
00032                          OF INDEXED-FILE-RECORD.
00033
00034
00035              DATA DIVISION.
00036              FILE SECTION.
00037
00038          SD   INTERNAL-SORT-FILE
00039               RECORD CONTAINS 98 CHARACTERS
00040               DATA RECORD IS INTERNAL-SORT-FILE-RECORD.
00041          01   INTERNAL-SORT-FILE-RECORD.
00042               02 LICENSE-NUMBER          PIC 9(6).
00043               02 FILLER                  PIC X(92).
00044
00045          FD   INPUT-FILE
00046               LABEL RECORDS ARE STANDARD
00047               BLOCK CONTAINS 100 RECORDS
00048               RECORD CONTAINS 98 CHARACTERS
00049               DATA RECORD IS INPUT-FILE-RECORD.
00050          01   INPUT-FILE-RECORD.
00051               02   LICENSE-NUMBER        PIC 9(6).
00052               02   FILLER                PIC X(92).
```

Program 18.2 (cont.)

```
00053
00054          FD   OUTPUT-FILE
00055               LABEL RECORDS ARE STANDARD
00056               BLOCK CONTAINS 0 RECORDS
00057               RECORD CONTAINS 98 CHARACTERS
00058               DATA RECORD IS OUTPUT-FILE-RECORD.
00059          01   OUTPUT-FILE-RECORD.
00060                 02   LICENSE-NUMBER        PIC 9(6).
00061                 02   FILLER                PIC X(92).
00062
00063          FD   INDEXED-FILE
00064               LABEL RECORDS ARE STANDARD
00065               BLOCK CONTAINS 0 RECORDS
00066               RECORD CONTAINS 98 CHARACTERS
00067               DATA RECORD IS INDEXED-FILE-RECORD.
00068          01   INDEXED-FILE-RECORD.
00069                 02 LICENSE-NUMBER          PIC 9(6).
00070                 02 FILLER                  PIC X(92).
00071
00072
00073          WORKING-STORAGE SECTION.
00074
00075          77   END-OF-FILE-ISF             PIC X(3).
00076               88 MORE-RECORDS-ISF VALUE IS 'OFF'.
00077               88 NO-MORE-RECORDS-ISF VALUE IS 'ON'.
00078          77   END-OF-FILE-IF              PIC X(3).
00079               88 MORE-RECORDS-IF VALUE IS 'OFF'.
00080               88 NO-MORE-RECORDS-IF VALUE IS 'ON'.
00081          77   COUNT-OF-RECORDS            PIC S9(8)
00082                                           COMP SYNC.
00083
00084          PROCEDURE DIVISION.
00085
00086               PERFORM SORT-RTN.
00087               PERFORM VALIDATE-ROUTINE.
00088               STOP RUN.
00089
00090          SORT-RTN.
00091               SORT INTERNAL-SORT-FILE
00092                   ASCENDING KEY LICENSE-NUMBER
00093                       OF INTERNAL-SORT-FILE
00094                   USING INPUT-FILE
00095                   OUTPUT PROCEDURE BUILD-INDEX-FILE.
00096
00097          VALIDATE-ROUTINE.
00098               PERFORM INITIALIZATION.
00099               PERFORM READ-AND-COMPARE
00100                   UNTIL NO-MORE-RECORDS-IF.
00101               PERFORM TERMINATION.
00102
00103          INITIALIZATION.
00104               CLOSE OUTPUT-FILE.
00105               OPEN I-O INDEXED-FILE.
00106               OPEN INPUT INPUT-FILE.
00107               MOVE 'OFF' TO END-OF-FILE-IF.
00108               READ INPUT-FILE RECORD
00109                   AT END MOVE 'ON' TO END-OF-FILE-IF.
00110               MOVE ZERO TO COUNT-OF-RECORDS.
00111
00112          READ-AND-COMPARE.
00113               MOVE LICENSE-NUMBER OF INPUT-FILE
00114                   TO LICENSE-NUMBER OF INDEXED-FILE.
00115               READ INDEXED-FILE RECORD KEY IS LICENSE-NUMBER
00116                   OF INDEXED-FILE.
00117               IF INPUT-FILE-RECORD NOT EQUAL
00118                   INDEXED-FILE-RECORD
```

Program 18.2 (cont.)

```
00119                    DISPLAY '***ERROR***'
00120                    DISPLAY LICENSE-NUMBER OF INPUT-FILE
00121               ELSE
00122                    COMPUTE COUNT-OF-RECORDS = COUNT-OF-RECORDS + 1.
00123               READ INPUT-FILE RECORD
00124                    AT END MOVE 'ON' TO END-OF-FILE-IF.
00125
00126          TERMINATION.
00127               DISPLAY COUNT-OF-RECORDS.
00128               CLOSE INPUT-FILE.
00129               CLOSE INDEXED-FILE.
00130
00131          BUILD-INDEX-FILE SECTION.
00132               PERFORM INITIALIZATION.
00133               PERFORM WRITE-SORTED-RECORDS
00134                    UNTIL NO-MORE-RECORDS-ISF.
00135               GO TO EXIT-PARAGRAPH.
00136
00137          INITIALIZATION.
00138               OPEN OUTPUT OUTPUT-FILE.
00139               MOVE 'OFF' TO END-OF-FILE-ISF.
00140               RETURN INTERNAL-SORT-FILE
00141                    AT END MOVE 'ON' TO END-OF-FILE-ISF.
00142
00143          WRITE-SORTED-RECORDS.
00144               MOVE INTERNAL-SORT-FILE-RECORD
00145                    TO OUTPUT-FILE-RECORD.
00146               WRITE OUTPUT-FILE-RECORD.
00147               RETURN INTERNAL-SORT-FILE
00148                    AT END MOVE 'ON' TO END-OF-FILE-ISF.
00149
00150          EXIT-PARAGRAPH.
00151               EXIT.
```

18.3.1 Program 18.2 Narrative

Program 18.2 reads the tape file called INPUT-FILE, sorts the records in ascending sequence by the record key, the LICENSE-NUMBER, and stores the incoming records as they are returned from the sort into the OUTPUT-FILE. Once the data base is created, it is closed and then reopened with ACCESS MODE IS RANDOM. The original tape file is also closed and reopened and its records read once again. As each record is read from tape, its license number is moved to the variable designated as the RECORD KEY of the INDEXED-FILE and a random read takes place. The records read from both files should be the same, and they are compared character by character. If all has proceeded satisfactorily, a count of the total number of records stored is printed. Note that there are two SELECT clauses for the Indexed I–O file, called OUTPUT-FILE and INDEXED-FILE. This is necessary in order to switch from ACCESS MODE IS SEQUENTIAL to ACCESS MODE IS RANDOM. It cannot be overemphasized that the only way to ensure that a file contains the data you expect it to is to compare its records with those on the source file character by character. Many programmers mistakenly print the records as they are written to the file being loaded. This proves nothing. It only echoes the records on the source file. The correct procedure is to close both the source and the new file, open both files again, and then read and compare the records in parallel.

The careful reader may wonder why we did not read both files with ACCESS MODE IS SEQUENTIAL. The reason for switching the Indexed I–O file to AC-CESS MODE IS RANDOM is to check that the system is capable of fetching the records given the keys. This checks the directory as well as the file.

18.4 CREATION OF INVERTED LISTS: THE STOLEN VEHICLE FILE

In order to implement a query facility for this data base so that the user is capable of quickly accessing all the records pertaining to a request for information such as "find all blue luxury cars from the state of Wyoming," it is necessary to use one of the query techniques discussed in Chapter 15. For each of these methods, whether it be the Hsiao–Harary scheme, the Trace algorithm, or the Binary Table approach, an inverted list is needed for each of the operands in a logical query. Recall that an inverted list is simply a sorted list of the addresses of records having a field value in common. A list of the addresses of records of blue cars is an example of an inverted list. In order to let VSAM create the inverted list for color, one merely creates an ALTERNATE INDEX, a path, and then invokes the BLDINDEX command. Un-fortunately, for the purposes of this data base, leaving it to VSAM to create the secondary keys is not acceptable. Do you recall why? The problem is that VSAM, though it creates its secondary keys in sorted sequence, does not maintain the sorted order of the secondary keys when the file is updated as this one is sure to be. It is up to the programmer to maintain the sorted order of the inverted lists, or the balance line algorithm will not work when the lists are combined.

To illustrate the building of inverted lists, we have decided to create inverted lists for type of vehicle, color, and state.

For purposes of design and discussion let us consider a typical inverted list, say, that of all compact vehicles in the stolen data base. This must be a list of all the addresses of vehicles that are designated as compacts. Since we are using an In-dexed I–O file, the actual physical addresses of the records are not very useful; in-stead, the lists will contain the license numbers of the associated records. This is really the equivalent of physical address because the record key in an Indexed I–O file is sufficient for record retrieval. If we were using a Relative I–O file, then the inverted lists would contain relative keys.

How long is the inverted list of compact cars? How many license numbers will it contain? How many bytes of storage will it occupy?

The answer to all three questions is that we have no way of knowing. A pro-gram could be written to count the current number on the file, but future thefts and hence inverted list sizes are unpredictable. We have no choice but to make an esti-mate. Guessing is a legitimate occupation for a computer scientist. Fortunately, guessing improves with experience.

Suppose we decide that the inverted list of compacts is unlikely to contain more than three quarters of the license numbers on the file, that is, 15,000 license

numbers. If each is stored as a PICTURE S9(8) COMPUTATIONAL SYNCHRO-
NIZED data item, the entire list will require 60,000 bytes of storage. Since no one
inverted list is different from another, in the sense that all are lists of license numbers, other lists may require the same amount of storage. Finding room on disk for
all the inverted lists probably will not present a problem, but finding room in memory for those inverted lists needed to answer a particular query may be another matter. Suppose, for example, that a given query is

WHITE AND COMPACT AND CALIFORNIA

requiring the manipulation of three inverted lists, and that there are 8,000 white
cars, 11,000 compacts, and 9,000 California registrations. The WORKING-
STORAGE requirements, at 4 bytes per license number for these 28,000 license
numbers, amounts to 112,000 bytes. A program capable of handling, say, six inverted lists may require twice this amount of storage. The programmer must keep in
mind that memory is needed for file buffers, program code, and other elements in
WORKING-STORAGE.

We can reduce the memory requirements by storing the inverted lists in segments. Instead of storing each inverted list in its totality, each list is stored as a
group of records chained together as a linear linked list. Each cell of the list is a
structure with room for up to 2000 license numbers. The COBOL structure for each
cell of this list is shown below.

```
01    INVERTED-FILE-RECORD.
      02   POSITION-POINTER PICTURE S9(8)
                      COMPUTATIONAL SYNCHRONIZED.
      02   INVERTED-LIST OCCURS 2001 TIMES
                             PICTURE S9(8)
                      COMPUTATIONAL SYNCHRONIZED.
      02   LIST-POINTER      PICTURE S9(8)
                      COMPUTATIONAL SYNCHRONIZED.
```

The element POSITION-POINTER is used in adding entries to the inverted
list, INVERTED-LIST is an array of 2001 entries,[1] the last of which is reserved,
and LIST-POINTER contains the address of the next segment or cell of the linear
linked list.

How many of these segments will there be? In the case study it was decided to
make room for 100 of them. This number was arrived at by deciding that there
would be some 69 or so inverted lists, 8 for the types of vehicles, 11 for the different
colors, and 50 for the states. Although there are 20,000 records in the data base, we
estimated that very few would require more than one segment. If the vehicles were

---

[1]In the 3rd Edition this will be increased to 2010.

evenly distributed over the states, for example, each inverted list would only contain 20,000 ÷ 50 = 400 license numbers.

18.4.1 Allocating Space for the Inverted Lists

Before a program can be written to store the inverted lists, it is necessary to request system allocation for storage space by using IDCAMS. It is also necessary to choose an appropriate file organization. The requirements in this case differ slightly from those of the stolen vehicle file. Random retrieval is necessary because different inverted lists will have to be fetched every time a query is made. Each record of this file is a cell of a linear linked list with a forward pointer. There is, therefore, no record key. Secondary keys are also not required. This is clearly an ideal situation for using a Relative I–O file. The address in the forward pointer of each cell is a relative key.

Program 18.3 allocates space for the inverted lists. Only the necessary IDCAM statements are shown.

```
DEFINE   CLUSTER-
          (NAME(COOPER.INVERT)  -
          RECORDS(100  0)  -
          FILE(***associated DD card***)  -
          VOLUMES(***your disk***)  -
          NUMBERED  -
          RECORDSIZE(8012  8012))-
          CATALOG(***your catalog***)
```

18.4.2 Program 18.3 Narrative

This program requests storage space for the 8012 bytes required by each cell of the inverted list. Note that no secondary extents are requested for space, as we will limit the number of cells to exactly 100. The next program will initialize only this number. It is often wise in programming to put some upper bound on the need for storage space. An overly large number of records can sometimes act as symptom for a complicated programming error. However, the programmer should clearly document how the size can be increased, if it should become necessary.

18.5 BUILDING THE INVERTED LISTS: PROGRAM 18.4

The purpose of Program 18.4 is to build the inverted lists and the directory which associates each inverted list with its corresponding name and relative key. The reader should study the program carefully, making use of the extensive narrative which follows it.

Program 18.4

```
00001          IDENTIFICATION DIVISION.
00002          PROGRAM-ID. PROG18P4.
00003          DATE-WRITTEN. 85/05/31.
00004          ENVIRONMENT DIVISION.
00005          CONFIGURATION SECTION.
00006          SOURCE-COMPUTER. IBM-3081.
00007          OBJECT-COMPUTER. IBM-3081.
00008        / ** CREATES INVERTED LISTS **
00009
00010          INPUT-OUTPUT SECTION.
00011          FILE-CONTROL.
00012
00013              SELECT INVERTED-FILE
00014                  ASSIGN TO DISK-DD1
00015                  ORGANIZATION IS RELATIVE
00016                  ACCESS MODE IS SEQUENTIAL
00017                  RELATIVE KEY IS RELATIVE-KEY.
00018              SELECT INVERTED-FILE-R
00019                  ASSIGN TO DISK-DD1
00020                  ORGANIZATION IS RELATIVE
00021                  ACCESS MODE IS RANDOM
00022                  RELATIVE KEY IS RELATIVE-KEY.
00023              SELECT INDEXED-FILE
00024                  ASSIGN TO DISK-DD2
00025                  ORGANIZATION IS INDEXED
00026                  ACCESS MODE IS SEQUENTIAL
00027                  RECORD KEY IS LICENSE-NUMBER
00028                      OF INDEXED-FILE-RECORD.
00029              SELECT DIRECTORY-TABLE-FILE
00030                  ASSIGN TO DISK-DD3
00031                  ORGANIZATION IS SEQUENTIAL
00032                  ACCESS MODE IS SEQUENTIAL.
00033
00034
00035          DATA DIVISION.
00036          FILE SECTION.
00037
00038      FD  INVERTED-FILE
00039          LABEL RECORDS ARE STANDARD
00040          BLOCK CONTAINS 0 RECORDS
00041          RECORD CONTAINS 8012 CHARACTERS
00042          DATA RECORD IS INVERTED-FILE-RECORD.
00043      01  INVERTED-FILE-RECORD.
00044          02  POSITION-POINTER           PIC S9(8)
00045                                         COMP SYNC.
00046          02  INVERTED-LIST OCCURS 2001 TIMES
00047                                         PIC S9(8)
00048                                         COMP SYNC.
00049          02  LIST-POINTER               PIC S9(8)
00050                                         COMP SYNC.
00051      FD  INVERTED-FILE-R
00052          LABEL RECORDS ARE STANDARD
00053          BLOCK CONTAINS 0 RECORDS
00054          RECORD CONTAINS 8012 CHARACTERS
00055          DATA RECORD IS INVERTED-FILE-R-RECORD.
00056      01  INVERTED-FILE-R-RECORD.
00057          02 R-POSITION-POINTER          PIC S9(8)
00058                                         COMP SYNC.
00059          02 R-INVERTED-LIST OCCURS 2001 TIMES
00060                                         PIC S9(8)
00061                                         COMP SYNC.
00062          02  R-LIST-POINTER             PIC S9(8)
00063                                         COMP SYNC.
00064      FD  INDEXED-FILE
```

Program 18.4   (cont.)

```
00065                    LABEL RECORDS ARE STANDARD
00066                    BLOCK CONTAINS 0 RECORDS
00067                    RECORD CONTAINS 98 CHARACTERS
00068                    DATA RECORD IS INDEXED-FILE-RECORD.
00069          01   INDEXED-FILE-RECORD.
00070                    02 LICENSE-NUMBER            PIC 9(6).
00071                    02 TYPE-OF-VEHICLE           PIC 9(1).
00072                    02 NOS-DOORS                 PIC 9(1).
00073                    02 MAKE                      PIC X(15).
00074                    02 YEAR                      PIC 9(2).
00075                    02 COLOUR                    PIC X(6).
00076                    02 DATE-STOLEN               PIC 9(6).
00077                    02 STREET-NO                 PIC 9(3).
00078                    02 STREET                    PIC X(19).
00079                    02 CITY                      PIC X(14).
00080                    02 STATE                     PIC X(13).
00081                    02 FIRST-INITIAL             PIC X(1).
00082                    02 SECOND-INITIAL            PIC X(1).
00083                    02 OWNER                     PIC X(10).
00084
00085          FD   DIRECTORY-TABLE-FILE
00086                    LABEL RECORDS ARE STANDARD
00087                    BLOCK CONTAINS 0 RECORDS
00088                    RECORD CONTAINS 1504 CHARACTERS
00089                    DATA RECORD IS DIRECTORY-TABLE-RECORD.
00090          01   DIRECTORY-TABLE-RECORD.
00091                    02 R-AVAIL-POINTER           PIC S9(8)
00092                                                 COMP SYNC.
00093                    02 R-DIRECTORY-TABLE
00094                         OCCURS 75 TIMES
00095                         INDEXED BY PTR2.
00096                         03 R-NAME-OF-LIST       PIC X(13).
00097                         03 R-LIST-LOCATION      PIC S9(8)
00098                                                 COMP SYNC.
00099
00100
00101          WORKING-STORAGE SECTION.
00102
00103          77   RELATIVE-KEY                      PIC S9(8)
00104                                                 COMP SYNC.
00105          77   END-OF-FILE-IF                    PIC X(3).
00106                    88 MORE-RECORDS     VALUE IS 'OFF'.
00107                    88 NO-MORE-RECORDS VALUE IS 'ON'.
00108          77   LIST-NAME-FROM-RECORD             PIC X(13).
00109          77   FOUND-FLAG                        PIC X(3).
00110                    88 FOUND VALUE IS 'ON'.
00111                    88 NOT-FOUND VALUE IS 'OFF'.
00112          77   COUNTER                           PIC S9(8)
00113                                                 COMP SYNC.
00114          01   DIRECTORY.
00115                    02  AVAIL-POINTER            PIC S9(8)
00116                                                 COMP SYNC.
00117                    02  DIRECTORY-TABLE
00118                        OCCURS 75 TIMES
00119                        INDEXED BY PTR.
00120                        03  NAME-OF-LIST         PIC X(13).
00121                        03  LIST-LOCATION        PIC S9(8)
00122                                                 COMP SYNC.
00123          01   WS-INVERTED-FILE-RECORD.
00124                    02  WS-POSITION-POINTER      PIC S9(8)
00125                                                 COMP SYNC.
00126                    02  WS-LIST OCCURS 2001 TIMES
00127                        INDEXED BY CTR.
00128                        03  WS-INVERTED-LIST
```

Program 18.4 (cont.)

```
J0129                                        PIC S9(8)
00130                                        COMP SYNC.
00131          02  WS-LIST-POINTER           PIC S9(8)
00132                                        COMP SYNC.
00133     01  TYPE-OF-VEHICLE-TABLE.
00134         02 TYPES-OF-VEHICLES.
00135             03 FILLER                  PIC X(13)
00136                 VALUE IS 'COMPACT      '.
00137             03 FILLER                  PIC X(13)
00138                     VALUE IS 'FOREIGN      '.
00139             03 FILLER                  PIC X(13)
00140                     VALUE IS 'LUXURY       '.
00141             03 FILLER                  PIC X(13)
00142                 VALUE IS 'NORMAL       '.
00143             03 FILLER                  PIC X(13)
00144                   . VALUE IS 'SPORTS CAR   '.
00145             03 FILLER                  PIC X(13)
00146                 VALUE IS 'STATION WAGON'.
00147             03 FILLER                  PIC X(13)
00148                 VALUE IS 'TRUCK        '.
00149             03 FILLER                  PIC X(13)
00150                 VALUE IS '4 WHEEL DRIVE'.
00151         02 TYPE-TABLE REDEFINES TYPES-OF-VEHICLES
00152                 OCCURS 8 TIMES         PIC X(13).
00153
00154
00155     PROCEDURE DIVISION.
00156
00157         PERFORM INITIALIZATION.
00158         PERFORM MAKE-THE-INVERTED-LISTS.
00159         PERFORM TERMINATION.
00160         STOP RUN.
00161
00162     INITIALIZATION.
00163         OPEN OUTPUT INVERTED-FILE.
00164         MOVE 1 TO WS-POSITION-POINTER.
00165         SET CTR TO 1.
00166         PERFORM SET-MINUS-ONES 2001 TIMES.
00167         MOVE 1 TO WS-LIST-POINTER.
00168         PERFORM WRITE-INITIAL-INVERTED-LISTS
00169             100 TIMES.
00170         CLOSE INVERTED-FILE.
00171     WRITE-INITIAL-INVERTED-LISTS.
00172         ADD 1 TO WS-LIST-POINTER.
00173         IF WS-LIST-POINTER EQUAL 101
00174             THEN
00175                 MOVE  -1 TO WS-LIST-POINTER.
00176         MOVE WS-INVERTED-FILE-RECORD TO
00177             INVERTED-FILE-RECORD.
00178         WRITE INVERTED-FILE-RECORD.
00179     SET-MINUS-ONES.
00180         MOVE -1 TO WS-INVERTED-LIST(CTR).
00181         SET CTR UP BY 1.
00182     MAKE-THE-INVERTED-LISTS.
00183         PERFORM INITIALIZE-DIRECTORY.
00184         OPEN I-O INVERTED-FILE-R.
00185         OPEN INPUT INDEXED-FILE.
00186         MOVE 'OFF' TO END-OF-FILE-IF.
00187         READ INDEXED-FILE RECORD
00188             AT END MOVE 'ON' TO END-OF-FILE-IF.
00189         PERFORM READ-AND-BUILD-LIST
00190             UNTIL NO-MORE-RECORDS.
00191     READ-AND-BUILD-LIST.
00192         PERFORM FIND-TYPE.
00193         PERFORM FIND-COLOUR.
```

Program 18.4   (cont.)

```
00194                PERFORM FIND-STATE.
00195                READ INDEXED-FILE RECORD
00196                    AT END MOVE 'ON' TO END-OF-FILE-IF.
00197            FIND-TYPE.
00198                DISPLAY INDEXED-FILE-RECORD.
00199                MOVE 'OFF' TO FOUND-FLAG.
00200                MOVE TYPE-OF-VEHICLE TO COUNTER.
00201                MOVE TYPE-TABLE(COUNTER) TO LIST-NAME-FROM-RECORD.
00202                PERFORM SEARCH-DIRECTORY.
00203                IF FOUND
00204                    THEN PERFORM ADD-LICENSE-TO-LIST
00205                ELSE
00206                    PERFORM GENERATE-NEW-LIST
00207                    PERFORM ADD-LICENSE-TO-LIST.
00208            FIND-COLOUR.
00209                MOVE 'OFF' TO FOUND-FLAG.
00210                MOVE COLOUR TO LIST-NAME-FROM-RECORD.
00211                PERFORM SEARCH-DIRECTORY.
00212                IF FOUND
00213                    THEN PERFORM ADD-LICENSE-TO-LIST
00214                ELSE
00215                    PERFORM GENERATE-NEW-LIST
00216                    PERFORM ADD-LICENSE-TO-LIST.
00217            FIND-STATE.
00218                MOVE 'OFF' TO FOUND-FLAG.
00219                MOVE STATE TO LIST-NAME-FROM-RECORD.
00220                PERFORM SEARCH-DIRECTORY.
00221                IF FOUND
00222                    THEN PERFORM ADD-LICENSE-TO-LIST
00223                ELSE
00224                    PERFORM GENERATE-NEW-LIST
00225                    PERFORM ADD-LICENSE-TO-LIST.
00226            INITIALIZE-DIRECTORY.
00227                MOVE 1 TO AVAIL-POINTER.
00228                SET PTR TO 1.
00229                PERFORM SET-DIRECTORY 75 TIMES.
00230            SET-DIRECTORY.
00231                MOVE 'DUMMY' TO NAME-OF-LIST(PTR).
00232                MOVE -1 TO LIST-LOCATION(PTR).
00233                SET PTR UP BY 1.
00234            SEARCH-DIRECTORY.
00235                SET PTR TO 1.
00236                SEARCH DIRECTORY-TABLE
00237                    AT END MOVE 'OFF' TO FOUND-FLAG
00238                    WHEN LIST-NAME-FROM-RECORD EQUAL
00239                    NAME-OF-LIST(PTR) MOVE 'ON' TO FOUND-FLAG.
00240            GENERATE-NEW-LIST.
00241                DISPLAY 'AVAIL POINTER--->' AVAIL-POINTER.
00242                MOVE AVAIL-POINTER TO RELATIVE-KEY.
00243                READ INVERTED-FILE-R RECORD.
00244                SET  PTR TO 1.
00245                SEARCH DIRECTORY-TABLE
00246                    WHEN NAME-OF-LIST(PTR) EQUAL 'DUMMY'
00247                        MOVE LIST-NAME-FROM-RECORD TO NAME-OF-LIST(PTR)
00248                        MOVE AVAIL-POINTER TO LIST-LOCATION(PTR).
00249                DISPLAY LIST-NAME-FROM-RECORD, AVAIL-POINTER.
00250                MOVE R-LIST-POINTER TO AVAIL-POINTER.
00251                DISPLAY R-LIST-POINTER.
00252                MOVE -1 TO R-LIST-POINTER.
00253                REWRITE INVERTED-FILE-R-RECORD.
00254            ADD-LICENSE-TO-LIST.
00255                MOVE LIST-LOCATION(PTR) TO RELATIVE-KEY.
00256                READ INVERTED-FILE-R RECORD.
00257                IF R-POSITION-POINTER NOT EQUAL 2001
00258                    THEN
```

Program 18.4 (cont.)

```
00259                    MOVE· LICENSE-NUMBER OF INDEXED-FILE-RECORD
00260                    TO
00261                    R-INVERTED-LIST(R-POSITION-POINTER)
00262                    ADD 1 TO R-POSITION-POINTER
00263                    REWRITE INVERTED-FILE-R-RECORD
00264               ELSE
00265                  IF R-LIST-POINTER EQUAL -1 THEN
00266                     MOVE AVAIL-POINTER TO R-LIST-POINTER
00267                     REWRITE INVERTED-FILE-R-RECORD
00268                     MOVE AVAIL-POINTER TO RELATIVE-KEY
00269                     READ INVERTED-FILE-R RECORD
00270                     MOVE R-LIST-POINTER TO AVAIL-POINTER
00271                     MOVE -1 TO R-LIST-POINTER
00272                     MOVE LICENSE-NUMBER OF INDEXED-FILE-RECORD
00273                     TO R-INVERTED-LIST(R-POSITION-POINTER)
00274                     ADD 1 TO R-POSITION-POINTER
00275                     REWRITE INVERTED-FILE-R-RECORD
00276                  ELSE
00277                     PERFORM FIND-LIST
00278                     UNTIL R-LIST-POINTER EQUAL -1
00279                     IF R-POSITION-POINTER EQUAL 2001
00280                        THEN
00281                        MOVE AVAIL-POINTER TO R-LIST-POINTER
00282                        REWRITE INVERTED-FILE-R-RECORD
00283                        MOVE AVAIL-POINTER TO RELATIVE-KEY
00284                        READ INVERTED-FILE-R RECORD
00285                        MOVE R-LIST-POINTER TO AVAIL-POINTER
00286                        MOVE -1 TO R-LIST-POINTER
00287                        MOVE LICENSE-NUMBER OF INDEXED-FILE-RECORD
00288                        TO R-INVERTED-LIST(R-POSITION-POINTER)
00289                        ADD 1 TO R-POSITION-POINTER
00290                        REWRITE INVERTED-FILE-R-RECORD.
00291               FIND-LIST.
00292                  MOVE R-LIST-POINTER TO RELATIVE-KEY.
00293                  READ INVERTED-FILE-R RECORD.
00294               TERMINATION.
00295                  OPEN OUTPUT DIRECTORY-TABLE-FILE.
00296                  MOVE DIRECTORY TO DIRECTORY-TABLE-RECORD.
00297                  WRITE DIRECTORY-TABLE-RECORD.
00298                  CLOSE DIRECTORY-TABLE-FILE.
00299                  CLOSE INVERTED-FILE-R.
00300                  CLOSE INDEXED-FILE.
```

18.5.1 Program 18.4: Narrative

Program 18.4 builds inverted lists for each of the types of vehicles, colors, and states. Each inverted list is a linear linked data structure with forward pointers. For purposes of discussion each cell of the linear linked list can be visualized as shown in Figure 18.2.

Available array position	An array of 2001 entries.	Forward Pointer

Figure 18.2

The actual COBOL code for a segment is labeled as WS-INVERTED-FILE-RECORD in the COBOL program. In order to understand Program 18.4, it is necessary to understand the way each of these cells is initialized and then used.

In the INITIALIZATION paragraph each of the cells is given an initial setting. The available array position is set to 1, each of the 2001 array elements are set to -1, and the forward pointer is set to the relative key of the next available cell. The first cell points to cell 2, cell 2 points to cell 3, cell 3 to cell 4, and so on. The last or 100th cell's forward pointer is set to -1. Once each cell is initialized, it is written to the Relative I–O file in sequential access mode. After initialization there are 100 relative records chained together. In data structure terminology these initialized cells would be called an *avail* list, which is a linear linked list of available cells.

Before any processing of the records on the Indexed I–O file takes place, a directory is initialized; this directory will point to the first cell of each inverted list and contains the name of the inverted list. The directory is initialized by placing the value 'DUMMY' in each inverted list name field and setting the associated pointer value to -1, indicating that no list yet exists. The AVAIL-POINTER is set to 1, since the first available cell is at relative key 1.

Once the avail list is prepared and the directory established, the program begins to build the inverted lists. In order to do this, each record of the Indexed I–O file is retrieved. Once retrieved its type is established using the translation table and the directory searched. If there is no such list, as is the case each time a type of vehicle is encountered that has never occurred before, a new cell is created; otherwise, a cell is read from disk and the license number entered. A cell is created by following the avail pointer of the directory to an empty cell and adding the name of the inverted list to the directory. Adding a record to a cell merely involves adding it to the array of 2001 entries using the first entry of the cell structure as the index value. The index value is incremented by 1 after entry. If the index value is 2001, a new cell must be allocated and the pointers updated. In the event that the AVAIL-POINTER becomes -1, the program terminates. In this event more than 100 cells are needed to establish all the inverted lists and the original design estimate was incorrect.

Once the type of vehicle inverted list has been updated, the program proceeds to do the same for color of the vehicle and state. Following this another record is read from the Indexed I–O file. The process terminates when end-of-file is reached on the INDEXED-FILE or when there are no more cells on the AVAIL list. On completion all files are closed and the directory is written out to a sequential file.

18.6 THE QUERY PROGRAM: THE STOLEN VEHICLE FILE

Now that the inverted lists have been created, a file query program can be designed. Any of the techniques discussed in Chapter 15, "File Query," can be used. For illustrative purposes we have chosen the BINARY TABLE QUERY. For convenience that algorithm is repeated here.

ALGORITHM: BINARY TABLE QUERY

1. Fetch each inverted list that appears as an operand in the body of the query.

2. Set a pointer to the head of each list. If any list is empty, set the pointer to infinity.

3. Set the active key to the smallest value pointed to by the inverted list pointers.

4. Generate a binary number by assigning a O digit (working from left to right in the order in which lists are given in the query) if the active key does not match a given pointer and a 1 digit otherwise. Use the binary number thus formed as the column index into the binary table whose row is given by the operators present in the query. Fetch the record whose key is the same as the active key if a 1 is found in the table; otherwise, ignore the active key.

5. Advance each list pointer whose current value matches the active key one position. If all lists are exhausted, stop. Otherwise, return to Step 3.

It would be a good idea to review the corresponding section in Chapter 15 if this algorithm is not completely familiar.

For purposes of design and discussion let us consider a typical query, say

BLUE OR BLACK AND ARKANSAS

Clearly there are several stages in handling this query. They are as follows:

1. The query must be resolved into its constituents. These are the three operands, BLUE, BLACK, and ARKANSAS, and the two operators, OR and AND.

2. Three inverted lists must be fetched into memory, one for each operand named.

3. An active key must be established and point to the smallest license number at the head of each of the three lists.

4. The binary table must be consulted, the operators determining which row and the operands with the active key determining which column.

5. If the key whose value is the active key satisfies the query, it is retrieved. Each list pointer is advanced if it points to a key matching the active key.

This process continues until all lists are exhausted.

Program 18.5 carries out this process. Carefully read the program, making use of the extensive narrative which follows it.

Program 18.5

```
00001          IDENTIFICATION DIVISION.
00002          PROGRAM-ID. PROG18P5.
00003          DATE-WRITTEN. 85/05/31.
00004          ENVIRONMENT DIVISION.
00005          CONFIGURATION SECTION.
00006          SOURCE-COMPUTER. IBM-3081.
00007          OBJECT-COMPUTER. IBM-3081.
00008        / ** QUERY PROGRAM **
00009
00010          INPUT-OUTPUT SECTION.
00011          FILE-CONTROL.
00012
00013              SELECT INVERTED-FlLE-R
00014                  ASSIGN TO DISK-DD1
00015                  ORGANIZATION IS RELATIVE
00016                  ACCESS MODE IS RANDOM
00017                  RELATIVE KEY IS RELATIVE-KEY.
00018              SELECT INDEXED-FILE
00019                  ASSIGN TO DISK-DD2
00020                  ORGANIZATION IS INDEXED
00021                  ACCESS MODE IS RANDOM
00022                  RECORD KEY IS LICENSE-NUMBER
00023                      OF INDEXED-FILE-RECORD.
00024              SELECT DIRECTORY-TABLE-FILE
00025                  ASSIGN TO DISK-DD3
00026                  ORGANIZATION IS SEQUENTIAL
00027                  ACCESS MODE IS SEQUENTIAL.
00028              SELECT QUERY-FILE
00029                  ASSIGN TO CARD-DD4
00030                  ORGANIZATION IS SEQUENTIAL
00031                      ACCESS MODE IS SEQUENTIAL.
00032              SELECT PRINT-FILE
00033                  ASSIGN TO PRNT-DD5
00034                  ORGANIZATION IS SEQUENTIAL
00035                  ACCESS MODE IS SEQUENTIAL.
00036
00037
00038          DATA DIVISION.
00039          FILE SECTION.
00040
00041          FD  INVERTED-FILE-R
00042              LABEL RECORDS ARE STANDARD
00043              BLOCK CONTAINS 0 RECORDS
00044              RECORD CONTAINS 8012 CHARACTERS
00045              DATA RECORD IS INVERTED-FILE-R-RECORD.
00046          01  INVERTED-FILE-R-RECORD.
00047              02  R-POSITION-POINTER       PIC S9(8)
00048                                           COMP SYNC.
00049              02  R-INVERTED-LIST OCCURS 2001 TIMES
00050                                           PIC S9(8)
00051                                           COMP SYNC.
00052              02  R-LIST-POINTER           PIC S9(8)
00053                                           COMP SYNC.
00054          FD  QUERY-FILE
00055              LABEL RECORDS ARE OMITTED
00056              BLOCK CONTAINS 1 RECORDS
00057              RECORD CONTAINS 80 CHARACTERS
00058              DATA RECORD IS QUERY-FILE-RECORD.
00059          01  QUERY-FILE-RECORD.
00060              02  QUERY                    PIC X(80).
00061
```

Program 18.5 (cont.)

```
00062          FD  INDEXED-FILE
00063              LABEL RECORDS ARE STANDARD
00064              BLOCK CONTAINS 0. RECORDS
00065              RECORD CONTAINS 98 CHARACTERS
00066              DATA RECORD IS INDEXED-FILE-RECORD.
00067          01  INDEXED-FILE-RECORD.
00068              02 LICENSE-NUMBER             PIC 9(6).
00069              02 TYPE-OF-VEHICLE            PIC 9(1).
00070              02 NOS-DOORS                  PIC 9(1).
00071              02 MAKE                       PIC X(15).
00072              02 YEAR                       PIC 9(2).
00073              02 COLOUR                     PIC X(6).
00074              02 DATE-STOLEN.
00075                 03 DAY-STOLEN              PIC 9(2).
00076                 03 MONTH-STOLEN            PIC 9(2).
00077                 03 YEAR-STOLEN             PIC 9(2).
00078              02 STREET-NO                  PIC 9(3).
00079              02 STREET                     PIC X(19).
00080              02 CITY                       PIC X(14).
00081              02 STATE                      PIC X(13).
00082              02 FIRST-INITIAL              PIC X(1).
00083              02 SECOND-INITIAL             PIC X(1).
00084              02 OWNER                      PIC X(10).
00085
00086          FD  DIRECTORY-TABLE-FILE
00087              LABEL RECORDS ARE STANDARD
00088              BLOCK CONTAINS 0 RECORDS
00089              RECORD CONTAINS 1504 CHARACTERS
00090              DATA RECORD IS DIRECTORY-TABLE-RECORD.
00091          01  DIRECTORY-TABLE-RECORD.
00092              02 R-AVAIL-POINTER            PIC S9(8)
00093                                            COMP SYNC. .
00094              02 R-DIRECTORY-TABLE
00095                 OCCURS 75 TIMES:
00096                 03 R-NAME-OF-LIST          PIC X(13).
00097                 03 R-LIST-LOCATION         PIC S9(8)
00098                                            COMP SYNC.
00099          FD  PRINT-FILE
00100              LABEL RECORDS ARE OMITTED
00101              BLOCK CONTAINS 0 RECORDS
00102              RECORD CONTAINS 133 CHARACTERS
00103              DATA RECORD IS PRINTER-FILE-RECORD.
00104          01  PRINTER-FILE-RECORD.
00105              02  FILLER                    PIC X.
00106              02  DATA-AREA                 PIC X(132).
00107
00108
00109          WORKING-STORAGE SECTION.
00110
00111          01  TYPE-OF-VEHICLE-TABLE.
00112              02 TYPES-OF-VEHICLES.
00113                 03 FILLER                  PIC X(13)
00114                    VALUE IS 'COMPACT      '.
00115                 03 FILLER                  PIC X(13)
00116                    VALUE IS 'FOREIGN      '.
00117                 03 FILLER                  PIC X(13)
00118                    VALUE IS 'LUXURY       '.
00119                 03 FILLER                  PIC X(13)
00120                    VALUE IS 'NORMAL       '.
00121                 03 FILLER                  PIC X(13)
00122                    VALUE IS 'SPORTS CAR   '.
00123                 03 FILLER                  PIC X(13)
00124                    VALUE IS 'STATION WAGON'.
00125                 03 FILLER                  PIC X(13)
00126                    VALUE IS 'TRUCK        '.
```

Program 18.5   (cont.)

```
00127                    03 FILLER                  PIC X(13)
00128                       VALUE IS '4 WHEEL DRIVE'.
00129                    02  TYPE-TABLE REDEFINES TYPES-OF-VEHICLES
00130                       OCCURS 8 TIMES          PIC X(13).
00131       77  I                                   PIC S9(8)
00132                                               COMP SYNC.
00133       77  J                                   PIC S9(8)
00134                                               COMP SYNC.
00135       77  K                                   PIC S9(8)
00136                                               COMP SYNC.
00137       77  L                                   PIC S9(8)
00138                                               COMP SYNC.
00139       77  N                                   PIC S9(8)
00140                                               COMP SYNC.
00141       77  M                                   PIC S9(8)
00142                                               COMP SYNC.
00143       77  NN                                  PIC S9(8)
00144                                               COMP SYNC.
00145       77  MM                                  PIC S9(8)
00146                                               COMP SYNC.
00147       77  II                                  PIC S9(8)
00148                                               COMP SYNC.
00149       77  JJ                                  PIC S9(8)
00150                                               COMP SYNC.
00151       77  KK                                  PIC S9(8)
00152                                               COMP SYNC.
00153       77  OPERATOR-COUNTER                    PIC S9(8)
00154                                               COMP SYNC.
00155       77  OPERAND-COUNTER                     PIC S9(8)
00156                                               COMP SYNC.
00157       77  RECORD-COUNTER                      PIC 9(4).
00158       77  LINE-NUMBER                         PIC S9(8)
00159                                               COMP SYNC.
00160       77  CNT                                 PIC S9(8)
00161                                               COMP SYNC.
00162       77  ROW-NO                              PIC S9(8)
00163                                               COMP SYNC.
00164       77  COLUMN-NO                           PIC S9(8)
00165                                               COMP SYNC.
00166       77  RELATIVE-KEY                        PIC S9(8)
00167                                               COMP SYNC.
00168       77  ACTIVE-KEY                          PIC S9(8)
00169                                               COMP SYNC.
00170       77  END-OF-FILE-QF                      PIC X(3).
00171           88  MORE-RECORDS     VALUE IS 'OFF'.
00172           88  NO-MORE-RECORDS VALUE IS 'ON'.
00173       77  VALID-FLAG                          PIC X(3).
00174           88  VALID VALUE IS 'ON'.
00175           88  NOT-VALID VALUE IS 'OFF'.
00176       77  ERROR-FLAG                          PIC X(3).
00177           88  ERROR-ON  VALUE IS 'ON'.
00178           88  NOT-ERROR VALUE IS 'OFF'.
00179       77  ABORT-CONDITION-FLAG                PIC X(3).
00180           88  ABORT-CONDITION  VALUE IS 'ON'.
00181           88  OK               VALUE IS 'OFF'.
00182       77  COUNTER                             PIC S9(8)
00183                                               COMP SYNC.
00184       77  TEMP-COUNT                          PIC S9(8)
00185                                               COMP SYNC.
00186       01  LIST-PTRS.
00187           02  LIST-POINTERS OCCURS 3 TIMES
00188                                               PIC S9(8)
00189                                               COMP SYNC.
00190       01  DIRECTORY.
00191           02  AVAIL-POINTER                   PIC S9(8)
```

Program 18.5 (cont.)

```
00192                                      COMP SYNC.
00193                02  DIRECTORY-TABLE
00194                    OCCURS 75 TIMES
00195                    INDEXED BY PTR.
00196                03  NAME-OF-LIST        PIC X(13).
00197                03  LIST-LOCATION       PIC S9(8)
00198                                      COMP SYNC.
00199          01  WS-INVERTED-FILE-RECORD.
00200              02  WS-QUERY-LIST OCCURS 3 TIMES.
00201                03  WS-POSITION-POINTER  PIC S9(8)
00202                                      COMP SYNC.
00203                03  WS-LIST OCCURS 2001 TIMES
00204                                       PIC S9(8)
00205                                      COMP SYNC.
00206                03  WS-LIST-POINTER     PIC S9(8)
00207                                      COMP SYNC.
00208          01  WS-OPERAND.
00209              02  OPERAND OCCURS 3 TIMES
00210                                       PIC X(13).
00211          01  WS-OPERATOR.
00212              02  OPERATOR OCCURS 3 TIMES
00213                                       PIC X(3).
00214          01  UNDER-SCORE.
00215              02  FILLER               PIC X(132)
00216                  VALUE ALL '-'.
00217          01  HEADER1.
00218              02  FILLER               PIC X(47).
00219              02  FILLER               PIC X(39)
00220              VALUE IS 'RESULTS FROM QUERY IN THE FORM OF'.
00221              02  FILLER               PIC X(46).
00222          01  HEADER2.
00223              02  FILLER               PIC X(47).
00224              02  OPERAND-NO1          PIC X(13).
00225              02  FILLER               PIC X(1).
00226              02  OPERATOR-NO1         PIC X(3).
00227              02  FILLER               PIC X(1).
00228              02  OPERAND-NO2          PIC X(13).
00229              02  FILLER               PIC X(1).
00230              02  OPERATOR-NO2         PIC X(3).
00231              02  FILLER               PIC X(1).
00232              02  OPERAND-NO3          PIC X(13).
00233              02  FILLER               PIC X(36).
00234          01  HEADER3.
00235              02  FILLER               PIC X(47).

00236              02  FILLER               PIC X(34)
00237              VALUE IS 'THE NUMBER OF RECORDS IN QUERY WAS'.
00238              02  FILLER               PIC X(1).
00239              02  HR-REC-COUNTER       PIC ZZ99.
00240              02  FILLER               PIC X(35).
00241
00242          01  BINARY-TABLE.
00243              02  ROWS.
00244                03  FILLER             PIC 9(7)
00245                    VALUE IS 0101010.
00246                03  FILLER             PIC 9(7)
00247                    VALUE IS 0000010.
00248                03  FILLER             PIC 9(7)
00249                    VALUE IS 1111111.
00250                03  FILLER             PIC 9(7)
00251                    VALUE IS 0011111.
00252                03  FILLER             PIC 9(7)
00253                    VALUE IS 1010111.
00254                03  FILLER             PIC 9(7)
00255                    VALUE IS 0000001.
```

Program 18.5   (cont.)

```
00256                02 TABLE-VECTOR REDEFINES ROWS.
00257                   03 ROW-VECTOR OCCURS 6 TIMES.
00258                      04 COLUMN-VECTOR OCCURS 7 TIMES
00259                                            PIC 9.
00260        01   NUMBS.
00261                02  NOS OCCURS 5 TIMES       PIC S9(8)
00262                                             COMP SYNC.
00263        01   WS-PRINT-RECORD.
00264                02   LICENSE-NUMBER          PIC 9(6).
00265                02   FILLER                  PIC X(1).
00266                02   TYPE-OF-VEHICLE         PIC X(13).
00267                02   FILLER                  PIC X(1).
00268                02   NOS-DOORS               PIC 9(1).
00269                02   FILLER                  PIC X(6)
00270                     VALUE IS '-DOOR'.
00271                02   MAKE                    PIC X(15).
00272                02   FILLER                  PIC X(1).
00273                02   YEAR                    PIC 9(2).
00274                02 FILLER                    PIC X(1).
00275                02 COLOUR                    PIC X(6).
00276                02 FILLER                    PIC X(1).
00277                02 DATE-STOLEN.
00278                   03 DAY-STOLEN             PIC 9(2).
00279                   03 FILLER                 PIC X(1)
00280                      VALUE IS '/'.
00281                   03 MONTH-STOLEN           PIC 9(2).
00282                   03 FILLER                 PIC X(1)
00283                      VALUE IS '/'.
00284                   03 YEAR-STOLEN            PIC 9(2).
00285                02 FILLER                    PIC X(1).
00286                02 STREET-NO                 PIC 9(3).
00287                02 FILLER                    PIC X(1).
00288                02 STREET                    PIC X(19).
00289                02 FILLER                    PIC X(1).
00290                02 CITY                      PIC X(14).
00291                02 FILLER                    PIC X(1).
00292                02 STATE                     PIC X(13).
00293                02 FILLER                    PIC X(1).
00294                02 FIRST-INITIAL             PIC X(1).
00295                02 FILLER                    PIC X(2)
00296                   VALUE IS '. '.
00297                02 SECOND-INITIAL            PIC X(1).
00298                02 FILLER                    PIC X(2)
00299                   VALUE IS '. '.
00300                02 OWNER                     PIC X(10).
00301
00302
00303        PROCEDURE DIVISION.
00304
00305            PERFORM INITIALIZATION.
00306            PERFORM QUERIES UNTIL NO-MORE-RECORDS.
00307            PERFORM TERMINATION.
00308            STOP RUN.
00309
00310        INITIALIZATION.
00311            OPEN I-O INVERTED-FILE-R.
00312            OPEN I-O INDEXED-FILE.
00313            OPEN INPUT QUERY-FILE.
00314            OPEN INPUT DIRECTORY-TABLE-FILE.
00315            OPEN OUTPUT PRINT-FILE.
00316            MOVE 'OFF' TO END-OF-FILE-QF.
00317            MOVE 'OFF' TO ERROR-FLAG.
00318            READ QUERY-FILE RECORD
00319                AT END MOVE 'ON' TO END-OF-FILE-QF.
```

Program 18.5 (cont.)

```
00320              READ DIRECTORY-TABLE-FILE RECORD
00321                  INTO DIRECTORY.
00322          QUERIES.
00323              MOVE 0 TO M.
00324              PERFORM CLEAR-NOS 5 TIMES.
00325              MOVE 0 TO M.
00326              PERFORM CLEAR-OPERANDS 3 TIMES.
00327              MOVE 0 TO M.
00328              PERFORM CLEAR-OPERATORS 2 TIMES.
00329              MOVE 'OFF' TO ABORT-CONDITION-FLAG.
00330              UNSTRING QUERY DELIMITED BY ALL '-' OR ALL '#'
00331                  INTO
00332              OPERAND(1)   COUNT IN NOS(1)
00333              OPERATOR(1)  COUNT IN NOS(2)
00334              OPERAND(2)   COUNT IN NOS(3)
00335              OPERATOR(2)  COUNT IN NOS(4)
00336              OPERAND(3)   COUNT IN NOS(5).
00337              COMPUTE RECORD-COUNTER = 0.
00338              PERFORM INITIALIZE-HEADER-RTN.
00339              PERFORM HEADER-RTN.
00340              COMPUTE COUNTER = 1.
00341              COMPUTE OPERAND-COUNTER = 0.
00342              COMPUTE OPERATOR-COUNTER = -1.
00343              COMPUTE CNT = 1.
00344              PERFORM FETCH-INVERTED-LISTS 3 TIMES.
00345              PERFORM DETERMINE-ACTIVE-KEY.
00346              PERFORM BALANCE-LINE-ON-LISTS
00347                  UNTIL ACTIVE-KEY EQUAL 1000000
00348                  OR ABORT-CONDITION.
00349              MOVE RECORD-COUNTER TO HR-REC-COUNTER.
00350              IF LINE-NUMBER > 45 THEN
00351                  MOVE SPACES TO DATA-AREA
00352                  WRITE PRINTER-FILE-RECORD
00353                      AFTER ADVANCING PAGE.
00354              PERFORM END-HEADER-RTN.
00355              READ QUERY-FILE RECORD
00356                  AT END MOVE 'ON' TO END-OF-FILE-QF.
00357          CLEAR-NOS.
00358              ADD 1 TO M.
00359              MOVE 0 TO NOS(M).
00360          CLEAR-OPERANDS.
00361              ADD 1 TO M.
00362              MOVE ' ' TO OPERAND(M).
00363          CLEAR-OPERATORS.
00364              ADD 1 TO M.
00365              MOVE ' ' TO OPERATOR(M).
00366          INITIALIZE-HEADER-RTN.
00367              MOVE OPERAND(1) TO OPERAND-NO1.
00368              MOVE OPERATOR(1) TO OPERATOR-NO1.
00369              MOVE OPERAND(2) TO OPERAND-NO2.
00370              MOVE OPERATOR(2) TO OPERATOR-NO2.
00371              MOVE OPERAND(3) TO OPERAND-NO3.
00372              MOVE SPACES TO DATA-AREA.
00373          HEADER-RTN.
00374              MOVE SPACES TO DATA-AREA.
00375              WRITE PRINTER-FILE-RECORD
00376                  AFTER ADVANCING PAGE.
00377              WRITE PRINTER-FILE-RECORD FROM UNDER-SCORE
00378                  AFTER ADVANCING 1.
00379              WRITE PRINTER-FILE-RECORD FROM HEADER1
00380                  AFTER ADVANCING 3.
00381              WRITE PRINTER-FILE-RECORD FROM HEADER2
00382                  AFTER ADVANCING 2.
00383              WRITE PRINTER-FILE-RECORD FROM UNDER-SCORE
00384                  AFTER ADVANCING 3.
```

Program 18.5   (cont.)

```
00385                     MOVE SPACES TO DATA-AREA.
00386                     WRITE PRINTER-FILE-RECORD
00387                         AFTER ADVANCING 1.
00388                     MOVE 10 TO LINE-NUMBER.
00389            FETCH-INVERTED-LISTS.
00390                     IF NOS(COUNTER) NOT EQUAL ZERO
00391                         PERFORM SEARCH-AND-FETCH
00392                         ADD 2 TO COUNTER
00393                         ADD 1 TO OPERAND-COUNTER
00394                         ADD 1 TO OPERATOR-COUNTER
00395                     ELSE MOVE 1000000 TO WS-LIST(CNT, 1).
00396                         MOVE 1 TO LIST-POINTERS(CNT).
00397                     IF ERROR-ON PERFORM ERROR-RTN.
00398                     ADD 1 TO CNT.
00399            SEARCH-AND-FETCH.
00400                     SET PTR TO 1.
00401                     SEARCH DIRECTORY-TABLE
00402                         AT END MOVE 'ON' TO ERROR-FLAG
00403                         WHEN OPERAND(CNT) EQUAL
00404                             NAME-OF-LIST(PTR) MOVE LIST-LOCATION(PTR)
00405                                 TO RELATIVE-KEY
00406                             READ INVERTED-FILE-R RECORD
00407                                 INTO WS-QUERY-LIST(CNT).
00408            BALANCE-LINE-ON-LISTS.
00409                     PERFORM VALIDATE-RECORD-RTN.
00410                     IF VALID PERFORM PRINT-RECORD.
00411                     COMPUTE I = 1.
00412                     PERFORM ADVANCE-POINTERS OPERAND-COUNTER TIMES.
00413                     PERFORM DETERMINE-ACTIVE-KEY.
00414            ADVANCE-POINTERS.
00415                     COMPUTE J = LIST-POINTERS(I).
00416                     IF WS-LIST(I, J) EQUAL ACTIVE-KEY THEN
00417                         COMPUTE LIST-POINTERS(I) = LIST-POINTERS(I) + 1
00418                         COMPUTE J = LIST-POINTERS(I)
00419                         IF WS-LIST(I, J) EQUAL -1 THEN
00420                             PERFORM CHECK-END-OF-LIST.
00421                     ADD 1 TO I.
00422            CHECK-END-OF-LIST.
00423                     IF WS-LIST-POINTER(I) EQUAL TO -1
00424                     THEN
00425                         MOVE 1000000 TO WS-LIST(I, J)
00426                     ELSE
00427                         PERFORM GET-NEXT-LINK.
00428            GET-NEXT-LINK.
00429                     MOVE WS-LIST-POINTER(I) TO RELATIVE-KEY.
00430                     READ INVERTED-FILE-R RECORD
00431                         INTO WS-QUERY-LIST(I).
00432                     COMPUTE LIST-POINTERS(I) = 1.
00433            VALIDATE-RECORD-RTN.
00434                     MOVE 'OFF' TO VALID-FLAG.
00435                     COMPUTE ROW-NO = 0.
00436                     IF OPERATOR-COUNTER EQUAL 1 THEN
00437                         IF OPERATOR(1) EQUAL 'OR' THEN
00438                             MOVE 1 TO ROW-NO
00439                         ELSE
00440                             MOVE 2 TO ROW-NO.
00441                     MOVE 0 TO L.
00442                     MOVE 0 TO K.
00443                     IF OPERATOR-COUNTER EQUAL 2 THEN
00444                         IF OPERATOR(1) EQUAL 'AND' THEN
00445                             MOVE 1 TO L
00446                             IF OPERATOR(2) EQUAL 'AND' THEN
00447                                 MOVE 1 TO K.
00448                     IF OPERATOR-COUNTER EQUAL 2 THEN
00449                         COMPUTE ROW-NO = 2 * L + K + 3.
```

Program 18.5 (cont.)

```
00450                    IF ROW-NO EQUAL 0 THEN MOVE 'ON' TO VALID-FLAG
00451                    ELSE
00452                    COMPUTE N = 1
00453                    COMPUTE MM = 4
00454                    COMPUTE COLUMN-NO = 0
00455                    PERFORM COLUMN-CALC 3 TIMES
00456                    IF COLUMN-VECTOR(ROW-NO, COLUMN-NO) EQUAL 1
00457                    THEN MOVE 'ON' TO VALID-FLAG.
00458            COLUMN-CALC.
00459                    COMPUTE J = LIST-POINTERS(N).
00460                    IF WS-LIST(N, J) EQUAL ACTIVE-KEY THEN
00461                       COMPUTE COLUMN-NO = MM + COLUMN-NO.
00462                    DIVIDE 2 INTO MM GIVING MM.
00463                    ADD 1 TO N.
00464            DETERMINE-ACTIVE-KEY.
00465                    COMPUTE II = 1.
00466                    COMPUTE JJ = LIST-POINTERS(II).
00467                    MOVE WS-LIST(II, JJ) TO ACTIVE-KEY.
00468                    PERFORM CHECK-OTHER-LISTS 2 TIMES.
00469            CHECK-OTHER-LISTS.
00470                    ADD 1 TO II.
00471                    COMPUTE JJ = LIST-POINTERS(II).
00472                    IF WS-LIST(II, JJ) LESS THAN ACTIVE-KEY
00473                       MOVE WS-LIST(II, JJ) TO ACTIVE-KEY.
00474            PRINT-RECORD.
00475                    MOVE ACTIVE-KEY TO LICENSE-NUMBER OF
00476                       INDEXED-FILE-RECORD.
00477                    READ INDEXED-FILE RECORD.
00478                    IF LINE-NUMBER > 50 THEN
00479                       PERFORM HEADER-RTN.
00480                    ADD 2 TO LINE-NUMBER.
00481                    ADD 1 TO RECORD-COUNTER.
00482                    MOVE CORRESPONDING INDEXED-FILE-RECORD TO
00483                       WS-PRINT-RECORD.
00484                    MOVE TYPE-OF-VEHICLE OF INDEXED-FILE-RECORD
00485                       TO KK.
00486                    MOVE TYPE-TABLE(KK) TO TYPE-OF-VEHICLE
00487                       OF WS-PRINT-RECORD.
00488                    MOVE WS-PRINT-RECORD TO DATA-AREA.
00489                    WRITE PRINTER-FILE-RECORD AFTER ADVANCING 2.
00490            TERMINATION.
00491                    CLOSE INDEXED-FILE.
00492                    CLOSE QUERY-FILE.
00493                    CLOSE INVERTED-FILE-R.
00494                    CLOSE DIRECTORY-TABLE-FILE.
00495                    CLOSE PRINT-FILE.
00496            END-HEADER-RTN.
00497                    MOVE SPACES TO DATA-AREA.
00498                    WRITE PRINTER-FILE-RECORD
00499                       AFTER ADVANCING 1.
00500                    WRITE PRINTER-FILE-RECORD FROM UNDER-SCORE
00501                       AFTER ADVANCING 1.
00502                    WRITE PRINTER-FILE-RECORD FROM HEADER3
00503                       AFTER ADVANCING 2.
00504                    WRITE PRINTER-FILE-RECORD FROM UNDER-SCORE
00505                       AFTER ADVANCING 2.
00506            ERROR-RTN.
00507                    MOVE 'ON' TO ABORT-CONDITION-FLAG.
```

Figure 18.3 Sample Output for Program 18.5

```
RESULTS FROM QUERY IN THE FORM OF

BLUE          AND SPORTS CAR    AND GEORGIA


010064 SPORTS CAR   2-DOOR MASSERATI     84 BLUE  23/03/84 215 KINGS COLLEGE ROAD ATLANTA   GEORGIA   E. E. CLARKE
133668 SPORTS CAR   2-DOOR AUSTIN MIGIT  84 BLUE  20/04/84 288 KITCHEN STREET     ATLANTA   GEORGIA   N. K. BARTLETT
305458 SPORTS CAR   2-DOOR TRIUMPH TR-5  84 BLUE  11/07/84 615 ARLINGTON CRESENT  ATLANTA   GEORGIA   Y. O. WATSON


         THE NUMBER OF RECORDS IN QUERY WAS   03
```

18.6.1 Program 18.5: Narrative

In the INITIALIZATION paragraph the directory and the first query are read in. The query itself is broken down into its components by the UNSTRING statement and an inverted list fetched for each of the operands encountered. The format for an incoming query is shown in the following example:

BLACK-OR-BLUE-AND-ARKANSAS#

with hyphens for delimiting operators and operands and # to terminate the query. A blank could not be used as a delimiter because of an operand such as 'STATION WAGON', which already contains a blank. Each list is fetched in the SEARCH-AND-FETCH paragraph by looking for its associated list name (an operand) in the directory and using the corresponding relative key to read an inverted list record from the Relative I–O file called INVERTED-FILE-R. Each inverted list is placed into one of the cells of an array called WS-INVERTED-FILE-RECORD. The program is capable of handling one, two, or three operands, as the reader should verify.

With three operands possible the standard binary table should contain 4 rows and 8 columns. The binary table used in this program has two additional rows appended to the front of the table to handle queries containing only one operator. A query with no operators is reduced to printing out all the records on a single inverted list. The calculation of which element of the binary table should be examined is made in the VALIDATE-RECORD-RTN. The ROW-NO is set to zero if there are no operators, and to 1 or 2 if there is one operator, corresponding to OR and AND, respectively. If there are two operators, the ROW-NO is set to 3,4,5, or 6 by translating each AND in the query to a 1 and each OR to a zero, considering the operators alone as a binary number, which is converted to decimal and then 3 added. For example, the preceding query has the operator combination OR AND, which is equivalent to the binary string 01. This becomes 1 in decimal and upon addition of 3 directs the program to row 4 of the binary table. The column calculation is made in a similar fashion, except that the binary string is calculated by assigning a 1 to an operand only if the license number at the head of its inverted list matches the active key and a 0 otherwise.

Once the binary table is consulted, it is necessary to increment each inverted list pointer by 1 if the leading license number at the head of the list matches the active key. This must be done carefully because the inverted list in memory is only one cell of a linear linked list. A cell is depleted if upon advancement the array value pointed to has the value of -1. When this condition occurs, it is necessary to check the link pointer of the cell. If this also is a -1, the entire inverted list has been processed; otherwise, it is necessary to fetch another cell of the inverted list into memory. If an inverted list has been fully processed, the -1 array value is changed in memory to the license number 1,000,000 representing infinity. Since the cell is never rewritten back to storage, the -1 indicating that the cell has no further entries is not destroyed on disk. If an additional cell must be fetched, the cell pointer is placed in the relative key and a READ issued. The list pointer is reset to 1. The result of all this for Program 18.5 is given in Fig. 18.3.

18.7 FURTHER CONSIDERATIONS

The system so far developed is a *static* system. It does not take into account that new records have to be added to the data base or that records must sometimes be moved to backup or deleted. Such a system is called a *dynamic* system. It reacts appropriately to change. Owing to space constraints we shall not change this system to a dynamic one. That is left as an exercise. We shall, however, discuss how the system can be made into a dynamic one.

The query program, as it now stands, can accept only one form of input, a query with up to three operands and two operators. In order to complete the system, there should be three more command structures:

1. add record command
2. delete record command
3. change record command

Adding and deleting records in an Indexed I–O file is straightforward. The WRITE and DELETE commands are fully described in Chapter 9. Great care must be exercised, however, in making sure that the corresponding inverted lists are updated. Deleting a license number from an inverted list is usually easier than adding a new one. There are several alternatives. One method is to change the license number to be deleted to another number, say, -2, and modify the other programs to skip over any -2s encountered. This is often referred to as *flagging* the value to be deleted. Another alternative is to remove the license number physically from the inverted list. Doing this is not complicated. One reads in the cells of the inverted list, following the link pointers from cell to cell, until the cell that contains the value to be deleted is located. Once it is found, the following license numbers are brought forward by one position to fill the vacated slot.

Adding a new license number is a little more difficult. First the cell must be found where the new value is to be inserted. This is exactly the same process as in the above paragraph. Now, however, room must be made to add the new value. One approach is to go directly to the last cell of the inverted list and move each license number ahead one position, moving backward through the lists until the cell is reached where the new license number is to be inserted. This is made much easier if the lists are equipped with backward pointers as well as forward pointers.

Another approach, which saves a great deal of manipulation, is to initialize the system so that only half of each cell of an inverted list is used. The rest of the cell is saved as free space. When a license number is to be added, it is only necessary to manipulate entries in the associated cell. When the free space in a cell is completely used up, a maintenance program can be run which copies the inverted list, cell by cell, into a new inverted list, leaving half of each cell free once again.

18.8 THE ROLE OF THE PROGRAMMER

If you look at the organization chart of a business that uses computers and is of any reasonable size, you will generally find the programmer's box drawn somewhere very close to the bottom of the chart, buried perhaps off to one side or even left off altogether. He is very far removed from the center of power in the corporation. Ahead of the programmer lies a long, winding, and tortuous climb up the ladder of success away from his origins. Advancement in the organization is very often blocked. A high barricade that can rarely be leaped is raised between those who program the computer and the senior positions of management. Senior management positions are reached only from areas of the company such as sales, marketing, advertising, research, finance, accounting, and production. This is a grim picture and to many an affront to the spirit of capitalism. Fortunately it is only a mental picture held by beginning programmers and bears no relationship to the real world. In fact, good programmers are extremely well paid and have unlimited futures, and can and do rise rapidly to areas of major corporate responsibility. But we should go back and underline the word "good." The dim picture just painted is certainly reality for the *poor* programmer. Why is it true that so many programmers—intelligent individuals, with college-level courses behind them, fired with ambition and opportunity— take off in their careers with great expectations and confidence only to fall flat on their faces to be buried alive forever inside the organization?

The answer is extremely simple. *The programmer, by the nature of his job, already has a share in corporate responsibility that he cannot afford to ignore.* If he cannot rise to the challenge of that responsibility, he can never be promoted into a position that would force him to assume a greater responsibility. It is just that simple.

What makes this seemingly universal requirement particularly applicable to a programmer is that there is no time to train him to accept responsibility as there is in so many other corporate positions. Once code starts to flow off the programmer's desk toward integration into production systems, he has implicitly assumed responsibility for the integrity of these systems. If his code fails, the systems fail. The more complex the system is and the more heavily the organization comes to depend on the programmer, the greater are the consequences of his failure. Neither the experienced nor the inexperienced programmer has the luxury of performing poorly on off days without the risk of exposure. *Poor coding is almost certain to be discovered.*

But the programmer is human and is going to make mistakes. How then does one succeed as a programmer? What differentiates the good programmer from the poor one?

RIE

Here Lies
the
Poor Programmer
Terminated
by
ABEND
OC4

Figure 18.4

A good programmer strives to reduce the frequency of failures, to minimize the consequences of failures, and, most importantly, to make it as easy as possible to recover from failures. This is true of all professions. A doctor cannot save every patient; a dentist cannot restore every tooth; a police detective cannot solve every crime; and a teacher cannot instruct every student. Professionals are measured by the percentage of successes they have in relation to their failures. This is a challenge that faces every good programmer, and it requires all the creative energy of which he is capable.

Since failure is something to be overcome, what is viewed as failure from the point of view of a corporation must be understood. For some reason one of the most frequently occurring problems among both novice and expert programmers is the failure to meet deadlines. What is even more shocking is the frequency with which such failures are discovered at the final hour. The bad news descends at the eleventh hour, often in spite of numerous promises and protestations to the contrary whenever the subject of the deadline is discussed. Often a deadline must be changed for perfectly good reasons but it is usually true that the consequences of changing a deadline vary in degree of severity as the deadline approaches; the closer the deadline the more severe the consequences of not making it. The shock waves of a missed deadline may reverberate throughout an organization, reaching sometimes to the senior executive level where a decision to dismiss those involved may be made (an event not nearly as rare as programmers believe). Programmers can avoid this most important of failures or at least minimize its consequences by communicating an accurate and truthful report of the status of a project as work progresses and by asking for changes in deadlines as early in the life of a project as possible with reasonable justification and with the expectancy that a deadline will not be reached.

Following these procedures will allow management to *minimize* the consequences of possible failure. A deadline that is missed because it was changed before it was reached is not as drastic a failure as one that is simply not met.

The second most important failure that a programmer must learn to avoid is the failure to accomplish that which was required. Such a failure *cannot* be blamed on management. It is the programmer's responsibilty to ensure that he understands what is expected of him. When in doubt, ask. The programmer who works hard, programs efficiently, and makes his deadlines is a failure if he has not done the job according to the specifications. Beginning programmers are particularly prone to this problem. The question, "Are there any questions?", often asked at the end of a meeting, should not be taken as a signal to prepare to leave the room. No question is considered stupid if it is asked at that point. Managers want to be sure you know how to proceed.

We should also caution the reader that both managers and programmers have the same memory problems as other people. Write project requirements down and send copies to all participants. Even if they lose them, do it again and again. Refer to such documentation from time to time.

The third failure that occurs widely among poor programmers is the failure to document work adequately. Documentation serves two purposes: First, it serves as a record of accomplishment. Managers rarely study code (although they would be well advised to do so) and documentation may be all that there is to indicate achievement; second, it enables individuals, including the programmer, to use, modify, and repair the code efficiently.

Documentation must be considered as part of the coding effort and must be developed in parallel with the code. Documentation should never be left to the end. Exactly what constitutes documentation is hard to define without a specific project in mind and without clear knowledge of the intended user. Those who use the documentation should be considered as the judges of what constitutes proper documentation.

A fourth failure that will ultimately lead to greater failure is the inadequate use of the resources available. In particular, avoid spending unreasonable amounts of time studying things or thinking through problems when there are people around who know the answers or have previously found solutions to the problems being faced. Ignorance should not be encouraged, and time is more important than pride. A programmer should never be afraid to ask.

Finally, the programmer should always provide adequate protection for routines that are thoroughly debugged and tested. Programs ready for production should be frozen and copies of them used for future modifications. All too often modifications cause formerly working versions to fail.

18.9 PROGRAM RUNNING TIMES

One of the great difficulties in running programs is in estimating how much time they are going to take. The authors find this a serious problem with students who are used to running in a student environment where the problems posed are constructed to require a small amount of CPU time. Usually, what is needed is an educated guess. The program which builds the inverted lists is a good example. It appears difficult, at first sight, to suggest an appropriate execution time, but a little analysis helps provide a suggestion. The program is driven by the number of disk operations involved. For every record on the Indexed I–O file three inverted list cells must be fetched, one for the type of vehicle, one for color, and one for state. The cell where the license number is to be placed may not always be the first cell on the inverted list, but let us suppose it usually is. There are 3 reads from the Relative I–O file for each of 20,000 reads on the Indexed I–O file. This means, then, 60,000 directory searches, 60,000 adds to the inverted lists, 60,000 updating of pointers, 60,000 re-writes, etc. A good approach, one that is sure to save money, is to do all testing on a small sample, say, 100 records. This is best accomplished by adding a counter to the program and forcing an end-of-file condition on the Indexed I–O file after the first 100 records are read. This short problem should run in less than 10 seconds. Once the job is working the actual CPU time can be found from the program listing. As a rough estimate one could expect this complete job to take 200 times as long. By doing this we estimated job time at two and half minutes on an IBM model 3081. We added a margin for error and requested 3 minutes. The job actually took two minutes twenty seconds.

Running small samples is a very good way to judge execution time and to correct errors. We have never found the approach of applying exact formulas, knowing how long one instruction takes to execute, and how long it takes the machine to do an I–O operation very useful in practice. Nevertheless, doing calculations to predict performance is useful because when the theoretical and experimental results differ an error may be present in the code or an inefficient solution chosen by the programmer. When programs run longer than predicted in theory, investigate.

18.10 CONCLUSION

In this chapter and in the preceding one we have looked at design and implementation from both a technical and a human perspective. The authors' advice contains what we have learned both from our own and others' mistakes and from inquiries when things went right as well as when they went wrong. We cannot guarantee that this advice will make everything our reader does turn out well, but we hope that it may save him a baptism by fire.

PROBLEMS

1. Modify Program 18.5 to handle the queries with the trace algorithm rather than the binary table query.

2. Modify Program 18.5 to handle additions and deletions of records from the Indexed I–O file. Use the current set of inverted lists.

3. Modify Program 18.4 to leave 30% of each cell of the inverted lists free for additions. Add backward pointers to the inverted lists and modify Program 18.5 to handle additions and deletions with this new inverted list structure.

4. Write a cleanup program that resets each inverted list cell back to 30% free space once a cell becomes full.

5. You have been hired by a hotel to write a small data base system to keep track of rooms and their occupancy. The hotel has 1200 rooms of various kinds, and naturally you will not have to keep the room assignments up-to-date yourself. You will, however, have to write the following COBOL programs.

(a) A program that creates an Indexed I–O file of room assignments. This file is to contain such information as room number, size of room (single, double, presidential suite, etc.), name of registered guest, number in party, his or her address, form of payment for room (i.e. check, cash, or credit card), cost of room, and one or more room charges and for what purpose (an example might be $2.40 PHONE, $8.00 BREAKFAST).

(b) Set up a few inverted lists such as OCCUPIED-ROOMS, SINGLE-BEDS, NUMBER-IN-PARTY, COST-OF-ROOM.

(c) Write a query program to handle such queries as

UNOCCUPIED and SINGLE-BEDS

and the more difficult

OCCUPIED and COST-OF-ROOM<$50.00

Basically we want you to design a nice little system that a hotel manager might like to have. If you want to get serious, visit a local hotel and discuss the project with a real manager. One of our students did, and a hotel chain gave him a job when he showed them the program.

19

Data Base Systems

So far we have considered a number of file organization techniques and examined the file structures available in COBOL. Advantages and disadvantages were discussed in the light of technical problems. As experience with large files has grown, a number of serious problems have been recognized as increasingly important. These we consider as metatechnical problems, in that they go beyond the kind of technical details we have so far discussed.

19.1 METATECHNICAL CONSIDERATIONS

The data base concept is an attempt to provide technical solutions to these metatechnical problems. A new file technology is developing that views data as independent of the programs that process it and as independent of physical storage.

We first discuss the metatechnical problems that have caused this shift and then we give an overview of a general data base system that arises as a reaction to these problems and, consequently, examine some of the major requirements for a data base system.

When we reconsider our study of file techniques in the previous chapters, we realize that we were concerned with only three essential functions:

- creation
- retrieval
- maintenance

The metatechnical problems we pose concern these three functions. How, for instance, do we minimize the creation of files? It is extremely expensive to create files, and it is foolish to add files that are largely redundant. Nevertheless, this is exactly what has happened time and time again. How can we efficiently access and use other people's files or indeed even our own when the file structure is no longer convenient? How do we maintain files that have multiple users? It is difficult to change files and programs, and it is difficult to query files when the query has not been anticipated. This can be nontrivial when the file definition is lost and the god-like creator has vanished. How can an enterprise best control the creation, dissemination, and protection of data consistent with its importance?

These problems are not necessarily new but were overshadowed by the difficulties of programming and of hardware technology or its lack. In the broadest sense, the problem is this: data stored in a computer is of no value if it is not accessible when required and at an acceptable cost. Conceptually, the data base solution is to integrate the data into a single rational system that can be defined and manipulated in a general way and easily accessed from an applications program. Although we are a long way from the pure concept of a data base, many working systems have been built.

19.1.1 The Data Definition Language

In the past, it has not been easy to share files. The problem has been recognized as essentially due to ownership of a file by its processing program or indirectly by the application programmer. The solution proposed is to make data independent of the processing programs and to centralize it. Obviously, some means of defining data external to such programs is necessary. This has resulted in the design and implementation of data definition languages. These languages allow us to model the data relationships that concern us. Such a descriptive representation of data is called a *schema*. Since an applications programmer may not be interested in the total schema, nor in the model of data provided, provision should be made to extract a submodel of the data pertinent to his use, and such a representation is termed a *subschema*. We consider these concepts in more detail, subsequently.

19.1.2 The Data Manipulation Language

As we have seen, hardware independence has been developed to avoid program change when a file is physically moved. A further step toward data base independence is logical independence of file storage structure. Since the program no longer owns the data, we wish to protect the program from changes in the structure of data as stored in the data base.

Data independence implies that the user no longer talks directly to the data base files but rather to logical files of the data base system defined in the user's subschema. For this, a *data manipulation language* (DML) may be necessary, and it is embedded in an application language which we regard as the *host language*. This is similar in nature to and could be the file control statements of the host language but then the user is forced to go through the data base for all file requirements. In our view the DML should be distinct from the file control statements of the application language. There are good reasons for allowing a file capability independent of the data base. These will become clear as we discover the complexity of the data base system overhead. The DML connects the program subschema to the physical data base via a schema.

19.1.3 The Data Base Administrator

Since the programmer no longer controls the data, he can no longer name it. The many uses of the same data require a data dictionary to provide the names, the relevant attributes of data, and its use and meaning within the enterprise. Who is to control data in the enterprise?

The responsibility for defining schemas, subschemas, actual file structures, and overall control is centralized in the *data base administrator* (DBA). Although often referred to as a person, this is a human function and in a large organization would be a department.

To execute his functions, the DBA has a system of software programs that control and manipulate the data of the data base. We will think of this software collectively as the *data base control* (DBC). Ideally, the DBA speaks to these programs via a data control language (DCL). The DCL would contain the DDL.

19.1.4 A Data Base Management System Architecture

The solution just proposed for the metatechnical problems can be represented in the data base architecture of Fig. 19.1. Solid lines indicate the flow of data or its definition; dashed lines indicate the flow of control. It must be emphasized that this is a general scheme and a particular data base architecture may differ. Since we show that the DBMS has access to the data base (DB), we will refer to all computer-stored data for an enterprise as a *data bank,* although "data base" is often used in this sense.

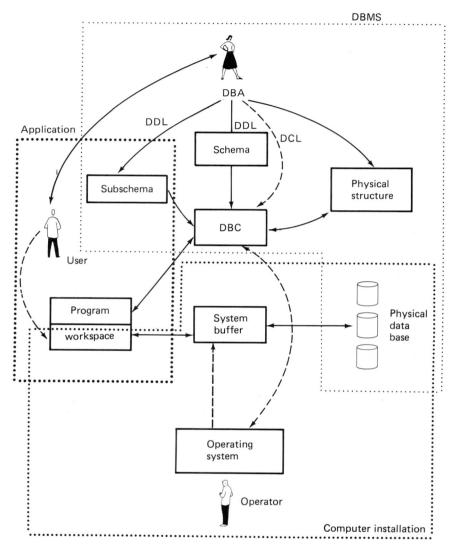

Figure 19.1   Data base architecture.

19.2 REQUIREMENTS AND OBJECTIVES OF A DATA BASE SYSTEM

With hindsight we can see that the prime objective of a data base system is the centralized control of data consistent with its importance. Secondary objectives and advantages are

- sharing of data files
- protection of processing programs and logical files against changes in physical files
- enforcement of standards
- ease of querying
- simplicity
- interface with future needs

The advantages of file sharing decrease data redundancy and inconsistency. By allowing new applications to use existing files, large savings can be made. We effectively share the cost of files over many applications, present and future. It is much easier to write processing programs than it is to create large files. There is a major disadvantage, and this results from the problems of concurrent access of files by multiple users. On-line systems have similar problems. Since files are shared and controlled external to an application, the data base can be structured to serve the enterprise rather than the individual. By balancing conflicting requirements, optimization occurs at the enterprise level rather than at the individual level.

The file techniques of previous chapters are data dependent. The physical file structure is built into the applications program. Any change in the physical file structure necessitates change in the program file access structure. Data independence separates the logical file of the program from the physical file structure, which is not the same as physical location of the file.

The enforcement of standards because of centralization of control provides increased security and integrity; conversely, these problems are of increased magnitude because of centralization. Integrity, security, and privacy of data require special attention in a data base. In the long run, installation and industry standards are economical, simplifying maintenance and data interchange. The DBA plays an essential role here. There is a vast difference between having standards and applying them. Responsibility for controlling data is centralized and assigned to the DBA.

To emphasize the potential advantages of a DBMS, we list some important qualities it should possess:

- access to data in a natural manner
- definition of relationships between files
- all data transactions logged
- standardization of data
- amortization of the cost of data over many applications
- versatile representation of data relationships that can be redefined independently of processing programs

- better availability of enterprise data
- reduced application program maintenance

It is equally important to list the following potential disadvantages of a DBMS:

- operational inefficiency due to software overhead
- higher storage cost of data and increased hardware requirements
- software cost
- organizational cost due to system complexity
- serious program failure if data incorrectly modified
- complicated security and integrity requirements
- vulnerability of all systems of an enterprise to a single DBMS failure

19.3 DATA MODELS

Given the real world, an observer does not see everything but only representative parts. How indeed are we to know that the images that impinge upon the brain are the real thing? Consider the person with defective eyesight. Certainly, without glasses he only sees a representation of what the normal viewer sees. A model is a representation that is necessarily incomplete. Language is a model for thinking. For instance, the word "house" is an abstract model for all the homes that exist.

More technically, a *model* is a representation of some reality that we can manipulate and expect the results to correspond to like changes in that reality. We deal daily with models; data files are models of the information we collect.

From an abstract point of view, a data base is a representation of the facts that pertain to an enterprise. Those facts that we collect and store in the data base we call *data*. Since it is not possible to collect all such facts, the data we have represents or models the collection of facts that is the enterprise.

No doubt the reader has perceived by now the different aspects of logical and physical realms. We have, for instance, an object, a name for that object, and a place where that object or a suitable representation of that object is located. That is, an entity is some item that we place in a field. Similarly, the problem of multiple aspects extends to facts or information. In discussing information, we can consider three viewpoints which we call *realms* [Mealy (1968)]. As with the logical and physical viewpoints, we tend to carelessly jump back and forth between these viewpoints and this often results in considerable confusion.

The first realm is the real world; the second is our perception of that world; and third is the data model we construct to represent that world. In the first we have entities and their properties; in the second we have attributes and attribute values; in the third we have data items and their values. Data models concern the relationships of the third aspect.

There are many ways that we can impose structure on a collection of data; what is important is that the structures we impose or the models we create bear a useful relation to the structure of facts concerning the enterprise that are perceived to be important by the enterprise now and in the future. Many models have been proposed for data files. At present, data models are divided into three general classes: hierarchical, network, and relational.

19.3.1 Hierarchical Models

A hierarchical model is one in which the data relationships are restricted to a tree structure. A hierarchical model, viewed abstractly, is a forest of trees. Although this may sound imposing, it is just the kind of abstract structure we can describe in the data division of COBOL. Many DBMS handle only hierarchical models, and this is perfectly satisfactory for many applications.

19.3.2 Network Models

A *network* is a generalization of a tree. Recall that in a tree the path from the root to any member is unique. Relaxing this restriction gives a network. Thus an element of a network may have more than one parent and interestingly can be fathered by its offspring. If that sounds circular, then you have got the point. Networks allow cycles or circular relationships. The most important attempt at DBMS standardization was the CODASYL DBTG report (1971), which is based on the network data model.

19.3.3 Relational Model

One of the most interesting models for data base organization is the relational model developed by E.F. Codd. Recently a great deal of interest has been shown in this model, chiefly because though it is based on simple principles, it can be analyzed with mathematics. This is revealing hidden characteristics in the structure of data which may prove of great assistance in effective systems design. Because we are convinced that the relational model is at the cutting edge of the new technology, we shall briefly describe some of the basic concepts which form the foundation for the overall model.

The relational model is based on the array data structure. Since this data structure is conceptually simpler than the tree, which underlies the hierarchical model; or the graph, which forms the basis of the network model, it is not surprising that the relational model has the advantage that it is easy to work with and easy to describe. This alone should guarantee its future.

In the relational model records are organized into arrays called *relations,* each record occupying one row of an array. A row is usually referred to as a *tuple.* Since the rows of an array have a fixed length, variable-length records are not permitted. The array or relation is the fixed-length record file of COBOL programming. Each

data item that represents a field of a record occupies one of the array columns and is
called an *attribute*. Two examples of a relation are shown in Figure 19.2.

The Schedule Relation

Flight Number	Destination	Departing	Time
TWA 234	LONDON	NEW YORK	0900
TWA 456	BRUSSELS	NEW YORK	0915
TWA 112	LONDON	NEW YORK	0925
TWA 334	TORONTO	NEW YORK	1000
TWA 667	LONDON	NEW YORK	1025
TWA 556	PORTLAND	NEW YORK	1120
TWA 888	TORONTO	NEW YORK	1145

(a)

The Flight Crew Relation

Flight Number	Pilot	Copilot
TWA 234	JOHNSON	COOPER
TWA 112	KNUTH	WIRTH
TWA 888	HOPCROFT	ULLMAN

(b)

Figure 19.2   (a) The schedule relation; (b) the flight crew relation.

The first relation lists some airline flights from New York to various cities.
The second relation assigns some pilots and copilots to the various flights.

There are very few operations one can perform on a two-dimensional array.
One can choose rows, which is equivalent in the relational model to record selection; one can choose to retrieve columns, which is called *PROJECTION;* and one
can choose only those rows whose fields have specific values, a process called *DI-
VISION*. If two or more arrays or relations are present, they can be joined together
when columns in each of the arrays store values in common, a process called a
JOIN. The result of any operation is another relation. *No rows of a relation are
allowed to duplicate any other row.* Surprisingly, these four simple operations make
it possible to extract a great deal of meaningful information from a set of relations.
As an example, suppose we PROJECT out the column labeled DEPARTING in the
schedule relation. This results in a relation consisting of the one column DE-
PARTING. Since duplicate rows are not allowed, the relation consists solely of the
row NEW YORK, the only city from which flights originate! If we project out the
column DESTINATION, the resulting relation is

Destination
LONDON
BRUSSELS
TORONTO
PORTLAND

Note that this yields the list of all flight destinations and that duplicate tuples have been removed. By joining the schedule relation with the flight crew relation over the common column FLIGHT NO we obtain the relation

Flight Number	Destination	Departing	Time	Pilot	Copilot
TWA 234	LONDON	NEW YORK	0900	JOHNSON	COOPER
TWA 112	LONDON	NEW YORK	0925	KNUTH	WIRTH
TWA 888	TORONTO	NEW YORK	1145	HOPCROFT	ULLMAN

If we now project out the columns DEPARTURE and PILOT, we have the relation

Time	Pilot	Copilot
0900	JOHNSON	COOPER
0925	KNUTH	WIRTH
1145	HOPCROFT	ULLMAN

We now have available the times our flight crews leave New York, information not originally present separately in either of the two given relations. The relations can each be updated separately by two different groups of people, those who schedule flights and those who schedule crews. In fact neither of these two groups has to be aware of the relation updated by the other.

These examples have illustrated some of the potential of the relational model. Other operations on relations are available, and we have oversimplified the concept of what constitutes a relation. Currently much research focuses on query languages, which would enable the retrieval of information by commands written in everyday English.

19.3.4 Perspective

Our view of data has been conditioned by the writing of COBOL programs. Records are groups of data items strung together in a contiguous line and made available to us by opening files and issuing READ statements. They may be fixed-length or variable-length. We may retrieve them sequentially, which is easy, or randomly, which is more difficult, when we want to obtain them randomly, we have to be able to specify which record we want. We do this in one of three ways: by specifying track addresses, by specifying relative addresses, or by specifying record or secondary keys. There are no other methods available to us in COBOL. But there are far greater drawbacks than this. Let us examine some of them.

Suppose we want to drop or add a field to a record. What a lot of work has to be done. The file has to be recreated. The record description in the DATA DIVISION has to be changed and the program recompiled. But not just one program; every program that uses the file has to be changed. The data is not independent of the application programs. In addition, every user who accesses a file has to have the same description of the records in his program as everyone else. But every user may not need the same fields for processing. And even the order of the fields in a record cannot be changed. This problem is often solved by having more than one copy of the file. The data is made redundant to satisfy each user. This regretfully leads to difficulty when data is updated. Forget to update one of the many copies and the several reports generated by all these user programs may be inconsistent. When users confront inconsistencies in their reports they may lose confidence both in the reports and in those responsible for preparing the reports.

An even greater drawback to COBOL data definition is that the language provides no facility for one type of record to have a relationship to another type or for a field to point to another record. For example, suppose we have a record detailing a part number, quantity on hand, price, and the names of one or more suppliers:

PART NO.	QTY	PRICE	SUPPLIER	SUPPLIER

Each supplier has a record specifying his address and a list of the part numbers of parts he manufactures. In COBOL, both of these record types have to be stored in separate files, and getting from a part number to the supplier records associated with it requires programming effort. Yet the association is, or ought to be, intrinsic. We would like to be able to say

```
FETCH RECORD FOR PART #5
OBTAIN ASSOCIATED SUPPLIER RECORDS
```

Logically, we see the record types as having a relationship with each other. Physically, they are on separate files, maybe on separate devices, and programming is involved to select the appropriate records. Data base technology is designed to overcome this problem.

The logical relationships among record types are specified by a data definition language and access to records is made (by means of statements very much like the FETCH above) with data manipulation languages. The DDL which describes the

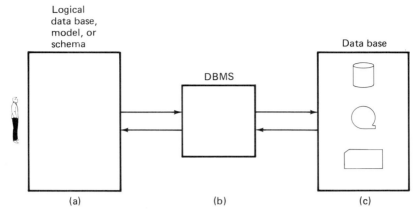

Figure 19.3   The DBMS interface: (a) user view of data; (b) system view of data; (c) physical data.

logical view of the data is said to provide a schema. In Fig. 19.3, we illustrate the overall process. The user sees his data logically through the model or subschema. The data base management system passes information back and forth from its physical reality via a schema to the user's program where the view is governed by the subschema instead of by its physical or actual schema structure.

Since the user is freed from knowing anything about the way data is really stored, his world can be involved with only the data important to his program. If he wants a record to have three fields, the data base management system can provide him with such a record although it may pull these three fields off three different files. Thus, in the future, the data division of COBOL will describe the user's view of data not the system's.

19.4 CODASYL DATA BASE MODEL

There are many implementations of DBMS. The first attempt at standardization was made by the CODASYL (Conference on Data Systems Languages) DBTG (Data Base Task Group) Proposal published in 1971. This work has evolved and is an important landmark in the development of DBMS.

Relational data models have achieved success in recent years, while the CODASYL proposals for a data base facility in COBOL have been slow in being approved as a standard. However, even if only for historical purposes, the CODASYL viewpoint is important. Regardless of which data model finally becomes standard, the problems addressed by CODASYL remain; no model that does not address and solve the problems that the CODASYL committee set out to delineate will be acceptable as a standard. In the Appendix, we give a brief overview of the CODASYL data base model approach.

19.5 CONCLUSION

When we consider a DBMS, we generally have in mind a rather large and complicated system. The potential advantages of such a large system involve many potential disadvantages. Such a large system is not always necessary.

At the very lowest level of a data base, we can begin by viewing data files as belonging to the enterprise and neither to the program nor, more dangerously, to the programmer. By considering files as a unified group and placing management control on their design and maintenance, the enterprise can begin to move toward a data base/data bank concept.

Many of the advantages claimed for DBMS are the result of defacto standardization instituted by the use of a single system. Manual standards and management control can also claim many of these advantages. Data base management as a philosophy has many manifestations. We would emphasize that if simple control can achieve the objectives of the enterprise, then more sophisticated control is not required. Indeed, we view simplicity as the golden rule of design.

REFERENCES FOR FURTHER READING

Codd, E.F. "Recent Investigations in Relational Data Base Systems." In *Information Processing '74*. Amsterdam: North-Holland, 1974.

Martin, James *Managing the Data-Base Environment*. Englewood Cliffs, N.J.: Prentice-Hall, 1983.

Mealy, A.H. "Another Look at Data," *Proceedings of the AFIPS 1967 Fall Joint Computer Conference,* vol. 31. Montvale, N.J.: AFIPS Press, 1968.

PROBLEMS

1. The intent of a DBMS is to isolate the application programmer from the storage structure of the data. Discuss the advantages that might be obtained. Are there any disadvantages?

2. Is a DBMS a better approach than a file management system?

3. What requirements must a DDL satisfy? Should it be a separate language?

4. What purpose is satisfied by inserting a DML in a host language? Give some reasons for making it a stand-alone language. Sketch how it might then be used.

5. Design high-level functional specifications for a *simple* DBMS.

6. What DBMS or file processing systems are available at your installation? What data models do they use?

Postscript

In our view many programming systems fail or are very unsatisfactory not because of insufficient technical knowledge but because of lack of discipline and understanding of the relative importance of the many facets of a project to the objectives of the enterprise. Computing as a relatively new discipline attracts those who enjoy the freedom to innovate attendant on a new area that does not have a well-defined rigorous body of knowledge that must be painfully acquired by a long arduous apprenticeship. Until programming changes from art to craft, the artist programmer will abound. If we are aware of the incredible amount of bad art, we will appreciate that the creations of the artistic programmer seldom are what they pretend to be. Few enterprises can afford to be patrons of artistic programming.

We realize that this attitude destroys much of the fun of programming. We do not expect the building of a bridge to be fun, and although we can appreciate the creativeness of a new bridge design, we do not want it to fall down or to exceed the cost estimates. Because of this, the building of bridges is a carefully controlled activity, indeed, a craft. The design of programming systems is developing as a craft to be practiced with discipline and understanding.

Appendix: CODASYL Database Overview

It should be noted that the CODASYL approach to database design is intended for a large general DBMS to be implemented by various vendors and consequently is quite complex. Current CODASYL documents should be referred to for precise reference.

An important design criteria of the CODASYL work is that it is to find practical application. In practice it is not easy to change existing procedural languages because of the large investment involved so that the data base application should be expected to be written in a host programming language. Although we may view a DBMS as a generalized file processing system, in practice a file is usually processed by well-defined applications and transactions run at high frequency; therefore, it is important that the DBMS application can be tuned for efficiency.

The DDL of CODASYL is a separate language and naturally enough is similar to COBOL in syntax. We examine some important features of DDL in the next section. In order to achieve efficiency and machine independence for the schema, a separate data storage description language (DSDL) has been conceived. DSDL defines the representation of a data base in storage. It defines how the data described in a schema may be organized in terms of an operating system and storage devices. The resulting description is known as a *storage schema,* and it is created by the data administrator (DA). Although the DSDL is important because its purpose, ideally, is to separate the logical description of a schema from its physical description and permits tuning for efficiency without alteration to other parts of the DBMS, we shall not consider it further.

The DML devised by CODASYL is embedded in COBOL and intended to interface with the CODASYL DDL.

CODASYL DATA DESCRIPTION LANGUAGE

The CODASYL data description language (DDL) is complex, and we make no pretense to examine it in detail. We do, however, propose to deal with several of its salient features that relate to its ability and limitations in dealing with modeling a data base. Any concern with syntax should be considered only as illustration. The objective of DDL is to describe the data contained in a database and their interrelationships or structure. Such a description is called a "schema" by CODASYL which refers to DDL as a "schema language."

A program that references a data base requires its own interpretation of the data; this interpretation is referred to as a subschema. In the CODASYL view, it is not necessary that the subschema language be the schema language. This has advantages in implementation when the syntax of a programming language does not resemble that of the DDL or the DBMS.

In Chapter 1 we discussed the need for and the definitions of various subgroupings of data and gave some general names for useful groups of data. In DDL there are seven ways in which we consider data: data item, data aggregate, record, set, area, schema, and data base. These are defined in Table A.1.

Record Type

The nature of a data base requires a more precise view of the different levels of abstraction. Recall that for a file we can distinguish three levels of the concept of a record: the record structure, a particular record associated with an entity or an occurrence of the record structure, and an instance of the record with values assigned to each of the record attributes. CODASYL refers to the record structure as a *record type,* the record associated with a particular entity as a *record,* and the set of values assumed by a record as an *instance of the record.* The COBOL definition of a *record type* is a collection of records described by a RECORD DESCRIPTION entry.

Thus we may have a record type AUTHOR and the occurrence of records for JOHNSON and COOPER. An instance of a JOHNSON record would contain fixed values for its attributes which would be expected to change with time.

Table A.1   CODASYL Data Groupings

Term	Definition
Data item	Smallest accessible unit of named data
Data aggregate	Named collection of data items within a record; they may be vectors or repeating groups
Record	Named collection of data items or data aggregates
Set	Occurrence of a named collection of records where one of the record types is said to be the owner record and the other record types are said to be members
Area	Named collection of unique records which need not preserve owner/member relationships
Schema	Complete description of a data base
Data base	All records, sets, and areas controlled by a particular schema; the contents of different data bases is assumed to be disjoint

The Set Concept

The nature of a data base requires a flexible way to relate records that is independent of physical or internal pointers in records. CODASYL introduced a simple one-to-many construct that forms the basis of DDL. This construct is called a *set* (an unfortunate choice; owner set might be a better choice) but is not a set in the set theory sense of the word. A set contains two kinds of records: an owner record of which there is exactly one and any number of member records. If there are no member records, the set is said to be *empty*.

The different levels of abstraction regarding a record also pertain to sets. The general form of a set is a set type and this consists of exactly one owner record type and a number of member record types. CODASYL defines a *set type* as a named relationship between record types. There may be many sets for a set type just as there may be many records for a record type. Again we distinguish between a set type and an occurrence of a set of that type: *set* will denote a set occurrence. There is a set whenever there is an owner record. A set is said to *empty* when there are no member records. Figure A.1 shows an example of this relationship.

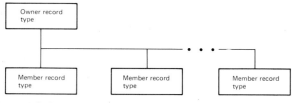

Figure A.1   Relationship of record types.

CODASYL COBOL DATA BASE FACILITY

CODASYL has defined a data base facility within COBOL. A DBMS environment for COBOL consists of a data base, a data base control system that provides an interface between the physical data base and the schema, a schema to describe the data base, a subschema to describe the data base as seen by the user, and a COBOL program containing instructions to manipulate the data of the subschema. Our purpose here is to examine some of the features of a data base facility within COBOL in order to gain insight into the requirements of a DBMS and, in particular, DML.

As in the previous chapter, we have chosen to follow the development in the *CODASYL Journal of Development* (1978) in order to facilitate more particular reference by the reader. As such, our purpose is a general overview of the important concepts of a DBMS as seen by an applications programmer. Our objective is twofold: insight into the requirements of a DBMS and a survey of necessary features as seen by CODASYL.

Data Base Records and Related Terminology

Although a data base record is conceptually like a record in a file, it is *not* necessarily a physically contiguous collection of data items. In fact some of the items may not physically exist but be derived in the act of access. A data base record type is described by a RECORD DESCRIPTION entry in the subschema.

Data Base Keys

Each data base record is uniquely identified by a *data base key* which is not part of the record. The data base key is a conceptual entity and, while the value pertaining to a record can be accessed by a COBOL program, this value is invariant for the life of the record.

Currency

The concept of currency is important to indicate the state of interaction of the program with the data base. Currency indicators are conceptual entities that act as pointers into the data base to keep track of record retrieval and storage. There is one currency indicator for each run unit.

Record Selection

In DB processing as well as file processing, the basic unit of data that we manipulate is the record and the basic problem is to select a record. To select a record we require some means of identifying the record we have chosen so that we can find it. In files, we can identify a record directly by its primary key and indirectly by logical position as, for instance, the next record of a sequential file.

The COBOL data base facility allows selection of records based on data base key value, logical position, or currency indicator. The rule for selection is based on a record selection expression of which there are seven formats. The selection expression can only occur in a FIND statement.

Simple Format of FIND

FIND *record-selection-expression*

Some Simple Record Selection Expressions

record-name DB-KEY IS *identifier*
NEXT *record-name* WITHIN *set-name*
CURRENT *record-name* WITHIN *set-name*

DML Verbs

Given a subschema, the user requires a data manipulation language to access the data he views through the subschema. As the user wishes to access the data base via his application language, the DML should be contained in the application language which is, thus, a host for DML. The commands of the CODASYL DML are COBOL verbs, fifteen in number, which provide for data base access in the PROCEDURE DIVISION:

ACCEPT
CONNECT
DISCONNECT
ERASE
FIND
FINISH
FREE
GET
KEEP
MODIFY
ORDER
READY
REMONITOR
STORE
USE

We briefly indicate the function of each DML verb and a sample format to indicate the possible manipulation of the data base by a user. For convenience of reference we have chosen alphabetic order.

1. ACCEPT accesses the contents of a specified currency indicator.

   ACCEPT *identifier* FROM CURRENCY

2. CONNECT places a record occurrence into a set or sets. Note that the record type must have been defined as a member of such a set.

   CONNECT *record-name* TO *set-name*

3. DISCONNECT logically removes or deletes a record occurrence from one or more sets.

   DISCONNECT *record-name* FROM *set-name*

4. ERASE logically removes one or more records from the data base.

   ERASE *record-name* PERMANENT MEMBERS

5. FIND establishes a specific record occurrence as the current record of the run unit. This prepares it for further manipulations.

   FIND *record-selection-expression*

6. FINISH terminates the availability of one or more realms to the program. It acts like CLOSE for a file. An affected realm must first be in READY mode. (Recall that you cannot close a file that is not open.)

   FINISH *set-name*

7. FREE removes records from extended monitored mode.

   FREE *record-name*

8. GET places part or all of a current record in its user work area. To retrieve a record, execute a FIND followed by a GET.

   GET

9. KEEP establishes an extended monitored mode for the current record of the run unit which must already be in monitored mode.

   KEEP

10. MODIFY changes the contents of the current record of the run unit in the data

base according to the contents of that record in the user work area.

MODIFY *record-name*

11. ORDER allows the logical reordering of the members of a set.

ORDER *set-name* ON DESCENDING
    KEY DB-KEY

12. READY prepares one or more realms for processing.

READY *set-name*

13. REMONITOR terminates a monitored mode or extended monitored mode followed immediately by the establishment of a new monitored or extended monitored mode for the same records.

REMONITOR *record-name*

14. STORE inserts a new record in the data base if its record type is defined.

STORE *record-name*

15. USE specifies procedures to be executed when the execution of a statement results in a data base exception condition. It must immediately follow a section header in the declarative portion of the PROCEDURE DIVISION and be followed by a separator period. The remainder of the section defines the procedure to be used.

USE FOR DB-EXCEPTION

We have done no more than highlight some major aspects of the CODASYL data base facility of COBOL in order to contrast the DBMS requirements with those of the file structures we have examined. It should now be clear that the potential increased flexibility of a DBMS is at the cost of increased complexity of programming record access and increased analysis of the data requirements of an enterprise.

When we consider a DBMS such as the CODASYL concept, we have in mind a rather large and complicated system. The potential advantages of such a large system involve many potential disadvantages. Such a large system is not always necessary.

References

Alexander, M. J. *Information Systems Analysis: Theory and Applications.* Chicago: SRA, 1974.

Brooks, F.P. *The Mythical Man-Month.* Reading, Mass.: Addison-Wesley, 1975. Essays on the design process based on the author's experience as project manager for the development of the IBM System/360. Supplements Chapters 17 and 18.

Cooper, R. H.; Cowan, D. D.; Dirksen, P. H.; and **Graham, J. W.** *File Processing with COBOL/WATBOL.* Waterloo, Ont., Canada: WATFAC, 1973.

Date, C. J. *An Introduction to Database Systems.* 3rd ed. Reading, Mass.: Addison-Wesley, 1981.

Inmon, W. H. *Effective Data Base Design.* Englewood Cliffs, N.J.: Prentice-Hall, 1981.

Knuth, D. E. *The Art of Computer Programming*. Vol. I: Fundamental Algorithms. 2nd ed. Reading, Mass.: Addison-Wesley, 1973.

Knuth, D.E. *The Art of Computer Programming*. Vol. III: Sorting and Searching. Reading, Mass.: Addison-Wesley, 1973.

Kroenke, D. *Database Processing*. Chicago: SRA, 1977. Considerable information on data base models and extant data base systems.

Lefkovitz, D. *File Structures for On-Line Systems*. New York: Spartan Books, 1969. An early book on techniques for direct access.

Lucas, H. C. *The Analysis, Design, and Implementation of Information Systems*. New York: McGraw-Hill, 1976. Readable management-level discussion related to Chapters 1, 17, and 18.

Lyons, S. K. *The Database Administrator*. New York: Wiley, 1976.

Martin, James. *Computer Data-Base Organization*. 2nd ed. Englewood Cliffs, N.J.: Prentice-Hall, 1977. Good general reference for many of our topics. It is language independent and very readable.

————. *Principles of Data-Base Management*. Englewood Cliffs, N.J.: Prentice-Hall, 1976.

————. *Security, Accuracy, and Privacy in Computer Systems*. Englewood Cliffs, N.J.: Prentice-Hall, 1973.

Meadow, C. T. *Applied Data Management*. New York: Wiley, 1976. A general reference that is language independent.

Philippakis, A. S., and Kazmier, L. J. *Advanced COBOL*. New York: McGraw-Hill, 1982.

Sprowls, R. C. *Management Data Bases*. New York: Wiley, 1976.

Tremblay, S. P., and Sorenson, P. G. *An Introduction to Data Structures with Applications*. 2nd ed. New York: McGraw-Hill, 1984.

Watson, R. W. *Timesharing System Design Concepts*. New York: McGraw-Hill, 1970.

Wiederhold, G. *Database Design*. 2nd ed. New York: McGraw-Hill, 1983. Highly technical treatment of files and data base concepts.

COBOL SOURCE DOCUMENTS

ANSI X3.23-1974, *American National Standard Programming Language* COBOL. New York: American National Standards Institute, Inc., 1974.

"CODASYL COBOL 1976." *CODASYL Programming Language Committee Journal of Development*. Hull, Que., Canada: Supply and Services Canada, 1976

"CODASYL COBOL 1978." *CODASYL Data Description Language Committee Journal of Development.* Hull, Que., Canada: Secretariat of the Canadian Government EDP Standards Committee, 1978. This is a working document of the Committee in preparation for the next version of the COBOL standard. It contains a definition of a COBOL data base facility within COBOL.

"Data Description Language 1978." *CODASYL Data Description Language Committee Journal of Development.* Hull, Que., Canada: Secretariat of the Canadian Government EDP Standards Committee, 1978.

Data Base Task Group (DBTG) of CODASYL Programming Languages Committee Report. New York: ACM (Association of Computing Machinery), April 1971.

INDEX